Latvia

The Transition to a Market Economy

The World Bank
Washington, D.C.

World Bank Country Studies are among the many reports originally prepared for internal use as part of the continuing analysis by the Bank of the economic and related conditions of its developing member countries and of its dialogues with the governments. Some of the reports are published in this series with the least possible delay for the use of governments and the academic, business and financial, and development communities. The typescript of this paper therefore has not been prepared in accordance with the procedures appropriate to formal printed texts, and the World Bank accepts no responsibility for errors.

The World Bank does not guarantee the accuracy of the data included in this publication and accepts no responsibility whatsoever for any consequence of their use. Any maps that accompany the text have been prepared solely for the convenience of readers; the designations and presentation of material in them do not imply the expression of any opinion whatsoever on the part of the World Bank, its affiliates, or its Board or member countries concerning the legal status of any country, territory, city, or area or of the authorities thereof or concerning the delimitation of its boundaries or its national affiliation.

The material in this publication is copyrighted. Requests for permission to reproduce portions of it should be sent to the Office of the Publisher at the address shown in the copyright notice above. The World Bank encourages dissemination of its work and will normally give permission promptly and, when the reproduction is for noncommercial purposes, without asking a fee. Permission to copy portions for classroom use is granted through the Copyright Clearance Center, 27 Congress Street, Salem, Massachusetts 01970, U.S.A.

The complete backlist of publications from the World Bank is shown in the annual *Index of Publications,* which contains an alphabetical title list (with full ordering information) and indexes of subjects, authors, and countries and regions. The latest edition is available free of charge from the Distribution Unit, Office of the Publisher, Department F, The World Bank, 1818 H Street, N.W., Washington, D.C. 20433, U.S.A., or from Publications, The World Bank, 66, avenue d'Iéna, 75116 Paris, France.

ISSN: 0253-2123

Library of Congress Cataloging-in-Publication Data

Latvia : the transition to a market economy.
      p.   cm. — (A World Bank country study, ISSN 0253-2123)
      Includes bibliographical references.
      ISBN 0-8213-2324-5
      1. Latvia—Economic conditions—1991– . 2. Latvia—Economic
policy—1991–   3. Mixed economy—Latvia. I. International Bank for
Reconstruction and Development. II. Series.
HC340.5.L28   1993
338.947'43—dc20   93-3018
                                              CIP

PREFACE

The World Bank Country Study contained in this volume is based on the work of two World Bank economic missions that visited Latvia in January and February 1992. These missions were undertaken in anticipation of Latvia's accession to membership in the World Bank, which took place on August 11, 1992. The World Bank wishes to thank the Latvian authorities for their excellent cooperation with the missions as well as for comments on an earlier draft of the study.

The study presents the first comprehensive assessment of the Latvian economy prepared by the World Bank. It is composed of two parts. Part I focuses on macroeconomic and systemic reform issues and Part II provides an overview and analysis of the main sectors. Quantitative information is presented in a statistical appendix.

The study was prepared by Mansour Farsad based on the work of the following mission members and staff:

First Mission

Adil Kanaan	Mission Leader
Roberto Rocha	Team Leader: Macroeconomy and Financial Sector
Rune Barneus	Financial Sector
Jaime Biderman	Macroeconomy
Andrew Bird	Public Investment
Boris Blazic-Metzner	National Accounts and Statistics
Barbara Dabrowska	Research, National Accounts and Statistics
Azita Dastgheib	Research, Fiscal and Financial Sector Issues
Mansour Farsad	Fiscal Issues and Balance of Payments
Mitja Gaspari	Financial Sector
Eric Manes	Foreign Exchange
David Tarr	Trade
Andrew Ewing	Team Leader: Enterprise Reform and Industry
David Kochav	Industry
Barbara Lee	Private Sector Development
Peter Hopcraft	Team Leader: Agriculture
William Meyers	Agriculture
Richard Johanson	Team Leader: Social Sectors; Education
Robert Holzman	Social Safety Net
Egon Jonsson	Health
Michal Rutkowski	Prices, Wages, and the Labor Market
David Mead	Legal Issues

Second Mission

Carolyn Gochenour	Mission Leader: Housing and Municipal Services
Bengt Turner	Housing and Municipal Services
Anders Willner	Housing and Municipal Services
Philip Blackshaw	Team Leader: Transport
Stig Lofberg	Transport
Marti Miettinen	Transport
Ann Ishee	Telecommunications
David Craig	Team Leader: Energy
Achilles Adamantiades	Energy
Laszlo Lovei	Team Leader: Environment
Clyde Hertzman	Environment
Robert Kapner	Environment
Stephen Lintner	Environment
Jack Schramm	Environment
Carlos Hinayon	Research, Macroeconomy; Statistical Appendix
Sophie Warlop	Mission Secretary and Document Preparation

Although statistical material has been prepared with care, data should be interpreted carefully. The report is based mainly on official data, but where appropriate it also uses estimates provided by various research institutes and outside official agencies including the World Bank. Efforts have been made to update the information provided to the missions in January and February 1992 with more recent data provided subsequently by the Latvian authorities to the World Bank. The rapidly evolving situation has made it impossible, however, to update all of the information in the report to a common point in time. Also, some of the most recent data, especially on international trade flows and the balance of payments, is based on preliminary estimates for 1992 that are still under revision.

GLOSSARY OF ABBREVIATIONS

AAQS	Average ambient air quality standards
BIS	Bank of International Settlement
BOL	Bank of Latvia
BOP	Balance of payments
CIS	Commonwealth of Independent States
CMEA	Council for Mutual Economic Assistance
EBRD	European Bank for Reconstruction and Development
EC	European Community
EIA	Environmental impact assessment
FDI	Foreign Direct Investment
FIAS	Foreign Investment Advisory Services (A joint service of IFC, MIGA and the World Bank)
FSU	Former Soviet Union
GATT	General Agreement on Tariffs and Trade
GDP	Gross Domestic Product
GNP	Gross National Product
G-24	Group of 24
GWh	Gigawatt Hour
IBRD	International Bank for Reconstruction and Development
IMF	International Monetary Fund
koe	Kilogram oil equivalent
kWh	Kilowatt hour
LPG	Liquid propane gas
MAC	Maximum allowable concentration
MER	Ministry of Economic Reform
MMA	Ministry of Maritime Affairs
MOA	Ministry of Agriculture
MoIE	Ministry of Industry and Energy
MOE	Ministry of Education
MOF	Ministry of Finance
mt	Mega ton
MTC	Ministry of Transport and Communications
MW	Megawatt
NMP	Net material product
OECD	Organization of Economic Cooperation and Development
PHARE (EC)	Pologne Hongrie Action pour la Reconversion Economique
PTA	Preferential Trading Area
RUR	Ruble
SIF	Social Insurance Fund
SOE	State-owned enterprise
toe	Tons of oil equivalent
VAT	Value added tax
WHO	World Health Organization

CURRENCY EQUIVALENTS

(as of December 31, 1992)

Currency unit	=	Latvian Rubles
USD 1.00	=	170
Latvian Ruble 1	=	USD 0.006

COUNTRY DATA - LATVIA

GNP per capita in USD in 1991	3,410

General

Area (square km)	64,600
Population, 1990 mid-year (thousands)	2,670
Growth rate, 1980-90 (percent)	0.6
Density, 1990 (per square km)	40

Social Indicators

Population characteristics

Crude birth rate, 1990 (per 1,000)	14.2
Crude death rate, 1990 (per 1,000)	13.0

Health

Infant mortality rate, 1990 (per 1,000 live)	10.8
Life expectancy at birth, 1990	70.5

Gross Domestic Product

	Current Prices (million rubles)		Real Growth Rates (annual % change)	
	1990	1991	1990	1991
GDP at market prices	12,201.0	28,665.0	-3.5	-8.3
Total consumption	8,226.0	16,198.0	N.A.	N.A.
Private consumption	6,888.5	13,249.6	N.A.	N.A.
Government consumption	1,337.5	2,948.4	N.A.	N.A.
Gross domestic investment	4,057.0	9,669.5	N.A.	N.A.
Fixed investment	3,337.9	N.A.	N.A.	N.A.
Change in stocks	719.1	N.A.	--	--
Net Exports	-82.0	2,797.5	--	--

Output, Employment and Productivity

	GDP in 1991		Employment in 1991		GDP per worker	
	mln RUR	% of total	thousands	% of total	rubles	% of average
Agriculture	5,739.0	20.0	226.6	16.2	25,326	123.4
Industry	13,907.0	48.5	433.6	31.0	32,073	156.3
Services	9,019.0	31.5	736.3	52.8	12,244	59.7
Total/Average	28,665.0	100.0	1,396.8	100.0	20,522	100.0

Government Finance

	Consolidated General Government, 1991	
	mln RUR	% of GDP
Total revenues	10,995.1	38.4
Total expenditures	9,154.4	31.9
Overall Balance	1,840.7	6.4

Money, Credit and Prices

	1990	1991
Broad money (mln RUR)	7,720.0	16,241.0
Domestic Credit	2,757.0	5,550.0
Annual percentage changes (%)	1990	1991
Consumer Price Index	10.5	172.2
Average Price of Goods Purchased	11.5	180.0

Balance of Payments Consolidated
(million rubles)

	1990	1991
Current Account	-647.0	1578.0
Trade balance	-827.0	762.0
Exports a/	4881.0	6895.0
Imports b/	5708.0	6133.0
Services Balance	745.0	1070.0
Unrequited Transfers, Net c/	-565.0	-254.0
Capital Account	-506.0	-106.0
Medium & Long-Term, Net	9.0	
Short-Term Capital, Net d/	-515.0	-106.0
Overall Balance e/	-1153.0	1,472.0

a/   Includes goods bought by tourists and other visiting populations from other Soviet Republics.

b/   Includes goods purchased by Latvians out of Latvia and supplies for the USSR Armed Forces, State Committee of Security and other Soviet organizations.

c/   Mainly taxes, profit of Latvian enterprises and the central budget transfers.

d/   Includes transfers.

e/   Latvia did not have its own national currency until 1992 and thus balancing position has been excluded.

Exchange Rates (Ruble per USD)

	May	June	July	1991 Aug.	Sept.	Oct.	Nove.	Dec.
Market Exchange Rates								
Buying	31.17	29.83	29.31	30.82	37.20	47.06	69.28	103.50
Selling	35.76	34.26	33.53	37.25	43.94	54.76	81.13	120.55

	April 6	May 4	1992 June 1	July 6	Aug. 3	Sept. 7	Oct. 6
Quoted by Bank of Latvia	125.00	125.00	119.35	129.20	136.00	159.05	160.07
Currency Exchange							
Buying	120	124	124	131	140	176	180
Selling	133	135	131	142	151	189	191

Composition of Exports and Imports in World Prices in 1989
(million rubles)

	Interrepublic		Extrarepublic		Total Trade	
	Exports	Imports	Exports	Imports	Exports	Imports
Industry	3,769	4,602	226	772	3,995	5,375
of which:						
Power	122	184	0	0	122	184
Oil and Gas	10	808	0	1	10	810
Coal	0	2	0	36	0	39
Other Fuels	0	0	0	0	0	0
Ferrous Metallurgy	123	388	14	19	137	406
Non-Ferrous Metallurgy	21	210	1	2	22	212
Chemical & Petroleum	517	438	9	60	525	498
Machinery	1,829	2,023	114	271	1,943	2,294
Sawmill & Lumber	78	99	16	13	94	112
Building Materials	62	86	3	2	65	88
Light Industry	281	131	10	105	291	236
Food Production	567	112	51	261	619	373
Other Industries	159	120	8	4	167	125
Agriculture	31	70	16	118	47	188
Other Prod Sectors	348	75	23	3	371	78
Total	**4,149**	**4,747**	**264**	**893**	**4,413**	**5,640**

CONTENTS

Text Figures

Text Boxes

EXECUTIVE SUMMARY

Latvia's annexation by the Soviet Union after World War II led to a radical transformation of its economy. Its comparatively well-developed infrastructure and skilled work force motivated Soviet central planners to establish some relatively sophisticated industries in the republic. As a result of the comparably higher efficiency of its economy, Latvia enjoyed one of the highest standards of living among the republics of the former Soviet Union, as indicated by a per capita income that was 30 percent above the Union average. However, as occurred elsewhere in the former Soviet Union, real economic growth steadily declined over the years. The abandonment of central planning by the Soviet authorities in the second half of the 1980s did not reverse this economic decline. Instead, the increasing economic and political turmoil aggravated macroeconomic imbalances and led the entire Soviet economy into crisis. Latvia's drive toward political and economic independence gained momentum during this period and led to its renewed independence in September 1991. This has enabled Latvia to take full control of its domestic economic policies.

Recent Economic Developments

The increased economic autonomy in the late 1980s allowed Latvia to abandon Soviet pricing policies and initiate comprehensive price reform in 1991, about one year before similar reforms were introduced in most parts of the former Soviet Union. The reduction in subsidies associated with the price reform was substantial, as indicated by the sharp drop in the ratio of subsidies to GDP from 13.7 percent in 1990 to 1.3 percent in 1991. At the same time, the price reform resulted in large price increases during 1991 as retail prices increased by 172 percent. Inflation accelerated considerably in late 1991 and early 1992 before decelerating during the second half of 1992.

Price reform in Latvia continued in several stages, and by mid-1992 fewer than 8 percent of goods and services in the consumer price index remained subject to price controls. The price reform brought relative prices more in line with world prices and reduced the excess demand for goods in Latvia. This reform was also an attempt to reduce spillovers of excess demand from other areas of the ruble zone and avoid internal shortages. The price reform had several important, but temporary, effects on the economy in 1991. First, the faster pace of price reform in Latvia relative to its main trading partners resulted in a significant improvement in Latvia's terms of trade and a corresponding shift in the trade balance, from a deficit of 6.8 percent of GDP in 1990 to a surplus of 2.7 percent of GDP in 1991. This was because the ruble prices for Latvia's exports to the former Soviet republics increased faster than the ruble prices that Latvia had to pay for imports from those republics. Second, the price reform contributed to an improvement in the financial position of Latvian enterprises, as they were able to increase their output prices substantially while still buying imported inputs from the former Soviet republics at relatively low prices. Third, it contributed to the sharp improvement in the government budget from a surplus of 2.0 percent of GDP in 1990 to 6.4 percent of GDP in 1991.

The improvement in the budget and in enterprises' financial situation occurred despite the severe contraction of economic activity: real GDP fell by 3.5 percent in 1990 and 8.3 percent in 1991. During this period, the decline in output was offset by the terms of trade gains and a substantial fall in real wages, allowing enterprises to retain their work force despite operating at low levels of capacity. As a result, the overall level of employment in 1991 remained at the previous year's level.

The severe contraction of output was essentially due to the collapse of trade relations with the republics of the former Soviet Union, particularly Russia. Such trade disruptions were caused by attempts by the republics to limit exports and avoid internal shortages, their reluctance to accept payment in rubles, and deficiencies in the payments mechanisms. The extent of the collapse of trade was indicated by the sharp decline in the ratio of imports to GDP from 47 percent in 1990 to 21 percent in 1991. Trade relations did not normalize in 1992 despite Latvia's efforts to conclude trade agreements with Russia and other former Soviet republics.

The macroeconomic situation worsened further during 1992. The depressing effect of trade disruptions on output was aggravated by the depleting stocks of raw materials and energy resources, the continued lack of foreign financial resources, and the sharp reversal of Latvia's terms of trade that resulted from the acceleration of price reforms in Russia and the other former Soviet republics. Industrial output in the third quarter of 1992 was 34 percent lower than a year before, compared with a decline of 31 percent in the first half of the year. Agricultural output was also affected by a severe drought in mid-1992. As a result, real GDP could have fallen by 30 percent in 1992. The worsening of the terms of trade not only depressed activity further, but also reversed the gains generated in 1991. The financial situation of enterprises worsened and unemployment, which was about 0.5 percent of the labor force during the first part of 1992, increased to 2 percent by early November 1992. Unemployment is expected to increase sharply in the near future as enterprises undergo restructuring. The unfavorable developments in 1992 also had an adverse impact on public finances. Profit and income tax revenues declined sharply and enterprises' tax arrears increased substantially. The negative impact of falling tax revenues, rising unemployment, and increased expenditure on social benefits is expected to put the fiscal deficit under strong pressure in 1993.

Latvia's decision to stay in the ruble zone did not contribute to resolving its economic difficulties during 1991 and early 1992. Instead, it resulted in increasing shortcomings, including the emergence of payments bottlenecks due to the interruption of regular deliveries of ruble notes from the Russian central bank. The payments bottlenecks resulting from the scarcity of ruble notes and the inefficiencies of the banking system prompted the Latvian government to issue an interim currency, the Latvian ruble, and accelerate plans to introduce the new national currency, the lats. However, on July 20, 1992, the government declared that the Latvian ruble was the sole legal tender in Latvia. This is expected to remain the case until the lats is put into circulation in 1993. The Latvian ruble was initially pegged to the Russian ruble at a ratio of one to one, but since July 1992 it has been allowed to float, and has appreciated significantly in relation to the Russian ruble. The floating of the Latvian ruble was in line with the government's policy of not imposing restrictions on foreign exchange transactions.

The Reform Efforts

Despite its macroeconomic difficulties, Latvia began introducing reform measures and has made significant progress in reforming various aspects of its economic system. Price reform has reached an advanced stage of implementation, with fewer than 8 percent of goods and services in the consumer price index remaining subject to price controls. These include energy, transport, telecommunications, rents, and other public services. However, some of these items have been severely underpriced. The underpricing of energy, particularly for residential use, has led to high energy wastage and large budgetary subsidies. The underpricing of transport and telecommunications has led to poor quality services and has hindered the development of services and export-oriented sectors. The lack of adjustment of rent to a level that covers maintenance costs has resulted in a deterioration of the housing stock and has increased housing-related subsidies. Therefore, the pricing of public services remains an important issue to be addressed by further price reform.

There has been considerable progress in the area of international trade policy in recent years. Importers do not need a license to import, the government does not ration convertible currency, and tariff barriers are negligible. However, there are still some restrictions on exports, for example, export taxes. Liberalization of the exchange regime has moved in parallel, and Latvia became the first republic of the former Soviet Union to establish a foreign exchange market free of any government restrictions or interventions.

The government has also made progress in the area of fiscal policy. The fiscal reforms replaced the distorted Soviet tax system with a modern tax system. The structure of expenditures has also changed significantly, with the drastic reduction of subsidies and transfers to enterprises. However, there is still scope for improvements as the government's capacity to collect taxes is still deficient and the expansion of extrabudgetary funds needs to be controlled.

The government has taken important steps toward the creation of a labor market. Wages have been liberalized and legal restrictions on firing workers have been substantially reduced. However, there is still a need to improve active labor market policies and increase the degree of labor mobility and the reallocation of labor across sectors.

Progress has been mixed in the area of privatization and private sector development. Relatively large advances in ownership change have been achieved in the agricultural sector by breaking up collective and state farms, transforming them into shareholding companies, and distributing shares to employees. Progress has also been achieved in privatizing small enterprises. However, progress in privatizing medium and large enterprises has been sluggish. The main reasons have been a lack of clear policy on citizenship issues, the restitution of property to previous owners, and the lack of a coherent privatization strategy. Parliament has adopted a resolution to provide an overall framework for the privatization program. However, major efforts will still be needed to privatize the vast majority of large enterprises and to commercialize those enterprises that remain in the state sector.

Progress in reforming the financial sector has been slow. There has been some initial progress in restructuring the Bank of Latvia and establishing a two-tier banking system. However, plans to deal with the non-performing commercial portfolio of the Bank of Latvia and to privatize its commercial branches are still lacking. Also, the legal and institutional framework regulating banking activities needs to be improved. The situation of the Savings Bank is also critical. This bank, which holds almost all household deposits in Latvia, is technically insolvent and probably illiquid.

Progress in reforming the social safety net has also been slow. A number of important measures have been introduced, such as the provision of unemployment benefits and allowances to poor families. However, the currently available financial resources for the social safety net will not be sufficient to meet the needs of the anticipated rise in unemployment due to restructuring and possible closure of enterprises. Some programs need to be streamlined to free resources for the expansion of other programs that are more urgently needed at this stage of the reforms. The financing of the social safety net system also needs to be re-examined, since it is excessively dependent on the wage base, thus inflating the cost of labor and discouraging employment.

An Agenda for Reform and Policy Actions

The successful transformation of Latvia's economy will require major actions in the areas of enterprise and financial sector reform, as well as measures designed to soften the impact of adjustment on the most vulnerable groups. The reform agenda is extensive, requiring the identification of priorities for policy actions in the short and medium terms. Moreover, the implementation of reforms at the microeconomic level needs to be preceded by efforts to improve the macroeconomic environment, as microeconomic restructuring cannot be implemented efficiently under high inflation and continuous trade-related shocks on output.

Currency Reform and Stabilization

Latvia's recent departure from the ruble zone has fulfilled some of the necessary conditions for the pursuit of an independent monetary policy and the successful implementation of a stabilization program. However, leaving the ruble zone is not by itself sufficient to control inflation. A successful program of economic stabilization in Latvia requires the adoption of restrictive fiscal and monetary policies, as well as the support of a well-designed incomes policy. Implementation of these measures will also create the preconditions for successful introduction of the new currency, the lats.

Fiscal policy needs to be strengthened, as it is the centerpiece of a successful stabilization program. For this purpose a considerable adjustment in both revenues and expenditures is needed so as to restrain the budgetary deficit. On the revenue side the measures should include eliminating the numerous exemptions from the turnover and profit taxes and strengthening tax collection, possibly by adopting presumptive methods to collect taxes from the growing number of small private enterprises. On the expenditure side the measures should include reducing the remaining consumer and agricultural subsidies; reducing residential heating subsidies; establishing a ceiling on the overall level of employment in the public sector; and identifying areas where expenditures can be reduced, such as civil service employment and remuneration.

Monetary and credit policies also have to be carefully designed. The expansion of credit should be controlled through various monetary policy instruments and linked to low inflation targets. Interest rate policy will also have to be carefully formulated to ensure the attractiveness of the new currency while avoiding excessively high real interest rates, which could aggravate portfolio problems in the banks. The interest rates on credits and deposits may have to be controlled initially, although they will have to be frequently adjusted to reflect inflation developments and allow for a reasonable intermediation margin.

The tight fiscal and monetary policies should be supported by (a) an appropriate exchange rate policy to help build up an adequate level of foreign exchange reserves to support the new currency, and (b) a restrictive (tax-based) incomes policy designed to avoid excessive wage payments by state enterprises and reduce inflationary inertia. The experience of other reforming economies indicates the need to maintain an incomes policy during the entire period of transition, until the ownership of enterprises is established and the financial discipline over enterprises prevents excessive increases in wages.

Finally, completing the price reform is essential to eliminate the remaining subsidies and to provide the correct signals to consumers and investors. To this end rents should be adjusted, the minimum support prices in agriculture should be eliminated, and the enterprises providing public services should start adopting cost-based tariffs. In particular, the underpricing of energy prices, which has a negative impact on the budget, should be corrected. Many of these measures are under consideration in the 1993 budget.

Complementary Policies and Structural Reforms

The implementation of a stabilization program will tend to have a depressing effect on output in the short run. Overstaffed state-owned enterprises will be particularly affected by the restricted access to credits and the charging of much higher interest rates. The unemployment rate is expected to increase significantly, as the growth of the private sector will not initially be sufficient to absorb the redundant labor discharged by state enterprises. Indeed, the experience of other countries indicates that the unemployment rate could increase well beyond 10 percent within a year or so. Output contraction and increased unemployment are unavoidable short-run effects of a successful stabilization program in the present Latvian context. However, the government needs to adopt complementary policies and deepen the reform efforts to avoid unnecessary output losses, to enhance the possibilities of an early supply response, and to soften the impact of adjustment on the population.

To minimize trade-related shocks on output and encourage the restoration of traditional trade links, the government should make efforts to engage in special trade arrangements with the other Baltic countries and republics of the former Soviet Union. It should also introduce a temporary increase in tariffs on imports from other countries. Such a temporary increase in tariffs would not only generate additional fiscal revenues, but would also help preserve critical trade links in the transition period during which trade will be reoriented. Intra-republic trade should not initially be subject to external tariffs, while extra-republic trade could be subject to tariffs of 15 to 30 percent, declining by a certain percentage per year to a lower level in the medium term. When the lower level is reached, intra-republic trade would also be subject to the tariff, and the preferential arrangement would be terminated.

Despite the temporary protection provided by the tariff, several state enterprises would likely experience severe financial difficulties, and would not be able to survive without support from the government or the banks. Closing all channels of financing and forcing these enterprises into bankruptcy would not be feasible, as a massive wave of bankruptcies would overwhelm the rudimentary court system, and would likely lead to an intolerable increase in unemployment. It could also lead to a very rapid increase in the stock of inter-enterprise arrears. However, the financing of inefficient state enterprises through the budget or the banking system postpones adjustment, deprives the emerging private sector from scarce resources, and retards the supply response. The best combination of policies probably includes providing a very selective and limited amount of budgetary support, imposing limits on bank lending to state enterprises, and, especially, adopting measures to accelerate transfers of state property to the private sector. Such transfers would stimulate some investment activity and facilitate the reabsorption of at least some of the discharged workers.

The delays in implementing a comprehensive program to privatize medium and large enterprises make it particularly important to accelerate the transfer of state property to the private sector through alternative channels. First, the government should facilitate the sale or lease of land, buildings, equipment, and even entire enterprises. Second, opening up various types of investment to foreign buyers would be a particularly valuable stimulus to attract foreign capital. Third, breaking up large, vertically integrated, industrial and commercial structures into smaller units would not only enhance competition, but would also facilitate privatization.

The adoption of a comprehensive plan to privatize large enterprises and the housing stock will still be needed, as will permission for land to be privatized. Branch ministries should expedite identification of the enterprises to be privatized and submit the privatization plans (developed at the enterprise level) for these enterprises as quickly as possible. After an initial round of privatization of a sample of enterprises, a more extensive privatization of large enterprises should be undertaken immediately.

Reform of the financial sector should be accelerated in view of the urgent need to channel external resources to the real sector and stem the decline in production. Financial sector reform should be focused initially on developing a plan to restructure the Bank of Latvia and to develop and implement a restructuring and privatization plan for the Savings Bank. The restructuring of the Bank of Latvia should involve developing a plan to restructure and privatize its commercial branches and strengthening its central banking and supervisory functions. The restructuring plan for commercial branches should be carefully designed and should involve the identification of healthy banks for immediate privatization and the restructuring of the rest through a restructuring agency. The restructuring and privatization of the Savings Bank should be implemented at a much faster pace, as its financial situation is fully known. The restructuring of this bank could be achieved by a conversion of deposits into vouchers or long-term bonds, or by placement of long-term bonds on the asset side of its balance sheet. Once this step is completed, its branches could be sold to the emerging private commercial banks.

Other financial reform measures that should be implemented in the short run include the implementation of international accounting and auditing standards, the improvement of the payment system, and the development of on-site and off-site bank supervision. To protect the new commercial banks against future bad loans, stricter prudential standards should be imposed, including a higher capital-asset ratio.

Social safety net reform should be focused initially on strengthening the system's capacity to meet the needs of the growing number of unemployed workers. To this end, local employment offices should be strengthened with additional resources, training and retraining programs should be improved, and the system of unemployment benefits must be streamlined in order to allow a growing number of dismissed workers to be covered. This can be achieved by eliminating benefits to new entrants in the labor force, restricting voluntary job leavers' access to unemployment benefits, and restricting the right to refuse job offers. These measures will help reduce costs and free resources for a possible extension of unemployment benefits beyond six months until an appropriate social assistance system is in place.

An appropriate social assistance system should be established soon to deal with a growing number of unemployed workers who will cease to receive unemployment benefits. The main actions required in this area are the determination of a more comprehensive poverty line, the periodic adjustment of the poverty line against rises in the price of a relevant basket of goods, and the establishment of a network of social assistance offices at the local level to help the most vulnerable groups more effectively.

Successful implementation of the reform program will also require (a) making progress in building institutional capacity for public sector management and coordination of policy development, including managing public expenditures and investment and managing and coordinating foreign external assistance; (b) improving the quality of statistical information and economic projections; and (c) establishing an appropriate legal and institutional infrastructure within which the private sector can operate effectively, including implementation of the bankruptcy law to permit systematic liquidation of non-viable enterprises.

In public investment the urgent need is to review the existing large portfolio of projects, in light of the changed role of the state and of the different economic environment. This review should identify projects that are to be retained and projects that should be abandoned as no longer being viable or appropriate for public investment. The government should also establish permanent mechanisms and processes for reviewing and monitoring the public investment program and for integrating it in the budget. A well-designed and managed public investment program will contribute to the development of the productive and commercial sectors and will increase Latvia's attractiveness to foreign investors. Experience in other countries indicates that an appropriately targeted public investment program, particularly in the infrastructure sectors and public works would contribute to a revival of investment in other sectors.

Reforming Major Sectors and their Investment Orientation

Complementing the structural reform measures mentioned above are specific programs of sectoral reform. Prospects for an adequate supply response will be poor if the rigidities and distortions in the sectors result in slow adjustment. The two key reform priorities that are common among all sectors in Latvia are (a) completion of the price reform and the privatization program, and (b) rationalization of investment policies and institution building. In addition, other measures deserve particular attention in each sector. These measures are summarized below.

Agriculture. The primary challenge facing the sector, which accounts for about 20 percent of GDP and 16 percent of employment in Latvia, is to increase its efficiency and export potential, and ensure that output markets are competitive and prices are not artificially suppressed. Trade relations with Russia should be restored and exports to the convertible currency areas must be expanded. Also, input prices for livestock feed, fertilizer, and other farm assets should reach market levels to reduce waste and encourage the introduction of efficient technologies. The resolution of ownership and compensation issues is of high priority to maintain production and promote investments. To encourage development of a commercially viable and competitive private farming structure, a well-functioning registration system that ensures the security and transferability of land rights is needed. The process of restructuring and privatizing state and collective farms and assets should be accelerated. It is also necessary to re-establish the agro-business support systems to provide a range of input supplies, financial services, repair and construction activities, and processing and marketing services.

Industry. Industry has been the fastest growing sector in Latvia, accounting for nearly half of GDP and less than one-third of employment. Therefore, in the short term, launching a successful privatization and restructuring program will be of the utmost importance to improve the sector and the economy as a whole. The government should also promote the growth of small and medium-sized enterprises and encourage large state enterprises to sell or lease part of their assets. In the medium term, the government should formulate policies to promote exports and to expose enterprises to competition. Other important medium-term measures include assisting enterprises to upgrade the quality of production and increase their efficiency and profitability.

Energy. Latvia has to import all its natural gas and oil products and about half of its electricity needs. Despite substantial adjustment in energy prices, underpricing still persists, creating a substantial burden on the budget. Industrial energy prices need to be adjusted to reach economic costs, and a program to eliminate household energy subsidies systematically should be introduced. A national electricity master plan should be prepared whereby plans for expansion are evaluated, analyzed, and prioritized. Investment proposals should be evaluated based on (a) their potential for efficiency and energy conservation, (b) the extent of rehabilitation and modernization of existing energy supply systems, (c) least-cost solutions for new plants, and (d) a commercial approach to borrowing. The government should initiate a strategy for attracting private investment to the energy sector. This strategy should include (a) liberalizing oil and coal imports; (b) adopting systematic approach to hard currency pricing of Latvia's natural gas storage services; (c) making a transition to cost recovery for electricity and heat producers; and (d) introducing legislation, tax codes, and contracts for licensing petroleum exploration. The government needs to rationalize its investment program in the sector by reviewing and prioritizing proposals within an overall framework of a public investment program.

Transport. Latvia's basic transport infrastructure is adequate, although parts of it have been neglected. In the short term, the government should undertake a review of public expenditure in the sector and develop a plan for focusing funds on priority projects. The financial performance of newly established enterprises should be monitored. Commercialization and privatization of other state transport enterprises should be pursued. The government should revise the maritime code and introduce mortgage and guarantee mechanisms. To enhance transport systems economic performance, transport pricing, and tariffs should be fully liberalized. Taxes on road users should be increased to generate enough funds for road maintenance and development. Local governments should become capable of assuming responsibility for road networks not covered by the National Roads Administration. In the medium term, improved decisionmaking tools should be applied throughout the sector. A strategy for promoting multi-modal transport should be developed and periodic road maintenance contracts should be introduced. Spare parts and other supplies are urgently needed in public transport, as well as investments in road maintenance, trucking, railways, aviation, and ports. Private roadside services should be encouraged.

Telecommunications. The telecommunications network is obsolete, provides only a moderate quality of service, requires labor-intensive maintenance, and uses spare parts that can only be purchased in the former Soviet republics. In the short term, the government should identify and prioritize its objectives in the sector within the framework of a strategic plan and evaluate commercialization and privatization policies in the sector. A regulatory review process should look into tariff and demand policy, legislative and contractual issues, technical standards, and taxation policy. The government should also re-establish supplies from the East. In the medium term, the government should conduct a study of tariffs to determine optimal levels to achieve objectives for the sector. Development plan for telecommunications should be rationalized in light of available resources and priorities. Initial investments could target services for high-paying costumers to ensure the availability of funds for expansion and quality improvements.

Housing and Municipal Services. This is one of the sectors in which price relations have been the most distorted. In the short term, the government needs to speed up the restitution process, raise rents on remaining government-owned apartments, and introduce a differentiated rent structure. The government should study the impact of the housing voucher system and investigate the experience of a social safety net in other countries. It should study requirements for a housing finance system, consider the introduction of tax credits, and clarify the revenue sharing formula for personal income taxes. In the medium term, the government should encourage the introduction of fees and charges to maintain buildings of mixed ownership. It should facilitate restructuring of the construction industries and plan for high priority urban investments. The government should provide incentives to stimulate investment in energy saving devices. Investments are required to maintain and upgrade municipal services, particularly water supply and sewerage services, and cost recovery principles should be introduced.

Health Care. The number of physicians in relation to population is high in Latvia by international standards. By contrast, the ratio of physicians to nurses and other paramedical personnel is low. The health care system needs to be restructured to achieve greater internal efficiency. Key elements of reform should include decentralized decisionmaking, budget responsibility, and consumer satisfaction. The principle of allocating health care funds should be changed to be based on the number of patients related to population served or on a per capita basis, and to include mechanisms to promote competition. Primary health care and sanitation should be reoriented to a more active role in health protection and reduction of preventable death and disease. Medical education should be reorganized and drug prices raised. A high priority should be given to maternal and child health care. At the same time, the quality of services needs to be enhanced while decreasing the emphasis on quantity and specialization.

Education, Training, and Research. Latvia has a rich history of educational development, and in 1990 extensive reforms were introduced to bring the system more in line with educational systems in Western Europe. In the short term, a priority is to develop a system to retrain adults expected to be displaced during the adjustment period. In addition, it is necessary to upgrade the skills of those presently employed. The government needs to define a comprehensive strategy to restructure vocational and technical training to make it more adaptable to changes in occupational demand. Measures are immediately needed to establish market-oriented courses in such fields as management, accounting, finance, and small business development. It is essential that Latvia preserves and exploits the best parts of its scientific research complex with greatest potential for Latvian development. In the medium term, a management information system should be developed to include improved data on financial inputs and learning achievements. In terms of higher education, the government should bring teaching content in all fields up-to-date and give priority to integrating teaching and research.

Environment. Latvia has a considerably lower level of air pollution than most other countries in Central and Eastern Europe. Many problems are the result of inadequate attention given to environmental issues in the development of urban areas and siting of industrial facilities. A national environmental strategy should be developed that would support a shift to proactive environmental management with a balanced focus on preventive and curative actions. The ongoing restructuring process provides an important opportunity to take a new approach to spatial planning that fully incorporates environmental concerns. Environmental planning issues should be a major factor in the preparation of environmental impact assessments. Industrial environmental audits should be conducted regularly. High priority should be given to the protection of the domestic water supply, a serious health concern. The Environmental Protection Committee and the Ministry of Agriculture should jointly identify actions to improve fertilizer selection, application, and storage. An evaluation of large-scale livestock and poultry complexes should assess their future and address their pollution effects. A waste management strategy should be put in place that addresses all dimensions of the problem and includes a detailed plan for management of the nation's hazardous wastes. Finally, an investment program should be developed that focuses on the future management of currently generated waste in all categories.

Balance of Payments Prospects and Financing Requirements

Latvia's current account deficit is projected to reach 12 percent of GDP in 1993. This deficit is associated with the deterioration of Latvia's terms of trade and the imports needed to prevent further declines in its economy. The current account deficit is expected to decline toward more sustainable levels during the second half of the 1990s as structural adjustment and reform measures begin to have an impact on economic performance, including on Latvia's exports to the convertible currency area. Latvia will need an estimated USD 350 million of external resources during 1992-93 to finance its current account deficit and build an adequate level of external reserves. Having only recently regained its independence and with no credit record, Latvia will need to establish full creditworthiness in the international financial markets. In view of the limited amount of private foreign capital in the short term, official disbursements will have to be the main source of foreign financing in the short term.

With implementation of the reform program and adjustment of the economy to the strong 1992 terms of trade shock, Latvia's current account deficits and the resulting financing requirement are projected to decline significantly to around 3 to 4 percent of GDP during the second half of the 1990s. Under these assumptions Latvia's level of debt service would stay within prudent bounds and would be manageable according to normal creditworthiness criteria.

Perhaps the most positive aspect of Latvia's stabilization and reform programs is its determination to carry them out even under deteriorating economic environment and external shocks. However, this process will not be easy and involves sociopolitical measures that could lead to major uncertainties and serious delays in policy actions. A major challenge facing the government is to develop capabilities within the government, particularly in the line ministries, in a relatively short time to implement the reform program. The reform program may also get derailed because of policy slippage in the areas of greatest sociopolitical sensitivity, such as introduction of an incomes policy designed to lower real wages. Other significant uncertainties facing the reform effort are the external economic environment and whether Latvia will be able to obtain the type of international support it needs.

Despite these risks, a probable medium-term scenario for output recovery based on the implementation of the reform program is feasible in terms of the availability of financing, with the help of the international financial community, and is sustainable in terms of Latvia's longer term export potential. Some slippage in the program with respect to the level and timing of the financing is quite possible. Additional efforts should be made to restore supplies of critical inputs from trading partners in the former Soviet Union and elsewhere, to find domestic substitutes for imports, and to shift into production lines that are less import intensive. With such efforts, and provided the desired financing becomes available, Latvia should be able to implement its economic reform policies effectively.

PART I

Macroeconomic and Systemic Reforms

CHAPTER 1

Background and Recent Economic Development

Background

The Republic of Latvia is situated on the eastern coast of the Baltic Sea, bounded by Estonia to the north, Lithuania to the south, and Russia and Belarus to the east. Latvia has a 500-kilometer coastline on the Baltic Sea, along which lie the ice-free seaports of Ventspils, Liepaja, and Riga, the capital.

Latvia has an area of about 25,000 square miles (about 64,600 square kilometers). A little less than half the country is arable. Woodlands cover about 40 percent of the territory and are an important source of timber. About 3.5 percent of Latvia consists of water. The longest river is the Daugava, and the largest lake, Lake Razna, has an area of around 53.5 square kilometers. Peat is the most important mineral resource. Other than peat, the country is poor in natural resources. Industry accounts for nearly 49 percent of GDP and 31 percent of employment. Agriculture accounts for about 20 percent of GDP and 16 percent of employment.

Latvia has a population of about 2.7 million people, of whom 1 million live in Riga. The composition of the population changed significantly during the post-World War II years: in 1935 over three-fourths of the population were of Latvian origin; by 1990 this figure had dropped to 52 percent, with Russians accounting for 70 percent of the rest. This dramatic transformation in ethnic composition is the result of Soviet policies that encouraged immigration from the nearby regions of Russia, Belarus, and Ukraine. Soviet policies also resulted in an increased share of the population moving to urban areas and away from agriculture. The population of urban areas increased from 37 percent of the total population in 1935 to 70 percent in 1990.

Latvia began to industrialize toward the end of the nineteenth century. By the early 1900s it was one of the most industrially developed provinces of Russia and had superior harbor facilities. During World War I, Latvia served as a battleground for the Germans and Russians. In 1920, a peace treaty was signed with the Soviet Union and Latvia's independence was recognized. Trade grew steadily throughout the 1930s, with the United Kingdom and Germany accounting for about three-fourths of Latvia's exports and imports. The Soviet Union played only a minor role in Latvia trade, accounting for only 3 percent. In 1940, the Soviet army invaded Latvia, and in August of that year Latvia was incorporated into the Soviet Union. The German occupation during 1941-44 interrupted the dominance of the Soviet Union in Latvia, but in 1944 Latvia was again occupied by the Soviet army. By the early 1950s its economy was fully integrated into the Soviet centrally planned system.

Rapid industrialization occurred during the period following World War II as a result of an aggressive capital formation strategy and forced labor movements from agriculture to industry and from other parts of the Soviet Union into Latvia. The republic's comparatively well-developed infrastructure and skilled work force motivated Soviet central planners to establish relatively sophisticated industries in the republic, including machine building, chemicals, electronics, wood, paper, food, and light industries. The agriculture sector was relatively well developed, and Latvia became an exporter of meat, dairy, and fish products to the other republics of the Soviet Union.

As a result of the relatively higher efficiency of its economy, Latvia enjoyed one of the highest standards of living among the republics, as indicated by a per capita income almost 30 percent above the Union average. However, as occurred elsewhere in the former Soviet Union, real economic growth steadily declined over the years. The technologies employed in civil industries became increasingly obsolete and the environment suffered. The shortcomings of the central planning model became more visible during the 1980s. Between 1981 and 1989, real GDP growth rates averaged 3.9 percent a year despite a level of fixed investment of around 25 percent of GDP. This implied an incremental capital output ratio twice as high as for the average developing country and great inefficiencies in the use of factors of production.

The gradual abandonment of central planning by the Soviet authorities in the second half of the 1980s did not reverse this economic decline. Instead, the increasing economic and political turmoil aggravated macroeconomic imbalances and led the entire Soviet economy into crisis. At the same time, Latvia's drive toward political and economic independence accelerated and led to the country's renewed independence in September 1991. This enabled Latvia to take full control of its national economic policies.

Recent Economic Developments

The increasing economic autonomy of the late 1980s allowed Latvia to abandon Soviet pricing policies and initiate comprehensive price reforms in 1991, one year before the implementation of similar reforms in most parts of the former Soviet Union. The Latvian price reform involved administrative price adjustments combined with a liberalization of an increasing share of commodities in the consumer basket. Price liberalization continued in several stages, and by early 1992 most prices had been liberalized, although government fears of monopoly pricing had also resulted in the imposition of maximum profit margins at the retail level. By mid-1992 those margins had been lifted, and less than 8 percent of goods and services in the consumer price index remained subject to price controls (mainly energy and municipal services).

The reduction in subsidies associated with the price reform was substantial: the ratio of subsidies to GDP decreased from 13.7 percent in 1990 to 1.3 percent in 1991, due mostly due to the reduction in price subsidies on food items. At the same time, the price reform resulted in a considerable increase in prices in 1991 compared to previous years. As shown in Table 1-1, during 1991 retail prices increased by 172 percent on an average annual basis and by 262 percent from December 1990 to December 1991. Table 1-1 also indicates the extent to which price reform in Latvia and the other two Baltic countries preceded that in the largest former Soviet republics. However, the situation reversed in 1992, with prices in Russia and the other large republics increasing faster than in Latvia.

Table 1-1. *Inflation in Selected Former Soviet Republics, 1991*
(percent)

Inflation	Baltic Republics				
	Estonia	Latvia	Lithuania	Russia	Ukraine
Average	211.8	172.2	224.7	90.4	84.2
December 1990/December 1991	303.0	262.0	376.2	152.1	136.9

Note: The figures shown are based on variations in the retail or consumer price indices.
Source: Latvian authorities and World Bank staff estimates.

The implementation of the price reform in 1991 was influenced by two major factors. First, the liberalization of prices and reduction of subsidies were correctly seen as fundamental components of a broader program of economic reform. The price reform contributed to the realignment of relative prices and reduced the excess demand for goods in Latvia. Second, the price reform was also a deliberate effort to reduce spillovers of excess demand in other areas of the ruble zone and to prevent internal shortages.

Nominal wages were also adjusted during 1991, but there was no attempt to index them fully to prices. As a result, average real wages decreased by 29 percent in 1991 after moderate increases in the previous years (Table 1-2). The decrease in real wages that followed the price reform was consistent with macroeconomic stability, since it reduced the excess demand for goods and the costs associated with redundant labor in the state-owned enterprises. Real wages continued their decline in 1992 (Figure 1-2).

Table 1-2. Average Changes in Retail Prices and Wages 1988-91
(percent)

Prices and Wages	1988	1989	1990	1991
Retail Prices	3.6	4.7	10.5	172.2
Nominal Wages	8.7	10.1	16.4	93.0
Real Wages	4.9	5.1	5.3	-29.1

Source: Latvian authorities.

The price reform had several important, but temporary, effects on the economy in 1991. For one, the faster pace of the price reform in Latvia relative to its main trading partners resulted in a significant improvement in Latvia's terms of trade, and a corresponding shift in the trade balance from a deficit of 6.8 percent of GDP in 1990 to a surplus of 2.7 percent of GDP in 1991 (Table 1-3). Second, the price reform contributed to an improvement in the financial position of enterprises, as they were able to adjust their output prices substantially while still buying imported inputs at relatively low prices. Third, it sharply improved the government budget from a surplus of 2 percent of GDP in 1990 to a surplus of 6.4 percent of GDP in 1991, although this improvement also reflected the introduction of new taxes under the 1991 tax reform.

Table 1-3: Selected Economic Indicators, 1989-91

Year	Average [a] Inflation (% p.a.)	Real GDP Growth (% p.a.)	Imports [b] (% of GDP)	Trade [b] Balance (% of GDP)	Fiscal Balance (% of GDP)
1989	4.7	5.7	51.4	-4.7	0.8
1990	10.5	-3.5	46.8	-6.8	2.0
1991	172.2	-8.3	21.4	2.7	6.4

a. Inflation measured by changes in the retail price index.
b. Includes inter-republican trade.
Source: Latvian authorities and World Bank staff estimates.

The improvement in the budget and in the financial situation of enterprises occurred despite the severe contraction of economic activity: real GDP fell by 3.5 percent in 1990 and 8.3 percent in 1991 (Table 1-3).[1] During this period, the decline in output was offset by the terms of trade gains and the 29 percent fall in real wages, allowing enterprises to retain their work forces despite operating at low levels of capacity. As a result, the overall level of employment in 1991 remained around the previous year's level. Although the faster pace of price reform in Latvia made it possible to avoid open unemployment, labor redundancy remained a serious problem.

The severe contraction of output was essentially due to the collapse of trade relations with the former Soviet republics, particularly Russia. Imported inputs and raw materials, especially oil products, declined from 46.8 percent of GDP in 1990 to 21.4 percent in 1991 (Table 1-3). Such trade disruptions were caused by attempts by the republics to limit exports and avoid internal shortages, their reluctance to accept rubles in payment, and deficiencies in payment mechanisms. Agriculture was the most affected sector (Figure 1-1). Agricultural output dropped by 17 percent in 1990 and 2 percent in 1991, mainly because of the lack of imported inputs and the drop in the output of state farms. Industry was the least affected sector and its production remained essentially unchanged from its 1990 level, partly because enterprises were able to draw down stocks, and partly because the increased production by cooperatives offset the decline in the output of state enterprises. Trade relations did not normalize in 1992, despite Latvia's efforts to conclude trade agreements with Russia and the other former republics.

Figure 1-1. Latvia: GDP Trends, 1985-91
(percentage growth)

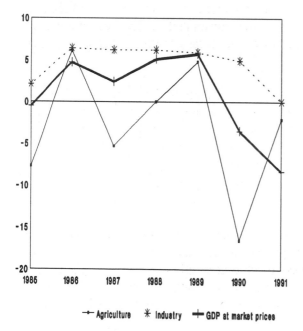

-◆- Agriculture   * Industry   -+- GDP at market prices

Source: Statistical Appendix Table 2.2.

Figure 1-2. Consumer Prices and Average Monthly Wage, January 1991-April 1992
(Index, Jan 1991 = 100.0)

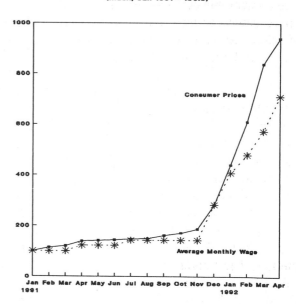

Source: Statistical Appendix Tables 6.1 and 6.4.

---

1.   Latvia's per capita income in 1991 is estimated at about USD 3,410. GNP estimates for Latvia, and all economies of the former Soviet Union, are not fully in accordance with the United Nations System of National Accounts and are subject to more than the usual range of uncertainty, and should therefore be regarded as preliminary and subject to revision.

The contraction of economic activity was accompanied by a sharp contraction in investment.[2] The fall in investment was due to a variety of factors, including political and economic uncertainties, increasing excess capacity in state enterprises, and the absence of an advocate for capital in decentralized state enterprises. Consumption did not fall as much because the government partly offset the reduction in subsidies and the fall in real wages with the provision of a compensation scheme in 1991.

Latvia's macroeconomic situation worsened further during 1992. The depressing effect of trade disruptions on output was aggravated by the depleting stocks of raw materials and energy resources, the continued lack of foreign financial resources, and the sharp reversal of Latvia's terms of trade, which resulted from the price reforms in Russia and the other former Soviet republics. Industrial output in the third quarter of 1992 was 34 percent lower than a year earlier, compared with a decline of 31 percent in the first half of the year.[3] Agricultural output was also affected by a severe drought in mid-1992. As a result, real GDP could have fallen by 30 percent in 1992. Inflation also accelerated in 1992, with monthly rates averaging 48 percent in the first quarter before declining to 13 to 15 percent in the second and third quarters. Monthly inflation rates are declining gradually and are expected to fall to 2 to 3 percent by mid-1993 under the current stabilization program.

The deterioration in Latvia's terms of trade in 1992 not only depressed activity further, but also reversed the gains experienced in 1991. The financial situation of enterprises worsened and unemployment started to rise, albeit from a very low level. Unemployment, which was about 0.5 percent of the labor force during first part of the year, increased to about 2.0 percent in November 1992. Unemployment is expected to increase sharply in the near future as enterprises undergo restructuring. The unfavorable developments in 1992 also had an adverse impact on public finances. Profit and income tax revenues declined sharply and tax arrears by enterprises increased substantially. The negative impact of falling tax revenues and rising unemployment and expenditures on social benefits is expected to put the fiscal deficit under strong pressure in the coming months.

Latvia's decision to stay in the ruble area did not contribute to resolving its economic difficulties during 1991 and early 1992. Instead, it resulted in increasing obstacles, including the emergence of payments bottlenecks due to the interruption of regular deliveries of ruble notes from the Russian central bank. The payments bottlenecks resulting from the scarcity of ruble notes and the inefficiencies of the banking system prompted the Latvian government to accelerate plans to introduce a national currency, the lats. However, the technical difficulties such as printing the lats in Germany, associated with the introduction of the lats led the authorities to introduce an interim currency, the Latvian ruble. The Latvian ruble was initially issued as a supplement to the Russian ruble, but was declared the sole legal tender on July 20, 1992. This is expected to remain the situation until the introduction of the lats in 1993. The government intends to stabilize the exchange rate for the Latvia ruble before circulating the lats. The Latvian ruble was initially pegged to the Russian ruble at a ratio of one to one, but since July 1992, it has been allowed to float, and has appreciated significantly in relation to the Russian ruble. Floating of the Latvian ruble was in line with the government's policy of not imposing restrictions on foreign exchange transactions.

---

2.   Preliminary national accounts estimates show a 10 percentage point drop in the investment to GDP ratio between 1989 and 1991.

3.   The decline may have been overstated as the national accounts data do not fully cover the rapidly rising private sector activity.

CHAPTER 2

Macroeconomic Issues

Latvia is implementing its economic reform program in an adverse macroeconomic environment, as indicated by declining output and deteriorating terms of trade. These developments are related to factors over which Latvia has limited control. The contraction in output is essentially the result of disruptions in the trade with the former Soviet Union (FSU). Normalization of trade relations in turn depends on the extent and pace of political and economic stabilization within the former Soviet Union. The reduction in trade is aggravated by the rise in unemployment and the sharp deterioration in the terms of trade. The emerging pressure on the financial position of enterprises has already been reflected on the budget through lower tax receipts and higher payments for unemployment benefits. These developments indicate that keeping fiscal policy under control, and normalizing trade relations will remain at the center of the main macroeconomic agenda in the foreseeable future.

Fiscal Policy

The Budgetary System under Central Planning

Under the Soviet central planning system, Latvia's budget was integrated with the All-Union budget of the former Soviet Union. Latvia shared its tax revenues with the All-Union budget and designed its expenditures according to Soviet guidelines. Revenue sharing with the All-Union budget involved the transfers from Latvia of (a) all profit taxes collected from All-Union enterprises, (b) all social security contributions, and (c) a share of the revenues from the turnover tax and personal income tax.

The Soviet fiscal system also involved transfers from the former Soviet Union to Latvia. For instance, social security expenditures were largely financed from All-Union budget transfers, and investments of All-Union enterprises were also financed from Moscow. Some of these transfers passed through Latvia's general budget, while others flowed directly between the All-Union budget and All-Union enterprises. The combination of budgetary and non-budgetary transfers made a precise assessment of the net transfer of resources impossible, although there seemed to be a net outflow of resources from richer republics, such as Latvia and the other Baltic republics, toward the poorer Central Asian republics.

The fiscal authorities mobilized a significant volume of resources, as indicated by the high ratios (about 40 percent) of tax revenues to GDP in the late 1980s. The ratio of total revenues to GDP was much higher (50 percent), although it was affected by some double counting due to the integration with the All-Union budget. As shown in Table 2-1, the tax burden in Latvia during the 1980s was significantly higher than the tax burden in countries with a similar per capita income: the ratios of tax and total revenues to GDP in developing countries were 19 and 26 percent, respectively. The ratios in Latvia were actually comparable to those in developed countries. Moreover, two-thirds of revenues were raised from the turnover tax and deductions of enterprise profits, resulting in a distorted tax structure.

Under the Soviet system, the allocation of fiscal resources followed central plan directives, and resulted in a substantial redistribution of resources across sectors. The price subsidies for food products were particularly large, accounting for over one-fifth of total expenditures during the second half of the 1980s. The integration of the Latvian and All-Union budgets lasted until 1990, when Latvia was granted some economic autonomy.

Fiscal Reform

The fiscal reforms implemented since 1990 have changed the structure of budgetary revenues considerably. The volume of revenues transferred to the USSR declined substantially in 1990 and was reduced to zero in 1991, the year that the first independent budget was introduced. The government also implemented a tax reform that replaced the Soviet tax structure by a Western type of structure and introduced several new taxes, including a profit tax, a personal income tax, and a tax on goods and services. Annex 1 to this report provides a more detailed account of the current tax structure and budgetary system, as well as of local government functions and finances.

The composition of expenditures also changed significantly. Price subsidies were reduced from 13.7 percent of GDP in 1990 to 1.3 percent in 1991 (Table 2-1). At the same time, several new expenditures related to tasks previously performed by the Union government, for example, police and defense, were added to the budget. Social security expenditures have been a growing item in the general government budget. Social security, previously financed to a large extent from USSR transfers, is now financed by payroll taxes and administered by the Social Security Fund.

The move toward independence was accompanied by increasing budgetary surpluses: 2 percent of GDP in 1990 and 6.4 percent of GDP in 1991 (Table 2-1). The fiscal accounts are not strictly comparable across recent years because of the former links with the All-Union budget and the presence of off-budget transactions before independence. However, several factors contributed to fiscal improvement in 1991, including: (a) the elimination of transfers to the All-Union budget; (b) the reduction in subsidies and transfers to enterprises; (c) the non-indexation of wage payments to inflation; (d) the introduction of new taxes, such as the personal income tax; and (e) the larger than expected revenues from the profit tax. This, in turn, was due to the terms of trade gain and the overestimation of enterprise profits under inflation and historic cost accounting.

The surpluses in the 1990 and 1991 budgets were exceptional and did not continue in 1992, for which a budgetary deficit of about 3 percent of GDP was expected as a result of the deterioration in the terms of trade and the continued decline in economic activity. In particular, the profit tax is expected to decline because enterprises will face reduced profitability resulting from a deterioration in the terms of trade and tighter credit conditions. The government is also experiencing difficulties in collecting taxes from enterprises. On the expenditure side, while the reduction in price subsidies has reduced the budgetary burden, other subsidies for residential heating are still a substantial burden. Also, the reform of the enterprise sector and the planned restructuring of the banking system will put extra pressure on budgetary resources (see Chapter 3). With a weak domestic revenue base and a limited scope for domestic debt financing, the continuation of a large budgetary deficit would undermine the government's ability to control inflation and to ensure the success of the new currency.

Table 2-1. International Comparison of General Government Operations, Selected Years

Government Revenues and Expenditures	Latvia [a]			Devel- oping [b]	Devel- oped	EEC	Poland	Hungary	CSFR	Bulgaria	Romania	USSR
	1985	1989	1990	1991	1987	1989	1989	1988	1989	1989	1981	1981	1989

General Government Revenues and Expenditures as Shares of GNP/GDP
Total Revenue	51.6	51.8	45.0	38.4	26.1	38.2	44.0	48.0	61.8	62.3	39.3	40.1	46.0
Tax Revenues	40.2	39.9	36.7	35.5	19.0	33.0	41.5	44.5	50.7	53.2	36.4	36.4	45.0
Non-tax Revenues	11.2	11.7	8.1	1.9	8.2	6.0	2.5	3.5	11.1	9.1	2.9	3.7	1.0
Total Expenditures	51.3	51.0	43.0	31.9	32.7	41.4	46.0	48.0	63.2	64.6	54.0	40.2	56.0
Subsidies	12.3	11.6	13.7	1.3					13.1	20.3			
Overall Balance	0.3	0.8	2.0	6.4	-6.0	-2.3	-3.0	0.0	-1.4	-2.4	-14.7	-0.1	-10.0
Composition of General Government Revenues (percentage of total)
Total Revenue	100.0	100.0	100.0	100.0	100.0	100.0	100.0	100.0	100.0	100.0	100.0	100.0	100.0
Tax Revenues	77.9	77.0	81.5	92.5			94.3	85.6	82.0	85.4	92.6	90.8	97.8
Enterprise Income Taxes & Transfers	28.5	27.5	25.9	19.0			9.1	29.8	11.8	17.6	42.8	11.6	39.1
Individual Income Taxes	6.9	7.4	8.4	9.4			20.5	2.1	9.2	11.1	8.3	20.4	8.7
Social Security	4.5	5.8	8.1	26.9			29.5	17.5	23.9	20.2	20.8	22.9	8.7
Domestic Taxes on Goods & Services	38.0	36.3	38.7	26.3			25.0	22.1	29.5	28.5	17.8	19.6	26.1
Revenue from International Trade	N.A.	N.A.	N.A.	0.1			0.0	4.2	6.8	2.9	0.0	3.0	13.0
Taxes on Property	N.A.	N.A.	N.A.	10.8			4.5	1.6	0.6	0.0	0.0	0.0	0.0
Other Revenue	22.1	23.0	18.5	7.5	31.3		5.7	14.4	18.0	14.6	7.4	9.2	2.2
Composition of General Government Expenditures (percentage of total)
Total Expenditures [c]	100.0	100.0	100.0	100.0	100.0	100.0	100.0	100.0	100.0	100.0	100.0	100.0	100.0
Current Expenditures [d]	94.4	92.6	90.9	90.6			91.3	89.0	89.2	88.7	96.8	83.5	85.7
of which: Subsidies and Transfers	61.0	59.0	41.3	39.9					51.6	53.3	7.1	49.4	
Capital Expenditures	5.6	7.4	9.1	9.4			8.7	11.0	10.8	10.9	3.2	16.5	14.3

a. Latvian data for 1991 are preliminary.
b. All data for the "Developing Countries" refer to 1987 except for total revenues, total expenditures, and overall balance, which are 1986 data.
c. Total Expenditures include repayments.
d. Current expenditures for Latvia also include expenditures on extra-budgetary funds.
Notes: - Totals may not add up because of roundings.
         - N.A. means not available.
Sources: Ministry of Finance and World Bank staff estimates.

Recommendations

Revenue Policies

The two-year tax holiday for newly established enterprises is too generous and should be reassessed, as it results in a serious loss of revenues from the *profit tax,* and because it may stimulate evasive behavior by enterprises. More generally, the exemptions and deductions from the profit tax should be eliminated. The current system of progressive rates should also be eliminated as it can lead to inefficiencies, such as enterprise splitting to shift the combined profits to lower marginal rates. Ideally, the government should introduce a single rate for the enterprise income tax, which should coincide with the top marginal rate of the personal income tax, thereby making the tax system neutral with respect to the decision to incorporate.

Frequent and regular adjustments of the value of fixed assets should be envisaged to allow depreciation allowances to increase in line with the increase in the cost of capital replacement. Other adjustments should also be introduced to avoid the distortionary effects of inflation on the profit tax.[1] In this regard, the experience of several developing countries in adjusting their enterprise income taxes for the effects of inflation would provide a useful guide (see Box 2-1).

The base of the personal income tax needs to be broadened to include non-wage income, especially rental and interest income. This measure would not only increase revenues, but would also reduce the distortions created by taxing only certain portions of income. Broadening the tax base would also improve the social incidence of the tax, as the share of interest income tends to increase with an individual's total income.

Similarly, there is scope for improving the design of the turnover tax, the excise tax, and the property tax. In the case of the turnover tax, the numerous exemptions, particularly for agriculture-related goods and services, should be eliminated, and the tax rate should be unified. In the case of the excise tax, the tax on furniture and microbuses should be eliminated as there is no justification for taxing these items. Also, imported inputs should not be taxed at a lower rate than domestic production. In the case of the property tax, the taxation of an enterprise's fixed assets as envisaged in the law may offset the depreciation allowances under the profit tax and discourage investment. Export taxes should be phased out and a flat rate import duty on all imports should be imposed. By not applying import duties, the government would give up the much needed revenue.

Attempts should be made to increase non-tax revenues through the adoption of cost-based tariffs on public services, such as electricity, transportation, and other municipal services. In general, tariffs, fees, and rents need to be adjusted, not only to avoid the growth of subsidies, but also to contribute significantly to the maintenance, rehabilitation, and replacement of capital equipment and facilities. In addition, the government should also consider introducing fees and other cost-sharing arrangements with the users of other public services, such as health and education. For instance, in the case of education the government should introduce moderate fees for admission to grades above compulsory levels. In the case of health the charging of moderate fees for outpatient visits would also generate some revenues.

---

1.   The need for inflation adjustments will obviously lose significance if inflation is reduced to single digit levels. However, if such a reduction does not materialize and the profit tax is not adjusted, inflation will continue to distort the measurement of profits and reduce enterprises' capacity to self-finance their investments.

Box 2-1. Inflation and the Enterprise Income Tax

Historic cost accounting produces a distorted measure of the real value of profits in the presence of inflation. Particular problems arise from the treatment of inventory appreciation, the depreciation of fixed assets, and the interest payments on net debt. The evaluation of inventories and fixed assets at historical cost leads to an understatement of the real cost of goods produced and the real cost of capital replacement. Thus, it leads to an overstatement of enterprises' real profits and to much higher effective tax rates. By contrast, the full deductibility of nominal interest payments leads to an overstatement of real interest expenditures, producing the opposite effect on taxable income. Although these effects work in opposite directions, it has frequently been the case that inflation produces a net increase in the tax burden. Moreover, such increase in the tax burden may be significant even at moderate rates of inflation.[a] Inflation may also distort the choice of debt versus equity finance, encouraging excessive use of debt. Thus, the impact of inflation on the corporate tax may result in excessive taxation and efficiency losses, with adverse consequences for economic growth.

To avoid such distortionary effects, countries with higher rates of inflation, such as Brazil, Colombia, Mexico, and Turkey, have indexed their corporate income taxes.[b] The most important adjustments involve:

- Revaluing fixed assets according to a relevant price index, with depreciation rules applied to the revalued stock.

- Introducing LIFO (Last In First Out) valuation of inventories, or adjustments in the more common FIFO (First In First Out) method.

- Allowing only the deductibility of real, as opposed to nominal, interest costs. To estimate real interest payments, the inflation component (which may measured simply by multiplying inflation in the period by the beginning of period debt stock) is subtracted from nominal interest payments.[c]

---

a.   See Bond, Devereux, and Freeman (1990); Matolcsy (1984) for analysis of the Australian case; and Feldstein, and Summers (1979), for an analysis of the U.S. case.

b.   See Thirsk (1991).

c.   A comprehensive description of internationally accepted corrections of financial statements is provided in Goldschmidt and Yaron (1991).

A well-designed tax policy must be accompanied by an effective tax administration system to achieve revenue objectives. The government should strengthen its administrative capacity to collect tax revenues from the growing number of small private firms and self-employed individuals. The growth of both is a major change from the past, when large state enterprises predominated. Policy actions are also needed to prevent augmentation of the extra-budgetary funds, which ultimately would become difficult to control. Extra-budgetary funds with designated sources of revenue are an expedient mechanism for financing some expenditures. However, a proliferation of funds with earmarked revenues could lead to excessive fragmentation and a lack of transparency and flexibility in the budget. They also weaken the ability of the government to use fiscal policy effectively and to exercise budgetary control. The number of new extra-budgetary funds should be minimized and the existing ones should be integrated into the budget. Similarly, the counterpart funds generated by food aid and commodity assistance should be used to support the budget. This step is particularly important because the slowdown in economic activities weakens the domestic revenue base in the short term.

Expenditure Policies

The government should take appropriate measures to keep public spending within the limits of available resources. In this regard, the remaining subsidies should be phased out. The phasing out of subsidies may require some increase in compensatory income transfers during the transition period. However, the government should restrict the eligibility for income compensation to specific target groups. Such a policy would generate net fiscal savings and enable the government to redirect resources to other high priority programs designed to mitigate the social costs of adjustment, for example, unemployment benefits and retraining.

As far as investment expenditures are concerned, enterprises that receive capital transfers from the budget to finance state investments now include not only providers of traditional public sector goods and services (such as infrastructure, education, and health), but also a number of industrial producers. The government should continue to phase out capital transfers to state enterprises producing goods and services that are privately provided in most market economies. In addition, enterprises providing public goods and services that remain in the public sector, for example, ports, railroad, airports, and electricity, should be subject to stricter financial discipline and should not receive funds from the budget on a grant or non-reimbursable basis. In view of the limited ability of the sectoral ministries and local governments to prepare and critically evaluate public investment programs, the government should initiate training in project preparation and evaluation (see Chapter 3).

Fiscal Policy and Planning

Transformation of the economy, especially the redistribution of functions among the state, local government, and the private sector, will lead to large shifts in budgetary accounts. Under these circumstances, the assignment of revenue and expenditure responsibility among the different levels of government and the system of transfers among them will undergo major changes. With the expected change in the scope and magnitude of revenues and expenditures, the risk is that the budget may come under increasing pressure. At present, it is difficult to predict the net outcome of the expected change in revenues and expenditures accurately as events are evolving rapidly. However, the net outcome will be substantially influenced by the speed of the government reform program and the speed and strength of the emerging private sector.

On the revenue side, a number of factors may result in a substantial change in tax revenues in the budget. Because enterprises have been publicly owned, the government has had direct access to their profits. Once these enterprises are privatized, this direct access will disappear and the revenue will be raised through taxes on the enterprises' profits. Initially, however, taxation of the private sector will result in only modest revenues. Moreover, as mentioned before, the tax administration is not well prepared to control and audit private sector activities and to prevent underreporting of profits, and consequently lower tax receipts. Therefore, it is likely that the share of the profit tax in total tax revenues will decline.

On the expenditure side, declines in some important budget categories are expected. With the anticipated increase in the share of private sector activities and the expected decline in the share of government involvement in the economy, employment in the public sector is expected to fall. As a result, total wage payments in the budget will fall. Similarly, further declines in subsidy expenditures are expected following adjustment of the prices of subsidized commodities and the government's intention to impose financial discipline on state enterprises. However, the expected increase in unemployment from its current low level will increase social security outlays in the immediate future. The planned restructuring of the banking system and the ongoing reform of the enterprise sector will also add extra pressure on budgetary resources. As a result, maintaining a budgetary balance or a sustained budget deficit without heavy recourse to the banking system or foreign financing will become more and more difficult. This underscores the need to design and implement a prudent fiscal policy that strengthens the tax administration system and concentrates on expenditure reduction as a mechanism to reduce budgetary deficit.

International Trade

Volume, Composition, and Direction of Trade

During the late 1980s, Latvia's exports and imports in relation to GDP were high, around 45 to 49 percent (Table 2-2). Such a high ratio might at first glance suggests a very open economy. However, the high ratio was more the result of the high economic integration with the former Soviet Union than the openness of the economy. As is shown in Table 2-3 the republics of the former Soviet Union accounted for nearly 90 percent of Latvia's foreign trade.[2] The remaining part was conducted on a barter basis with the governments of Bulgaria, Czechoslovakia, China, Cuba, and Romania, and limited volume of trade with convertible currency area.

Because of its integration with the Soviet economy, Latvia was highly dependent on inputs from the former Soviet republics, especially Russia. Latvia was a net importer of primary and intermediate products and a net exporter of food and finished products (Table 2-4). This structure of trade was a mirror

Table 2-2. Current Account, 1987-91
(rubles millions)

Trade	1987	1988	1989	1990	1991
Former Soviet Union	-1,613	-1,114	-913	-357	1,467
Exports	4,342	4,300	4,843	4,692	6,642
Imports	4,700	4,616	4,729	4,779	5,324
Services & Transfers, Net	-1,255	-798	-1,027	-270	149
Other Countries [a]	46	118	-179	-290	111
Exports	275	302	264	189	253
Imports	589	621	893	929	809
Services & Transfers, Net	360	437	450	450	667
Total Account Balance	-1,567	-996	-1,092	-647	1,578
Memorandum Items:					
As percentage of GDP					
Current Account Balance	-16.6	-10.0	-10.0	-5.3	5.5
Trade Balance	-7.1	-6.4	-4.7	-6.8	2.7
Exports to FSU	45.9	43.2	44.3	38.5	23.2
Imports from FSU	49.7	46.4	43.3	39.2	18.6

a. Includes foreign currency accounts with the former Soviet Republics. Services balance partly in world market prices (mainly shipping and transport) and partly in ruble (rest of services).
Note: The trade data differ from the balance of payments data because of differences in coverage and timing.
Source: State Committee for Statistics, World Bank staff estimates.

---

2.   By 1992 this ratio had dropped to 50 percent, reflecting a rapid decline in trade with the former Soviet republics and a substantial increase in developing trade relations with the West.

image of the structure of production, which was oriented toward machinery, chemicals, and the metal processing industries, along with textiles, food processing, and some consumer electronics industries.

During the 1980s, the balance of trade with the former Soviet Union was negative, with net imports financed mostly by various transfers from the center. However, the trade figures in Latvia should be viewed cautiously, as they are subject to a large margins of error for a number of reasons, including incomplete reporting of information by enterprises, which in the absence of customs controls were the only source of information, and the presence of Soviet military

Table 2-3. Geographical Distribution of Trade, 1991 (percentage of total)

Country	Exports	Imports
TOTAL	100.0	100.0
Interrepublican	96.8	87.2
Russia	54.4	44.5
Ukraine	12.0	8.7
Belarus	6.9	5.9
Lithuania	5.4	10.1
Estonia	3.2	5.2
Others	14.9	12.7
CMEA Countries [a]	0.3	1.7
Other Countries	2.9	11.1

a. Council for Mutual Economic Assistance.
Source: State Committee for Statistics.

personnel in Latvia, who were financed with transfers from Moscow, and who had a negative impact on trade balance. Moreover, relative prices were distorted and bore little relation to relative scarcities, resulting in great differences between domestic and international prices. In particular, the relative price of energy was extremely low by international standards.

The trade balance with Russia was also distorted by the inclusion of the large turnover tax and of subsidies, which were embodied in the price data, in particular, in the prices of finished industrial goods relative to food products. Also, the inclusion of subsidies in the price of exports underestimated the value of those exports. Since Latvia was a net exporter of food and food products, which were heavily subsidized, the value of those exports was understated. However, since the turnover tax fell more heavily on finished goods, of which Latvia was also a net exporter, the ruble value of its industrial exports was overstated. The net results showed a loss to Latvia as the negative impact of the food subsidies was far greater than the positive impact of the turnover tax.

Latvia's trade deficit would have been much larger had trade been conducted at international prices. It is estimated that a complete shift to international prices would have generated a drop of about 24 percent in Latvia's terms of trade based on prices in 1990. However, due to lower energy prices in 1989 and 1988, the decline in the terms of trade would have been 17 and 16 percent, respectively.[3] Since trade accounts for nearly 50 percent of GDP, the income loss associated with this deterioration in the terms of trade would have been between 8 and 12 percent.

As discussed in Chapter 1, the move toward independence was actually accompanied by an improvement in the terms of trade and a sharp shift of the trade balance, from a deficit of 6.8 percent

3.   Brown and Belkindas (1992) for 1987 and 1988; Tarr (1992). These estimates are based on trade volume and prices prevailing in the years of the estimates. The drop in the terms of trade would have been 19.7 percent if 1987 volumes and prices were used. The terms of trade deterioration for Estonia and Lithuania may be even larger, in the 30 to 35 percent range for 1989 and 1990, with the larger estimates again based on 1990 data.

Table 2-4. Commodity Composition of Trade, 1987-91
(percentage of total)

Exports and Imports	1987	1988	1989	1990	1991
TOTAL EXPORTS	100.0	100.0	100.0	100.0	100.0
Electricity	1.9	1.5	1.5	1.7	1.6
Fuel	0.2	0.2	0.1	0.1	0.2
Ferrous Metals	2.3	2.4	2.2	1.9	1.2
Nonferrous Metals	0.3	0.3	0.3	0.2	0.1
Chemicals	13.5	13.6	12.8	12.4	8.2
Machinery & Equipment	28.6	28.7	28.0	27.9	24.8
Forest Products	3.5	3.4	2.7	2.6	5.4
Building Materials	1.3	1.3	1.5	1.4	2.5
Textiles	19.1	16.6	16.2	17.3	12.9
Food Products	23.5	22.4	22.1	21.6	20.5
Agricultural Products	2.2	2.3	2.6	2.1	1.1
Others	3.6	7.2	10.0	10.9	21.5
TOTAL IMPORTS	100.0	100.0	100.0	100.0	100.0
Electricity	2.3	2.4	2.0	1.8	5.6
Fuel	9.2	9.2	8.5	7.6	8.8
Ferrous Metals	7.1	7.4	5.8	5.6	3.2
Nonferrous Metals	2.3	2.4	2.3	2.2	1.2
Chemicals	12.4	12.8	11.6	11.6	14.4
Machinery & Equipment	29.1	30.0	30.2	31.3	13.7
Forest Products	2.8	2.9	2.6	2.4	4.1
Building Materials	1.4	1.4	1.5	1.1	1.1
Textiles	15.2	13.6	14.5	16.3	22.0
Food Products	11.1	10.7	11.5	9.9	8.3
Agricultural Products	4.8	4.7	5.9	4.6	5.3
Others	2.3	2.5	3.5	5.6	12.4

Source: State Committee for Statistics.

of GDP in 1990 to a surplus of 2.7 percent of GDP in 1991.[4] However, the gain in the terms of trade and the trade surplus experienced in 1991 were both transitory, having resulted simply from the much faster pace of price reform in Latvia relative to its main trading partners during that year. Indeed, the reverse happened in 1992: the price reforms in Russia and the other republics generated a sharp deterioration in Latvia's terms of trade. However, this deterioration was offset by a sharp decline in the volume of imports from the former Soviet republics, with the result that Latvia's overall trade with those republics was in balance.[5]

---

4.   If trade with the convertible area had been measured at the market exchange rate (as opposed to the statistical exchange rate), the overall trade balance in 1991 would have been negative. However, the large overshooting of the market exchange rate in 1991 reduces its relevance as a conversion factor during that year.

5.   While imports were down in absolute amounts in 1992, they were higher relative to GDP than in previous years due to the expected 30 percent decline in GDP for 1992.

Trade Policies

Trade with the Convertible Currency Area

As a small country, Latvia must rely on open international competition to establish a rational set of prices, ensure competitiveness in its markets, and provide for long-run growth. With respect to imports, Latvia has taken many steps to implement an open competitive market. As of January 1992 it eliminated all controls on imports from any region. Imports were not subject to licensing, there were only small customs processing fees, and no customs duties. Foreign exchange is allocated principally through market methods. These include retention of convertible currency earnings from enterprise exports and purchase of convertible currency through licensed convertible currency dealers or at commercial banks.

The right to engage in foreign trade was generally open to any firm. Thus, access to imports was relatively open and free from restraints. However, by January 1992 restraints on exports were widespread. Licenses were required for exports of timber, metal, scrap, cotton, all raw materials, and all food products to convertible currency areas. Licenses were required for all products exported to the republics of the former Soviet Union. In February 1992 export taxes replaced export licenses to the convertible currency area for timber and wood products. Henceforth, exporters of these products only had to pay the export tax in convertible currency.

In March 1992 the government abolished the foreign exchange surrender requirement and replaced it with taxes on hard currency transactions. Before the abolition exporters had been allowed to retain 60 to 82 percent of their foreign exchange earnings. The rest, with the exception of exports by joint ventures, had to be sold at a rate of 1.8 rubles per dollar.[6] By late 1992 most export taxes had been lifted and the rest were expected to be removed in early 1993. This has been an important step in the direction of developing an effective export market.

Trade with Republics of the Former Soviet Union

In late 1991, as the centralized system of control in the former Soviet Union was being dismantled, Latvia started to negotiate trade agreements with the republics of the former Soviet Union to help assure supplies. However, in most cases the agreements were not finalized, and those that were finalized were not completely fulfilled.

Trade with republics of the former Soviet Union takes place either under an "obligatory list," which includes the most important products traded between the governments, or under an "indicative list," which includes trade on an enterprise to enterprise basis. Valuation of products under the obligatory list is ostensibly on the basis of ruble equivalents of world market prices, but involves negotiations on a product by product basis. The implementation of bilateral trade agreements has been plagued by the lack of fulfillment of the obligatory deliveries.

---

6.   Joint ventures with foreign capital did not have to surrender convertible currency on their exports, except for a very limited number of industries (notably timber). Enterprises that exported to convertible currency areas paid a profits tax in both convertible currency and rubles. A separate accounting was carried out to decompose their profits into profits from convertible currency operations and ruble operations.

The agreement signed with Russia in February 1992 identified thirty commodities under the obligatory list for government to government trade.[7] These included mostly meat and dairy products, gasoline, diesel oil, and gas. During the first five months of 1992, however, the trade volume on both the export and import sides was underfulfilled. Table 2-5 shows the actual quantity and value of trade in the first five months of 1992. The table indicates that while Russia has been accumulating arrears vis-a-vis Latvia, Latvia has been making prepayments for imports of key petroleum products. The accumulation of these arrears, as discussed in Chapter 3, will have important macroeconomic implications for both enterprises and banks.

Trade agreements with republics of the former Soviet Union other than Russia also involve indicative lists of export products. Under these agreements, until June 1992 virtually all exports were subject to export licenses. Enterprises that wanted to export under the agreements were subjected to an export quota defined for that enterprise, with the export license generally granted up to the amount of the authorized export quota.

Table 2-5. State Trade Between Latvia and Russia, January-May 1992

Product	Actual Delivery (percentage of agreement)	Value of Deliveries (rubles millions)	Actual Amount Paid (rubles millions)
Imports from Russia			
Liquified Petrolem Gas	56.8	194.2	161.9
Gasoline	19.5	14.9	0
Diesel Fuel	23.2	68.0	0
Fuel Oil	22.9	43.8	0
Subtotal		126.7	399.7
Natural Gas	115.4	962.6	1,173.8
TOTAL		**1,283.5**	**1,735.4**
Exports to Russia			
Hydrocylinders	10.1	6.2	0.5
Transmission Chains for Bicycles, etc.	89.6	256.9	5.8
Integrated Circuits	150.0	476.5	247.6
Rough Corded Textile	153.3	1,776.9	71.7
Lubricating Equipment	92.7	15.1	3.4
Meat and Meat Products	35.0	193.9	127.6
Milk and Milk Products	57.6	276.5	45.3
Eggs and Egg Products	60.6	11.8	10.6
TOTAL		**3,713.8**	**512.5**

Source: Ministry of Foreign Trade.

---

7.   The preliminary trade agreement with Russia called for maintaining trade at about 70 percent of the trade volume during the same period of 1991.

The Foreign Exchange Market

Before independence, as in the other republics of the former Soviet Union, the exchange rate quoted in Latvia was set by the States Bank of the former Soviet Union.[8] Since independence, the foreign exchange market has been based on a laissez faire policy stance. As of mid-1992, the foreign exchange market has been organized around the commercial banks, private foreign exchange dealers, and auctions organized at two stock exchanges (Riga and Latvia). There are no barriers to entry into the market and no restrictions or interventions in the market by the government. While the institutional structure allows foreign exchange transactions through an interbank system, many of the foreign exchange transactions are carried out by private organizations. In addition to a private agency with a network throughout the ruble zone, other small competitors are entering the market for foreign exchange transactions, which goes beyond Latvia's borders and takes into account developments in Moscow's foreign exchange market. The two stock exchanges hold weekly auctions, but only a small amount is traded in these two markets (Annex 2 provides a full description of Latvia's foreign exchange system and its developments).

Since independence Latvia's policy has been to impose no restrictions on foreign exchange transactions. However, there have been large differences in the exchange rate depending on the type of transaction and the market. In the market where individuals have exchanged convertible currency for ruble bank notes, the exchange rate has been determined on the basis of supply and demand. This rate has provided a basis for the exchange rate quoted by the Bank of Latvia. In the other market, which has been dominated by enterprises, convertible currency has been exchanged for bank deposits. The exchange rates between these markets have differed by a margin of about 30 percent or more since the beginning of 1992. The difference has been essentially explained by the limitation of bank deposits as a substitute for cash rubles as a means of payment.

Recommendations

Trade with the Convertible Currency Areas

The requirement of export licenses to convertible currency areas hurts Latvia because the country loses the value of the convertible currency. With the exchange rate of over 100 rubles to the U.S. dollar that prevailed in early 1992, Latvian workers were earning only about USD 10 per month, a demonstration of the very high value of convertible currency in Latvia. The restrictions on exports are, in effect, an implicit tax on imports because they decrease the domestic price of exports relative to imports and reduce the foreign exchange available to import key inputs. This may have adverse consequences, such as inducing the closure of some industries that rely on imported inputs.

Export restrictions can only be justified on a temporary basis and in very few cases, such as where domestic prices of essential commodities are below world market prices. Even in these few cases restrictions should not be imposed through quotas and licenses. Export taxes are preferable to export licenses as a second-best policy to free exports. First, export taxes are more transparent (the government and the public know how much the export tax is costing in foregone foreign exchange per unit sold).

---

8.   Under that system there were essentially three exchange rates: the official exchange rate fluctuated at around 0.6 ruble per U.S. dollar; the commercial rate, introduced in November 1990, was about 1.8 rubles per U.S. dollar; and the tourist rate, introduced in July 1991, was about 32.0 rubles per U.S. dollar.

Second, exporters are able to engage in contracts being certain of their ability to deliver (subject to the tax). Third, a licensing system leads to wastage of resources through lobbying for the licenses. The surrender requirements for exporters to convertible currency areas at below market exchange rates also amounts to a tax on those exports, and probably reduces the incentive to export to those areas.

Given the importance of diversifying Latvia's export markets so as to earn additional convertible currency for diversified imports, the government should avoid reintroducing the surrender requirements. The government should also support exports to the convertible currency area by selective investments in the infrastructure needed to export, and by legal and institutional reforms aimed at attracting foreign capital and encouraging the formation of joint ventures. The recent action taken by the government to replace all export quotas and licenses by a system of export taxes is commendable. The government should further review this system with the objective of eliminating these taxes as soon as possible. Pending the observed export supply response after the elimination of all export restrictions, additional policy measures to facilitate exports may be advised in the context of further studies of the trade sector in Latvia.

Trade with Republics of the Former Soviet Union

Since a substantial portion of Latvia's international trade is conducted with the republics of the former Soviet Union, maintenance of trade linkages with these republics is of paramount importance to prevent further decline of production and employment in the short run. In the long run, it is likely that the extreme dependence on the markets of the former Soviet Union will be reduced, with the situation reverting to something more like Latvia's pre-World War II trading pattern. The problem is that in the short run it will be very difficult for Latvia to switch sales of much of its output to the convertible currency markets. Thus, it must look to the republics of the former Soviet Union for markets for these products, in return for which it can import supplies of many crucial inputs from them, such as refined petroleum products and many metal products.

The government's attempt to facilitate trade with the republics of the former Soviet Union is encouraging. Trade with the republics of the former Soviet Union should be conducted as freely and with as much enterprise autonomy as possible, avoiding governmental obligations at the enterprise level and the use of state orders. This would increase the role of the market economy, and over time help increase the efficiency of Latvian enterprises. State orders are a legacy of the central planning system and are incompatible with the long-run development of a market economy, since obligatory state trading implies that those products under state orders remain under state control. Countries such as Finland, Hungary, and Poland have shown that trade with the former Soviet Union can be conducted on the basis of indicative lists without state obligations or orders.

The main problem in moving away from such lists is that some goods that are important in interstate trade remain under price controls and adjust to world prices gradually. If these products are to be supplied at less than world market prices in interstate trade some kind of state commitment may be required. Otherwise, exporting firms would raise the price to the market price. This underscores the importance of reducing the number of goods subject to price controls. Contrary to practice, however, a state obligation to export does not imply the need to impose a system of state orders and quantity regulations for producing enterprises. Instead, the state could use procurement agents for the purchase of goods for interstate trade that are subject to price controls. The agents would be authorized to pay a price slightly above the controlled domestic price, which should induce sales to the procurement agents. Except for these products, and possibly for a basket of goods exported in return by the oil importing countries, there is no justification for export controls.

Latvia should encourage its commercial banks to establish correspondent accounts in commercial banks of other republics of the former Soviet Union. This will be necessary to facilitate enterprise to enterprise trade, especially as Latvia and the other republics introduce new currencies. Once new currencies are introduced, participation in a clearing union that involves the Baltic countries and other republics of the former Soviet Union would be desirable to permit simultaneous settlement of claims among participating central banks: claims that arise from enterprise to enterprise trade among the various republics.[9]

Such a mechanism demands relatively little convertible currency to facilitate trade, but still permits enterprise to enterprise trade. In a clearing union, only the multilateral balance within the union would be settled in convertible currency, not all the bilateral balances, and transactions at the level of the enterprise would be conducted in national currencies. Settlements among the central banks would be made in convertible currency after short intervals, needed so that the credit outstanding is limited.

Such a system would economize greatly on the use of scarce hard currency reserves required to conduct interrepublican trade, since considerably less would be needed to settle multilateral imbalances than if all the transactions had to be denominated in hard currency and conducted through international banks. Moreover, since only the multilateral balance is important to members of a clearing union, the incentive to balance trade bilaterally would be removed.[10] It should be emphasized that these arrangements are no substitute for moving to internal convertibility. Convertible currency settlement, even within a clearing union, will probably reduce the demand for goods from others. The reason is it will transform incentives among enterprises in different states. Payment would ultimately be required in convertible currency even in a clearing union, so governments will not be able to pay for trade deficits by creating ruble credits through the banking system.

Given the increasing difficulty of trade with the states of the former Soviet Union because of the risk of severe disruptions, it is important to accelerate efforts to diversify into export markets in convertible currency areas. With convertible currency earnings diversification of sources of imports will be relatively easy.

Establishment of Special Trade Arrangements

The Baltic states have reached an agreement regarding the formation of a preferential trading area (PTA). However, they have not yet decided whether it will be a customs union, with common external tariffs on both the import and export sides, or a free trade area, which would require certificates

---

9.   It is important to distinguish a multilateral clearing union from a clearing arrangement or a payments union. A clearing arrangement is the type of arrangement that characterized CMEA trade in the state trading era. Strongly criticized, it involves substantial inter-governmental bartering of goods for goods, with no mechanism for settling imbalances. A payment union differs from a clearing union in the provision of substantial amounts of credit. This creates the problem of funding for a payment union, and introduces distortions in the trade regime (see Michalopoulos and Tarr 1992).

10.   For details, see Michalopoulos and Tarr (1991, 1992). An alternative mechanism has also been proposed (Sachs and Lipton 1992; Williamson 1992). In this scheme commercial banks in the states introducing new currencies would open correspondent ruble accounts in commercial banks of Russia, and Russian commercial banks would maintain correspondent ruble accounts in commercial banks of these countries. An essential feature of the system would be that countries introducing their own currencies would have to allow a free market between their national currency and the ruble, and trade would be predominantly denominated and settled in rubles. An important condition for such a scheme is the stability of the ruble.

Box 2-2. Costs and Benefits of Preferential Trade Arrangements a

A customs union is a particular type of preferential trade arrangement whereby the members of the union eliminate all tariffs and other barriers on trade among themselves, and set a common tariff on trade with the rest of the world. A customs union can improve or worsen the welfare of member countries, depending essentially on whether it leads to trade creation or trade diversion. That, in turn, depends on individual trade policies prevailing before the union and the degree of protection provided by the union. Trade creation occurs when inefficient domestic production of a member country is replaced by lower cost imports from another member country. Trade diversion occurs when lower cost imports from outside the union are replaced by higher cost imports from a union member.

A customs union is likely to result in trade creation and increased welfare (a) the higher the pre-union trade barriers of member countries (b) the lower the union's common barriers on trade with the rest of the world, (c) the greater the number of countries forming the union and the larger their size, (d) the closer geographically the union members are, and (e) the more competitive rather than complementary the economies of member countries are.

It should be cautioned, however, that the experience of preferential trade areas in the developing world has not been encouraging. Except for the Central American Common Market (CACM), preferential trading areas have generated very little trade, and the internal trade of the CACM was predominantly of the costly trade diverting type.

---

a. A simple exposition of preferential trade arrangements is found in Salvatore (1983). A thorough survey of the subject is provided in Corden (1986).

---

of origin. In addition, preferential access to markets in Scandinavia and the European Community is being negotiated. The latter may require the introduction of a certificates of origin system in the Baltic states with preferential access to the Western market.

It has also been suggested that the region that encompasses the former Soviet Union is a good candidate for a PTA. In principle, a permanent PTA could be readily justified if the scope for trade creation is considerably greater than the scope for trade diversion. The evidence strongly indicates, however, that there is a need in the long run for a major reorientation of inter-industry trade, with much more trade with the rest of the world and less with the other republics of the former Soviet Union. Thus, based on traditional static trade creation and trade diversion considerations, it appears ill advised to suggest a permanent preferential trade area for the former Soviet Union (see Box 2-2).

However, a preferential trade area during the transition might be warranted. Given the high degree of specialization in the former Soviet system, there is a strong argument for preserving traditional trade links in the transition period during which trade will be reoriented. That is, importing from the convertible currency area may be feasible after a short adjustment, because Latvian enterprises should be able to accommodate the higher quality Western products as inputs. By contrast, many Latvian enterprises may be unable to adjust the quality of their products to sell in the convertible currency market in the short term. This means that the existing production linkage may be broken before Latvian enterprises are able to compete on world markets.

Temporary preferential trading arrangements will encourage the maintenance of these links during the transition. The Baltic countries and the other republics of the former Soviet Union are simultaneously removing their non-tariff barriers to imports. Given the likely presence of unemployment, as these republics collectively remove their non-tariff barriers to imports, moderate transitional tariff protection for positive value added industries would be warranted because the opportunity costs of primary factors are very low and many industries would be expected to contract significantly under open world competition. With the disintegration of the former Soviet Union and the independence of the Baltic countries, the only way that transitional tariff protection can protect the formerly domestic market of the union is through a temporary preferential trade area. If preferences are based on tariffs, intra-union trade would initially not be subject to external tariffs. Extra-union trade, however, would be subject to moderate tariffs initially. In the longer term, and after a suitable transition period, the preferential trade area could be terminated through a combination of lowering tariffs to third countries and raising them to members of the preferential area.

It is important to avoid high preferential tariff rates even on a temporary basis, however, because high tariff rates may result in the continued operation of industries with negative value added, which would raise rather than reduce the adjustment costs to the economy. Moreover, strong trade preferences for intra-union trade dramatically increase the dangers of costly trade diversion (see Box 2-2). Provided only a moderate level of protection is employed, a temporary preferential trade could facilitate both the long run reorientation and the short-term transition.[11]

Although the formation of a preferential trading area among the Baltic countries will help preserve traditional trade links among them, the potential benefits will remain relatively restricted due to the limited size of the trading area. The potential gains from a temporary preferential trading area would increase substantially if the area could be extended to include Russia and the other former Soviet republics. Indeed, most of the disruptions in trade have been associated with trade between Latvia and the non-Baltic countries. Therefore, the argument to introduce temporary preferential arrangements in order to ease adjustment from traditional links during the transition would acquire much greater significance if the trading area could be enlarged. It is possible that the Baltic countries may form a customs union, but trade with the countries of the former Soviet Union as part of a larger free trade area.

In summary, to minimize trade-related shocks on output and encourage the restoration of traditional trade links, the government should make efforts to engage in special trade arrangements with the Baltic countries and the former Soviet republics and introduce a temporary increase in tariffs applied to imports from non-former Soviet Union countries. Such increase in tariffs would not only generate additional fiscal revenues, but would also help preserve critical trade links in the transition period during which trade will be reoriented. Intra-union trade should not initially be subject to external tariffs, while extra-union trade could be subject to tariffs of 15 to 30 percent, declining by a certain percentage per year over a period of three to five years. When the long-run lower level is reached, intra-union trade would also be subject to the tariff, that is, the preferential arrangement would be terminated.

---

11.   The transitory external tariff would also generate modest budgetary revenues during the initial stages of the reforms, which is precisely the period when the budget will be subject to strong adverse pressures. Since most external trade is with countries of the former Soviet Union, however, tariff revenues cannot be expected to be large if a broad preferential trade area is formed that includes most of the states of the former Soviet Union.

Balance of Payments and External Financing

Balance of Payments Prospects, 1992-93

Latvian trade is heavily influenced by energy imports, which account for about a quarter of total imports. The country has to import all its natural gas and oil products and most of its electricity needs. Gas and oil products have traditionally been supplied by Russia. However, with the disruption of trade between the two countries and as the prices of these commodities started to increase toward international levels, oil and gas imports from Russia have dropped significantly. Supplies of oil products from alternative sources have increased, which has been possible because the port of Ventspils is equipped to handle part of such imports. Nevertheless, Russia is expected to remain a major supplier of gas and oil products for some time. These developments represent a significant shift in the geographical structure of Latvia's energy imports. Among other factors, this shift partially explains why Latvia's trade deficit in 1992 and 1993 is expected to be primarily with the non-FSU countries (Table 2-6).

The preliminary data for 1992 show a significant decline in the volume of trade with the FSU. However, the overall decline in Latvia's FSU exports has been less than the decline in imports. The larger reduction in imports from the FSU has been mainly due to the general sharp production declines in the FSU republics, attempts by these republics to limit exports and avoid internal shortages, deficiencies in payment mechanisms, and the terms of trade shock. The reduction in imports has been a crucial factor in the sharp drop in production and output in 1992.

Projections for 1993 assume a gradual resumption of trade relations with the FSU. Such a situation appears plausible in view of the expected reduction in government involvement in interstate trade and the possibility of the revival of enterprise to enterprise trade, given the long established trade links between enterprises in Latvia and the FSU, as well as the signing of a major trade agreement with Russia in 1992. Energy imports would be expected to stabilize in volume terms, non-energy imports would be expected to grow, and most import prices would be expected to rise to world market levels in 1993. The improved availability of imported inputs would also permit a rise in export volumes. Because of the low volume of trade in 1992, both imports and exports could show substantial growth in 1993. After this initial increase, exports and imports would grow more moderately and would be in line with the growth prospects of the economy. Non-FSU exports could, on average, grow by about 7.4 percent a year and imports by 7.0 percent a year between 1993 and 1997. Some trade diversification is expected in the non-energy sectors in line with the reorientation of trade with the convertible currency areas. As Latvia's trade with convertible currency areas grows, trade with the FSU would stabilize at a much lower level than in the past, and stay at around 55 percent of total exports by the late 1990s.

Expanding Latvia's trade with the convertible currency area remains one of the most important medium-term challenges for the growth of the economy. Latvia needs to build up a level of convertible exports that will, after a transition period of say three to four years, begin to pay for most of the convertible imports. The success in achieving this objective depends on the ongoing structural reforms and on removing some remaining constraints on exports, for example, export taxes.

Latvia's wood industry is already competitive in world markets. Other products such as textiles, light machinery, building materials, and fisheries may also be competitive in non-FSU markets given the currently depreciated exchange rate of the Latvian ruble against the U.S. dollar. The sectors that could have a better chance for penetrating the hard currency markets include building materials, wood

Table 2-6. Trade and Balance of Payments Projections, 1992-93
(USD millions)

Balance of payments	1992 [a]	1993
Exports	800	1,320
FSU	410	800
Non-FSU	390	520
Imports	900	1,630
FSU	420	870
Energy	280	380
Other	140	490
Non-FSU	480	760
Energy	80	110
Other	400	650
Trade Balance	-100	-310
FSU	-10	-70
Non-FSU	-90	-240
Services (net)	105	70
of which: Interest	0	15
Current Account Balance	5	-240
Capital Account	40	305
Official Grants	30	40
Direct Foreign Investment	0	10
Medium- & Long-Term Capital Flows	40	255
Disbursement	40	260
Amortization [b]	0	5
Other Capital [c]	-30	..
Change in Reserves [- = increase]	-45	-65
Memo.		
Reserves as months of imports	2	2

.. = not significant.
a. The 1992 data are provisional. The balance of payments situation has been evolving rapidly, particularly since the last quarter of 1992. It is believed that once the final data become available, the current account may show a significant surplus for 1992.
b. Includes debt service on projected new borrowing from multilateral and bilateral sources.
c. Change in correspondent account balances with ruble area central banks.
Source: Latvian authorities and World Bank staff estimates.

working, light industries, and fisheries. However, the reorientation of exports toward the convertible currency areas will take time for a number of reasons, including the low quality of products, the large investment needs to upgrade and expand export industries, and the lack of marketing know-how and export finance. Transport services and tourism also have good potential to earn hard currency for Latvia.

The overall trade deficit in 1992 has been moderate largely because the foreign exchange requirements to cover the needed imports did not materialize. In 1993, however, Latvia is expected to be able to cover a considerably larger trade deficit than in 1992. A further collapse of output can be avoided and recovery of exports could be possible if imports increase substantially in 1993. While merchandise trade is expected to show a deficit, net service income is likely to be positive, due mainly to foreign exchange receipts on maritime and shipping services, port service fees for exports of Russia's crude oil, and a low initial stock of debt on which interest is owed. The overall current account is, therefore, projected to show a deficit of about USD 240 million in 1993.

These projections, however, are tentative and subject to large margins of error, given the uncertainties regarding the impact of currency reform on trade and payments relationships, the external economic and political environment, and the speed with which Latvia can normalize its trade relations with the FSU and expand its exports to convertible currency markets. Quantifying the balance of payments is itself complicated by data problems: statistical systems are still weak and are undergoing a transition from the Soviet system to Western and worldwide standards.

External Financing Requirements

In 1993, Latvia requires substantial external resources to cover its current account deficit, stem the decline in production, and build up adequate reserves to support the new currency. Latvia will also have to begin servicing its emerging external debt and to cover modest trade fluctuations. About one-third of the current account deficit would be due to trade with the former Soviet republics. Total gross financing requirements are estimated at about USD 350 million for 1992 and 1993 (Table 2-7). Of this amount, USD 220 million would be needed to finance the non-interest current account deficits and about USD 110 million is for reserve build-up. Debt service payments are expected to remain small during this period, about USD 20 million.

With implementation of the reform program and adjustment of the economy to the strong 1992 terms of trade shock, Latvia's current account deficit and the resulting financing requirements are expected to decline significantly in the mid-1990s, while remaining large through 1994, and probably 1995.

Sources of Financing

Private flows are not likely to be of significant importance in short term, but will increase in the medium term. However, official flows from multilateral and bilateral sources will be an essential part of the financing plan in short term (Table 2-7). The possible sources of financing for 1992-93 are described in the following paragraphs.

Private foreign borrowing required to close the financing gap will be negligible given Latvia's lack of a credit history in international financial markets. So far, most commercial lending to Latvia has been in short-term trade credits, and the outstanding amounts have not been increasing.

Direct foreign investment has already commenced in Latvia, particularly by the Nordic countries. Investments are being made by foreign enterprises in the hotel, fish processing, furniture, and wood industries. However, the impact of such inflows on the balance of payments will not be significant in 1993 since investments will generally be implemented over a longer time period.

Multilateral institutions are estimated to provide about USD 180 million in 1992 and 1993. Of this amount, nearly half is expected to be provided by the International Monetary Fund (IMF), largely as reserves financing, and the rest by the World Bank, the European Bank for Recontruction and Development (EBRD), and Nordic Investment Bank (NIB).

Financial support from bilateral sources is essential for the success of the government's reform program. Without such funding the reduction of imports will be even more severe, which would

Table 2-7. Financing Plan, 1992-93
(USD millions)

Financing	1992	1993	Total
Financing Requirement	40	310	350
Non-Interest Current Account	5	-225	-220
Debt Service [a]	0	20	20
Amortization	0	5	5
Interest	0	15	15
Reserve Build-Up [b]	45	65	110
Financing Sources	40	310	350
Private Sources	..	10	10
Direct Foreign Investment	..	10	10
Commercial Credits (excluding export credit agencies)	..	..	..
Official Sources	70	300	370
Official Transfers	30	40	70
Medium- and Long-Term Disbursements	40	260	300
Multilateral	40	140	180
Bilateral			
(including export credit agencies and EC)	..	120	120
Other capital [c]	-30	..	-30

.. = not significant.
a. Includes projected debt service payments on multilateral and bilateral loans.
b. Assumes IMF standby arrangement fully disbursed into reserves.
c. Mostly enterprises export earnings deposited abroad.
Source: Latvian authorities and World Bank staff estimates.

lead to an even more serious fall in output and consumption. It is therefore assumed that the balance of financing requirements will be provided by bilateral sources. USD 120 million is anticipated for 1993 from the bilateral donors, including export credit agencies.

Export credit agencies (ECAs) are expected to become a significant source of financing over the next several years. Trade credit facilities have been established by Canada, Denmark, and Germany. In the current distorted and uncertain environment, export credit agencies will need to pay particular attention to the financial and economic viability of projects proposed for financing under export credits. Significant opportunities for cofinancing projects with multilateral institutions will be present and the involvement of these institutions could help to provide additional assurances of the economic merit of such investments.

Most ECAs, as well as private commercial creditors, are expected to provide medium- and long-term credit provided the country has accumulated an adequate level of foreign exchange reserves and has established a track record of success in implementing structural programs. Therefore, the government's commitment to implementing the economic reform program would be essential to attract a considerable share of the financing needs from these sources.

In addition to external resources required to fill the balance of payments gap, substantial resources are needed to help finance Latvia's technical assistance requirements. Major potential sources of funds include the Nordic countries and the EC's PHARE program.

Aid coordination will play a vital role in assuring the success of the sustained scenario. Although a combination of budgetary constraints in donor countries and problems in implementing the reform program could raise difficulties, there is reason to believe that the necessary resources can be mobilized. The World Bank and the IMF have worked closely to identify possible sources of financing from private and official donors. This has included contacting representatives of potential donor countries, working within the G-24 framework to coordinate assistance to the Baltic countries, developing a framework for identifying investment priorities, and participating in the coordination of technical assistance.

Matching Financing Requirements and Sources

Matching By Source

The need to match financing to Latvia's trade and balance of payments requirements underscores the need for a well-managed foreign aid coordination process during the next few years. Foreign exchange provided by official sources is usually tied to imports from a particular country, a specific investment project, or technical assistance. Likewise private financing is normally tied to a specific project or product.

While part of Latvia's gross financing requirements for 1992 and 1993 arise from trade deficits with the FSU, particularly Russia, virtually all external assistance is from convertible currency sources outside the former Soviet Union. A significant portion of these funds, especially those from official sources, may be tied. To the extent that they cannot be used to finance FSU imports and the associated trade deficits, the hard currency export earnings will have to be the primary source of financing these deficits. This matching, however, may not be a serious problem, since Latvia's hard currency export earnings are expected to more than cover the trade deficit with the FSU during 1992-93, as discussed below.

In 1992-93 non-FSU exports are projected to total about USD 910 million, and another USD 175 million are expected from net service exports and private transfers, bringing the amount of available foreign exchange to about USD 1,085 million (Table 2-6)[12]. For the same period, the total trade deficit with FSU is estimated at about USD 80 million. Therefore, the total hard currency export earnings for these two years would more than cover the trade deficits with FSU. There will be some USD 1,005 million left to finance part of the non-FSU imports of USD 1,240 million for those two years. Thus, USD 235 million of the non-FSU imports will have to be financed through the capital account in the form of flows from both multilateral and bilateral sources. The amount of foreign exchange needs to finance the FSU trade deficit could become larger if following the resumption of trade relations with the FSU

---

12. Services and private transfers are treated on a net basis in the absence of more detailed information regarding their composition. Thus, gross foreign exchange from exports of goods and services plus private transfers might be somewhat higher.

Latvia imports all its energy needs from that market in 1993. In that case, the total trade deficit with the FSU in 1993 could increase to USD 180 million instead of USD 70 million.

Matching by Type

In the short term Latvia's pressing foreign exchange needs are for balance of payment support to obtain critical imports and stabilize the economy. If this type of financing can be obtained Latvia would gain flexibility in managing its foreign exchange flows. Well-designed project support will also be needed, particularly related to bank and enterprise restructuring, which could be important in stimulating a supply response in the short term. Likewise, project financing from private foreign sources, especially through direct foreign investment would also be helpful and desirable. Within the next year or two, the government can then launch a carefully targeted public investment program that addresses the serious underinvestment in public services during the past few years.

Although Latvia's external debt is still small, it will be important to adopt an appropriate external debt strategy to prevent an excessive debt service burden in the future. In the short term, flows from official sources should play a major role in meeting the external financing requirements for the next several years, given the time that will be required to develop Latvia's capacity to earn foreign exchange from convertible currency markets. The prospects for obtaining such financing are enhanced by (a) the sympathy of donors for the need to maintain imports to avoid further economic compression and the consequent risk of serious social and political problems, (b) the steps to assure short-term stabilization as evidenced by the agreement on a standby arrangement with the IMF, and (c) a solid economic reform program that has the support of international financial institutions.

Latvia will also need a substantial amount of technical assistance in the short term and donor support for such assistance is being actively sought. However, technical assistance funds normally make little contribution to the balance of payments. Technical assistance funds have therefore not been included in the balance of payments in Table 2-6, and related financing requirements would be in addition to those shown in Table 2-7. Several governments have already committed technical assistance to Latvia. The IMF has proved technical assistance in various areas of fiscal policy, monetary policy, and economic statistics. Also, the World Bank, in the context of its rehabilitation loan to Latvia, has identified technical assistance requirements related to key areas of the government's structural reform program.

External Debt and Creditworthiness

As a republic within the former Soviet Union, Latvia was allocated responsibility for over USD 1 billion of the external debt of the former Soviet Union. However, in mid-March 1992, the chairmen of the supreme councils of the three Baltic states issued an official declaration that their countries are not legal successors to the former Soviet Union, and therefore cannot take responsibility for servicing and paying off its external debt. Discussions between the governments of Latvia and Russia on this issue continue.

Since regaining independence in September 1991, Latvia has undertaken only negligible new debt obligations. However, the government and state enterprises will soon have access to foreign credit, starting with loans from multilateral institutions and the establishment of short-term credit lines with export credit agencies.

Latvia's debt service is projected to stay within a prudent level of 5 percent of non-FSU exports in 1993. Having only recently regained its independence and with no credit record, Latvia will need to establish full creditworthiness in the international financial markets. The projections shown in Table 2-6 imply current account deficits of about 12 percent of GDP in 1993. Over the longer term, if reforms are sustained and the economy fully adjusts to trade at world market prices, the current account deficits could be reduced to about 3 to 4 percent of GDP by the late 1990s. Under these assumptions, Latvia's level of debt service would equal less than 7 percent of total exports or 15 percent of non-FSU exports and would be manageable by normal creditworthiness criteria.

Although the level of debt and debt service would be manageable if reform is sustained, Latvia could build up new debt relatively quickly and could become, under an adverse macroeconomic scenario, a moderately indebted country by the end of the decade even if exports grow reasonably fast. As mentioned above, Latvia will need to borrow substantial sums of foreign exchange during the next several years to help assure the success of its economic transformation program. If the funds are borrowed on normal commercial terms, the debt service ratio could rise above sustainable levels in the medium term to roughly 25 percent of non-FSU exports by 1997.

Recommendations

Fast resolution of the external debt issue is important to improve Latvia's access to foreign capital. Financial institutions may find it difficult to provide Latvia access to new credit in the presence of continued uncertainty about the remaining outstanding debt. The government needs to ensure fast access to complete and up-to-date information about all its external financial obligations, including those contracted directly and those that it has guaranteed. To this end, the government should assign the task of collecting, registering, and processing all external debt information to one unit in the government, probably in the Ministry of Finance. This unit would also project future debt service obligations and work closely with the other units in charge of identifying and managing the budgetary and external financing needs of the government. Similarly, the Bank of Latvia should develop a capacity for balance of payments accounting and for monitoring trade and capital flows and should work closely on such issues with the Ministry of Finance and other responsible agencies.

To make full use of possible credits under the export credit line agreements with Western creditors, the government should, through the Ministry of Finance, define and formally adopt guidelines for government guarantees of loans contracted by both state-owned and private Latvian enterprises. In principle, it is important that guarantee policies be transparent and non-discriminatory.

The breakdown of the centralized trade regime will have implications for the economy both in terms of the market effect and the terms of trade effect. While the terms of trade effect will reflect the change in relative prices of imports to exports, the market effect will indicate losing trade with the other FSU republics who prefer to import from other countries with higher quality products, and probably lower prices. The economy also needs to adjust to the elimination of various explicit and implicit transfers from the former Soviet Union, which in effect were a form of external financing. The implication is that Latvia not only needs to gain access to foreign borrowing, but also needs to generate larger exports to finance its import needs. This would underscore the need to pursue a trade strategy with a strong export orientation. Adoption of this strategy is particularly important at this stage in view of Latvia's close proximity to Europe, its highly skilled labor force, and its relatively low wages of skilled workers. Such a trade strategy should aim at eliminating state orders, promoting enterprise to enterprise trade, facilitating enterprises' direct engagement in international transactions, adopting an active exchange rate policy, and eliminating export restrictions and replacing export taxes with tariffs. Moreover, to maintain creditworthiness in the medium term, it will be essential to ensure through aid coordination activities that as much of the foreign assistance as possible is on a grant basis. The coordination of foreign external assistance is elaborated on in the next chapter.

CHAPTER 3

Systemic Reforms

Transformation to a market economy requires fundamental changes in the structure of production and in the relationship between resource allocation and use. While some important policies of the command system have been abandoned, further institutional and policy reforms are needed for proper functioning of a competitive market economy in Latvia. In particular, reforms are needed to (a) reinstate private ownership, privatize existing state enterprises, expand private sector activities, and introduce competition through the breakup of existing monopolies; (b) put in place a modern financial system suitable for a market economy; (c) establish a properly functioning labor market; (d) establish a safety net system for the most vulnerable groups to minimize the social cost of adjustment; and (e) improve public sector management and strengthen capabilities for evaluation and implementation of public investment programs. The transition process takes several years and its management poses a serious challenge to the Latvian authorities.

The Enterprise Sector

Development of the Private Sector

The Business Environment

To support Latvia's transition to a market economy, a strong private sector must be developed. At present, private activity in Latvia consists of new small businesses, a limited amount of privatization, and foreign investment, mainly through joint ventures. Private initiatives are constrained by economic instability, legal inconsistencies, and the absence of adequate support institutions. While some uncertainty is inevitable during a transition, protracted political and economic instability can seriously disrupt the implementation of reforms, development of the private sector, and transition to a market economy.

Although Latvia has begun to enact legislation to encourage commercial activity, major gaps and inconsistencies exist. Many laws date from before World War II, while others were adopted prior to independence. Some laws provide unnecessary detail about day-to-day business operations, and a few include provisions that actually hamper new entry into business. The progress made and areas needing further elaboration are summarized in Table 3-1.

A market economy needs more than simply a legal framework; it also needs institutions to enforce agreements and commitments. The best drafted laws are of little value if there is no means to enforce them or resolve disputes. Investors need assurance that disputes will be resolved promptly and fairly. The judicial system will need to be strengthened to handle the complex disputes likely to emerge in a market economy. Substantial training will be required to reorient and expand the capacity of the legal system. In cooperation with universities and the emerging private sector, the government should introduce more relevant courses and training programs in law schools and expand the opportunity for overseas study by lawyers, judges, and professors.

Table 3-1. Status of the Legal Framework for a Market Economy

Property rights, including ownership rights and property transfers

Existing laws on restitution cover land, housing, and enterprises, but rules governing restitution (i.e., compensation) not fully determined. Law on Privatization of Small Municipal Enterprises enacted November 1991 and amended in 1992.

Areas that need elaboration and or enactment of legislation include (a) comprehensive property law defining who may own property and on what conditions, and providing equal protection for all property regardless of ownership and permitting expropriation only after carefully defined public purpose and with adequate and full compensation; [a] (b) a system for recording all property rights, including titles, transfers, mortgages, and other secured transactions; (c) laws governing intellectual property (patents, trademarks, and copyrights).

Competition legislation, including development of a comprehensive commercial law, entry and exit, and the control of monopolistic practices

Existing laws include laws on Entrepreneurship Activity (September 1990), Limited Liability Companies (January 1991), Partnerships (February 1991), and Shareholder Associations. Foreign investment activity regulated by Law on Foreign Investments (November 1991). Bankruptcy and anti-monopoly laws are in place (December 1991).

Areas that need elaboration include comprehensive company law (or trade law/commercial law, if commercial transactions will also be included) setting the rules for formation and registration of companies, capital requirements, company management, minority shareholders protection and financing institutions for implementation and enforcement, public company register, mortgage/liens register, bankruptcy courts, and alternative dispute resolution system. None of the existing laws in this group is modern, organized, and easy to implement.

Company legislation, including contract law and related judicial rules.

Existing Laws (pre-World War II) set forth general governing principles, but need to be adapted to the new market-oriented system. Current transactions do not easily fit into the old structure.

Areas that need elaboration include legislation governing the sale of goods, credit transactions, secured transactions, collateral, negotiable instruments, and securities. The civil and criminal procedure codes need redrafting to allow the judicial system (which previously handled mostly criminal cases) to deal with complex commercial transactions.

a.   Citizenship in Latvia is not yet defined as criterion for property ownership. Several proposals have been made to parliament and are under discussion.

Source: World Bank staff.

Small Business Development

With little promotional effort, the private sector in Latvia has grown quite rapidly. Most new activity has been in trade and other services, although a few small manufacturing firms exist. At the beginning of 1992, nearly 7,000 registered firms were operating, and 20,000 rural enterprises were providing services for the agricultural sector. The interests of this emerging sector are represented by a group of five associations, which lobby regularly with the government.[1] New business establishment is also being enhanced by the privatization of small enterprises in trade, catering, and services. In addition, the sale of moveable assets and separable activities of state-owned enterprises has been permitted in order to stimulate small business establishment. The government also plans to address the contracting out of public services more systematically. The government has established a division in the Ministry of Economic Reform (MER) to foster private sector development, but neither its mandate nor its responsibilities have been clearly defined.

Although there are no overt barriers to private sector development and the registration of new enterprises is said to be relatively straightforward, obstacles to the development of small businesses remain: a lack of equal access to land and suitable premises, difficulty in securing funds to establish and expand a small business, a perception that the regulatory framework is confounding and inconsistent, and a lack of business skills and business information. In addition, Latvian entrepreneurs encounter cultural and institutional difficulties given the absence of private sector activity under the communist system.

Foreign Investment

By 1992 Latvia had attracted only small amounts of foreign capital, and many of the joint ventures have focused on trade. For some Latvian partners, the motivation for forming joint ventures may have been to minimize taxes and gain access to export markets. Yet foreign investment is essential to provide capital and access to new technology and markets. Larger amounts of capital are not likely to be forthcoming until confidence in the Latvian ruble increases. Since independence, more than 1,000 enterprises with foreign partners have registered in Latvia (see Table 3-2). Clearly, there is considerable scope for increasing the level of foreign investment.

Privatization

The Latvian program for ownership reform comprises three stages: municipalization, denationalization (or restitution), and privatization.

The first step is to return state-owned property to the municipalities, which will be responsible for its subsequent privatization. The municipalization was largely completed by mid-1992.

The second step is to return property nationalized or otherwise confiscated after 1940. The government has promised to restore such property to former owners or their descendants or to pay compensation in cash, vouchers, or comparable property when the property itself cannot be restituted. Three separate restitution programs have been going on for housing, enterprises, and land. The process has proceeded at varying speeds due to different claim deadlines: deadlines for enterprises and land were July 1992, but for housing is October 1994. Delays have been also caused because the rules for compensation for unreturnable property have not been defined. These delays have slowed down

---

1.   The Small Business Confederation, the Small Business Association, the Latvian Entrepreneur's Union, the Craftsmen's Union, and the Latvian Rural Business Association are independent groups representing different types of small businesses. These associations are themselves grouped under an umbrella organization, the World Association of Latvian Entrepreneurs.

Table 3-2. Foreign Investment in Latvia as of the First Quarter of 1992

Joint Venture Country	No. of Enterprises	Foreign Capital		Partners' Share (%)
		Rubles millions	USD millions	
United States	88	19.7	83.8	49.2
Germany	159	148.3	3.6	43.0
Sweden	67	103.3	1.9	55.4
Poland	72	2.8	0.3	49.3
Other	618	284.4	29.6	42.5
Total	1,004	558.5	119.2	43.0

Note: In addition, there are 400 registered joint ventures with partners from the republics of the former Soviet Union. In such cases the foreign investment may be in equipment rather than in foreign exchange.
Source: Ministry of Economic Reform.

privatization and enterprise restructuring efforts. The government intends to move ahead with the privatization of medium and large enterprises by reserving shares of enterprises for claims by former owners and privatizing the rest. In other instances where claims by the former owners have not been received by the time of privatization, cash or alternative compensation will be permitted. Implementation of these mechanisms should ensure that potential restitution claims will not continue to slow down the privatization process.

The third step is to sell state and municipal property. In November 1991 a law on the privatization of small enterprises was passed and municipalities were instructed to privatize systematically businesses in trade, services, and catering under their jurisdiction. In conjunction with this program small state-owned enterprises were converted to municipal ownership. This program began with a very narrow focus: the original legislation stipulated that enterprises eligible for sale must be municipally owned, operate in the areas of trade or service, be no more than 100 square meters in size, have a maximum seating capacity of thirty people in the case of restaurants, and have no more than ten employees. This legislation was amended in 1992 to increase the scope of the small privatization program by eliminating the size restriction on entities that could be sold. Businesses are auctioned for cash. To be eligible bidders must have resided in Latvia for a minimum of sixteen years. In some cases preferential rights are granted to employees.

The program started slowly in early 1992, but has gained momentum since then. The municipalities are responsible for privatizing small enterprises. During the first quarter of 1992, some 80 to 100 businesses were sold under this program, generally accompanied by leases for the property. Parliament instructed municipalities to privatize 35 percent of retail businesses under their purview by September 1992. By the beginning of November, nearly 60 percent of enterprises eligible for privatization under the purview of seven municipalities had been privatized. In the city of Riga, for example, nearly two-thirds of municipality-owned commercial and trade outlets, restaurants, and service enterprises had been privatized or leased.

Progress on other aspects of privatization continues to be slow mainly because of a lack of clear policy on citizenship and the restitution of property to previous owners. In March 1992 parliament passed a resolution broadly outlining guidelines for and an approach to privatization and instructing the government to prepare legislation for the privatization of large enterprises. The resolution specified four possibilities for the privatization of large enterprises: (a) transferring them into joint stock companies and subsequently privatizing them, (b) selling them to an individual or legal entity, (c) selling them to foreign private investors or firms, and (d) leasing them with an option to buy. Parliament also approved the use of vouchers for privatization of state and municipal properties. However, implementation procedures for voucher privatization have yet to be defined. A handful of large enterprises are currently being prepared for pilot privatization with external assistance.

Clearly, the primary obstacles to progress on privatization are political ones. The government has been unable to design a comprehensive approach to privatization methods, and key issues such as restitution mechanisms and questions of citizenship have not been resolved. The lack of progress has fueled uncertainty about the direction and stability of the entire reform program. Not only is privatization moving slowly, but spontaneous privatization and arbitrary deals have reportedly been enacted at various levels of government.

The institutional arrangements for privatization have also been in a state of flux. In the early stages, the Department of Ownership, which reported directly to the Council of Ministers, carried out privatization activities, primarily program design. These activities are now being coordinated by the MER. However, an earlier government program had decentralized much of the decisionmaking, and as a result, ministries such as Finance and Justice contained divisions of privatization. More important, the branch ministries have been mandated to play a key role in implementation in terms of selection and sales of medium and large enterprises. Branch ministries have identified enterprises under their purview to be privatized and were mandated to submit privatization plans (developed at the enterprise level, including possible pre-privatization corporatization and restructuring) for these enterprises by November 1992. These numerous governmental organizations have caused confusion about basic questions such as who is authorized to carry out privatization, what forms of privatization are permitted, and how information is reported and collected.

Public Enterprise Reform

Because of the slow progress on privatization, many enterprises will remain in the public domain in the short to medium term. During this transition, reforms are needed to improve the economic and productive efficiency of these enterprises. Several issues will have to be addressed, namely: (a) clarification of ownership rights; (b) demonopolization and deconcentration; (c) establishment of a commercially-oriented method of operation, including financial autonomy; and (d) the growing size of enterprise arrears.

Ownership

The question of enterprise ownership has become increasingly complicated. Most issues involve complex interests. For example, the final years of Soviet rule saw the creation of new enterprises, for example, cooperatives independent of Moscow. Employees in some organizations believe they have ownership rights to the assets with which they work. Government responses to these claims have been inconsistent. Latvia has taken possession of some 140 All-Union enterprises, which have been placed under the sectoral ministries. There is an ongoing program to assign property rights to local and state governments. Foreign participation in state companies is now permitted.

Many of these ownership issues are beginning to be resolved. The former All-Union enterprises are now under Latvian control. The process of municipalization (decentralizing ownership to the municipalities) is mostly complete and ownership through joint ventures is being established in a fairly straightforward way. However, managerial and worker interests are still ambiguous, so that arbitrary decisions over ownership rights are possible. These issues must be addressed soon.

Demonopolization and Deconcentration

Latvian enterprises are, on average, much larger than those in market economies. Many enterprises in Latvia are vertically and horizontally integrated. Large industrial *combinats* exist where there is no justification based on economies of scale requirements. In addition to fostering monopolistic tendencies and anti-competitive behavior in selling goods, these entities tend to purchase inputs from other members of the *combinat*, thus discouraging the development of competitive independent suppliers. The breakup of these enterprises into smaller, viable units should be a top priority. The government has introduced proposals in a number of the large (formerly All-Union) enterprises to separate technologically distinct units, including breaking up large industrial *combinats* into financially autonomous entities that could purchase inputs and sell products outside their former organization. This is a positive step toward eliminating cross-subsidization within large enterprises and encouraging individual enterprises with potential for privatization. However, links should exist only between the newly created subsidiaries and headquarters. All forms of ownership or other arrangements between subsidiaries should be avoided.

An anti-monopoly law was passed by parliament in December 1991, and a department to deal with demonopolization has been established in the MER. Its role is to prepare plans for individual cases of demonopolization to be presented to the Council of Ministers. Work is in progress to improve implementation of the anti-monopoly law. The program of demonopolization will be closely coordinated with the program of corporatization to avoid further integration of enterprises and to increase competition and efficiency.

Commercialization

Even when enterprises remain in state hands, they should be run on a commercial basis. To do so requires appropriate arrangements for governance, including exercise of ownership rights, and strict financial discipline, including severing all ties (subsidies and investment funds) with the state budget.

Commercialization has been implemented only partially. The steps that have already been taken to instill a commercial orientation in existing state-owned enterprises include (a) the elimination of state orders except those needed to fulfill interstate agreements; (b) the removal of privileges to enterprises that are suppliers to the state; (c) the elimination of budgetary support to enterprises, including implicit subsidies from all levels of government; and (d) the elimination of the system of administrative guarantees on loans to enterprises and its replacement with a system of commercial guarantees.

Despite a directive by parliament to complete legislation for corporatization (to transform state-owned enterprises into state stock companies), this process was formally tied to privatization until late 1992, and, as such, little or no corporatization had occurred. Some forms of managerial autonomy, such as the ability to hire and fire employees, were being exercised. In late 1992 the government decided to corporatize the majority of state-owned enterprises, but commercialization is still moving slowly.

Enterprise Arrears

There have been substantial changes in the financial relationship between enterprises and the government. At present, the budgets of state-owned enterprises are independent of the ministries. Subsidization of working capital has been eliminated, and the government has taken a firm stand regarding governmental financing of investment projects in the industrial sector. However, input shortages resulting from the collapse of FSU trading arrangements and the high cost of non-FSU imports, together with falling internal and external demand, have produced substantial losses for Latvian enterprises since early 1992. Combined with failures of the FSU payments system, this has resulted in significant and growing inter-enterprise arrears. Many firms seem to be reaching the limit of the arrears that they are willing to absorb from other firms in order to stay in business. As a result, Latvian enterprises are turning increasingly to pre-payment schemes and other temporary arrangements to stem the flow of arrears.

One important aspect of the accumulation of arrears is a risk that enterprises may be left with uncollectible debt if their counterparts in the other republics of the former Soviet Union were to collapse. Under these circumstances, the banking system would also be adversely affected by non-performing assets. Loss-making enterprises will, however, continue to exist during the transition period. Inter-enterprise arrears, both domestic and interrepublican, are likely to remain for some time to come, and efforts should be made and guidelines developed to prevent the further accumulation of these arrears.

Recommendations

Development of the Private Sector

To encourage a sound environment for commercial activities and development of the private sector it is crucial that the legal framework provide clear rules concerning property rights; market entry and exit; trade and competition, including bankruptcy law, anti-monopoly legislation, and accompanying regulations; and commercial law, including company law, contract law, banking law, and related rules governing the settlement of commercial disputes. Other areas where legal reform needs to continue to improve the business environment and enable market transactions include citizenship, recording and transfer of property, the creation and trading of securities, and intellectual property rights. In addition to a clear legal framework, investors need confidence in the enforceability of agreements. Delays in enforcing laws and agreements between private parties will impede the efficient functioning of economic activities. The judicial and dispute settlement system needs to increase its efforts to handle the complex disputes that are likely to emerge.

To promote competition by stimulating small business development, several measures need to be taken to promote new businesses. In particular, to relieve the problems with access to office and other commercial space, the government should consider a tax on unused or underused office space in state enterprises. A survey of excess space in government-owned buildings that could be leased to small businesses would be useful.

To overcome financing problems, the government should consider introducing measures to stimulate the availability of credit to small businesses.[2] Such measures include (a) tax incentives to banks that make such loans; (b) special lines of credit that take into account the higher cost and potentially higher risk of this type of lending; and (c) a guarantee, which should be only partial so that banks have an incentive to scrutinize and collect on the loan. However, enterprises should be encouraged to prepare viable and bankable projects and not to rely on the government to overcome financing problems.

To ease information bottlenecks, the government should supply updates of policy and regulatory changes and help businesses contact suppliers, distributors, and foreign investors. With the assistance of donor funds, the government should also support the development of business associations; the initiation of private initiatives to disseminate information and services by publishing business directories; the establishment of business centers that provide fee-based services to businesses; and the development of training institutions and other facilities that can hold seminars, workshops, and so on to familiarize people with entrepreneurial skills.

To expand small business development opportunities, the government should expand contracting activities between state-owned enterprises and the emerging private sector. Small businesses can provide resources and services to large manufacturing enterprises and to state and local governments.

The government should coordinate its policy on private sector development to ensure a coherent approach and to stimulate appropriate development during the transition. The division for private sector development in the MER should be a logical place for such initiatives. The function of this division should be limited to analyzing the implications of government policies for private entrepreneurs, liaising with business associations, coordinating external assistance for private sector development, and assuring that basic reference materials for business start-up and compliance with regulations are easily available.

Foreign Investment

Further measures are also needed to promote the inflow of foreign investment that is crucial to Latvia's growth and export prospects in the future. The Foreign Investment Law provides the usual protection to foreign investors and offers tax incentives to attract foreign capital.[3] Modifications should be made to this legislation to make foreign investment as attractive in Latvia as in other reforming socialist economies. Two requirements are simplification of the licensing procedures and removal of the special regulatory requirements.

Other ways to improve the environment for foreign investment include opening up privatization to foreign investors, removing export taxes, improving the infrastructure (telecommunications and transport) that potential foreign investors need, and establishing a one-stop agency for foreign investors that would help establish linkages with Latvian enterprises and provide all

---

2.   The experience with extending credit to small businesses in other countries has not always been positive. However, under the conditions that prevail in Latvia, temporary government programs to improve access to credit would be appropriate.

3.   The law provides full tax relief for three years and partial tax relief for an additional five years, depending on the amount and share of foreign ownership.

necessary information concerning legal and other requirements for foreign participation. The Foreign Investment Advisory Service (FIAS) of the World Bank has undertaken a diagnostic study of foreign direct investment to assist in identifying ways to promote foreign investment, including strengthening institutional capacity and developing investment promotion capabilities.

Privatization

To accelerate privatization the government should follow up on the parliamentary resolution outlining the privatization plan and quickly implement a consistent and coherent privatization program with the objective of rapid movement to a market economy, and within an overall framework of an export-oriented growth strategy. More specifically, the government should:

- Prioritize its objectives, for example, increase efficiency, create widespread private ownership, generate revenue, return property to previous owners, and reduce the financial burden of enterprises on the state;

- Address all types of state-owned property, that is, large enterprises, small enterprises, separable assets, land, and housing;

- Put more emphasis on selling assets and identifying potential owners (institutions, the general public, employees, and domestic and foreign investors);

- Select the privatization methods best suited to each type of property and determine how privatization will tie in with other aspects of enterprise reform (for example, selecting those enterprises to remain state-owned and breaking up enterprises), and reform of the enterprise environment (financial sector, private sector development, and macroeconomic reforms);

- Identify institutions to exercise ownership rights over state-owned enterprises and agents to initiate, approve, monitor, and implement privatization;

- Determine the use of proceeds from sales, for example, budget support, reduction of public debt, and promotion/administration of privatization, and develop alternative financing plans to facilitate privatization (installment payments and debt/equity swaps);

- Set goals for the number and types of enterprises to be privatized annually and identify those that should be liquidated;

- Identify the technical assistance and appropriate counterparts necessary to implement the program.

To effect a successful privatization program the government should expedite the sale or transfer of state property. In doing so it should not emphasize such elements as full valuation of enterprises and revenue generation, but rather transparency, consistency, and speed. Some of the privatization methods and their tradeoffs are outlined in Table 3-3.

The government should not wait for the completion of all legislation to begin selling enterprises. Early sales will serve several purposes: demonstrating to the public that privatization, including sales to foreigners, is necessary and can be politically palatable; increasing domestic capacity to undertake transactions in the future; and indicating to the government what objects will or will not require restructuring prior to sale (the latter will provide valuable information to develop further the institutional and financial arrangements for eventual restructuring). The government could benefit from technical assistance in these areas and in the pilot privatization of some large enterprises. While it is clear that technical assistance is urgently needed to broaden and deepen all aspects of the privatization program, responsible counterpart agencies must be identified and technical assistance must be placed within an overall framework of aid management.

Experience from privatization programs in Eastern and Central Europe indicates that there must be a mixture of decentralized and centralized authority to design and carry out the privatization program. For centralized functions, such as drafting legislation, monitoring transactions, and in some cases performing the ownership function of enterprises in the privatization stream, a central ministry or agency is most appropriate. In Latvia, the most suitable institution to carry out these functions is the MER. While this ministry has played a key role in privatization activities to date, its mandate must be more clearly defined, its role vis-a-vis other ministries and agencies explicitly delineated, and its authority strengthened.

Public Enterprise Reform

The government should address remaining unclear ownership claims, especially regarding managerial and workers' interest in public enterprises. The government also should clarify the institutional responsibilities for reforming public enterprises. Delineation of the responsibilities of the branch ministries, core ministries, and the legal system must be established, with a comprehensive demonopolization program implemented thereafter.

The demonopolization authority should address issues of both industrial structure and firm behavior. On the structural side, conglomerates should be broken up unless there is reasonable evidence of efficiency gains from their remaining together. In addition, mergers that would result in a market share above a predefined level should be reviewed. However, given the small size of the Latvian economy, high concentration is likely to be the most efficient solution in certain sectors due to economies of scale. In these sectors, low barriers to international trade are likely to provide the best antidote to monopoly behavior. In terms of firm behavior, the demonopolization authorities should prevent horizontal cartel agreements among competitors, particularly in the distribution sector, to fix prices or divide markets. They should, however, refrain from focusing on vertical restraints (such as predatory pricing) as they are vague, difficult to enforce, and may permit unjustified interference in competitive market behavior.

Contractual arrangements with enterprise managers should include incentives linked to an enterprise's performance, and other commercialization measures should be implemented systematically. The government has acknowledged the need to deepen these measures and intends to review proposals for further measures in the coming months. Technical assistance has been requested to strengthen corporate governance.

Table 3-3. Privatization Methods

	Restitution	Free Distribution	Auctions	Public Offering	Private placements	Management contracts/leasing
Objectives	Restoring pre-war property	Quick, widespread private ownership; equitable (initial) distribution of wealth	Revenue maximization	Widespread share of ownership; revenue generation	Revenue generation; concentrated ownership; improved efficiency improvements	Improved efficiency
Suitable property	All forms of property	All forms of property	Most suitable to small enterprises, separable units, & equipment (should be accompanied by enterprise breakup)	Large enterprises	Medium to large enterprises; can be initiated at the enterprise level	Large enterprises not immediately privatizable
Future Owners	Pre-war citizens and heirs thereof	All citizens	Highest bidder; (concessions can be made to employees; may have citizenship restrictions)	Domestic/foreign shareholders; partial sales and preferential shares to employees possible	Primarily foreign/ corporate	Foreign/domestic or management/ employee groups
Consequences	Some property privatized quickly; many property disputes; no revenue generation	Speedy privatization; emergence of capital markets; no capital inflow or revenue generation; dispersed corporate governance; risk of inflationary pressure	Transparent procedure; speedy process; demonstrates progress	Case by case, thus a slow form of privatization	Greatest potential for capital infusion but case by case sales, therefore slow	Can lead to eventual sale
Problems	Need to determine compensation for nonreturnable property; burden on judicial system	Resource-intensive system; need institutions for secondary trading; possible need for intermediary ownership bodies	Opposition from employee groups; favors cash-endowed buyers	Administratively intensive (may need outside assistance); requires valuations and development of capital market case	Complex contract negotiations (may need outside assistance); need enterprise valuation; possible lack of buyers	Administratively intensive (need contract for maintenance/ investment responsibilities); slow case by case process

Source: World Bank staff.

A number of steps will be needed to deal with loss-making enterprises during the transition period. Bankruptcies, as politically feasible and logistically possible with an undeveloped legal infrastructure, will have to be tolerated. To enforce financial discipline further and permit liquidation of non-viable enterprises the institutional framework for implementation of the bankruptcy law must be developed. Liquidation of non-profitable enterprises is intended to begin soon. Some limited budgetary transfers are also likely to be inevitable, however, these should be extremely selective and of an explicitly temporary nature. Finally, bank credit will likely be involved to finance loss-making enterprise. As mentioned before, this should be avoided to the extent possible, but where unavoidable should involve careful audits and restructuring plans for the borrower enterprises in order to minimize the negative effects on banks' viability.

The Financial Sector

The Financial System under Central Planning

The Latvian financial system was a regional component of the Soviet financial system until 1988, when the first reforms were introduced. Until that year, the Latvian financial system was institutionally limited to the regional branches of the large Soviet banks: Gosbank, the Savings Bank, the Construction Bank, and the Foreign Trade Bank.[4] The financial system did not play an independent role under the Soviet central planning system. Instead, it mobilized and allocated resources according to the decisions of the central planning authorities in Moscow.

The mobilization and allocation of resources by the Soviet central planning authorities involved three basic steps: first, the absorption of tax revenues and financial resources from the various republics; second, the amalgamation of those resources at the federal level; and third, the allocation of the total volume of resources through both financial and fiscal channels according to central plan directives. The regional branch of Gosbank in Latvia was the main channel for allocating resources through the financial system. The fiscal transfers were channeled from the Union budget to the Latvian budget and directly to All-Union enterprises in Latvia.

Overall, Soviet policies seem to have resulted in a net transfer of resources from the richer republics, such as Latvia, to the poorer Central Asian republics, although the mix of financial and fiscal flows makes it difficult to assess the magnitude of the net transfer. In addition, the fact that only a share of the resources mobilized by Latvian banks came back through the financial system resulted in an accumulation of net financial claims on the Soviet Union on the balance sheets of Latvian banks. These financial claims on the Soviet Union were mostly held by the regional branch of the Savings Bank in Latvia, since this institution mobilized household deposits and transferred them to Gosbank.

Most enterprise credits were provided through the regional branch of Gosbank in Latvia. These credits were used to finance short-term working capital, since enterprise investments were mostly financed from the All-Union and republican budgets. Some investments were financed from long-term credits extended by the Construction Bank.

The main objective of the financial sector reforms introduced by the Soviet authorities in early 1988 was to establish a two-tier banking system. The reforms included the separation of commercial banking operations from Gosbank, the introduction of three new specialized banks--the Agriculture Bank, the Industry and Construction Bank and the Social Bank--and permission to establish commercial banks. The Savings Bank continued its former operations.

---

4.   The Foreign Trade Bank was established in April 1989. Before that its operations were carried out by Gosbank.

Latvia began to nationalize the financial system immediately after it declared its independence. The regional branches of the Soviet banks were nationalized and the authorities transferred the responsibilities of Gosbank to the Bank of Latvia (BOL) as the central bank. In September 1991, the BOL took over the activities of Gosbank and four other state-owned banks (the Industrial, Agriculture, Social, and Foreign Trade banks), becoming the dominant bank in Latvia and engaging in both commercial and central activities. Since then several other commercial banks have been established in Latvia.

The Current Structure of the Financial System

Latvian Financial Institutions

As of early 1992, the Latvian financial sector comprises the BOL; the state-owned Savings Bank; thirty commercial banks; one state-owned insurance company; eight small private insurance companies; and a large private foreign exchange dealer. As shown in Table 3-4, the system is dominated by the BOL and the Savings Bank, which account for more than 90 percent of total financial assets.

Table 3-4. Structure of the Latvian Financial System

Bank	Number of Banks	Number of Branches	Assets (% of total)	Credits (% of total)	Capital (% of total)	Ownership	Number of Employees
Bank of Latvia	1	48	65.0	87.9	80.9	State	2,679
Savings Bank	1	37	27.3	1.6	0.0	State & enterprise	2,389
Commercial Banks	30	N.A.	7.7	10.5	19.1	State & private enterprise, private individuals	N.A.
Total	32	N.A.	18,276	6,770	914		N.A.

N.A. means not available.
Source: Latvian authorities.

The Bank of Latvia is in charge of monetary policy, management of the payments system, and prudential control and regulation. Since taking over the functions of Gosbank in September 1991, it has also performed commercial activities. It has over 2,600 employees, forty-eight branches, and assets amounting to 65 percent of the combined assets of the banking system. The BOL has little experience with monetary policy, since these functions were either conducted by the head office in Moscow or were simply non-existent under central planning. It does not carry out its prudential functions efficiently either, since it still lacks an appropriate regulatory framework and skilled staff. Its loan portfolio, whose quality is unclear, includes subsidized lending to the agricultural sector and investment and commercial loans made under the former central planning system. In June 1992, parliament adopted legislation that allowed the BOL to separate its commercial banking functions by December 1992.

The Savings Bank has thirty-seven branches and holds more than 95 percent of all household deposits in Latvia. Before independence the resources mobilized by the Savings Bank were all transferred to the head office of Gosbank in Moscow and then channeled back according to central plan directives. As a result, at the end of 1991 the Savings Bank held claims on Moscow amounting to almost RUR 5 billion. Since the All-Union banks, including Gosbank and the Savings Bank, have been liquidated, technically this bank is insolvent. It is also nearly illiquid because Gosbank Moscow interrupted interest payments to this bank at the end of 1991.

The commercial banks were first introduced in 1988, and by early 1992 their number has increased to thirty institutions, although some banks have not yet started operations. Moreover, only two or three banks have achieved a notable share of the market, and the share of the commercial banks in total assets is less than 8 percent. Overall, the growth of commercial banks seems to be constrained by the lack of a branch network and restricted access to household deposits. These banks have generally been established by one or more enterprises to address their financial needs. However, the shareholding of the commercial banks is gradually becoming more private.

The Latvian Investment Bank was established in mid-1992 with the assistance of the EBRD and the NIB to provide long-term financing for investment projects in the industrial sector and to help develop expertise in the appraisal of investment projects.

Resource Mobilization and Allocation

Under central planning and repressed inflation, the overall efficiency of the financial system in the mobilization and allocation of resources cannot be assessed with the same criteria employed for a market economy. As shown in Table 3-5, the ratio of M2 to GNP at the end of 1990 was 55 percent, a high ratio by international comparison. However, that indicated the existence of a monetary overhang rather than efficiency in resource mobilization. By the same token, the decrease in the ratio during 1991 reflects the impact of the price reform rather than financial disintermediation. In particular, the sharp drops in the ratio in the first and fourth quarters of 1991 reflect the large increase in prices during those periods. Note that the stock of rubles in the form of currency also appears on the asset side of the monetary survey, since it represents a potential claim on the former Gosbank Moscow.[5]

It is noteworthy that the Latvian financial system holds a large net creditor position relative to the former Soviet Union, as indicated by the large stock of foreign assets in non-convertible currencies. Indeed, even deducting the stock of currency in circulation the stock remains very high: RUR 8,866 million in the last quarter of 1991. This basically reflects the large net creditor position of households and the associated claims of the Savings Bank on Gosbank Moscow. The large stock of foreign assets in convertible currency also reflects some other claims of state-owned banks on former Soviet banks.

Note that enterprises hold a very moderate net debtor position in the banking system, a reflection of the fact that most investment expenditures were financed by budgetary transfers, as opposed to bank loans. The stock of enterprise credits and deposits reflects primarily a closed circuit within the enterprise sector through which short-run surpluses were used to finance short-term working capital needs.

---

5.   Right after the introduction of the lats, the government will express the outstanding stock of currency in lats, and the BOL will hold a commensurate stock of foreign assets denominated in rubles. Further agreements with the successor of the former Gosbank will determine the final settlement of these claims.

Table 3-5. Monetary Survey
(rubles millions, end of period)

Monetary Aggregates	1990-Q4	1991-Q1	1991-Q2	1991-Q3	1991-Q4
Net Foreign Assets	5,005	5,502	8,424	10,880	13,442
Foreign Assets	6,410	9,250	9,814	11,008	13,442
- Convertible	13	14	106	185	576
- Nonconvertible [a]	6,397	9,236	9,708	10,823	12,866
Foreign Liabilities	1,405	3,748	1,390	128	0
Net Domestic Assets	2,715	2,872	2,398	1,665	6,569
Domestic Credit [b]	2,757	3,038	3,449	4,123	5,550
Credit to Households	190	188	186	163	179
Credit to Enterprises	3,213	3,695	4,837	5,777	7,740
Other Items, Net	-42	-166	-1,051	-2,458	1,019
Revaluation, Net	9	9	100	177	
Other Assets, Net	-543	-613	-1,745	-2,580	
Capital and Reserves	242	382	823	1,186	
Interbanking Transactions	249	56	-229	-1,242	
Broad Money (M2)	7,720	8,374	10,822	12,545	16,241
Currency in Circulation	2,128	2,300	2,464	3,000	4,000
Deposits of Enterprises	1,962	2,360	3,517	4,391	6,300
Deposits of Households	3,630	3,714	4,841	5,154	5,941
Memo Items:					
Household deposits/GDP [c]	26.1	22.0	23.0	22.0	15.0
M2/GDP [c]	55.0	48.3	52.0	53.0	40.1

a. Includes the counterpart of currency in circulation, claims of the Savings Bank on Gosbank Moscow, and other claims, including reserve requirements on All-Union banks in Moscow.
b. Credits to households and enterprises plus net credits to the government (not shown).
c. Defined as $m_t/gdp_t = (M_t/GDP_t)(P'_t/P_t)$, where mt and M_t are the real and nominal money stocks, and gdp_t and GDP_t are real and nominal GDP, respectively. P_t is the retail price index at t and P'_t is the average value of the index in the respective year.
Source: Bank of Latvia and World Bank staff estimates.

To summarize, the Latvian financial system has a much greater stock of domestic liabilities than domestic assets. The difference is explained by foreign assets in convertible currencies and claims of doubtful value on financial institutions of the former Soviet Union. In addition, the household sector holds a large net creditor position and the enterprise sector holds a very moderate net debtor position in the banking system. These are essential features to consider in designing a financial restructuring program.

Other Institutional Aspects

Banking institutions and activities in Latvia are regulated by the Latvian banking law and the charter of the BOL, which was adopted on May 27, 1992. The banking law defines the functions of the commercial banks, principles of bank operations, role of the BOL, and bank secrecy. The law does not specify prudential regulations, but does authorize the BOL to set up rules and to establish obligatory reserves for commercial banks. The banking law gives discretionary power to the BOL in all these matters.

The abandonment of Soviet accounting practices was not followed by the adoption of clear accounting standards. As a result, the reporting of financial transactions is inadequate, the financial statements of individual institutions are not strictly comparable, and it is very difficult to determine the quality of banks' portfolios. Internal auditing is not practiced. The Bank of Latvia processes payments within the country, clearing them electronically at its computer center, while settlement is conducted manually at its accounting center. The procedures are cumbersome, and the manual settlement causes errors and delays.

Although some bank managers have been oriented to some aspects of international banking, the general level of banking expertise is quite low, since most of the banking staff have not been trained in modern banking methods. Experience in managing credit, interest, and foreign exchange risks and in assessing the quality of loan portfolios is limited. There is no organized training system for bank staff in Latvia.

Major Reform Issues

The problems in the financial system will prevent it from playing a central role in the allocation of scarce resources and may lead to a financial crisis with adverse macroeconomic implications. Reform of the financial sector must solve the large imbalance between performing assets and liabilities and enable financial institutions to identify and finance the most dynamic sectors of the economy, particularly the emerging private sector. Doing so will require a strong and independent central bank, well-capitalized private commercial banks, and a modern regulatory and supervisory framework.

The major reform issues to be addressed following the separation of the BOL's central banking and commercial banking activities are the strengthening of the BOL as a central bank, and the restructuring and privatization of the commercial branches of the BOL and the Savings Bank. It is also important to increase private sector participation in the ownership of commercial banks so as to reduce the influence of the state-owned enterprises on these banks.

Separation of the commercial and central banking activities of the BOL was an important step for two reasons: first, to avoid serious conflicts of interest and interference in the conduct of monetary policy; and second, to allow its management to concentrate on the establishment of the institutional framework required for efficient conduct of monetary policy.

Restructuring and privatization of the commercial branches of the BOL and the Savings Bank are also essential for two reasons: first, to prevent the emergence of serious financial problems that could jeopardize monetary control; and second, to introduce more competition into the financial system and increase the efficiency of resource allocation.

The ownership structure of some commercial banks is cause for concern. The influence of state-owned enterprises on their lending decisions could lead them to deviate from profitability criteria and lend to state-owned enterprises in financial distress. The recent decision to allow private individuals to own shares in commercial banks is an important initial step in privatizing the financial system. However, a more substantial reduction, or even elimination, of the ownership of state-owned enterprises in commercial banks is necessary.

Recommendations

Restructuring and Strengthening of the Central Bank

A strong, independent central bank that focuses on monetary policy and bank regulation and supervision is the core of a stable and efficient financial system. Separation of the commercial and central banking activities of the BOL should be implemented promptly as planned. To this end, the commercial activities of the bank should be transferred immediately to a separate balance sheet. The loan portfolio and deposits, as well as some branches, should be offered for sale to new and existing private commercial banks.

The management and staff of the BOL need to acquire much greater familiarity with monetary management. It is likely that initially monetary management will have to rely on direct credit controls, while the institutions and instruments required for indirect control of monetary aggregates are being developed. However, the BOL and its staff should concentrate on setting up mechanisms and putting in place regulations that will allow the instruments of indirect control to become operational. Staff must acquire much greater familiarity with foreign exchange operations, including management of the country's foreign exchange reserves.

Finally, the BOL is responsible for bank regulation and supervision. Establishment of adequate on-site and off-site bank supervision will require a substantial strengthening of staff skills and expertise and of financial reporting by the banks. Improvement of BOL performance in all these areas will require substantial assistance from other central banks and private financial institutions, possibly with coordination by the IMF and the World Bank.

Restructuring and Privatizing the Savings Bank and the BOL's Commercial Branches

In the restructuring of the state-owned banks, the Savings Bank should be treated separately, since it holds the deposits of the population and has practically no assets besides claims on extinct Soviet banks. The restructuring of the Savings Bank has to be conducted under tight political constraints. The point of departure must be that the deposits of the population are honored in some way. At the same time, the resolution of the Savings Bank problem cannot result in an excessive burden on public finances.

Several solutions can be considered for the Savings Bank. A first solution is to convert the household deposits into privatization vouchers. These vouchers would enable households to bid for houses, land, or enterprise shares. A second solution is to convert the household deposits into interest-yielding bonds with long-term maturities issued by the government. A third solution is to replace the claims on Moscow on the asset side of the Savings Bank's balance sheet with government bonds with long-term maturities. Table 3-6 provides a schematic comparison of the three solutions and their impact on other areas of the economy.

As indicated in Table 3-6, the first two solutions allow immediate liquidation of the Savings Bank. They would force households gradually to deposit their "new" savings in commercial banks, so that these banks would develop the deposit base necessary to expand their operations. Mobilization of new household savings could be facilitated by the sale of the fixed assets of the Savings Bank (such as buildings) to the commercial banks. Under the third solution the Savings Bank would not be liquidated immediately. That step would only take place after the sale of its branches to the

Table 3-6. Assessment of Alternative Restructuring Schemes for the Savings Bank

Solution	Impact on Savings Bank	Fiscal Impact	Impact on Privatization
Vouchers in exchange for deposits	Immediately liquidated	Some foregoing of revenues from property sales	Contribution in real sector and financial sector
Government bonds in exchange for deposits	Immediately liquidated	Fixed interest on government bonds	Contribution in financial sector only
Government bonds in the balance sheet of the Savings Bank	Gradual sales of branches to private banks	Interest on government bonds linked to cost of funds	More moderate contribution in financial sector

Source: World Bank staff.

commercial banks. In this case, the commercial banks would absorb the deposits together with the fixed assets and the bonds. Although purchase of the branches would give commercial banks the means to expand their operations, the government would have to offer a very attractive yield on the bonds.

The impact of the three alternative solutions on the government's budget may be quite different. The first solution implies foregone revenues from the sale of state properties, while the second and third imply interest expenditures for the government's budget. The amount of foregone revenues would depend on how quickly the government privatizes state assets. The faster it does so, the lower the revenues that can be expected from such sales.

The second solution could offer reasonable and predictable costs, since the government could fix the interest rates on the bonds. If the rate of inflation were to exceed the interest rate on the bonds, however, bondholders would, in effect, face a capital levy. This situation would not affect resource mobilization at the margin or create financial difficulties for the banks. The third solution is probably the most costly, since the government would have to keep interest rates on the bonds at least equal to the average cost of bank deposits plus operating costs. In a scenario of relatively high inflation and nominal interest rates, the budgetary costs could be very high, particularly in the first years.

Finally, the first solution would result in further privatization of the real sector and would give the commercial banks an enhanced role. It would force households to bid for state property while allowing immediate liquidation of the Savings Bank. As mentioned, households would have to channel their savings to the commercial banks. The second and third solutions would contribute to the second objective, but not to the first.

The conversion of deposits into vouchers is probably the most effective solution, although the political scope for implementing a full conversion of the stock of household deposits is unclear. The political implications of the second solution are also unclear for similar reasons. The third solution is the most feasible politically, since it would safeguard the deposits in the Savings Bank. However, the potential fiscal problems this solution could generate must be assessed carefully.

The choice of a solution to the Savings Bank must also take into account inflation developments before and after the currency reform. Ruble inflation reduces the real size of household deposits and the potential costs of a fiscal solution. Household deposits in the Savings Bank were still significantly large in 1991--around 20 percent of GDP--but have declined since because of the high ruble inflation. However, even if a continuation of ruble inflation further reduces the real size of household deposits, the costs of a fiscal solution may still be significant if the new currency is not immediately stabilized. If it is not stabilized, nominal interest rates will also be high, so that the initial costs will be high, even under a low ratio of deposits to GDP.

This point may be illustrated by assuming that the ratio of household deposits to GDP declines to 10 percent while inflation and interest rates remain at 50 percent a year after the introduction of the new currency. In this case, interest payments on the stock would amount to 5 percent of GDP in the first year, which would impose an excessive burden on public finances. Interest payments in the first year could be reduced substantially by indexing the principal of deposits to inflation, but that solution could create other complications. Government attempts to refinance the interest through new issues of bonds could also prove difficult, given the absence of developed markets for securities. These figures illustrate the problems that could be generated by an attempt to maintain the Savings Bank and the household deposits in their current form.

As concerns restructuring and privatizing the commercial branches of the BOL, four basic factors must to be addressed. First, the BOL has two different groups of clients: the government and state-owned enterprises (SOEs) on the one hand, and private enterprises, firms, and farmers on the other. Second, the quality of its loan portfolios varies substantially, with the bulk of non-performing loans having gone to SOEs. Third, the quality of the loan portfolio across the BOL's branches also seems to vary significantly. Fourth, the restructuring of the BOL's commercial branches should not disrupt the financing of working capital in the enterprise and agriculture sectors.

Before considering specific restructuring and privatization strategies, it is essential to assess the scope for a substantial reduction in the size of the balance sheets through a concerted write-down of loans and deposits to the government and SOEs. Politically, a concerted write-down may be easy to accomplish, since these operations are conducted within the public sector. In addition, if the net creditor and debtor positions across SOEs are not associated with past enterprise efficiency, but rather with pricing and allocation through central planning, a concerted write-down may well be justified on economic grounds. It would reduce the overall size of potential portfolio problems by narrowing the number of enterprises that need to be liquidated or financially restructured.

A write-down can proceed in several ways. First, there are no political and economic constraints on a write-down of assets and liabilities to the same SOEs. Second, once state ownership of the former All-Union enterprises is definitely established, there may be scope for writing-down loans to the former republican enterprises, which are mostly net debtors, against the deposits of the former All-Union enterprises, which are mostly net creditors. However, even if all loans to SOEs are written-down, a large stock of SOE deposits will remain, the counterpart being claims on extinct Soviet banks. Enterprise deposits could be written-down further, but doing so would require a commensurate write-down of the capital of these enterprises. Alternatively, enterprise deposits and the claims on Moscow could be transferred to a special government financial institution.

After the write-down, the healthiest branches could be identified and sold to commercial banks. In cases where the net worth of the branch is slightly negative, the government could consider some recapitalization before the sale. Branches with a largely negative net worth should have their accounts initially frozen and submitted to more prolonged intervention by a restructuring agency created for this purpose. However, that step should not prevent the sale of the fixed assets of the branches and the transfer of some personnel to the commercial banks.

If the size of the balance sheets cannot be substantially reduced through a concerted write-down, the government may have to consider a temporary freeze on the balance sheet of the commercial activities of the BOL while it implements a more definite solution. The loan portfolio should be carefully audited and customers given an opportunity to open new accounts in the commercial banks.

Assessment and management of the frozen balance sheets would have to be overseen by a restructuring agency. That agency would try promptly to identify the healthier branches and sell them to the commercial banks. After concluding this step and finalizing the collection procedures for non-performing loans, the government would liquidate the remainder. The existence of net claims on Moscow implies that the final liquidation might require some fiscal support, for example, replacing such claims with bonds and safeguarding the deposits. Otherwise, loans and deposits would have to be written off against enterprise capital.

The privatization of enterprises has potentially important connections with financial restructuring. There is little sense in restructuring the domestic banks if most enterprises remain in state hands. The restructuring and privatization of the financial and real sectors should proceed in parallel, and possibly include connecting elements whenever that proves feasible and efficient. For instance, the proceeds from sales in the agricultural and industrial sectors could be channeled to the restructuring agency and used to write off bad loans (see Box 3-1).

Box 3-1. The Links Between Enterprise and Banking Reforms

The restructuring and privatization of enterprises and banks lies at the core of the transformation of a socialist economy. As the financial problems of enterprises and banks are closely related, the restructuring and privatization of both types of institutions should follow a consistent design and proceed at roughly the same pace. There is little sense in restructuring and privatizing banks if most non-financial enterprises remain in state hands. Experience from other reforming socialist countries has shown that state enterprises have little incentive to respond to interest rates and to honor their financial obligations. Under these conditions, the potential benefits of financial sector reform do not materialize and bad loans eventually reappear.

There is widespread agreement that a program of bank restructuring and privatization cannot ultimately succeed without parallel reforms in the real sector. However, there is less agreement on the need for the restructuring and privatization of banks and enterprises to be explicitly and tightly connected. Although it is possible to design some connecting elements, all reforming socialist countries have experienced difficulties in designing fully integrated strategies that are both simple and efficient.

Implementing a concerted write-down of loans and deposits of state enterprises in Latvian banks, as suggested in this section, does not constitute a complete strategy in itself, but could be a useful component of a broader and consistent strategy of enterprise and bank reform. Such concerted write-down would not interfere with the government's plans to privatize large enterprises through various methods, including vouchers. In addition, this across-the-board measure would facilitate the restructuring and privatization of state-owned banks. Finally, this measure could also generate immediate efficiency gains, as the incentives for banks to keep financing bankrupt enterprises would decrease in line with the decline in their loan exposure to these enterprises, and with the emergence of private non-financial enterprises. The voucher solution proposed for the Savings Bank could also be linked with the privatization program.

Whatever solution is implemented, it is essential that fundamental banking services not be disrupted during the restructuring. Maintenance of a minimum level of banking services during the transition could be achieved by carefully coordinating the sale of branches and the transfer of personnel to expanding banks. This point is particularly important in those rural areas where a single branch provides banking services to farmers.

Strengthening the Commercial Banks

Restructuring the BOL's commercial activities along the lines suggested would promote the growth of the commercial banks and greatly enhance their role in financial intermediation. However, greater efficiency in resource allocation can only be ensured if the commercial banks can make decisions independently. In this regard, the ownership structure of some commercial banks is a concern, since these banks could easily be induced to lend to SOEs in distress; a practice that would reduce the private sector's access to scarce financial resources.

One way to reduce the relative position of SOEs in the ownership of commercial banks is immediately to write off state enterprise loans against their share capital and deposits in the banks. Where the state-owned enterprises still have a dominant position in a commercial bank, the government could implement further measures, such as sales of these shares to the private sector or to foreign banks.

It may be also necessary to introduce safeguards while SOEs are still important shareholders in the commercial banks. During this period, commercial bank lending to state enterprises should be restricted, particularly where the enterprises hold a substantial share of the capital. The distribution of commercial bank profits to state enterprises should also be restricted. These measures would allow the commercial banks to increase their capital and would liberate resources for the private sector. As a general principle, it is recommended that lending to shareholders be limited to avoid conflicts of interest and to prevent enterprises from getting preferred access to credit.

The entry of foreign banks could contribute significantly to reform of the financial sector. Foreign banks should be allowed to participate in the financial system by injecting additional capital into emerging commercial banks or by purchasing the shares of SOEs. Foreign banks would introduce modern banking practices and stimulate management and staff to adapt to international financial standards more quickly.

Other Institutional Aspects

The minimum capital for opening a commercial bank should be increased considerably. The licensing should include an investigation of the owners and their plans for the bank. The present licensing process seems to be pro forma.

In addition to increasing minimum capital requirements, the capital/asset ratios should be raised to the levels recommended by the Bank of International Settlement (BIS). Exposure to single borrowers should be limited to 10 to 15 percent of capital and to groups of borrowers to 30 to 50 percent. The banks should be prevented from giving new loans or holding additional equity in enterprises if that would mean exceeding these limits.

Special consideration should be given to deposit insurance regulation. International experience in this area suggests that it is advisable to develop an insurance scheme that limits the amounts covered.   In addition, banks should be charged insurance premiums and the proceeds channeled to a separate insurance fund.   These resources would be used to finance future restructuring.

Prudential supervision needs to be strengthened and conducted under rule of law.   The banking and central bank laws must specify the central bank's supervisory functions and criteria for classifying of bank loans, and should empower the central bank to enforce the provisions for doubtful loans.

The financial reforms must improve the payments system and introduce internationally accepted accounting standards.   International consulting firms have gained experience with restructuring the basic banking routines of several formerly planned economies.   It may be worth using such firms to help introduce standard accounting rules and establish an efficient payments system.[6]   International auditing of at least the largest private commercial banks would introduce greater transparency and help attract foreign capital into the Latvian financial system.   Also, the payments clearing system needs to be improved to reduce present delays of up to several weeks in clearing domestic payments.

Finally, establishment of an institution or a school for studies in banking, accounting, and auditing would accelerate the acquisition of modern banking techniques and procedures.   This institution should be linked to one or more similar institutions abroad, with possible cooperation by a foreign bank and the assistance of international institutions.   As an alternative, individual banks should be encouraged to enter into an agreement with one or more foreign banks for twinning, that is, for long-term technical assistance, with or without ownership participation.

 The Labor Market

Wages

Under the Soviet system, abandoned in 1991, wages were determined according to a long and detailed list of job classifications.   During 1991, the government introduced different rules for wage formation inside and outside the budget, with all rules involving some form of indexation.   Wages in the budgetary sector were linked to the minimum wage, which was initially set by the government, but revised every six months according to changes in a basket of essential goods and services.   Wages outside the budgetary sector were freed from ceilings, but subjected to minimum compensation for price increases.   During the year, the government forced enterprises to increase wages by a certain amount of rubles per worker.   The ruble amount was set at different levels for different groups of recipients.   As mentioned in Chapter 1, despite several adjustments in nominal wages, real wages dropped significantly in 1991 and 1992.

The structure of workers' earnings in Latvia is poorly related to their education, which reflects the low financial returns on investment in education.   The sectors with the lowest pay are education and health, which have the highest number of university graduates.   The two sectors with the highest pay are construction and industry, in which most of the work force has no secondary education.[7]

---

6.   A new accounting law was adopted in late 1992 to be effective in January 1993.

7.   Statistical Appendix Table 6-4.

The wage differentials among managers, specialists, and workers vary by sector, but tend to be small. The recent rules on indexation involving higher coefficients for lower wages have compressed the salary schedules even further.[8]

Employment

Latvia shares several demographic and employment characteristics with other Eastern European countries. The share of the population that is economically active is high; more than 50 percent of the population is employed, compared with 40 percent in Western Europe. The share of people employed in agriculture and industry is also high, 16 and 31 percent, respectively. The share of people employed in services is correspondingly low, especially in the banking and insurance sectors, where it is negligible by Western standards.[9] The share of people employed in services is to some extent underestimated, since many workers nominally employed in agriculture and manufacturing perform service tasks, such as equipment repairs, cleaning, and transportation. However, the numbers confirm that Latvia's employment structure follows the pattern of the other former socialist countries, including an undersized services sector.

Under the Soviet central planning system, demand for labor at the enterprise level was, in principle, regulated by a set of production coefficients. However, enterprises' employment plans had to be accepted by the respective sectoral ministry. Since labor mobility was severely limited by bureaucratic hurdles and housing problems, enterprises applied for permission to employ more people than necessary to avoid labor shortages. Thus, a large number of underemployed workers were maintained on the payroll. The fact that the number of vacancies was always higher than the number of registered unemployed was misleading, since state enterprises operated within a soft budget constraint.

In 1991 the government started to implement a number of measures to cope with the expected increase in unemployment. They included the development of a small network of labor exchanges and various other active and passive labor market policy measures. However, the number of registered unemployed remained negligible in the first quarter of 1992. In March 1992 the rate of unemployment was about 0.2 percent, corresponding to 2,500 people.[10] Of this number 556 persons were receiving unemployment benefits, up from 294 in February. In April the number of recipients of unemployment benefits went up to 751. At the same time the number of vacancies was about 10,000, most for blue-collar workers. In the second quarter of 1992 the unemployment rate increased significantly: at the end of June over 20,000 people were actively seeking employment. About 9,524 had already registered as unemployed, and some 2,500 were receiving unemployment compensation.[11] Unemployment grew further, reaching 2 percent by November 1992. In that month, 36,600 people were

---

8. For instance, in December 1991 the employee at the highest level, level 24 was earning 13 times more than the employee at level 1. This difference has since been reduced to 9.

9. Statistical Appendix Table 1.2.

10. These figures are not a true reflection of the unemployed labor force as they exclude those looking for a job and those who work at plants running on a reduced operating schedule.

11. Among the unemployed 50 percent were women. Among them, 15 percent were older than fifty, and 48 percent were women who had been working longer than ten years. More than 70 percent were white-collar employees.

looking for jobs, 23,300 were unemployed, and 20,500 getting unemployment benefits.[12]   However, there is considerable hidden unemployment in Latvia because a number of workers have been sent on unpaid holidays. After adjusting for these working short hours (49,000 according to some estimates), the unemployment rate could reach 6 percent.

Aside from frictional unemployment, the fact that the rate of unemployment remained negligible in 1991 despite a sharp drop in output is partly explained by a temporary improvement in the financial position of enterprises in that year. Another explanation is the negative net migration observed in recent years. The steeper decrease in employment compared to the rise in unemployment in 1991 and for the first part of 1992 may reflect tougher criteria for classifying a worker as unemployed. However, as mentioned above, during the second half of 1992 unemployment growth accelerated, and was accompanied by a rising number of enterprises putting workers on unpaid leave or declaring bankruptcy.

The Latvian labor market could turn out to be highly segmented when unemployment rises. In addition to the usual segmentation resulting from professional differences and low labor mobility mainly because of housing constraints, the Latvian labor market is characterized by a high number of single employers in medium and small cities, often producing on the basis of raw materials obtained from Russia, and with the production sent back to Russia. In such places, where the share of national minorities is often high, unemployment could be particularly high and the possibilities of moving the unemployed is severely limited. For instance, if the gloomy forecasts of high unemployment in the city of Daugapils come true, it would be extremely difficult to move the unemployed to other areas. It may soon be necessary to differentiate labor market policies across regions, with different sets of regulations for unemployment benefits and active labor market policies.

As mentioned before, the deterioration in the terms of trade in 1992 was substantial, and the implementation of a stabilization program is likely to have an initial adverse impact on output. Enterprises will experience severe shocks and will have to shed a significant number of workers, despite the fact that the system is not fully equipped to cope with a large number of unemployed at this stage. In November 1992, for example, thirty enterprises put all their workers on unpaid or half-paid leave.

Recommendations

Wages

The fact that wages increased more slowly than prices in 1991 and 1992 indicates that the influence of workers on wage determination has been somewhat limited. However, the experience of other reforming socialist countries, notably Poland and former Yugoslavia, indicates that the decentralization of state enterprises may rapidly lead to an excessive increase in wages. Such an increase may occur at the expense of investment or may lead to a serious deterioration in the financial condition of enterprises.

This possibility suggests a need for close monitoring of wage developments, particularly during the period when the privatization program is being implemented and a large share of enterprises are still owned by the state without effective ownership control. To prevent excessive wage increases, the authorities, in agreement with the IMF, introduced a tax-based incomes policy in July 1992. The

---

12.   In November the number of long-term unemployed, that is, those out of work for more than six months, reached 1,150.

objective of this tax is to penalize enterprises that raise wages above a specified ceiling, and to prevent a wage-price spiral from emerging.[13]

In the longer run, a proper collective bargaining scheme is of primary importance for a small, open European economy. Such a scheme should be negotiated and the Act on Collective Bargaining should be approved. The Swedish style of collective bargaining, based on centralized relations between the government and the unions, may be reasonable for Latvia. It may allow more serious involvement of the trade unions in supplementary unemployment compensation, improvement of industrial relations, and issues of labor productivity.

Employment

Since the beginning of 1992, expenditures for unemployment have been paid out of the Social Insurance Fund. Since proper measures for reducing unemployment involve the use of active labor market policies, for example, retraining and selective wage subsidies, they should not be financed from the same fund that provides the unemployment benefits. Experience in other countries (Germany, Poland) shows that in these cases active labor market policies are given a second order of importance, and are frequently crowded out by other labor-related expenditures. Besides, there is no contribution of local funds to labor exchanges whatsoever, and an inappropriate separation of financing and effective control. The costs of the labor exchanges should be co-financed locally. An Employment Fund should be created to handle unemployment benefits, while active labor market policies would be covered either directly by the state budget or by other funds.

Unemployed people should be encouraged to search for employment in other occupations, particularly during the first six months of benefits. In present circumstances, when the need for restructuring the economy is large, restricting job searches only to people's current occupations would unnecessarily delay adjustment of the labor force. The only active labor market policies mentioned explicitly in the Employment Law are retraining and temporary public works. However, the concept of temporary works is unclear. Although the Employment Law suggests actions similar to public works, it also points out that employers should, in principle, cover all costs, with possible participation by the employment offices in certain cases. This proposal contradicts the idea of public works and becomes similar to wage subsidization. Clarification of these concepts is necessary. If the government is going to use public works, then public works should be organized either by employment offices or by local authorities and should involve the production of public goods.

The current system of training is limited to state-owned institutions and is not linked to potential employers. To make training and retraining schemes efficient, a variety of institutions should be involved, including private ones. In Latvia this process has not yet happened. Increases in the demand for certain skills, for example, private commercial banking or data processing, are on the rise, and retraining funds would be well spent in these areas. Many of the trainees would easily find employment in the private sector. However, these schemes need to be targeted carefully. Employment officers are often tempted to admit the most promising people to training and retraining schemes, for instance secondary school or university graduates with short periods of unemployment, as this approach

---

13.   State-owned enterprises are allowed to raise wages only to 70 percent of the forecasted price increases. Excessive growth is taxed at the rate of 150 percent for 1 to 2 percent above the threshold, or 300 percent for more than 2 percent above the threshold.

ensures a high rate of success for the employment office. Consideration should be given to establishing a training fund, financed jointly by employers and a direct budgetary contribution. In the case of employers, their contribution would be reduced to the extent that companies train their own workers. Among the needed training measures is proper job search strategies. These would be much easier to provide if a well-developed information system were in place. Foreign technical assistance will be particularly helpful in this area.

The government has lifted administrative constraints to labor mobility inside Latvia, although both the housing constraint and the fact that various benefits are provided by the enterprises still limit labor mobility. This seems to be one of the reasons that instead of layoffs enterprises tend to send workers on unpaid holidays. The government should undertake more active steps to transfer provision of these benefits to local authorities.

The government should develop better statistical coverage of the labor market, including unemployment. It is essential to supplement the simple unemployment numbers with statistics of inflows, outflows, and duration of unemployment. This task will require the development of labor force surveys and direct collection of information from households. A breakdown of unemployment by various categories (age, sex, and nationality) should be part of the unemployment statistics.

The Social Safety Net

The social security system in Latvia was fully integrated with the social programs of the Soviet Union until 1990. In 1990, the Latvian government began to change the structure and administration of the social programs it had inherited.[14] The government wanted its new system to reflect national preferences and to allow a clear accounting of social expenditures and earmarked revenues. In January 1991, a new social security system was initiated, that introduced a pension system and substantially increased family benefits. In January 1992 unemployment benefits were also introduced. However, the system is not yet prepared to provide a minimum social safety net for a large number of beneficiaries in a cost-effective manner. The main social programs are currently being restructured to make them compatible with the transformation of the economy.[15]

Essentially all cash benefits are funded and administered by the newly established Social Insurance Fund (SIF). The Employment Fund will provide support to the labor market. It receives earmarked contributions channeled through the SIF and occasional transfers from the state budget.

The Social Security System

At the beginning of 1991, the Latvian government removed the fiscal operations of most social programs from the state budget and handed them over to the SIF. The SIF operates the following

---

14.   For a short description of the social programs in the Soviet Union, see for example, IMF and others (1991); U.S. Department of Health and Human Services (1991).

15.   Comparing the new and old systems in terms of design, implementation, and administration is hazardous, particularly because before 1990 the data are very fragmented. In addition, reform of these social programs is incomplete, and many inconsistencies and gaps exist.

four programs: (a) pension benefits;[16] (b) family benefits, including maternity leave, birth grants, child care allowances, and kindergarten substitution allowance;[17] (c) sick pay, including sick care leave; and (d) unemployment benefits.

The SIF is financed by social security contributions paid by (a) employers (37 percent) and employees (1 percent) based on the firm's total wage bill; (b) the self-employed, small business people, and private farmers (19 percent of declared earnings or twice the minimum level of living); and (c) voluntary contributors (1 percent of wage).[18] There is no contribution ceiling on wages. However, given that Latvia has introduced a minimum wage, an implicit contribution floor does exist.

In 1991, total expenditures by the SIF were equivalent to 9.2 percent of GDP. More than 80 percent of these expenditures were disbursed as pension benefits; sick pay and family benefits (excluding family allowances) accounted for the remainder. Spending by local authorities on social assistance programs was less than 0.2 percent of GDP. At the local level the system is still undeveloped.

The SIF budget for 1992 included additional outlays for unemployment benefits and family allowances. The unemployment benefits are funded through the allocation of 1.5 percent of the social security contribution rate.

Pensions

As of January 1, 1991, a new pension law was enacted that essentially provides all residents with a non-contributory (social) pension. The new law also enacts an insurance plan that combines the eligibility criteria of the old system (as regards retirement age and contribution record) and a generous new benefit formula, particularly with regard to disability. The new law stipulates that the standard minimum pension should not be below the minimum level of living.

Qualifying criteria for old-age pensions are age and a minimum record of service (five years). The standard retirement age is sixty for men and fifty-five for women. Lower retirement ages are available for those working under dangerous or stressful conditions. Depending on the occupation, retirement can occur as early as age fifty for men and forty-five for women. About 10 percent of Latvians work in occupations where early retirement is possible. Withdrawal from the labor market is not required to qualify for an old-age pension, but some retirement testing does apply under the new law.

For disability pensions, the two main qualifying conditions are a medical certificate and a minimum service record, depending on the age of the disabled. The latter condition is waived in the case of a disability attributable to a work-related injury or disease. Three groups of disabled are differentiated depending on their work capacity and need for attendance. No further differentiation based on the causes of the disability (such as general sickness, work injury, or professional disease) is made.

---

16.   Data on the state budget before 1990 indicate additional expenditures on social security pensions of about 3 percent of GDP. The nature of these expenditure could not be clarified.

17.   The family benefit was introduced in 1991 and financed by the state budget that year. In 1992 it came under the SIF budget.

18.   Essentially women rearing children in order to qualify for pension benefits.

In principle, a wide range of family members (spouse, children, sisters, brothers, and parents) are eligible for survivor's pensions if they are dependents and are too young, disabled, or too old to work. In the case of the spouse's survivor's pension, no differentiation is made by gender. However, an employed spouse who is below the retirement age is not eligible. If retired, the spouse may only receive her/his pension or the survivor's pension, whichever is higher. Children are eligible for a survivor's pension if younger than eighteen (twenty-four if in higher education).

The benefit formula for all three pension benefits (old-age, disability, and survivors) is two-tiered: a flat-rate (basic) pension and an earnings-related pension. The first tier puts the basic pension at 80 percent of the minimum level of living, or RUR 1,200 in November 1992. The second tier (for old-age pensions) is a function of the person's service record and salary (determined by the best consecutive five years within the last ten years before retirement). The standard term of service is twenty-five years for men and twenty for women; the minimum is five years. For fewer years of service the pension is reduced pro rata. The second tier is limited to twice the minimum level of living (except for special groups, who constitute 6 percent of pensioners). If the retiree continues to work, the basic pension is suspended. The remaining earnings-related pension, however, may not be reduced below the flat-rate pension.

The disability pension combines the basic pension and various earnings-related and flat-rate additions. The benefit levels compare favorably with the old-age pensions and with wages. For each survivor, the pension benefit consists of the basic pension plus 40 percent of the pension base of the deceased. If there are several survivors, the total sum of the pension cannot exceed the pension base.

A pension is also granted to those aged sixty-five (men) and sixty (women) and older with no other income. It amounts to 80 percent of the minimum level of living. Pension benefits, as with other social benefits, are not subject to the income tax. If retirees continue to work, their salary is taxable, but not their benefits.

Family Benefits

Currently, the system provides various benefits: (a) maternity leave, (b) birth grant, (c) child care allowances, (d) family allowances, and (e) kindergarten substitution allowance. A few minor programs for children operate under other social programs, such as the disabled child allowance (handled by the pension program), foster children allowance (Ministry of Education), child care sick leave (sickness program), and lump sum payments (social assistance programs at the local level).

Maternity leave applies to the period fifty-six days before and fifty-six days after birth. However, under the new regulations, the leave can be changed to seventy days/forty-six days, and under certain circumstances to seventy/seventy days. The benefit amounts to 100 percent of the average wage in the prior two months. The enterprise disburses the benefit and is reimbursed by the SIF. The birth grant is based on the estimated costs of a basket of baby necessities. The child care allowances, for newborns to three-year-olds, are disbursed by firms only to women who return to work after their maternity leave. A universal family allowance amounted to RUR 140 in December 1991 for a child up to age eight and RUR 160 for a child age eight or older until high school graduation. A kindergarten substitution allowance is for children not attending kindergarten. The initial rationale was the lack of kindergarten spaces; a problem that has now been resolved. Nevertheless, the allowance has continued, and no working test on the mother is applied. The allowance is paid for children after eligibility for the child care allowance ends (age three) and before school age (seven or younger).

Sickness Benefits

Sickness benefits, largely unchanged from the former Soviet-wide system, have three components: (a) sick pay; (b) maternity benefits (discussed above); and (c) sick care leave (for children and other family members). In addition, benefits cover orthopedic devices or compensation payments for stays in sanatoria. The SIF finances all these sickness benefits.

Sick pay is graduated according to the person's service record. Employees who have worked less than five years receive 60 percent of their last wage, those who have worked for five to eight years receive 80 percent, and those who have worked more than eight years receive 100 percent. In the case of a work injury, no service requirement applies, and the replacement rate is 100 percent. Employees can receive sick pay up to 120 days per year, subject to a physician's verification, and can take up to 7 days (14 days in the case of a child up to age fourteen) to nurse a sick family member. No separate worker's compensation program exists. Industrial accidents and work-related health problems are covered under the normal sickness benefits for short-term problems and under disability for long-term problems. Sick pay is not subject to income tax.

Unemployment Benefits

Unemployment benefits were paid for the first time on February 15, 1992. They are part of an overall employment policy package comprising passive and active labor market policies (essentially retraining and public works). Three groups of the population are covered by unemployment benefits: (a) former workers, (b) new entrants to the labor market, and (c) women returning to the labor market after taking time off to care for their children. According to the Law on Employment, there is a mandatory two months' advance notice prior to lay-off, and firms must continue to pay salaries (severance pay) for three months. Local employment offices administer these benefits. There are currently thirty-six such offices with a total staff of 257.

There are two types of unemployment benefits: the unemployment allowance and the stipend allowance. The unemployment allowance for dismissed workers amounts to 90 percent of the minimum wage (RUR 1,350 in June 1992) or 70 percent for first-time job seekers. This allowance is paid for no more than six months, except that the period of eligibility is extended in the case of sickness. For job seekers undergoing retraining, a stipend allowance equal to the unemployment allowance is paid for a maximum of six months. During this period, payment of the unemployment allowance is suspended but it may be resumed later, with a possible total allowance period (unemployment allowance and stipend allowance) of one year. For individuals below age twenty-one, the Ministry of Education finances the stipend allowance.

Every unemployed person has a legal right to training or retraining; the decision on which depends on the local employment office. Local governments, enterprises, or other organizations can also organize public work. In this case a job agreement is signed with the unemployed person for two months: extensions are possible, but the work can last no longer than six months. During this period the unemployment allowance is temporarily suspended. People whose unemployment allowance or stipend allowance and supplements fall short of their average wage from the last place of employment can receive monthly supplements equal to 50 percent of the minimum wage from the local employment office. This regulation, which may result in an unemployment allowance of 140 percent of the minimum wage, essentially applies to unemployed people with dependents. About 50 percent of the eligible unemployed qualify for this supplement, according to the mission's estimates.

Recommendation for the Short Term

As the Latvian government begins to reform its social programs and to prepare for economic transition, it should ensure that its programs continue to:

- Shelter vulnerable groups in society against the most adverse effects of the economic transition, particularly the loss of employment and high inflation;

- Be cost-effective and consistent with the budget constraints;

- Be consistent with a market-oriented environment and be financially sustainable, yet put no undue burden on the productive sector.

Although many of the reforms under way are to be commended--they support the lowest income groups, provide work incentives, are easy to administer, and are cost-effective--they fall short in such areas as financial sustainability, indexing, and providing social assistance benefits. The Ministry of Social Welfare, Labor, and Health recently announced plans to improve the system of benefits.

Closing the Social Safety Net

The purpose of a social assistance program is to grant income support to all people with insufficient means of their own who are not covered by other social programs, and who would otherwise live in poverty. To deal with the issue of poverty sufficiently, either the social security system must be more generous, or else support for poor households (subsidies or direct provision of basic foods) should be reintroduced.

Latvia has only the rudimentary elements of a social assistance system to provide income support. No mechanism is in place to raise low-income individuals above the poverty line (the minimum level of living). The system is unprepared to cope with a rising number of poor, especially compared with the old system, which guaranteed employment and provided basic goods and services at low prices or for free. The few social assistance benefits consist of meal coupons, food coupons, and non-recurrent lump sum payments. There is no network of social assistance offices.

To establish a viable social assistance system will require various measures. First, a minimum poverty line has to be established and regularly reviewed against a basket of goods to maintain its value in real terms. The poverty line should be (a) minimal, but sufficient to ensure adequate nutrition, health, warmth, and other basic needs; (b) adjusted for family size and age or gender composition; and (c) reflect the differences between rural and urban areas.

Once a minimum poverty line is established, it should trigger policy actions, individual claims, and standardized regulations (application rules, screening and disbursement procedures) and ensure equal treatment of the poor. An assessment of the poverty gap under alternative economic scenarios is also needed. To ensure that the local authorities have sufficient means and incentives to spend on the poor, matching grants from the central budget are recommended.

Rationalizing Indexation

The adjustment of the minimum wage, the minimum level of living, and social benefits to changes in prices in Latvia follows established rules whose economic rationale is sometimes questionable. A rational indexing procedure is needed. In periods of high inflation, quarterly, or even monthly, indexing may be required. If necessary, different indexes for families and for the elderly than a general consumer price index may be applied to secure the real purchasing power of the benefits.

Adjusting the Pension System

The pension system introduced in January 1991 combines a modern, Western-oriented system of old-age income support with major elements of the old system. As a result, the retirement provisions are rather generous, but pay little attention to incentives or financing constraints. If inflation remains high, periodic indexing of benefits may be needed. However, with rising unemployment and falling output, the resources to finance such a system may not be available.

Under the old system, pension expenditures were 6 percent of GDP, much higher than in some Western industrialized countries such as Australia, Canada, or Japan. Under the new system, this share is up to almost 9 percent of GDP, a level close to the average in Organisation for Economic Co-operation and Development (OECD) countries. Once inflation subsides, this share of pension expenditures could reach 15 percent of GDP or higher, requiring substantial contributions to finance the program.

The current ratio of pensioners to those employed is high: two workers support one pensioner. This ratio is the result of a low standard retirement age (sixty for men, fifty-five for women) compared with the average in OECD countries (older than sixty-four for men and sixty-two for women) and easy access to disability benefits in the forty-six to sixty age group.

In view of the need to provide a minimum social safety net for the elderly at a time of high inflation and of the longer-term financial unsustainability of the new pension system, a transitory pension plan is recommended. It would pay flat-rate benefits during periods of high inflation, but would be indexed on a monthly basis. Meanwhile, a comprehensive pension reform should be prepared, following a review of the retirement age and benefit formula and a costing of reform options under alternative economic and demographic scenarios.

Restructuring Sick Pay Provisions

The way sick pay provisions are set up in Latvia seems to invite abuse. The social security budget absorbs the financial burden of sick pay, and employers therefore have little incentive to question the legitimacy of sick-day claims. In contrast, in periods of sluggish demand employers may have an incentive to reduce their wage bill; behavior that may increase as the number of small-scale and private enterprises grows. For employees too there may be a slight incentive: a sick worker is paid in full, but is not taxed, whereas a healthy worker is paid and taxed at an average marginal rate of 20 percent.

In most industrialized countries, the income risk from sickness is distributed: the risk is borne by the individual for the first few days, and by the employer for the next four to six weeks. Only in cases of prolonged illness does the social security system bear the burden of sick pay. An alternative method often used in the United States allows employees to accumulate the sick leave days granted every year. If these days prove insufficient, employees use their annual leave.

Given the likelihood of future abuse of sickness benefits and the positive experience with alternative systems in other countries, the government should consider making employers responsible for sick pay. This would lower the rate of contributions paid to the SIF. Furthermore, sick pay should be subject to income tax, as should other social benefits that replace income.

Reviewing Unemployment Benefits

Unemployment benefits are necessary given the disturbances in the Latvian economy, but the eligibility criteria, benefit structure, and administrative procedures should be reviewed. The right to turn down job offers with lower qualifications, for instance, may not be appropriate during a period of economic restructuring. Providing benefits to new or re-entrants into the labor market (students who leave school or women returning from maternity leave) is neither justified nor efficient. Setting retraining benefits at the same level as unemployment benefits does not provide an incentive to retrain. Finally, local employment offices have neither the staff, physical facilities nor equipment needed to service large numbers of unemployed, nor does the Employment Fund have the budgetary means to finance the required start-up costs.

To enhance the social efficiency and cost-effectiveness of the unemployment benefits given the tight budget constraints, several measures seem appropriate:

- Strengthening eligibility criteria, particularly with regard to refusals of job offers;

- Setting retraining benefits at, say, 50 percent more than unemployment benefits to provide incentives for the unemployed to participate in retraining programs;

- Graduating the length of time allowed to receive benefits on the basis of service record and age to prepare for the rising numbers of long-term unemployed;

- Eliminating unemployment benefits for new or re-entrants into the labor market, but allowing both groups to benefit from retraining programs.

Budgeting in Inflationary Environments

Although preparing a budget under conditions of high inflation, rising unemployment, and uncertain output is difficult, a revenue and expenditure plan is needed to determine the required policy decisions and the scope of the fiscal operations in the economy. Such a plan has to make assumptions on both sides of the budget and should be based on reasonable projections. The calculations have to anticipate lags in the collection of contributions and disbursements of expenditures, which critically influence the balance in any given month. To allow the SIF to operate better in an uncertain economic environment, the authorities need to (a) provide it with consistent economic forecasts and budgeting guidelines; (b) base its annual budget on monthly revolving projections, taking into account the major lead and lag structures in expenditures and revenues; and (c) control the accounts of the SIF and every social program on a monthly basis.

Securing Revenue Collection

The central source of revenue for all social programs is the social security contributions collected by the SIF. Because of the other expenditure responsibilities of the state budget, these contributions may be the only revenue available to finance social benefits. Consequently, the authorities must ensure that the contributions from enterprises are collected. However, substantial arrears are likely to emerge for the following reasons: (a) the dual position of firms as disbursers of and contributors to benefits complicates application of simple control mechanisms; (b) the current penalty and interest rate on late payments--0.1 percent per day or 3.0 percent per month--is too low in view of the current rate of inflation; and (c) the lack of fines and criminal charges to levy against enterprises and management in arrears and of bankruptcy procedures.

To secure the collection of these funds, the following measures should be taken: (a) increasing dramatically the monthly penalty and interest rate, for example, 1.5 times the inflation rate of the preceding month; (b) reducing the lag for collections by putting private farmers, the self-employed, and small business people on a monthly payment basis; (c) introducing penalty charges against managers of firms more than two months in arrears; (d) initiating bankruptcy procedures by the SIF against enterprises more than three months in arrears; and (e) strengthening SIF staff to monitor compliance under an expanded program.

Recommendations for the Medium Term

Over the medium-term, the government must prepare plans that address the following issues: reform of the pension system, review of family benefits, and rationalization of the operations of social programs.

Pensions

Although the new pension law is an improvement over the prior system, many distortions remain. To ensure the new system is financially sustainable, a comprehensive reform should consider the following:

- Increase the effective retirement ages for both genders and eliminate the differentiation between them;

- Review those occupations that permit lower retirement ages and reconsider the need for this provision;

- Establish lower pension levels for workers who choose to retire at an early age;

- Consider introducing private (occupational and personal) retirement provisions.

Family Benefits

The provision of universal family allowances and other benefits can be an effective instrument for reducing the risk of poverty, and thus cushion the effects of economic restructuring. However, given the structure of family benefits, many families, particularly at the higher income levels, may be compensated twice, first through higher than average real wage changes, and second, through real increases in the value of family benefits. In addition, a fall in the prices of non-basic consumer goods could further benefit upper-income groups.

The entire structure of the family benefits program should be reviewed and the following steps should be taken:

- Devise methods to target benefits, possibly using a two-tier system;

- Include benefits in the income tax base;

- Drop other allowances, for example, the kindergarten substitution allowance, once an established system of social assistance services allows for a more equitable approach;

- Review the generous terms for sick care leave, which may inadvertently lead to discrimination in the labor market against mothers with young children.

Rationalizing Administration and Financial Operations

The division of the expenditure and revenue responsibilities between the state budget and the extrabudgetary funds handling social programs should be rationalized. The following central issues should be addressed:

- Currently, the SIF finances earnings-related benefits (such as pension benefits) and important flat-rate benefits (such as child care and family allowances), which are only marginally linked to prior labor market participation. Those program benefits not related to contributions should be moved out of the SIF budget to compete with all other public programs and should be financed directly by the budget.

- At the local level, administration of the benefits for working and non-working people is divided. A new system needs to be established to disburse benefits to both groups in a unified manner.

- Contributions to the Social Security Fund should be divided more fairly between employers and employees.

- Contributions should be fully tax deductible under the profit or income tax and the resulting pension benefits should be tax exempt.

In summary, the government has made progress in restructuring social programs to shelter vulnerable groups from the most adverse effects of the economic transition. To strengthen the social safety net, however, additional measures are needed in the following areas: indexation, the poverty line, social assistance benefits, budgeting of social programs, and collection of revenues for social funds. The entire system of social benefits must be consistent with, and supportive of, the other reforms and with the new market-oriented economy. Reform of the pension system is especially critical. The current system is a heavy burden on the economy, jeopardizes the objectives of the reform, and makes no allowance for private provision of pensions, which would be an important step toward increased saving and economic growth.

 Public Sector Management

Like other former Soviet republics, Latvia faces two vast challenges: the radical transformation of the economic system and the building of independent national institutions. However, unlike most other former Soviet republics, Latvia enjoys a living memory of market-oriented independent institutions and of legal and regulatory precedents that--although fifty years old--may still be a basis on which to build for the future. Despite this advantage, the task of institutional development is considerable.

The term institution encompasses both the basic rules and the organizations that function by those rules, in the private sector as well as in the government. Development of institutions in this broad sense has a diffuse and long-term economic impact, and depends on the efforts of all segments of society. Although private sector institutions are key to a market economy, the reform of public sector institutions also has a major impact on the efficiency of economic resources in the medium term. The guiding principle of public sector reform is a reorientation in the role of the state from directing to facilitating economic activity, from repressing to enabling the private sector.

The private sector and the economy as a whole need not only smaller government, but better government. Better government means disengagement from directly productive and commercial activities, and a stronger and more effective role in other public activities. These public activities mainly comprise economic and social infrastructure, basic administrative services, and the establishment and enforcement of a policy and regulatory framework for a competitive market economy, all of which are essential for the development and efficiency of the private sector. Various reforms in this direction--in the financial sector and in other main economic sectors--are identified elsewhere in this report. This section focuses on the governmental institutions that are directly responsible for the management of the economy.

Core economic management functions of the central government include central banking, external debt management, tax administration, planning and budgeting, collection and management of statistical data, and macroeconomic forecasting. The government has launched a comprehensive review and assessment of economic management institutions and of the civil service. It is already clear, however, that Latvia has two areas of economic management where fairly rapid improvement is possible and urgent. Successful reform in these areas would have the additional advantage of providing an example and a model that could facilitate subsequent reform of other institutions. These two areas are (a) the coordination and management of external aid; and (b) the programming, monitoring, and execution of public investment.

Aid Management

Latvia is expected to receive a significant amount of foreign grants and loans for technical assistance, balance of payments and emergency support, and investment projects over the next few years. Foreign assistance will support many government programs and will involve a number of government agencies. To benefit fully from this assistance, it needs to be effectively managed and coordinated by the Latvian government.

To manage its aid program effectively, the government needs to assign clear responsibilities among ministries and departments. The nature of the aid management problem is such

---

Box 3-2. Lessons from Aid Management in Other Countries

   • The success or failure of aid management depends very much on individuals, their commitment, and their capabilities. Quality and continuity of staffing is therefore critical.

   • Each country needs to adapt aid management arrangements to suit its own political and administrative culture.

   • Good aid management goes hand in hand with good macroeconomic management, a clear sense of direction, and clear expenditure priorities.

   • Close and effective links between the core economic management agencies and effective higher-level coordination committees improves aid management.

   • Functioning government accounting systems are necessary for good aid management.

   • The inclusion of all aid-funded activities in the annual budget and the separation of development and recurrent budgets improves aid management.

   • Firm control and monitoring of foreign borrowing by the public sector, including public enterprises, and a well-functioning debt reporting system makes for better aid management.

---

that no institutional configuration can be perfect, and the World Bank's experience indicates that arrangements may vary from country to country (Box 3-2). However, it needs to be clear (a) who is responsible for overall aid policy, (b) where the authority resides within the government to make day-to-day decisions on aid, and (c) what are the channels of communication between aid agencies and the government. Agencies designated to carry out specific aid management functions need to enhance their capacity to do so, and may require technical assistance for this purpose.

   Responsibility for relations with donors in Latvia is currently divided among three ministries: the Ministry of Economic Reform, which is in charge of World Bank and EBRD activities; the Ministry of Finance, which is responsible for IMF activities, and the Ministry of Foreign Affairs, which is in charge of other foreign economic and financial relations, including technical assistance. A committee headed by the deputy minister of foreign affairs, and including among others representatives of the Ministry of Finance, the Ministry of Economic Reform, and the Bank of Latvia, coordinates the overall foreign financial relations of Latvia. The current situation is complex, lines of responsibility are unclear, and foreign assistance is not managed effectively. The government is actively considering a streamlined and more effective institutional arrangement. Such an arrangement would place responsibility for aid coordination in the Ministry of Finance, and would meet the following criteria:

   • Foreign donors need to have direct access to and work directly with implementing agencies, particularly when the assistance is for investment projects or technical assistance, or with core ministries when the assistance is related to macroeconomic stabilization or adjustment. The aid coordination unit should facilitate such interaction, but should also be the focal point for relations with donors.

   • The unit should not duplicate the macroeconomic and sectoral expertise of the economic and sectoral ministries. One way of avoiding such duplication would be to organize the unit's staff along donor rather than sectoral lines. The unit's familiarity with donors and donor programs would complement the sectoral and economic specialization of ministries and agencies.

- The unit should be the focal point in the government for donor coordination and cover all types of assistance such as grants and loans, financial and technical, and so on. Any dilution of such responsibility will lead to confusion and reduce the effectiveness of aid coordination and of the aid itself.

Public Investment

Because a major part of external aid is normally used to help finance public investment, a badly programmed or misdirected program of public investments is a weak basis for attracting foreign aid and directing it to priority areas, no matter how efficient the aid management mechanism may be.

Previously, the State Planning Committee was responsible for coordinating the investment programs of the state administration and non-Union enterprises. After 1985, SOEs were required to invest their surpluses (subject to State Planning Committee approval), and the state budget financed investments of the ministries, the local councils, and SOEs that were either non-commercial or did not generate a sufficient surplus. In 1985-90, the budget financed about one-fourth of state investment, local SOE's about one-half, and All-Union SOEs the remaining one-fourth.

Currently, SOEs no longer need government approval for investment out of their own funds. Slightly over half of state investment is now through the central budget and the remainder from local government budgets. Local governments' investment, in turn, is financed almost equally by state transfers and a share of taxes collected locally. However, the difficult economic situation, particularly the collapse of revenues, and the urgency of fiscal and financial stabilization, have led to a sharp decline in state investment to levels even below replacement needs. Maintenance provisions are also insufficient. This has resulted in large numbers of uncompleted construction projects and some deterioration in economic and social infrastructure. Thus, it is clear that state investment must gradually recover from its current minimal level, which is estimated, on a per capita basis, at about one-seventh the level of Poland. It is equally clear, however, that (a) public sector investment as a whole needs to be far smaller than it was under central planning, (b) its composition will be very different, (c) the approach to project evaluation needs to be changed, and (d) the institutional arrangements for investment programming and monitoring require reform and improvement.

Concerning the scale of public investment, the fundamental reorientation in the role of the state--from directing to facilitating economic activity--means that an expansion of the economy's productive capacity must eventually come more and more from the private sector. Although public investment in social overhead capital will remain crucial for the efficient functioning of the economy and the profitability of the private sector, the state's disengagement from directly productive activities necessarily entails an optimal level of public investment much lower than under the previous system. Thus, reallocating investments from obsolete or inappropriate projects to public investments of genuine priority for a competitive market economy is fundamental for establishing an appropriate public investment program within a reduced resource envelope.

The composition of public investment cannot remain the same in the face of the different role of the government and of major changes in the economic environment, especially in the structure of prices and of external trade. The most urgent task for the government is to take a fresh look at the large overhang of projects currently in the investment program to decide which projects should be completed in their present form when financing becomes available, which should be scaled down or redesigned, and which should be abandoned altogether, and if so in what manner. For practical reasons, this review could initially focus on the larger projects. Also, the prompt application of good judgment and reasonable priorities are more important in this phase than standard rate of return calculations or other technical requirements. Such a review will certainly lead to a substantial contraction in the investment program and focus it on rehabilitation and other investments with short gestation periods and high returns. This is particularly true for state enterprises in the commercial sector, where as a general rule new investments should be postponed until the enterprises have been privatized. It must be recalled, however, that only a small fraction of the public investment program is currently being funded in any case. The extent of underfunding is illustrated by the Riga City Council, which estimated its investment requirements at 25 times the amount budgeted for the first half of 1992.

A new approach to project evaluation is a must for both the screening of the existing portfolio and the realization of new investment opportunities. While Latvia has many civil servants with substantial technical expertise, their training and approach to project evaluation are, almost by definition, unsuitable to the requirements of a market-oriented economy. Under central planning, partly because of the distortions in the price system, there was no critical evaluation of costs and benefits and project preparation was dominated by engineering inputs. Therefore, project evaluation and selection criteria should be introduced (and appropriate training provided) that adequately reflect economic and financial costs and benefits of the project with due regard to uncertainties and risks and taking into account recurrent costs.

These urgent measures, although important, cannot have lasting results in the absence of institutional reform. At present, the MER is responsible for aggregating and appraising investment proposals from the various sectors. However, personnel and expertise are lacking. The MER's Public Investment Department has only five staff members. A reorganization and strengthening of the function is needed. Also needed is a public investment program (PIP) process to provide continuity and some predictability in the management of public resources (see Box 3-3).

The PIP would show all state investment projects, including those of state enterprises, envisaged to require funding over a certain period of years (normally three), along with their financial requirements, source of funding and some indication (to the extent possible) of recurrent cost implications. The PIP would be rolled over annually. Despite the uncertainties of Latvia's economic outlook, all efforts should be made to formulate a realistic investment program to allow a smooth stream of projects and their review over time. The projects would normally originate in the sectoral ministries or state enterprises, but central coordination by the core ministry must be systematic and substantive. Also, it is the core ministry's responsibility to assure that (a) all projects included in the PIP are compatible with the new role of the state and with established priorities in the major sectors, (b) projects meet standard appraisal criteria, and (c) total funding is consistent with the overall macroeconomic framework.

The PIP is mainly a tool to improve resource planning and allocation. Investment projects included in the PIP need to be submitted to regular feasibility studies before going ahead. As such, the PIP need not have formal legislative approval. However, the year's public investment expenditure must be reflected in the budget and be specifically approved. Hence, if the structure of financing shown in the PIP is realistic and internally consistent, budgetary investment requirements will correspond to the local and foreign funding of the year's tranche of the PIP. It is highly advisable, therefore, to annex the

PIP formally to the draft budget or, at the very minimum, to schedule discussion of the PIP at the same time as discussion of the budget. It also advisable to develop multi-year expenditure plans covering recurrent and investment expenditure to provide a longer-term framework for the annual budget exercise.

To improve the core economic management function, in particular, making the PIP process work properly, a number of other institutional issues need to be addressed. The most important of these are:

- The classification and management of the budget by capital and recurrent expenditures, by project with clear separation of foreign and local counterpart funding, and by clear identification of budgetary subsidies for SOEs;

- The improvement of government accounting systems and systems for the effective monitoring of the physical and financial execution of the PIP;

- The policies and procedures for providing government or government guaranteed credit to SOEs and the private sector;

- The policies and procedures for technical assistance to support the development and implementation of the reform and investment programs;

- A clearer definition of responsibilities between central and local government for the planning, implementation, and funding of the PIP.

Box 3-3. Preparation of a Public Investment Program (PIP)

A PIP shows the investments a government intends to implement over a three- to five-year period. A well-prepared and realistically sized PIP can serve several functions:

- Assist *economic management* by ensuring that macroeconomic and sectoral strategies are translated into programs and projects within a realistic assessment of resources.

- Facilitate *aid coordination* by enabling aid inflows to be maximized and channeled to priority areas.

- Encourage sound *public sector financial management* by making it easier to balance commitments with resources.

- Strengthen the *project cycle* by providing a framework within which the preparation, implementation, monitoring, and evaluation of investment projects can take place.

There are three main steps in preparing a PIP:

- *Establishing the framework of available resources and their allocation among sectors and subsectors.* Typically this step involves (a) estimating total investment resources over the PIP period, (b) determining intrasectoral investment priorities and resource allocations, and (c) determining investment priorities and resource allocations within sectors. As external financial assistance programs get under way, there are prospects for Latvia to increase substantially the funding of the PIP. The allocation of these resources will need to reflect the changing role of the government within sectors and subsectors and the relative demand for investment resources.

- *Building up a portfolio of investment projects to be matched against available resources.* These comprise (a) existing commitments against ongoing projects; (b) pipeline projects that have been prepared and are awaiting funding; and (c) new projects that are in various stages of identification and preparation, and that can be expected to be implemented later in the PIP. The limited availability of investment resources and the transformation to a market economy require that both ongoing and pipeline projects be subject to detailed review before resources are committed.

- *Screening of investment proposals for inclusion in the PIP.* This task involves an iterative process to determine the ranking of projects against financial resources at the subsector, sector, and aggregate PIP levels. Determining the ranking is complicated by the wide differences in the types of projects to be considered and their stages of preparation. It relies on a combination of formal investment appraisal methodologies, such as cost-benefit analysis, and more judgmental approaches that seek to match projects for their consistency with sector policies and strategies.

The end result of a PIP preparation exercise is typically:

- A set of brief project descriptions each including a table showing (a) the planned lifetime of each project, (b) its total estimated cost, (c) the investment incurred prior to the start of the PIP period, (d) the planned expenditures in each financial year, (e) the balance of expenditure required to the complete the project in subsequent PIPs, (f) the long-term recurrent costs to the government budget (if applicable), and (g) the general terms under which the financing is to be provided (grant, loan, government guarantee, credit, and so on).

- A series of summary tables that aggregate capital and recurrent costs by (a) subsector and sector; (b) council, department, and ministry; and (c) main sources and types of financing.

- The incorporation of the annual expenditures under the agreed public investment program into the annual budget exercise.

CHAPTER 4

An Agenda for Transition and the Medium-Term Outlook

This chapter identifies the major elements of Latvia's reform agenda and examines the macroeconomic conditions under which the rest of the reform program will be implemented. It draws extensively on the analysis and recommendations of the previous chapters, and the sectoral analysis contained in Part II of this report to outline an agenda for reform and to assess Latvia's likely macroeconomic prospects.

Stabilization, Structural Reforms, and Sequencing

Latvia remained in the ruble area until recently because of political constraints and other difficulties associated with the introduction of a new currency. Due to these constraints, the authorities concentrated their efforts on implementating structural reforms, while making preparations to issue a new currency and stabilize the economy. Although this implementation sequencing has been somewhat different than in most other reforming economies, where stabilization measures were implemented in the early stages of the reform, the outcome has not been discouraging. The fact that the price and trade reforms are already at an advanced stage of implementation actually facilitates the tasks of stabilization and of enterprise restructuring. The tax reform has broadened the tax base and should also contribute to stabilization, although the capacity to administer the new taxes needs to be greatly improved. However, further delays in implementing a comprehensive privatization program will retard the potential supply response, and will eventually complicate the task of stabilization (see Box 4-1).

Latvia left the ruble area in July 1992, and thus fulfilled some of the necessary conditions for the pursuit of an independent monetary policy and the successful implementation of a stabilization program. However, the government has been also aware that leaving the ruble area is not by itself sufficient to control inflation, and has agreed with the IMF on a program of economic stabilization. Policymakers now face the challenge of consolidating the stabilization efforts and designing a reform agenda for a rapid transition to a market economy. Therefore, establishing priorities for the short and medium term is crucial for the success of this economic transformation program.

An Agenda for Reform and Policy Actions

In the short-term (mid-1992 through mid-1993), policymakers should focus on stabilizing the economy and on adjusting the economy to the adverse impacts of the terms of trade shocks. In the medium-term complementary actions are needed to minimize output losses, increase the possibilities for an early supply response, and reduce the initial impact of the adjustment on the population. The following two subsections examine priorities for policy actions in the short and medium term.

Box 4-1. The Design and Sequencing of Reforms

In recent years, there has been a great effort by many economists to examine questions of reform design and sequencing and to review the experience of early reformers.[a] As a result of such efforts, consensus has emerged over some aspects of reform design and implementation. For instance, there is agreement that stabilization should come at the early stages of the reform program, in coordination with price and trade reforms. There is somewhat less consensus on the position of privatization in the sequencing of reforms. Although there is widespread agreement that privatization is at the core of the transformation process, and that a fast privatization program increases the likelihood of an early supply response, it is frequently argued that privatization is not strictly required to ensure the success of stabilization.

The opposite view is that privatization is a fundamental component of stabilization, since non-privatized enterprises do not respond to price signals and behave in a way that is ultimately inconsistent with stabilization. For instance, excessive wage payments, the accumulation of inter-enterprise arrears, and widespread defaults on bank loans may seriously undermine stabilization efforts. Moreover, these phenomena are more likely to occur in the absence of early privatization.

The experience of Eastern European countries has been mixed. In most countries state enterprises have created some difficulties for stabilization, although the Czechoslovak case indicates that there can be initial success at stabilization before privatization. The view that seems to be emerging is that a stabilization program rooted in fiscal and monetary discipline and supported by an incomes policy may be initially successful in reducing inflation. However, if such initial success is not promptly reinforced by widespread privatization and a fundamental change in microeconomic behavior, the supply response will be delayed and the stabilization program may ultimately fail.

a. See, for instance, Fischer and Gelb (1991); Hinds (1991).

Currency Reform and Stabilization

A successful program of economic stabilization in Latvia requires the adoption of restrictive fiscal and monetary policies, as well as the support of a well-designed incomes policy. These policies, together with the maintenance of a liberal exchange system, would also make substantial contributions to the process of external adjustment in Latvia.

Fiscal policy needs to be strengthened as it is the centerpiece of a successful stabilization program. To this end, the government must adjust both revenues and expenditures so as to curtail the budgetary deficit. On the revenue side the measures should include eliminating the numerous exemptions from the turnover and profit taxes; introducing a moderate flat-rate import tariff; and strengthening tax collection, possibly by adopting presumptive methods to collect taxes from the growing number of small private enterprises. On the expenditure side the measures should include reducing the remaining consumer and agricultural subsidies; reducing residential heating subsidies; establishing a ceiling on the overall level of employment in the public sector; and identifying areas where expenditures could be reduced, such as civil service employment and remuneration.

Monetary and credit policies also have to be carefully designed. The expansion of credit should be controlled through various monetary policy instruments and linked to low inflation targets, while also meeting the needs of the emerging private enterprises. Interest rate policy will have to be carefully formulated to ensure the attractiveness of the new currency, while also avoiding excessively high real interest rates that could aggravate portfolio problems in the banks. The interest rates on credits and deposits may have to be controlled initially, although frequently adjusted to reflect inflation developments and allow for a reasonable intermediation margin.

The tight fiscal and monetary policies should be supported by (a) an appropriate exchange rate policy to help build up an adequate level of foreign exchange reserves to support the new currency, and (b) a restrictive (tax-based) incomes policy designed to avoid excessive wage payments by state enterprises and reduce inflationary inertia. The experience of other reforming economies indicates the need to maintain an incomes policy during the whole period of transition until the ownership of enterprises is established, and the financial discipline over enterprises prevents excessive increases in wage payments.

Finally, completing the price reform is essential to reduce budgetary subsidies further and to provide the correct signals to consumers and investors. Such reform will require actions in various areas:[1]

- Energy prices must be corrected to rationalize energy use and avoid the rising budgetary costs associated with energy subsidies. This is particularly important in residential use.

- Minimum support prices in the agriculture sector should be phased out and the prices of agricultural inputs (including livestock feed, fertilizer, and farm equipment) should be free of controls to ensure their efficient use.

- Enterprises providing public services should start adopting cost-based tariffs: railway tariffs should fully cover costs, including depreciation, and road maintenance costs should be covered by levying taxes on road users, including a special tax for heavy vehicles.

- Telecommunication tariffs will need to be raised substantially to allow for needed investments in expansion and improvement of services. Tariffs will probably need to be raised in several stages and with differentiation among different customer groups, some of which should be charged full cost-based tariffs immediately.

- Rents for public housing need to be raised to cover maintenance and economic costs and to allow the replacement or rehabilitation of old equipment and facilities.

Important steps have already been taken in the direction of such an economic stabilization program and the government has reached agreement with the IMF on a standby arrangement (see Box 4-2).

Complementary Actions and Structural Reforms

The implementation of a program of stabilization and currency reform will tend to have a depressing effect on output in the short run. Overstaffed state-owned enterprises will be particularly affected by the restricted access to credits and the charging of much higher interest rates. The unemployment rate will increase significantly, as the growth of the private sector will not initially be sufficient to absorb the redundant personnel discharged by state enterprises. Indeed, the experience of other countries indicates that the unemployment rate could increase well above 10 percent within a year

---

1.   For detailed analysis and discussion of price policy in various sectors, see the chapters on sectoral reforms.

Box 4-2. Summary of the Stabilization Program under the IMF Standby Arrangement
(July 1992-June 1993)

Principal Targets

To reduce the monthly rate of inflation to 3 percent by December 1992 and to 1-1/2 percent by June 1993, to limit the fall in real GDP to less than 20 percent in the program year, to have an external current account deficit of USD 300 million in the program year, and to increase gross official international reserve equivalents to one month of imports by the end of the program year.

Principal Policies

Fiscal Policy: Limit the general government deficit to less than 2 percent of GDP in 1992 through the implementation of the following measures: eliminating almost all consumer subsidies; curtailing subsidies and transfers to agriculture; capping the overall level of employment in the public sector combined with implementating an incomes policy to help restrain the wage bill; eliminating most exemptions from the value added tax and increasing the basic rate from 10 to 12 percent; imposing a flat-rate import duty of 15 percent on all imports regardless of origin, except for a very limited number of products; reducing the number of exemptions from the profits tax and unifying the basic tax rate; strengthening tax administration; and improving cash management of the budget.

Monetary Policy: An increase in the refinancing rate of the Bank of Latvia from 50 to 80 percent, an increase in the reserve requirement ratio from 15 to 20 percent, liberalization of deposit rates in the branches of the Bank of Latvia, elimination of interest rate subsidies through the banking system, and requirement that the branches of the Bank of Latvia observe all stipulations of the Law on Banks.

External Policies: Introducing flexible exchange rate policy, establishing a foreign exchange department in the Bank of Latvia and centralizing official foreign exchange holdings in the Bank of Latvia; abolishing the foreign currency budget, eliminating all export quotas and licensing requirements and the bulk of export taxes, introducing a flat-rate import duty (see under fiscal policy); and conducting international economic relations on a nondiscriminatory basis in line with multilateral principles prevailing in the world economy.

Structural Policies: Removal of price regulations for fuel oil, liquified gas, and coal for industrial purposes; implementation of competition and anti-monopoly legislation; privatization of state enterprises as quickly as possible; and adoption of a new accounting law and development of regulations and institutions to put the Bankruptcy Law into effect.

---

or so, a rate substantially higher than the present 2 percent. Output contraction and increased unemployment are unavoidable short-run effects of a successful stabilization program in the present Latvian context. However, the government needs to adopt complementary policies in the short and medium term to avoid unnecessary output losses, to enhance the possibilities of an early supply response, and to soften the impact of the adjustment on the population. The thrust of these policies is summarized below and is based on the analysis and recommendations of the previous chapters.

Reforming the Enterprise Sector

Essential to the transformation of the economy into a market-based system is a progressive expansion of the role of the private sector. This requires actions in many areas: promoting small businesses, expediting privatization of large enterprises, commercializing those enterprises that remain in the state sector, and promoting competition and breaking up monopolies as quickly as possible.

Small business development should be promoted largely through completing the small privatization program, the sale of moveable assets and separable activities of state-owned enterprises, and the contracting out of public services. To accelerate the privatization of large enterprises, the government should allow the sale of these enterprises to both domestic and foreign purchasers through a variety of techniques. After an initial round of privatization of a sample of large enterprises, further and more extensive privatization of large enterprises should be undertaken immediately. For those enterprises that remain in the state sector or will take a longer time to privatize, measures should be taken to enhance their commercial practices and impose strict financial discipline on them. For this purpose, the past practice of financing enterprise losses should be stopped. To promote competition further and encourage the entry of new enterprises, an active program of demonopolization of wholesale and retail businesses through breaking up monopolies and multi-plant enterprises should be initiated as quickly as possible. The program of demonopolization needs to be closely coordinated with the program of corporatization to avoid further integration of enterprises and to increase competition and efficiency.

Reforming the Financial Sector

Experience with other reforming economies indicates that reform of the financial sector is critical to the stability of the economy in general and to the reform of the enterprise sector in particular. Reforming the financial sector in Latvia requires a two-track approach: developing a plan to restructure the BOL and its commercial branches, and strengthening the central banking and supervisory functions of the BOL. The restructuring of the Savings Bank should start immediately since its portfolio situation is fully known and its branches could be sold to the emerging private commercial banks.

The restructuring plan for commercial branches of the BOL should be based on an evaluation of their portfolios and should cover financial, management, and ownership issues. The restructuring plan should identify ways of adapting the banking system to the needs of a market economy and, in particular, of increasing private ownership of the banks. The restructuring plan should also be complemented by imposing stricter prudential standards, including a higher capital-asset ratio, and development of on-site and off-site bank supervision.

The development of an independent central bank with strong supervisory functions is essential for the success of the new currency and is another aspect of financial sector reform that deserves particular attention in the medium term. This would involve further enhancement of the BOL's authority to regulate and supervise commercial banks and to conduct monetary policy through a more extensive use of indirect monetary policy instruments.

The banking system restructuring should be closely linked with the restructuring of illiquid and loss-making enterprises, since the poor portfolio of the banks is most likely the result of the poor performance of their enterprise clients. However, restructuring of enterprises would mean closing down the loss-making and illiquid enterprises and forcing these enterprises into bankruptcy. Such actions may not be politically feasible in the short run as they involve massive lay-offs and lead to increases in inter-enterprise arrears. However, financing these losses through the budget or the banking system limits resources to new and more efficient enterprises, delays enterprise reform, and jeopardizes the objectives of the stabilization program as this would ultimately involve inflationary financing through allocating credits to inefficient users and loss makers. Perhaps limited but transparent budgetary support, together with some limits on bank lending, would help ensure a smoother process before state property is fully transferred to the private sector.

Creating a Labor Market and Social Protection

The shift of labor to the most dynamic sectors is essential to increase productivity and reduce segmentation in the labor market. For this purpose, the reallocation of labor should be facilitated through strengthening the employment offices and improving the training and retraining programs. Labor mobility should also be stimulated by the privatization and development of a housing market and the establishment of a sound system of housing finance.

The increased mobility of labor should be accompanied by a social safety net system (social assistance and benefits, unemployment benefits, pension benefits) that prevents the adjustment costs from falling disproportionately on the most vulnerable groups of the population. The current system of social assistance is insufficiently targeted. Therefore, the government should define a more comprehensive poverty line, taking into account international experience, as a benchmark for all future programs of social assistance. The poverty line should be revised regularly to maintain its value in real terms. The medium-term objective should be to assure that individuals receive payments sufficient to bring their income at least to the poverty line. Also, a network of social assistance offices should be developed to help channel the necessary help to the most vulnerable groups. To make the social benefit system more compatible with the practice of market economies, the government should take a number of measures to tighten eligibility requirements for social benefits. These measures should include raising the retirement age and changing the sickness benefit scheme so that both employees and employers share its cost.

To cope with the rising budgetary costs, the government should modify eligibility criteria that would exclude new entrants and re-entrants into the labor market. The budgetary cost of the current earnings-related pension system is unsustainable. In the medium term, the system of pension benefits should be thoroughly revised, including retirement provisions, social contributions, and pension benefits. The government should also evaluate options for the establishment of private pension schemes. The financing of the safety net system, which is based entirely on the wage bill, should be restructured, taking into account that the system increases the cost of labor to enterprises excessively and discourages employment in a period of structural transformation and large increases in unemployment. The government should also restructure the system of contributions to the social benefit program, increasing employees' contributions and reducing employers' contributions until they pay equal shares.

Managing the Public Sector and the Public Investment Program

The successful implementation of the reform program will also require (a) progress in building institutional capacity for public sector management and coordination of policy development, including the management of public expenditures and investment and the management and coordination of foreign external assistance; (b) improvement in the quality of statistical information and economic projections; and (c) establishment of an appropriate legal and institutional infrastructure within which the private sector can operate effectively, including implementation of the Bankruptcy Law to permit systematic liquidation of non-viable enterprises.

In public investment, the urgent need is to review the existing large portfolio of projects in light of the changed role of the state and of the different economic environment. This review should identify projects that are to be retained and projects that should be abandoned as no longer viable or appropriate for public investment. The government should also establish permanent mechanisms and processes for reviewing and monitoring the public investment program and for integrating it in the budget. A well-designed and managed public investment program will contribute to the development of the productive and commercial sectors and will increase Latvia's attractiveness to foreign investors. Experience in other countries indicates that an appropriately targeted public investment program, particularly in the infrastructure sectors and public works, would contribute to a revival of investment in other sectors.

Sectoral Reform Policies

Complementing the structural measures mentioned above are specific programs of sectoral reform. Prospects for an adequate supply response will be poor if the rigidities and distortions in the sectors result in slow adjustment. The sectoral policies and programs, as well as investment priorities, are discussed in Part II of this report. The two key reform priorities that are common among all sectors in Latvia are (a) completion of the price reform and the privatization program, and (b) rationalization of investment policies and institution building. In addition, other issues deserve particular attention in each sector. Those issues, which are drawn from the more extensive sectoral discussions in Part II, are as follows:

- In the agriculture sector, property rights should be transferable and a competitive trading system for inputs and outputs should be established.

- In industry, enterprise restructuring and privatization are the key reform priorities. Also, the development of small and medium enterprises and an increase in competition and export orientation are important priorities in the sector.

- In the energy sector, energy subsidies should be eliminated and rationalization of the investment program should receive priority attention.

- In the infrastructure services sector, which includes transport, telecommunications, housing, and municipal services, cost-based tariffs and a consistent medium-term public investment program are the major concerns.

- In education, the reform should focus on training programs that support the functioning of a market economy, while in the health sector they should be directed at preventive diseases and improved quality of health-related services.

- As concerns the environment, a national environmental strategy for proactive environmental management should be designed and priority should be given to the conduct of industrial environmental audits.

A summary of the main actions for sectoral reforms in the short and medium term are presented in Table 4-1.

Table 4-1. Summary of Main Actions for Sectoral Reforms in the Short and Medium Term

Sector	Short-Term Actions	Medium-Term Actions
Agriculture	• Resolve questions of ownership and compensation for land and farm assets and ensure transfer of land rights • Establish a network of support services • Restore trade with traditional suppliers and explore new markets in convertible currency areas	• Encourage development of commercially viable farming • Ensure output markets are competitive and allow input prices to reach market levels
Industry	• Convert large state-owned enterprises to joint stock companies and operate them on a commercial basis • Refrain from bailing out unprofitable enterprises and prepare comprehensive programs for restructuring • Appoint supervisory boards of directors in state-owned joint stock companies and arrange for proper selection and training • Resume trade with former Soviet republics and seek subcontracting arrangements with Western firms • Promote growth of small and medium-sized enterprises	• Formulate industrial policy, enforce anti-monopoly policy, and prevent wastage of scarce resources • Accelerate large-scale privatization program • Facilitate institutional framework that provides modern banking and financial services to industrial enterprises • Initiate reorganization of scientific and technological institutes
Energy	• Adjust all industrial energy prices to world market levels • Decontrol prices of coal and fuelwood and introduce a mechanism to adjust prices of natural monopolies regularly • Transfer ownership of heating companies to municipalities	• Eliminate household energy subsidies • Introduce unified tariffs and metering equipment • Make regional distribution companies independent • Encourage private parties to explore renewable energy resources • Implement strategy for attracting private investment: transition to full cost recovery; introduction of planned legislation, tax codes, and contracts; liberalization of coal imports; and systematic approach to hard currency pricing of natural gas storage services
Transport	• Review public expenditures and develop priority projects • Monitor financial results of newly established aviation, maritime, and rail enterprises and develop corporate strategy for Latvian Airlines • Pursue commercialization and privatization of state transport enterprises	• Develop local government capacity for road network not covered nationally • Conclude performance contract and corporate plan for Latvian Railways • Implement strategy for promoting multi-modal transport • Introduce periodic road maintenance by competitive contracts • Promote private investment in roadside services

Sector	Short-Term Actions	Medium-Term Actions
Telecommunications	• Develop strategy and identify priority objectives for sector • Revise tariff policy and regulations • Review Lattelecom's development plan in light of technical, financial, and managerial capabilities and possible joint venture arrangements	• Determine optimal levels of tariffs to achieve long-term objectives of sector • Clarify roles of Lattelecom and government in setting tariffs • Establish a detailed plan to reorganize Lattelecom • Implement human resource policy in Lattelecom and complete retraining plan for staff • Introduce new financial and accounting policies and practices and implement computerization plan for Lattelecom
Housing and Municipal Services	• Raise rents to cover costs and make government-owned apartments more attractive for sale • Investigate experience of social safety net in other countries • Study requirements for housing finance system with appropriate lending instruments • Clarify formula for municipalities' sharing revenues from taxes • Speed up restitution process	• Introduce charge for maintaining apartments, in buildings of mixed ownership • Convert construction industry into smaller companies to increase competition • Prioritize investments in water supply, sewerage and sanitation, and urban transport • Undertake study of leakage into groundwater at Riga landfill site
Health Care	• Develop comprehensive maternal and child health care program	• Restructure health services system to achieve internal efficiency and effectiveness • Reorient primary health care and sanitary stations to prevention and reduction of death and disease • Reorganize medical education and alter medical school curriculum
Education, Training, and Research	• Develop affordable and effective system for adult training • Define comprehensive strategy to restructure vocational and technical training • Reform existing market-oriented course	• Establish management information system, including improved data on inputs and outputs • Prepare strategy for financing costs of sector improvements • Upgrade teaching content through improved training, supplies, equipment, and access to literature from abroad • Enhance quality of teaching in general schools
Environment	• Protect domestic drinking water supply and assure adequate treatment • Provide materials and equipment to operate water supply and wastewater systems • Include environmental concern in spatial planning • Design an environmental protection plan based on a completed environmental audit	• Devise national environmental strategy for proactive environmental management • Conduct industrial environmental audits • Implement viable water conservation program • Complete partially finished wastewater treatment plants • Develop joint plan with Ministry of Agriculture to improve fertilizer selection, application, and storage • Design and implement a waste strategy that integrates solid, industrial, sludge. and hazardous wastes • Agree on investment program that focuses on management of currently generated waste in all categories

Medium-Term Prospects

The success of the government's stabilization and structural reform programs will ultimately depend on political support, effective implementation, and timely provision of external assistance. Although uncertainties and economic difficulties will continue in the short term, the reform program should result in a progressive improvement of Latvia's overall economic situation in the medium term. Latvia's growth prospects and its links with external financing and trade are elaborated below. The projections presented here are only indicative and are subject to large margins of error.

The downturn in output that began in 1990 and accelerated in 1992 is expected to have led to a cumulative loss of output of around 40 percent over 1991 and 1992. Assuming that trade relations with the former Soviet Union begin to normalize and that entry of new private ventures continues, the output contraction could start easing in 1993 and a gradual recovery could begin in early 1994. With much faster progress with privatization during 1993 and 1994 and with the adoption of an export-oriented growth policy and a well-designed public investment program in key sectors, a new investment cycle could materialize in the mid-1990s. As a result, the economy could start growing faster in the second half of the decade, and by late 1990 GDP growth could average 3 to 4 percent a year.

Consumption will be negatively affected by the stabilization-oriented macroeconomic and demand management policies that the government intends to pursue during 1992-93. Overall consumption is likely to fall in real terms, but less than the fall in GDP. There is thus a need to prevent further decline in real consumption and a dramatic fall in the standard of living of the population. The projected deficit in current account in 1993 is associated with this need as well as with the maintenance of production in the short term. This deficit in relation to GDP is estimated to be about 12 percent in 1993. With the increase in economic activities starting in 1994, consumption is expected to rise in real terms, although less than the rise in GDP. As a result, consumption as a share of GDP is likely to fall gradually during the second half of the 1990s. At the same time, with investment activities picking up from their present low levels, the share of investment in GDP is projected to increase during the second half the decade. This rise in investment would partly offset the positive effect of the decline in consumption on the current account. The current account deficit is, therefore, expected to decline gradually and stay around 3 to 4 percent of GDP by the late 1990s.

Financing of imports would initially have to rely on external sources, but is expected to be largely financed by increased exports to the convertible areas in the second half of the 1990s. Although Latvia's foreign trade to the convertible currency areas is growing, it is still essentially geared to the markets of the former Soviet Union. This pattern of trade should change and Latvia should adopt policies to reorient its trade and integrate competitively in the international markets. One way to achieve this objective would be through accelerating the privatization program and improving the environment for foreign investment and joint ventures. Greater efforts would also be needed to remove the remaining constraints on exports, for example, impose export taxes, expose domestic producers to foreign competition, and improve the quality of products and marketing techniques.

The sectors with potentially the most significant export capability include the wood, food, building materials, and textile and leather industries, and a small number of machine building and electronics industries. For most industrial subsectors increasing their export capability will require a shift to higher skill-based production in accordance with Latvia's competitive advantage. Participation in preferential trade areas and bilateral trade agreements would also facilitate Latvia's reorientation of trade to foreign markets. The Baltic Free Trade Agreement concluded in March 1992, the Free Trade Agreement with Sweden, and the ongoing discussions with Finland and Norway are positive moves in this direction.

Every effort must also be made to minimize further trade disruptions with the former Soviet Union in the short term and to restore supplies of critical inputs. In this respect, the government should reduce its involvement in the state-to-state trade and promote direct trade among enterprises.

Latvia will require substantial external resources to cover the current account deficits mentioned above and to build an adequate level of external reserves (see Chapter 2). Having only recently regained its independence and with no credit record, Latvia will need to establish full creditworthiness in order to borrow from the international financial markets. Therefore, in view of the limited private foreign capital in the short term, official disbursements will have to be the main source of foreign financing. With the anticipated decline in the current account deficit by the late 1990s, Latvia's level of debt service would stay within prudent bounds and would be manageable according to normal creditworthiness criteria.

As mentioned in Chapter 2, Latvia could build up new debt relatively quickly under an adverse macroeconomic scenario. This situation could occur if the funds that Latvia needs for the implementation of its reform program are borrowed solely on normal commercial terms. In that case, the debt service ratio could easily rise above sustainable levels by the end of the decade even if exports grow reasonably fast.

Major Uncertainties

The simultaneous implementation of stabilization and structural reform measures is probably the best vehicle for the economy to recover, and ultimately to achieve sustainable growth. However, the process will not be easy. Major uncertainties exist in implementation capacity, policy implementation due to sociopolitical pressures, availability of external financing, and the external environment.

Implementation Capacity

Despite highly skilled and motivated manpower, mainly in the technical fields, Latvia lacks the specific skills needed to transform to a market economy, and this problem is likely to hinder the pace of implementation of the reform. A major challenge facing the authorities is how to develop capabilities within the government, particularly in the line ministries, in a relatively short time. Priority areas that require strengthening include the management of public expenditures; the general ability of the legal system to implement laws and supervise their enforcement; the quality of statistical information and economic projections; and the adoption of international standards and practices in accounting, auditing, procurement, and so on. The government is making special efforts to ensure that a substantial program of technical assistance is implemented in key areas of reform. Multilateral institutions and bilateral donors are also providing a wide range of technical assistance.

Political and Policy Slippage

The reform program may also get derailed because of policy slippage in the areas of greatest sociopolitical sensitivity, such as the introduction of an incomes policy designed to lower real wages and the implementation of strict financial discipline on enterprises, which will lead to much higher levels of unemployment than at present. Citizenship is also a very sensitive issue that, as discussed in Chapter 2, affects progress in the areas of restitution, ownership, and therefore privatization. The combination of these factors may lead to significant policy backsliding that would make the transition more difficult, and eventually more costly. In such an environment the government would lose credibility, enterprise reform would be delayed, domestic bank credits would be diverted to finance increases in wages and enterprise losses, and the stabilization and reform program would be compromised.

Resource Availability

A significant uncertainty facing the reform effort is whether Latvia will be able to obtain the type of international support it needs. In large part because of the program of policy reform the government has announced, the country enjoys broad support in the international financial community, and prospects for obtaining the financing requirements are reasonably good.

External Environment

Latvia also faces challenges from its external economic environment, over which it has limited control. The pace of political and economic stabilization within the FSU will be of prime importance to a normalization of Latvia's trade with the former Soviet Union, and thus its overall economic recovery. Political and economic stability within the FSU will affect the financial viability of many of Latvia's enterprises and the degree to which the hard currency that it earns from non-FSU exports will be used to cover trade deficits with the FSU. While some import and export diversification will be possible in the medium term, the experience in other reforming economies indicates that this will inevitably be a long-term process. Latvia will continue to depend on critical inputs from the FSU as well as FSU markets for its exports for some time. The present continuing political tensions and economic contraction in many republics of the former Soviet Union suggest that the risk of a slow pace of normalization of trade with the FSU is fairly significant.

Despite these risks, the medium-term scenario outlined above is feasible in terms of the availability of financing, with the help of the international financial community, and is sustainable in terms of Latvia's longer-term export potential. Some slippage in the program with respect to the level and timing of the financing is quite possible. However, additional efforts should be made to restore supplies of critical inputs from trading partners in the former Soviet Union and elsewhere among the former CMEA countries; to find domestic substitutes for imports; and, most important, to shift into production lines that are less import intensive. With such efforts, and provided the desired financing becomes available, Latvia should be able to implement its economic reform policies efficiently and forcefully.

PART II

Sectoral Reforms

CHAPTER 5

Agriculture

The Latvian agriculture sector accounts for 20 percent of GDP and employs about 16 percent of the labor force. The sector traditionally produced an exportable surplus, which was mainly delivered to the other republics of the former Soviet Union. In 1990, Latvia exported 22 percent of its dairy production, 10 percent of its meat production, and 1 percent of its egg production to other republics of the former Soviet Union. In turn, it received nearly all its fuel and agricultural machinery, and a large share of its fertilizer, feed grains, and farm finance under the FSU's centralized procurement plan.

With the dissolution of the Union, the collapse of the central planning and distribution system, and the radical changes in the domestic policy environment, the sector became involved in a profound internal transition. Simultaneously, it faced a series of major external shocks relating to trade relationships, critical prices, and the entire financial and currency system. The combination of these events has been disrupting the sector and imposing heavy adjustment costs on it. However, these events have also given Latvia an opportunity to develop a significantly more efficient, productive, and commercially viable agricultural sector, better integrated with the rest of the world, and more competitive and diversified in its economic relationships.

Background to the Current Transition

As with much of Eastern Europe and the former Soviet Union, most agricultural sector activity in Latvia was forcibly collectivized or taken over by the state in the early years following the Soviet invasion.[1] In this process, individual rights to land and other productive assets (buildings, machinery, livestock, and so on) were generally curtailed, and markets for such assets and for the complete range of agricultural inputs and outputs were suppressed. In theory, the objective was to give the state control over these assets with a view to garnering what were expected to be large-scale economies, and allocating these resources more fairly and efficiently in the interests of society as a whole. In practice, the motivation had more to do with a mistrust of independent market processes, an effort to ensure an adequate flow of low cost-supplies, and an aim of centralizing economic decisionmaking with regard to agricultural production and resource use while operating through large, monopolistic agencies.

In this context of central control, planners and government officials typically saw little or no role for functioning markets, market-determined prices, or independent initiatives by producers or intermediaries based on market signals. Instead, such institutions and activities were generally viewed as counterproductive, antisocial, and even criminal. Collective and state-owned farms and the various agencies for storage, processing, transport, marketing, and trading of both inputs and outputs constituted links in the chain of agricultural production and distribution by command. Some of the farms and other

---

1.   In theory, state farms have employees who earn a wage, whereas collective farms have members who receive their share of aggregate farm earnings. In practice, however, with the substantial share of collective farm income that could come from budgetary allocations and farms' dependence on state directives, allocations, and controls, any distinction between them becomes somewhat academic.

organizations, such as the large poultry and hog establishments, were technically internally managed more or less on a par with agro-industrial enterprises in the rest of the world, but without the market pressures and opportunities that face such businesses elsewhere. More typically, however, they became chronic victims of conflicts of interest, free rider, and other incentive problems where neither the managers nor the operatives of the system had the motivation to consider costs, efficiency, or productivity in a rational fashion. No one made cost-minimizing or profit-maximizing decisions. The result was that costs and inefficiencies escalated to the point that the entire system became non-functional, with employees making a large part of their living at the expense of the enterprise as a whole rather than as a result of its productive performance.

The incentive and management problems of the state and collective institutions responsible for production and trading were evident virtually from their inception, and became the subject of perennial efforts at reorganization, both internally and in the external systems of management and control to which they were subjected. As the communist period came to an end, it became evident that fine-tuning and tinkering with marginal aspects of these institutions might be necessary to preserve productivity in the short run. For the medium and longer run, a more radical restructuring involving clear and secure land rights and production would be necessary. In the current indeterminate situation, the management and husbanding of the resources of these large enterprises, as well as their structural and ownership transition, has become a major challenge.

Reform and Restructuring Tasks Ahead

The central task of the post-communist reform period is to permit the re-establishment of both the incentives and institutions necessary for rational economic decisionmaking decentralized to the level of the producer and the market intermediary enterprise. These include secure, transparent, and tradable property rights, and competitive marketing and trading systems for inputs, outputs, and factors of production, particularly land, shares, and other instruments of enterprise or asset ownership. Re-establishing the competitiveness of markets is a particular priority for policymakers so that credible commodity and factor prices can emerge that reflect both trade opportunity costs and a consensus of the various agents in the domestic market as to actual and anticipated scarcities and values. The emergence of such a price system, derived from open markets and trade, would send appropriate signals to producers, traders, and consumers as to the optimal mix of commodities and technology. It would also facilitate the resolution of a number of potentially contentious ownership issues.

Latvia has no recent experience with well-functioning markets and trading systems or with the price relationships that they imply. As prices move toward world market levels, producers have been facing a severe terms of trade shock (comparable to the real income shock faced by consumers), with sharp rises in the costs of the most critical imports: fuel, equipment, feed, agro-chemicals, and veterinary pharmaceuticals. Adjusting production systems to these new price relationships is, in many ways, the central challenge of the transition to a market economy.

Once the above changes are under way, or are at least governed by a consistently applied set of laws, policies, and regulations, the entrepreneurial and commercial development process will become self-generating and self-sustaining.[2]   In the presence of such growth, there are multiple opportunities for fruitful assistance and, as necessary, reorientation.

Agricultural Production and Land Use

In 1990 the aggregate value of agricultural production consisted of livestock (71 percent) and crops (29 percent) (Table 5-1).   Within the livestock subsector, dairy production was the largest component (38 percent), followed by beef (26 percent), pigs (20 percent), and poultry (6 percent).

Crops.   In 1990 Latvia produced 1.6 million tons of grain and 1.8 million tons of fodder crops, including 1 million tons of corn.   In addition, Latvia produced over 1 million tons of potatoes, 439,000 tons of sugar beets, and more than 190,000 tons of a wide range of other vegetables and fruit. More than three-quarters of the grain and half the potatoes were used as animal feed.   Despite such a large flow of produce into the livestock sector for feed, Latvia still had to import about 1 million tons of feedgrain and 200,000 tons of protein feed.

Livestock.   The livestock subsector has been by far the most prominent in agriculture, but has recently been affected by a shortage of feed.   Although there were increases in livestock on individual plots and farming enterprises, the number of animals on state and collective farms declined by as much as 23 percent from 1990 to 1991.   The largest declines were for pigs, sheep, goats, and horses and the smallest were for poultry.   As a result, total pig numbers declined by 11 percent and cattle by 4 percent.   The major factors causing these declines were shortfalls in feed and rising costs.   Other factors included disruptions associated with privatization and the loss of managers from the collective and state farms.   As a consequence of the decline in livestock numbers, meat production also declined by 6.0 percent in 1991, milk products by 7.0 percent, and eggs by 6.6 percent.   Because of delivery commitments to the former Soviet Union, exports declined by a smaller proportion, and production shortfalls were felt most strongly at home.   Latvia exported livestock products, mostly to St. Petersburg and Moscow.   Latvia traditionally had to import around 1 million tons of grain each year from the former Soviet Union, but such supplies are now becoming increasingly uncertain.

The outlook for livestock in 1992 was uncertain.   The estimated feed shortage was expected to be over 600,000 tons.[3]   Feedgrains have been subsidized for many years, with the predictable result that such feed is used inefficiently.   Therefore, removal of this subsidy would be a pre-requisite for achieving efficient feeding practices that would also lead to rational use of forage and other feed materials.

---

2.   It is important to move firmly away from administratively determined or discretionary systems of regulation and licensing, and toward transparent and predictable systems with a clear civil code and access to the courts. The latter reduce rent-seeking opportunities and provide a more secure environment for investment and growth.

3.   As of January 1992, the only contract for imported feed was for 100,000 tons of corn under the US Agency for International Development (USAID) grant aid to be sold for local currency.

Table 5-1. Agricultural Production, Selected Years

General Data	1985	1987	1989	1990	1991
Population, of which	2,604	2,647	2,681	2,686	2,680
Rural Population (thousands)	768	770	774	773	773
Meat and Livestock					
Livestock Numbers (thousand head)					
Cattle	1,485	1,481	1,472	1,439	1,383
Cows	563	552	544	535	531
Pigs	1,721	1,718	1,555	1,401	1,247
Sheep	177	165	159	165	190
Production Deadweight (tons thousands)	324	338	331	309	292
of which: Beef and Veal	127	133	129	125	125
Pig Meat	152	157	154	138	123
Eggs					
Production (millions)	880	921	890	819	765
Eggs per Hen	198	215	219	210	205
Poultry					
Flock (thousand head)	12,667	12,487	11,246	10,321	10,395
Poultry Meat Production (tons thousands)	40	43	43	40	38
Milk					
Production (tons thousands)	1,957	1,988	1,977	1,893	1,760
Yield per Cow	3,417	3,573	3,636	3,476	3,289
Animal Feed					
Field Food Crops Area (hectares thousands)	789	820	819	820	843
Maize Area (hectares thousands)	48	49	46	45	40
Production (tons thousands)	1,395	1,123	1,534	967	785
Cereals and Pulses					
All Cereals Area (hectares thousands)	727	697	680	686	657
Production (Barn Weight) (tons thousands)	1,294	1,630	1,597	1,622	1,336
Wheat (Winter and Spring)					
Area (hectares thousands)	94	102	118	141	70
Production (tons thousands)	217	296	360	370	186
Spring Barley					
Area (hectares thousands)	397	402	332	307	397
Production (tons thousands)	711	907	700	693	762
Potatoes					
Area (hectares thousands)	94	90	85	80	82
Production (tons thousands)	1,272	1,135	1,315	1,016	944
Yield (dt/ha)	135	126	155	127	115
Sugar Beet					
Area (hectares thousands)	14	14	14	15	15
Production (tons thousands)	356	352	395	439	378
Yield (dt/ha)	263	259	294	299	258
Vegetables					
Total Area (hectares thousands)	12	12	11	11	13
Total Production (tons thousands)	217	194	219	169	209
Fruit					
Production, Fruit/Berries (tons thousands)	75	32	121	23	100

Source: State Committee for Statistics; Ministry of Agriculture.

Land. Most of Latvia is flat, with about 43 percent covered with forest, and many small rivers and lakes (cumulative river length is 37,500 kilometers). It has 2.6 million hectares of agricultural land, of which nearly 1.7 million is arable. As shown in table 5-2, more than a million hectares of agriculture land have been converted into forest since 1935. This shift appears to have been state and collective farm land going out of production (perhaps due to the lack of interested and responsible parties) rather than a deliberate policy of forest expansion. In the past decade, cultivated land for grain and the area planted with field crops for animal feed declined. In 1990, about 50 percent of the arable land was used for fodder crops, 42 percent for grain, 5 percent for potatoes, and less than 2 percent for flax and sugar beet.

Table 5-2. Land Resources

Resource	1935	1990	% change
	(ha thousands)		
Agricultural Land	3,775	2,567	-32%
Fields	2,114	1,687	-20%
Pastures	751	598	-20%
Meadows	905	246	-73%
Forests	1,747	2,803	+60%
Other Land and Water	1,057	1,089	+3%
Agricultural Land per Capita (ha/capita)	1.93	0.96	-50%

Source: Ministry of Agriculture.

During the Soviet years, massive state investments resulted in a network of state and collective farms. These farms controlled the majority of agricultural land and appropriated virtually all agricultural inputs and other resources. These farms are still responsible for the overwhelming share of agricultural production despite their legendary inefficiencies. In January 1991 there were 413 collectives and 210 state farms. Many of the large collective farms are simply several small farms that were once separate collectives.

Individual household plots on these large state and collective farms have traditionally made substantial contributions to total output, especially in terms of livestock and vegetables. In 1991, the household plot sector held 87 percent of the sheep and goats, 35 percent of the dairy cows, 28 percent of the cattle, 21 percent of the pigs, and 12 percent of poultry. Although many plot-holders are now in the process of establishing their own private farms, some rural (and urban) people maintain the tradition of intensive production on these plots. The plot tradition runs deep, and in all likelihood household plots will continue to make significant contributions to family incomes, welfare, and aggregate food production.

Agricultural Productivity

Measured in terms of yields and conversion ratios, Latvian agriculture is not competitive with other Western and Central European countries, although it is relatively more productive than the average in the former Soviet Union (see Table 5-3). Labor intensity is substantially higher than in Western countries. Such differences suggest that in the short run, Latvia is likely to continue using more labor-intensive commodities and techniques than its Western partners. The sudden escalation in the prices of fuel and capital equipment in Latvia, auguring a period of extreme scarcity of these resources, is likely to accentuate this tendency.

Table 5-3. Productivity Comparison, 1989

Commodity	Finland	Latvia	USSR	Democratic Republic of Germany
Grain (quintals/ha)	29.3	23.5	19.0	44.0
Potatoes (quintals/ha)	219.0	155.0	20.0	233.6
Sugar Beet (quintals/ha)	320.3	294.0	249.0	302.3
Milk (kg/cow)	5,246.0	3,636.0	2,600.0	3,821.0
Eggs (units/hen)	N.A.	219.0	N.A.	220.0
Feed conversion (pigs)	3.2	9.8	N.A.	N.A.
Inputs				
Labor/100 hectares	7.9	11.4	N.A.	8.2
N/ha	100.0	91.5	N.A.	141.3
P/ha	30.0	71.4	N.A.	56.4
K/ha	56.0	123.8	N.A.	94.4

N.A. = not available.
Note: N = nitrogen; P = phosphorus; K = potassium.
Source: Ministry of Agriculture.

Despite its importance, the productivity of animal feed is relatively low. The feed to meat conversion ratio for pigs, for example, is about twice that of Finland. This difference is primarily due to an inadequate supply of high quality animal feed and a lack of vitamin and mineral supplements. Given that livestock accounts for almost three-quarters of agricultural production, improvement of feed availability and quality would substantially improve the sector's performance.

Farm equipment is still available in the country, much of it still under the control of state and collective farms and in need of repair. For the existing stock of machinery to become generally available, the equipment and workshop privatization process must be carried forward to set up the firms that would manage, maintain, and rent various types of equipment. The next step would be to adjust to the sharp rise in costs and rental rates.

Government Reform Programs

Early Reforms

Beginning in 1989, the Latvian government initiated a series of reforms designed to re-establish private ownership and management of the food and agricultural sector, to eliminate government subsidies, and to free both producer and consumer prices. Although the legal framework and the implementation mechanisms are still incomplete, the transition process is well under way. Since independence in September 1991, the somewhat haphazard process of disintegration and restructuring occurring in the rest of the former Soviet Union has created enormous difficulties and uncertainties with regard to prices, deliveries from, and supply relations with the East.

Land Rights and Private Farming

The initial legal innovations with regard to land rights were introduced in the Council of Ministers' resolution in 1988. By 1990, when the first legislation was enacted, land use rights had been provided free of charge to some 7,500 individuals who wished to establish their own farms. Land allocations under this law generally involved parcels that were not regarded as essential to the operations of the state or collective farms, and typically went to those with known claims on the land and the strongest desire to establish their own farms. The law was designed to allow private farming under the ownership constraints imposed by Soviet law. Soviet law permitted ownership of buildings, but rights to the land rights were usufruct, heritable but not tradable. These rights provided the basis for developing private farming operations. By denying tenure security and transferability, however, they did not permit the development of a market in land nor the ability to mortgage the land to acquire money to develop it.

Subsequent land laws in July 1990 and June 1991 provided for full private ownership by individuals to take place in two phases. The first phase provided land that claimants could use, but it did not give them full ownership rights. The second phase, effective January 1, 1993, and extending for ten to fifteen years, allows for ownership title to the land. Restitution provisions specify that previous owners who possessed land before the occupation in 1940 can receive their previously owned parcel if it is available, equivalent land in another location, or compensation. These former owners have the first priority for claiming land and receive it without payment. Excluded areas include land already containing developed farms, orchards, subsidiary (individual) plots, homes, other existing structures or land needed to maintain the productivity of livestock or other assets formerly belonging to state and collective enterprises; for environmental or historical reasons; or for universities, agricultural schools, research institutions, and experimental stations.

Second in line for land claims would be present users or new petitioners with plans for the following, in order of priority: (a) expanding existing individual farms and subsidiary plots, (b) constructing individual homes for present land users that have none, (c) expanding towns, and (d) adding land to state and collective farms. Local land commissions have been set up in each district to implement the land reform, but the process has been contentious. About 112,000 people requested land for private farms averaging 24 hectares each. Their requests would absorb 38 percent of the available land. By January 1992, a total of 17,538 private farms had been established with an average area of 18.5 hectares, including 9.0 hectares of arable land (see Tables 5-4 and 5-5).

The short-run effects of breaking up the farming system have been to disrupt farm production. Many farmers are confused and apprehensive.[4] In the longer run, however, the development of a well-informed, voluntary, and open system of land rights can be expected to serve a variety of different types of farms, provide the basis for well-functioning land and asset markets, and enormously improve the productivity with which land is allocated and farming is organized.

---

4. Surveys of collective farm members indicate that most members do not wish to strike out on their own. In view of the extreme shortages of supplies, equipment, and finance available to private farmers, these results should not be surprising, but neither should they be taken as signs of entrepreneurial (or moral) deficiency.

Table 5-4. Private Farm Development, 1989 and 1991

Unit	1989	1991
No. of Private Farms	3,931.0	17,538.0
Total Area (ha thousand)	65.6	186.2
of which:		
Agriculture Land	48.7	132.2
Usable Land	36.1	96.7
Total Sown Area (ha thousand)	12.8	89.3
of which: Cereals	5.0	38.3
Cattle (thousand head)	15.1	62.5
of which: Cows	5.9	25.7
Pigs (thousand head)	7.0	43.0
Sheep (thousand head)	6.4	28.0
Production (thousand mt)		
- Cereals	10.8	89.7
- Potatoes	14.4	77.8
- Milk	9.5	73.5
- Meat (live weight)	2.2	13.9

Table 5-5. Farm Sizes as of January 1, 1992

Area (hectares)	No. of Farms	Percentage of Total
TOTAL	17,538	100.0
< 10.0	3,422	19.5
10.0 - 19.9	7,003	39.9
20.0 - 29.9	4,300	24.5
30.0 - 39.9	1,643	9.4
40.0 - 49.9	680	3.9
50.0 or more	490	2.8

Source: Ministry of Agriculture.

Price Liberalization

Latvia began price reform measures in agriculture in March 1991 with substantial increases in prices: retail food prices rose 100 to 300 percent and were accompanied by income subsidies and wage increases. Initially retail prices were increased more than producer prices in order to reduce government subsidy costs. However, producer prices caught up and increased faster than retail prices during the rest of the year, responding to rapidly increasing costs of inputs and pressure from producers. As a result, the subsidy costs to the government rose again.

On December 10, 1991, a law was passed to deregulate food and agricultural prices. The government continued minimum support prices for agricultural products, but these were well below market prices. As of early 1992, producers and processors negotiated the producer prices in each region on a weekly basis. Producers were free to sell products wherever they wished, but they usually had limited options. The December 10 law limited processors' profit markup to 15 percent of total production costs. Similarly, the combined markup of the wholesale and retail distributors was limited to 15 percent for meat products, 20 percent for dairy products, and 25 percent for bread. Export licensing was established to control the outflow of essential food products. Thus, despite all the price liberalization measures, the market was still not fully functioning or competitive.

The impact of the December 1991 price liberalization on farm and food prices can been seen in Table 5-6. Producer prices increased substantially from December 1, 1991, to the end of 1992. Retail market prices have also increased proportionally. These price changes have led to a marked increase in the share of total expenditure going for food, and a shift away from higher priced commodities (livestock, fruit, and vegetables) and toward lower cost and more income inelastic components of the consumption basket. A consequence of these price changes has been a significant reduction in the ratio of private market prices to prices in state shops.

Table 5-6. Producer Prices, Selected Dates
(RUR per million tons)

Product	Before Dec. 10, 1991	March 8-15, 1992	July 1, 1992	December 31, 1992
Milk	1,050			14,600
Low		6,500	7,000	12,500
High		8,000	7,800	13,300
Cattle (top quality)	7,300		26,000	31,600
Low		20,000	19,400	22,900
High		27,000	23,100	27,300
Pigs (1st quality)	7,700			
Low		35,000	38,600	32,500
High		40,000	49,500	107,200
Broilers	5,500		22,300	51,600
Low		20,000	NA	NA
High		22,000	NA	NA

NA = not available.
Source: Latvian authorities.

Short- and Long-Term Prospects

During the transition period, output declines will be significant, especially in the state and collective farms sector. The share of the private farm sector will increase, but farm finance and other problems are likely to slow the initial expansion. The most serious potential constraint for short-term cropping is uncertainty about the availability and price of fuel, fertilizers, veterinary pharmaceuticals, spare parts and equipment, and other production inputs formerly obtained from the former Soviet Union.

In the longer term there are two directions in which the sector can be expected to develop and grow. The first is increasing agri-business activities in response to the various domestic and foreign market opportunities that arise. Much of the entrepreneurial drive for such growth can already be seen as new farmers seek to enhance their income by getting into a variety of processing and marketing activities that generate income and add value to what they produce. These initiatives can be expected to coalesce into a dynamic and competitive system of businesses, many of them initially quite small, that vigorously seek out additional employment and profit opportunities. Entering the world market with exports and competing with more sophisticated imports in traditional domestic and regional markets is going to involve a great deal more emphasis on the quality and specific market orientation of particular products. In recent decades, the growth and sophistication of the domestic agri-business sector was suppressed by the monopolistic and bureaucratic nature of the state's activities, including an implicit de-emphasis on product quality. Especially in export markets, and as incomes increase in domestic markets, this pattern is likely to change. The critical policy approach in support of this change is ensuring an open and competitive structure, with unrestricted entry and exit, in every phase of the marketing chain (processing, storage, wholesale, transport, and retail). Income opportunities would then attract new entrants, new finance, new technologies, new products, and new packaging and marketing approaches.[5]

The second direction is increasing efficiency. In a competitive context there is a strong tendency to phase out institutions that result in less efficient or less sustainable asset management, this essential exit option was not available under the Soviet system. With decentralization of decisionmaking at the level of both farm production and market intermediary enterprises, including ownership and management arrangements that transmit appropriate incentives, economic pressures would drive these agencies to engage in the economizing and cost-saving measures that constitute efficiency. The Soviet-style structure resulted in a range of microeconomic decisions that led to inefficient use of labor, equipment, fuel, feed, fertilizer, and other inputs and resources. The aggregate effects of a pricing and exchange rate regime that did not respond to the market and of production and trading institutions that did not respond to economic signals was a sector whose overall growth was dragged down by inefficiency.

A further set of institutions that can be expected to exert concerted pressure for greater efficiency is the development of a network of markets for the various resources and factors used in agriculture, including land, equipment, livestock, technological expertise, and labor. These markets depend on a predictable and widely understood system of contract enforcement and secure and tradable property rights that facilitate the various transactions. They generate a transparent system of prices for these resources that create strong incentives to put them to their best use, and manage and husband them appropriately. With greater efficiency in the use of the sector's considerable resources, and a burgeoning of new enterprises and product lines, the sector can be expected to play a dynamic part in the country's recovery, and make a significant contribution toward growth.

Recommendations

Prices and Markets. Efforts toward price liberalization should continue and price subsidies to the sector should be phased out as soon as possible.

Farm Equipment and Other Inputs. In the case of farm equipment, the top priority is repair and maintenance of existing equipment. Small, local firms are needed for servicing, maintaining, and renting the available equipment and for deciding whether to salvage and repair items or to replace them. Price and institutional adjustments are needed before allocation improvements can be expected. In the short run, it is hard to predict whether output prices will be adequate to generate significant demand for tractors and fuel at the adjusted prices. The policy response to the costs of inputs, however, must ensure that output markets are competitive and prices are not artificially suppressed. The alternative would be a squeeze on farm incomes and profits, severely undermining farm investment and productive activity.

Agricultural Inputs. Questions of demand and efficient use also apply to livestock feed, fertilizer, and other farm assets and inputs. Allowing the prices for each of these to reach their market

---

5.   A comparable range of activities can also be expected on the "backward linkage" side of agriculture, with more sophisticated services and input supplies in the area of biological and mechanical technology, repair, construction, finance, accounting, management, and other contracting services as farming itself becomes more sophisticated. In some countries employment and incomes in this sector rival those of production agriculture.

levels would reduce their wasteful use and encourage the substitution of more efficient and low-cost technologies. Examples include the more economical and nutritionally balanced use of livestock feed and grazing and more careful use of fertilizer, especially its timing and placement, and the complementary use of manure and other organic matter.

The immediate problem facing the sector is maintaining trade relations with Russia, the major source of energy, equipment, and agrochemicals and the principal market for meat, fish, poultry, and dairy products produced in Latvia. If this trade is restored at world market prices, the sector is likely to suffer a significant terms of trade loss (import prices increasing more than export prices). Trade relations with other republics of the former Soviet Union have not deteriorated to the same extent, but are still insecure. Western markets for Latvia's main agricultural exports have a variety of import barriers, export subsidies, and quality standards that inhibit access and reduce prices. While every effort should be made to expand exports and capture specialty markets in convertible currency areas, restoring market links with the former Soviet Union appears to be the major challenge.

Land and Asset Ownership. The resolution of ownership and compensation questions relating to land and other farm assets is of high priority. Maintaining production in the short run and promoting long-run investment would be very hard in circumstances of unresolved or conflicting ownership claims. Full ownership rights should be granted as soon as possible, including the elimination of any restrictions on transactions relating to land, shares, or any other assets by new owners. The security and transferability of land rights requires the development of a well-functioning registration and information system as the basis for a well-informed and open land and asset market. Such a market would facilitate a range of functional transactions and contracts, for example, mortgaging, selling, renting, sharecropping, consolidating, and subdividing. It is critically important that such transactions are facilitated rather than inhibited by the legal, policy, and procedural environment. In particular, any approach that requires administrative discretion or permission must be carefully avoided as such approaches are susceptible to rent seeking, favoritism, and corruption.

Establishing a policy and regulatory environment that is neutral with respect to organizational arrangement or size of holding would encourage the development of a commercially viable and competitive private farming structure. It would also reduce future pressures for government protection or budgetary support from inefficient or high-cost farms. Small plots have served the country well, and may well continue to do so, both for intensive and part-time operations. Other operators may have the management, financial, and technical capacity for much larger operations, employing a significant work force, and consolidating holdings with a variety of purchase, rental, sharecropping or contract arrangements. Facilitating these adjustments without discriminatory measures aimed at protecting or subsidizing particular firms or farm sizes, and allowing both the entry and exit of individual enterprises depending on their commercial performance, can help mold a structure that is both efficient and truly voluntary. Limits on the size of holdings, constraints on potentially functional transactions, or arbitrarily targeted subsidies are likely to bias the new structure of farming toward less efficient farm units and are also likely to politicize the process.

Restructuring and Privatization. Latvia is in the process of establishing and implementing mechanisms for restructuring and privatizing state and collective farms and their assets. Continuing uncertainties about the future status of these assets is continuing to erode productivity. These farms still provide a large share of marketed supplies of agricultural products, and husbanding their resources is critical for both the short and the longer run. Delays in the process also slow the resolution of ownership claims by private farmers and the overall development of private farming. The privatization process should encourage either individuals or farms to take ownership of the assets and should be neutral with respect to farm size. In the current situation of capital scarcity, it is important that existing production assets, including workshops, means of transport, and farm equipment, be available for full commercial use through new ownership, rental, or contractual arrangements. It is also important that joint stock companies, partnerships, and the like continue to have full flexibility to adjust both the scale of their operations, their land holdings, and their internal ownership and organizational structure in response to their emerging experience and to changing economic conditions and incentives. Clear and tradable ownership rights for land, shares, and other assets would facilitate this process.[6]

The Agricultural Processing and Marketing System. The concentration of Latvia's processing and distribution system and the wide margin between farmgate and consumer prices are major sources of concern to producers and consumers. The government has responded by putting limits on processor profits and retailer margins, and even by placing specific ceilings on prices. In general, such price limitations narrow the scope for competition and product differentiation.

While regulating processing and marketing margins may be needed in the face of large monopolies, a more effective way to enhance market power would be to facilitate free entry, expansion, and exit of individuals or firms. Such openness to new entrants would ensure a more competitive market structure. Price or margin controls are likely to impede this development, generating dual or parallel pricing systems with mixed signals. Privatizing individual retail shops, as well as wholesale, storage, and transport enterprises, would generate increased competition, driving down marketing margins and promoting greater efficiency at each level of the marketing chain. Anti-collusion legislation may also help. Providing options to producers and other agents so that they can choose among alternative processing and marketing channels would help limit the price setting power of large processing plants and of the state and cooperative retail systems.

Export Licenses. The government should reconsider its licensing system for agricultural exports. This system imposes high implicit taxes on producers; reduces the incentive to earn foreign exchange; and impedes the ability of enterprises to develop new markets, obtain necessary resources, and develop healthy commercial relationships in the critical export markets. The system does not bring any revenue, yet generates significant gains for the license holder. For this reason, discretionary licensing creates a climate of insecurity for potential exporters. It also inevitably creates strong pressures for rent seeking, corruption, and other non-productive ways of earning income.

Support Services. Private farming requires a network of commercial, technical, and financial services oriented toward farmers. Such a network includes input supply, construction, and machinery rental and repair services as well as a range of alternative marketing channels, including private processing, wholesale, and retail enterprises and a series of advisory services, market information systems, and competing financial intermediaries. State agencies provided these services under the old system. For private farmers this network hardly exists as yet. An important first step would be privatizing existing services, which would then have clear business incentives to provide good service. The efficiency of this network would improve with competition as economic opportunities and incentives attract new entrants.

---

6.   Experience in other reforming economies suggests that the ability of the individual to withdraw from a producer association or some other corporate arrangement provides extremely useful pressures on such associations to perform in a useful fashion. Conversely, locking individual producers into such associations can be a prescription for poor performance.

A clear distinction must be made between viable rural credit operations -- which require commercial evaluation of the ability to repay, specific repayment schedules, and sound financial practices -- and subsidized lending to selected farmers with no requirement to maintain the commercial viability of the lending agency. Financial support to farmers, whether in the form of subsidized credit or other grants, is in short supply, and sustaining such a system would hinder the development of sound rural credit agencies. Pending banking reforms and the development of independent financial institutions, short-term finance can be provided through commercially self-sustaining credit unions. Long-term credit, meanwhile, would most likely be provided through the banking system, but this would require clear land rights, mortgage and bankruptcy laws, extensive banking reform, and a more stable currency.

Institutional Development. The prime task of government is to provide a secure, transparent policy and regulatory environment that supports efficient production activities. Many of the institutions that facilitate these activities need to be updated to become more responsive to a market economy. The research focus needs to be modified based on the changing needs of the private farming system. Restrictions on importation of equipment, seeds, and agrochemistry would inhibit the process of technological change in agriculture. Much of this process typically arises from direct access by farmers and other agents to new technologies and supplies in other countries. More emphasis in the research and training system is needed on economic management, marketing, financial strategies, and decisionmaking. Extension or farmer advisory services need to be developed to link research efforts with the problems of farmers.

New data collection and dissemination systems need to be developed. The old reporting system, which is no longer very effective even for the remaining state and collective farms, is breaking down as central planning gives way to a decentralized, private farming structure. New statistical methods and approaches need to be developed for sectoral data, and the Ministry of Agriculture needs to create a comprehensive system for collection, analysis, and dissemination to serve the needs of government, farmers, agri-business firms, traders, and the public.

Finally, Latvia should diversify its sources of input supplies and markets for food and agricultural products. Even if trade relations with the former Soviet Union are restored, Latvia and the other Baltic countries may have the same status as former CMEA countries in Central and East Europe. Under these circumstances, Latvia should be competitive in selling food to the former Soviet Union, but would be relatively disadvantaged by the export subsidies and soft credit sales that the West provides to the former Soviet Union. If the Uruguay Round of GATT negotiations is successful in reducing Western market protection and subsidized sales, Latvia would be a major beneficiary. In the meantime, segments of the agri-business industry that now have or can develop product and input market links in convertible currency areas should be encouraged. Better foreign investment laws would help firms with export potential improve their access to foreign capital and technology, potentially improving their efficiency, product quality, and access to convertible currency markets.

CHAPTER 6

Industry

Before World War II, the industrial sector contributed relatively little to Latvia's economy: in 1930, for example, only 13.5 percent of the labor force worked in industry. Major industrial subsectors at that time included food processing, light industries, woodworking, and building materials. In the 1950s Latvia began to industrialize, and eventually became the most industrialized Baltic state. By 1990 the industrial sector accounted for nearly half of the GDP and a little less than one-third of employment.

Structure and Performance

Characteristics

The central Soviet authorities emphasized industrial development in the following areas: machine building and the electronics, chemicals, and electric power industries. Changes in the structure of the Latvian industrial sector are shown in Table 6-1.

Table 6-1. Share of Industrial Output and Employment by Subsector, Selected Years
(percent)

Subsector	Share of Industrial Output					Share of Employment
	1970	1975	1980	1985	1990	1990
Electric Power	1.4	1.2	1.6	1.8	2.1	1.8
Engineering (including machine building and electronics)	21.3	21.8	25.5	25.9	26.3	38.9
Chemicals	5.9	6.2	6.6	7.2	7.2	5.7
Wood and Paper	7.7	5.8	5.1	6.0	5.6	9.6
Building Materials	3.5	3.8	3.0	3.2	3.2	4.6
Light Industries	25.2	25.1	22.6	20.1	18.0	17.0
Food Industries	27.6	27.7	25.8	25.8	24.9	12.7
Other (including research and technical colleges)	7.4	8.4	9.8	10.0	12.7	9.7
Total	100.0	100.0	100.0	100.0	100.0	100.0

Note: The figures shown are probably underestimated due to underreported production for military use.
Source: State Committee for Statistics.

The share of the engineering subsector, which was insignificant in the early 1950s, had increased to 21.3 percent of industrial output by 1970. By 1985, engineering had become the largest industrial subsector, and by 1990 it contributed 26.3 percent to industrial output and almost 39 percent of industrial employment. The share of communication equipment and electronics increased from less than 6 percent of industrial output in the 1970s to more than 9 percent by the end of the 1980s.

Altogether in 1990, the non-traditional industries of engineering and chemicals contributed more than 33 percent to industrial output and more than 44 percent to industrial employment.

During the 1970s, the industrial sector grew by an annual average rate of 5 to 6 percent (in constant prices). In the 1980s, the growth rate decelerated to about 3 to 4 percent per year. Taking account of the increase in the industrial labor force, which was moderate, as well as the rapid increase in capital stock per worker, the net increase in productivity in the 1980s appears to have been low, indicating low efficiency in the use of capital and human resources. Table 6-2 shows the number of enterprises in each subsector, total employment, and the average number of employees per enterprise.

Table 6-2. Enterprises and Employment in the Industrial Sector, 1990

Industrial Subsector	Number of Enterprises	Number of Employees	Average Employees per Enterprise
Metallurgy	4	3,284	821
Engineering, of which	82	79,772	973
Electronics	5	39,044	7,809
Chemicals	15	19,192	1,279
Forest Industries	55	24,478	445
Building Materials	30	13,248	442
Light Industries	74	63,563	859
Food Industries	89	37,071	417
Other	55	30,766	580
Total	407	310,418	763

Source: Latvian authorities.

The major characteristics of Latvian industrial enterprises are as follows:

- *Large average size*. The largest enterprises are concentrated in the communications, electronics, chemical, and machine building subsectors. However, even in light industries, Latvian enterprises employ many more people than firms in West European countries. The relatively large size of Latvian enterprises is due to several features common to Soviet-type enterprises: (a) large-scale production of components and final products designed to supply the former Soviet Union as a whole, particularly in the communication equipment and electronics and engineering subsectors; (b) vertical integration, with in-house design, construction, transport, and other services to reduce dependence on unreliable suppliers and services; (c) horizontal integration, with plants in the same subsector grouped into a single enterprise, not only in machine building, but also in food and light industries (the objective of this policy was to create monopolies as well as to facilitate central planning and control); and (d) prohibition of private ownership, resulting in a lack of small enterprises.

- *Predominance of central Soviet ownership and control*. About ninety of the industrial enterprises in Latvia were All-Union, owned and controlled by the Soviet Union. These enterprises, generally in engineering and chemicals, operated almost as subcontractors within the Soviet industrial system. These enterprises were provided with equipment and inputs of raw materials or components and were required to supply specific quantities of output to the Soviet Union. All major decisions were taken by the central authorities in Moscow. Another sixty-five enterprises (about 16 percent of all enterprises) were Union-Republican, under joint ownership of the Soviet Union and Latvian ministries. In practice these enterprises were also largely controlled by Moscow. Prior to independence, only 46 percent of the enterprises in Latvia were controlled by the Latvian authorities.

- *Monopolistic or oligopolistic position.* As shown in Table 6-3, several machine building and electronics enterprises in Latvia were the major supplier, sometimes the sole supplier, of certain products and components to the former Soviet Union. In addition, several enterprises in food and light industries had a monopolistic or oligopolistic position in the Latvian market.

- *A high degree of integration with Soviet industry.* The high degree of integration was true for both inputs and outputs. Lacking any mineral resources and having limited indigenous energy resources, Latvia needs to import all its metal needs and almost all its energy needs from other parts of the former Soviet Union. All bulldozers, tractors, and excavators, as well as 95 percent of the cardboard, 77 percent of the mineral fertilizers, more than 60 percent of the paper, more than 40 percent of the cement and most of the cotton and wool used in Latvia were imported. Almost all the output of several major machine building and electronic enterprises were destined for former Soviet republics. [1]

- *High share of military products.* A large share of the output from electronics industries and shipyards consisted of products and components for military use. Although data on the military share are not published, according to an authoritative estimate, more than 15 percent of

Table 6-3. Importance of Latvian Products in Former Soviet Markets

Products with 100 percent of former Soviet markets

1. Passenger minibuses
2. Milking equipment
3. Chain belts for bicycles, motorcycles and agricultural combines
4. Spare parts for metal cutting machines
5. Electrical equipment for electric trains
6. Automatic telephone switchboards, electronic or quasi-electronic
7. Zinc white pigment
8. First-aid minibuses

Products with more than 50 percent of former Soviet markets

1. Telephone sets
2. Industrial belts
3. Signal anemometers for railways

Source: Ministry of Industry and Energy.

---

1.   Of total output in 1990, the share of exports to the former republics was as follows: telephone exchanges, 98 percent; motorcycles, 93 percent; minibuses, 92 percent; washing machines, 89 percent; railroad cars, 88 percent; radio sets, 79 percent; telephone sets, 77 percent; and diesel generators, 71 percent.

the labor force in Latvia in 1985 was employed in military production, higher than in Lithuania and three times higher than in Estonia.

Disintegration of the Old System and Foundation of a New System

Since mid-1990, the Latvian industrial sector has undergone drastic changes, due in part to the disintegration of the Soviet economic system and in part to measures taken by the Latvian government. The major changes were the following:

- *Reduced supplies of essential inputs.* Supplies of energy and raw materials to Latvia have been sharply curtailed due to the disintegration of the Soviet economic system. The government of Latvia attempted to secure vital supplies through difficult negotiations with Russia and other former republics, but on the whole, the inputs delivered in 1991 fell short of levels agreed upon in negotiations. Despite efforts to hoard inputs, by early 1992 several engineering and electronics enterprises had raw materials for no more than two weeks. Shortages of energy and basic chemicals forced a sharp reduction of production in chemical enterprises.

- *Curtailment of demand.* Demand for Latvian-made civilian equipment and components has been curtailed due to the decline in investments in the former republics. In addition, the demand for some consumer appliances made in Latvia has been reduced due to competition from East Asian and Western products.

- *Takeover of All-Union and Union-republican enterprises.* In August 1991, the Latvian government took over the All-Union and Union-republican enterprises. About half of the Russian managers of large enterprises were not reappointed. All enterprises were required to pay taxes only to the Latvian government.

- *Change of industrial oversight structure.* The Latvian Ministry of Planning and ministries for the industrial subsectors were abolished, and a Ministry of Industry and Energy was established with a mandate to coordinate the industrial and energy sectors. In addition to its departments of Economics, Coordination, and Information, the new ministry, with a staff of 120, has five subsectoral divisions. The ministry does not exercise direct control over enterprises, but focuses on formulating industrial policy and preparing restructuring programs.

- *Price liberalization.* Since January 1992, the prices of most industrial products have been liberalized. Trading organizations were permitted to charge a maximum margin of 25 percent of ex-factory prices. Price margins were eliminated in June 1992.

De-monopolization. Parliament passed an antitrust law in December 1991 and a department to deal with de-monopolization was created in the MER. The Ministry of Industry and Energy has begun to work on splitting up large enterprises to facilitate their eventual privatization and introduce competition, but progress has been slow.

Phasing out budgetary subsidies and investment financing. The government has phased out the provision of budgetary subsidies to industrial enterprises, as well as the financing of investments in industrial enterprises. In sharp contrast with the previous system, the present government policy is that industrial enterprises should finance investments out of retained profits. Under inter-republican trade agreements, enterprises producing goods or components needed for vital inputs were required to fulfill state orders. State orders were eliminated in 1992. Although the government does not provide direct budgetary subsidies to industrial enterprises, it has granted exemptions from profit taxes.

- *Recent performance.* The output of state-owned industrial enterprises declined by 5 percent in 1991. However, privately-owned enterprises and joint ventures increased their output by 34 percent in 1991. Thus, total industrial output declined by less than 1 percent in 1991. The relatively modest decline in the output of state enterprises was due to several measures. A number of machine building enterprises turned to subcontracting for Western firms. Many enterprises made direct deals with firms in the former Soviet Union, selling their products in some cases for foreign exchange, but mostly based on barter deals. In those deals they not only supplied their own products, but also sweetened the transactions by giving the FSU workers food or consumer appliances, which they bought for rubles from other Latvian enterprises. Most enterprises did not lay off workers even though the law allowed them to do so. Nevertheless, the labor force in state enterprises was reduced somewhat by early retirements and by voluntary resignations of workers who preferred to join new private firms. The situation deteriorated substantially in 1992, with industrial output dropping by 34 percent in the third quarter compared to a year before. In 1991, most industrial enterprises registered profits due mainly to the favorable terms of trade situation. According to preliminary figures, only one industrial enterprise had a loss in 1991 (RUR 3.3 million). There is strong evidence that enterprises used their monopolistic position to raise output prices more than was warranted by increases in costs. Some enterprises even hoarded their output in anticipation of further price increases following a probable currency reform. The situation changed in 1992 as the terms of trade deteriorated and most enterprises showed losses and accumulated arrears. Inter-enterprise arrears rose rapidly, not only within Latvia, but also with enterprises in other FSU republics. Financial flows to enterprises were also limited by the continued problems with payments system in the republics of the former Soviet Union.

- *Short-term outlook.* Many engineering and electronics enterprises, as well as enterprises in light industries, for example, textiles, are left with few raw materials. It is unlikely that conditions in the former Soviet Union will improve in the short-term or that supplies of inputs to Latvian enterprises will increase. Projections indicated a decline of about 40 percent in total industrial output in 1992. Some enterprises, facing a decline in demand for military products or severe shortages of inputs, might even have been forced to reduce their output by 50 percent or more in 1992. Some Latvian enterprises are the sole suppliers of products or components for the former Soviet Union. Indeed, some of these enterprises appear to have a strong bargaining position, given that their products are vital inputs and cannot be supplied from other sources for technical reasons. Such enterprises might be able to secure both orders and supplies of inputs. However, several of the Latvian monopolistic products consist of equipment or components that are not vital for the former Soviet republics in the short-term. In brief, the short-term prospects for Latvian industrial enterprises, particularly those dependent on the former republics, are bleak. Such enterprises are facing sharp declines in production, and even bankruptcy.

Constraints on Competitive Performance

Latvian officials and enterprise managers recognize the need to start formulating and implementing a comprehensive strategy for gradual integration into the international economy. However, there are major constraints on competitiveness in international markets that need to be removed.

To begin with, many of the Latvian enterprises in engineering, chemicals, and electronics are heavy users of scarce resources, such as energy and raw materials, that were supplied at a fraction of world prices. These enterprises had produced goods and components needed by the Soviet economy, but because of their low quality, these goods could not be sold in international markets. Only about 6.6 percent of Latvia's industrial output was sold in Western markets in 1991, generally at low prices. On the basis of international prices for inputs and output, it is doubtful that many Latvian enterprises generate any value added. Such conditions characterize not only machine building and chemical enterprises, but also some textile enterprises. For example, cotton and wool have been imported at very low prices from Asian republics for processing into low quality fabrics and garments that could be sold only in the protected markets of Latvia and of the former Soviet republics.

Some of the Latvian machine building and electronics enterprises are extremely vulnerable to changes in the economies of the former Soviet republics. Several enterprises have specialized in producing components tailor-made for the needs of enterprises in the former Soviet republics. Facing sharp declines in the demand for military products and investment goods, they need to change their product mix drastically and upgrade the quality to Western standards.

Latvian enterprises have not been exposed to competition and have generally operated on a cost-plus basis. Enterprises in light industry, food processing, and woodwork have been grouped together, which has prevented any competition in the domestic market. Implementation of a de-monopolization program, a process that has begun, and eventual import liberalization are needed to expose Latvian enterprises to effective competition.

With a few exceptions, most equipment used in Latvian enterprises is of low quality. According to an official estimate, 85 to 90 percent of the equipment used in Latvian enterprises does not meet modern technological standards.[2]

Extreme distortions in prices are another major constraint on competitive performance. For example, the current price of fuel is still only a fraction of the world market price. Moreover, there are extreme uncertainties with respect to the structure of costs and prices after the currency reform.[3] Implementation of macroeconomic reform should provide enterprise managers with proper signals on the structure of costs and prices and eliminate some uncertainty about future trends.

Enterprise managers generally appear to have technical competence, but have little, if any, experience in overall management. Under the previous system, enterprise managers had no direct contact

---

2.   Department of Foreign Economic Relations (1991).

3.   The exchange rate differences between Latvia and other republics of the former Soviet Union has led to substantial losses for enterprises.

with suppliers of either equipment or raw materials, nor with their major clients. They lack training and experience in marketing, procurement, finance, and other aspects of business management. Another problem is the dependence of enterprise managers on workers' councils. Although the supervising ministry appoints the managers, these appointments still require the consent of the workers' councils.[4] The contracts recently drawn up between the government and enterprise managers have established salary ranges that are too low to induce the performance needed to turn the enterprises around. Moreover, managers are not paid bonuses for outstanding performance.

State-owned companies do not have supervisory boards of directors, and it is up to the supervising ministries to exercise state ownership rights over management.[5] Considering that managers lack business experience and are subject to potential pressure from the workers, the absence of an external board of directors represents a serious weakness in the corporate governance system of state enterprises.

Finally, as in the other Baltic countries, the telecommunications and transport systems in Latvia are inadequate to facilitate the integration of the industrial sector into international markets. The banking system is also incapable of providing the necessary financial services.

Potential for Strengthening Competitiveness

On the positive side, Latvia has a potential for strengthening the competitiveness of its industrial sector, based on its skilled labor force, potential for research and development (R & D), low labor costs, and basic industrial strategy.

The Latvian labor force is recognized to have higher skills than the labor forces in the other former republics. Moreover, there are some indications that the average skill level of Latvian workers is higher than that of workers in the other Baltic countries. As stated above, the share of workers employed in production for military use was higher in Latvia than in the other Baltic countries. It is well known that the technical standards of products for military use in the former Soviet Union were much higher than the standards for civilian products. Since military goods were produced in enterprises that also produced civilian products, it is likely that workers in such enterprises have skills that can be carried over to other industrial enterprises.

Latvian R & D institutes appear to have potential for designing quality products. One example is the R & D institute of the VEF in Riga, the largest Latvian company specializing in producing telecommunications equipment. This institute, which employs 1,500 workers, had been the leading institute of its type in the former Soviet Union. It designed high precision measuring instruments used in the Calgary Olympic Games. Several other academic and industrial institutes appear to have impressive R & D potential.

---

4.   Moreover, workers' councils appear to have the right to petition the ministry for removal of the manager if the latter cannot secure raw materials.

5.   The government began corporatization of state-owned enterprises in November 1992.

As for the low costs of labor, in early 1992, the monthly wage for an average industrial worker was RUR 1,000, and for a highly skilled worker RUR 1,700, a low wage by international standards.

Latvia's basic industrial strategy should be to shift production toward skill-intensive goods. Production based on intensive use of energy and imported raw materials should be scaled down and, in extreme cases, may have to be completely phased out. In order to increase exports to international markets, Latvian enterprises must produce high quality goods that can be sold in these markets. The basic criterion for decisions on restructuring existing enterprises and investing in new ones must be their capability to create value added on the basis of international prices of inputs and outputs.

This basic strategy has important implications for future links with the former republics' markets. Although links with the former republics should be maintained both as sources of supplies for inputs and as markets for outputs, the importance of such links is bound to diminish in the medium-term as the republics begin trading on the basis of international prices for raw materials and products. Under these circumstances, Latvian enterprises would not necessarily have an advantage in purchasing inputs from the former republics. Instead they should purchase inputs from the best available source in terms of a quality/price ratio. Similarly, Latvian products will face competition from products made in Western and Asian countries. The implication for Latvian industries is that they need to produce high quality goods competitively and not distinguish between Western and former republics' markets.

Upgrading the quality of industrial production and integrating into international markets requires close cooperation with Western companies, which should provide technological skills, marketing expertise, management support, and as much financial investment as seems feasible.

The government's industrial policy is to move production away from energy-intensive goods and toward higher value added goods for export. In the chemical subsector, for instance, priority is given to developing pharmaceuticals and biotechnology. In the woodworking industry, the government wishes to promote furniture production, primarily for export. These priorities are fully consistent with the need to shift to skill-based and higher value added production for exports to international markets. However, the government has promoted investments based on the criterion of available domestic raw materials. Yet the mere availability of domestic raw materials is neither a sufficient nor a necessary condition for justifying investments in industrial processing. Investments in industrial processing must be justified by prospects of making competitive products, either for external markets or for an unprotected domestic market.

The government also wishes to develop production of machinery for agriculture and food processing, mainly for use in the domestic market, but it is doubtful that machinery production would be profitable without heavy subsidies, either directly, or indirectly by high protection.

Recommendations

Implementing a strategy to integrate the Latvian industrial sector into international markets will be a gradual and lengthy process. Short-term measures are needed to enable the industrial enterprises to survive during this difficult period. These survival measures should be consistent with making further progress in the transition to a market economy.

The government should take the following measures to help enterprises survive and prepare for comprehensive restructuring:

- Implement a macroeconomic stabilization and reform program that would give the right signals to enterprises on prices, exchange rates, and interest rates.

- Design and implement a privatization program for SOEs.

- Require all large enterprises to convert to holding companies, with semi-autonomous divisions registered as subsidiary joint stock companies. Such decentralization would facilitate privatization by selling off the joint stock companies.

- Refrain from bailing out enterprises that become unprofitable unless they have strong prospects for successful restructuring. Enterprises that are not viable should be liquidated and their assets sold off.

- Increase the financial incentives for enterprise managers, including bonuses for meeting targets.

- Appoint supervisory boards of directors in state-owned joint stock companies and arrange for a proper selection process and for training prospective directors.

- Arrange for funding the preparation of restructuring programs for enterprises by consultants, the training of enterprise managers and directors, and the establishment of domestic consulting services.

Enterprises should not rely on government financial assistance for survival. Instead they should take the following measures:

- Intensify efforts to restore commercial contacts with enterprises in the FSU. In the short-term, such deals might provide Latvian enterprises with raw materials in exchange for their products.

- Seek subcontracting agreements and other arrangements with Western firms that could use their capital and human resources.

- Lay off excess workers. Despite a concern for the welfare of their workers, enterprises cannot afford their current number of employees if the projected declines in output in 1992 were realized.

- Seek to improve cash flow by selling hoarded output, renting out space, and reducing non-essential expenditures, including those for workers' welfare.

- Prepare comprehensive restructuring programs with the assistance of experienced consultants.

- Convert to holding companies with subsidiary joint stock companies (for large concerns). The necessary preparatory work of splitting up assets and liabilities should be undertaken as soon as possible.

Although enterprises should initiate the preparation of restructuring programs while still state owned, implementing these programs, particularly when investments in modern equipment are needed, will require private ownership. Implementing a comprehensive program for privatizing SOEs is the major role of the government and is a pre-requisite for integrating Latvian industry into international markets. This program falls under medium-term measures.

Export growth should be promoted by a proper exchange rate policy. Exposing industrial enterprises to competition requires import liberalization and enforcing an anti-monopoly policy. Positive real interest rates should prevent the wastage of scarce capital resources.

The government should facilitate the creation of an institutional framework that can provide modern banking and financial services to industrial enterprises. It should also initiate reorganization of scientific and technological institutes to assist enterprises with upgrading design and quality of production. The government should not attempt to prepare restructuring programs for industrial enterprises. Preparing such programs should be left to the enterprises themselves, with the assistance of advisory services.

The government should actively promote the growth of small and medium-sized enterprises. For their part, enterprises should help accelerate the growth of privately owned small and medium-sized enterprises by selling off or leasing plant and equipment to their workers. A network of industrial small and medium-sized enterprises would help create a more balanced and less centralized industrial structure, which has proved to be extremely efficient in market economies.

CHAPTER 7

Energy

Latvia is strategically located at the crossroads of East-West energy trade. Large volumes of crude oil and refined products travel through Latvia by pipeline and rail and are exported from the port of Ventspils. Coal from Russia is also exported from Latvian ports. Large volumes of natural gas from Russia are pumped into underground storage in Latvia during the summer for use in the winter and some re-exports to neighboring Baltic countries.

These trade and traffic patterns will probably undergo major changes as the region makes the transition to world energy prices. Latvia is already changing its port facilities to accommodate more imports. In the future, Latvia may import coal from the world market, particularly if coal proves to be the least-cost way to reduce Latvia's dependence on imported electricity. Latvia's gradual liberalization of its domestic energy market will ease the adjustment to higher energy prices and create suitable conditions for private investors to participate in Latvia's energy supply and energy transit industries.

Structure and Recent Performance

Statistical data on energy consumption are very limited. The energy balance (Table 7-1) was compiled from official statistics, information from Latvian experts, data from All-Union institutions and World Bank staff estimates. However, it is preliminary and subject to change when more information becomes available.

Domestic consumption of energy grew quickly in the 1970s and early 1980s, but stabilized between 1985 and 1990 at approximately 9 million tons of oil equivalent (toe). Energy consumption per capita in 1990 was 3,668 kilograms of oil equivalent (koe), which is average by European standards, but high in relation to GDP. Twenty-one countries were chosen with climatic conditions similar to Latvia's (see Table 7-2), and using data from the World Bank's 1992 *World Development Report*, a cross-country analysis of the relationship between energy consumption and GDP was carried out. The results indicate that in 1990 Latvia used about 35 percent more energy than would be expected on the basis of its GDP (see figure 7-1).

One of the important features of Latvia's energy system is its deficiency in generating electricity. The Latvian generation system consists of three hydropower stations (capacity 1,500 MW) on the River Daugava and two thermal power stations (capacity 500 MW) burning heavy fuel oil or natural gas in the Riga area. In 1991, about 43 percent of Latvia's electricity needs were imported from neighboring countries.

Industry is responsible for 32 percent of final energy consumption in Latvia, which is similar to that in Western European countries. The household and commerce/service sectors combined consume 29 percent of final energy. However, transport's share of energy consumption is estimated at about 11 percent, substantially lower than in developed countries, but higher than in most Eastern European countries.

Table 7-1. Energy Balance 1990
(petajoules)

Production and Consumption	Hard Coal & Briquettes	Coke	Raw Oil	Gasoline	Diesel	Fuel Oil	Other Liquid Products from Oil	LPG	Natural Gas	Other Primary	Hydro-Electricity	Electricity	Heat	Total
Indigenous Production	..	..	..	..	..	..	..	..	..	17.7	43.8	64.8	122.6	249.0
Imports	25.2	0.5	561.6	35.6	455.4	78.5	25.7	3.9	114.2	0.0	..	69.6	..	1370.0
Exports	-0.09	..	-561.0	-7.4	-398.1	-1.1	-1.5	-0.2	-5.2	..	..	-34.7	..	1009.0
Stock Change	0.7	..	..	0.0	-7.7	0.0	..	..	..	..	..	..	..	-7.0
Total Energy Requirements	**25.6**	**0.5**	**0.6**	**28.2**	**49.6**	**77.4**	**24.2**	**3.7**	**109.0**	**17.7**	**43.8**	**99.7**	**122.6**	**603.0**
Final Use in Energy Industry (with own consumption)	0.0	0.0	0.0	0.0	0.0	0.0	0.0	0.0	0.0	0.0	0.0	..	0.0	..
Coal Industry	..	..	..	..	..	..	..	..	..	..	..	..	..	..
Other Fuels Industry	..	..	..	..	..	..	..	..	..	..	..	..	..	..
Power and Heat Industry	..	..	..	..	..	..	..	..	..	..	..	..	..	..
Energy Inputs into a Gross Outputs from Transf. Processes	**12.2**	**0.0**	**0.0**	**0.0**	**2.7**	**-50.1**	**-4.9**	..	**-70.4**	**-3.6**	..	..	..	**144.0**
Blast Furnaces	..	..	..	..	..	..	..	..	..	..	..	..	..	..
Oil Shale & Peat Refineries	..	..	..	..	..	..	..	..	..	..	..	..	..	..
Petroleum Refineries	..	..	..	..	..	..	..	..	..	..	..	..	..	..
Public Power & Heat Plants	..	..	..	..	..	..	..	..	-29.5	..	..	..	..	-30.0
Industrial Power Plants	..	..	..	..	..	..	..	..	..	..	..	..	..	..
Industrial Heating Plants	..	..	..	..	..	..	..	..	..	..	..	..	..	..
Municipal Heating Plants	..	..	..	..	..	..	..	..	..	..	..	..	..	..
Distribution Losses	-0.1	..	..	..	..	..	..	..	..	..	0.0	11.5	3.1	15.0
Total Final Consumption	**9.8**	**0.5**	**0.0**	**28.0**	**33.5**	**28.8**	**33.4**	**3.7**	**30.7**	**11.3**	**0.0**	**86.3**	**119.5**	**386.0**
Total Industry	**0.8**	**0.5**	**0.0**	**1.9**	**3.1**	**10.7**	**1.9**	**0.0**	**18.9**	**0.4**	**0.0**	**38.0**	**54.7**	**131.0**
Ferrous Metallurgy	..	0.1	..	..	..	1.2	..	..	4.4	..	..	1.4	1.4	8.5
Non-Ferrous Metals	..	..	..	..	..	..	..	..	..	..	..	..	..	0.0
Electroengineering Industry	..	..	..	..	..	..	..	..	..	..	..	1.0	..	1.0
Chemical Industry	..	..	..	..	..	0.2	..	..	..	..	..	8.8	6.7	16.0
Minerals Industry	..	..	..	..	..	..	..	..	..	..	..	..	..	0.0
Wood Industry	..	..	..	..	..	0.6	..	..	0.5	..	..	3.1	7.7	12.0
Machinery	..	0.4	..	..	0.1	1.3	..	..	4.6	..	..	7.0	9.8	23.0
Other Industry	..	..	..	0.1	0.2	3.2	1.4	..	3.4	..	..	10.7	16.3	38.0
Construction	..	..	..	1.8	2.6	4.2	0.3	..	5.9	..	..	2.0	6.2	20.0
Total Transport	**0.2**	**0.0**	**0.0**	**9.1**	**16.9**	**17.0**	**26.2**	**0.7**	**1.4**	**0.0**	**0.0**	**3.4**	**2.1**	**77.0**
Road	0.54	..	..	9.1	16.9	..	15.8	..	..	..	..	2.2	..	27.0
Rail	..	..	..	..	..	..	4.2	..	..	..	..	1.2	..	6.0
Sea	0.0	..	..	..	..	17.0	6.2	..	..	..	..	0.0	..	23.0
Unspecified	..	..	..	..	..	..	..	..	1.4	..	..	..	2.1	3.5
Total Other Sectors	**8.8**	**0.0**	**0.0**	**10.7**	**11.8**	**0.9**	**5.3**	**3.0**	**10.4**	..	**0.0**	**43.9**	**61.5**	**156.0**
Agriculture	0.5	..	..	5.5	6.1	0.7	0.4	3.0	1.6	1.4	..	14.0	9.8	42.0
Residential & Commercial	8.2	..	..	3.8	5.5	0.2	4.8	2.9	7.9	9.5	..	26.1	46.5	116.0
Other	0.1	..	..	1.4	0.2	..	0.1	..	0.9	..	..	3.8	5.2	12.0

Notes: Totals may not add up to due to rounding. One petajoule PJ = 1 quadmillion joules = 0.95 trillion btu = 0.24 trill kcal = 24,000 toe. LPG = liquid petroleum gas.
Source: Latvian authorities.

Figure 7-1. Energy Consumption and GNP, 1990

Energy Consumption/Capita (koe thousands)

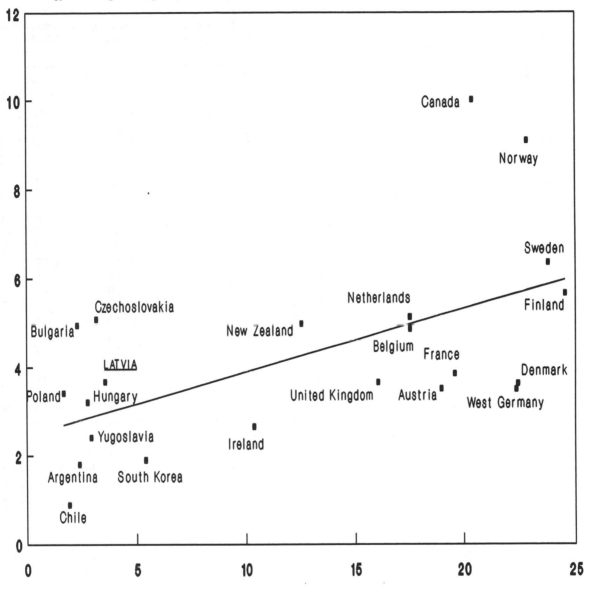

GNP per Capita (USD thousands)

■ Actual —— Regression

Source: Latvian authorities, World Bank staff estimates; World Bank, and *World Development Report 1992.*

Table 7-2. International Comparison of Energy Consumption, 1990

Country	Energy Consumption per Capita (koe)	GNP (USD millions)	Population (thousands)	GNP/capita (USD)	Energy Consumption/GDP (koe/USD 1,000)
Latvia	3,668	8,975 [a]	2,670	3,410 [a]	1,091
Argentina	1,801	77,590	32,300	2,400	750
Bulgaria	4,945	20,460	8,800	2,320	2,127
Poland	3,416	64,480	38,200	1,690	2,024
Chile	887	25,620	13,200	1,940	457
Hungary	3,211	29,330	10,600	2,780	1,160
Yugoslavia	2,409	82,310	23,800	2,940	697
Czechoslovakia	5,081	49,920	15,700	3,190	1,598
Republic of Korea	1,898	231,130	42,800	5,400	351
Ireland	2,653	36,320	3,500	10,370	256
New Zealand	4,971	41,940	3,400	12,570	403
United Kingdom	3,646	922,720	57,400	16,110	227
Netherlands	5,123	262,440	14,900	17,570	291
Belgium [b]	4,852	175,000	10,000	17,580	277
Austria	3,503	146,500	7,700	19,000	184
France	3,845	1,102,300	56,400	19,590	197
Denmark	3,618	116,700	5,100	22,440	158
Canada	10,009	540,700	26,500	20,380	491
Federal Republic of Germany	3,491	1,400,240	62,000	22,363	155
Sweden	6,347	203,540	8,600	23,780	268
Finland	5,650	122,360	5,000	24,540	231
Norway	9,083	96,920	4,200	22,830	394

a.   GNP estimate for Latvia is for 1991. GNP estimates for economies of the former Soviet Union are subject to more than the usual range of uncertainty, and should therefore be regarded as preliminary and subject to revision. Other GNP and GNP per capita data were calculated using the Atlas methodology.

b.   Energy consumption per capita for Belgium in 1989 was 4,804 koe. The 1992 *World Development Report* reported energy consumption per capita for Belgium in 1990 of 2,807 koe, clearly an underestimate. An increase of 1 percent over the 1989 figure has been used until a final calculation is made.

Note: koe = kilograms of oil equivalent.

Sources: World Bank staff estimates; World Bank, *World Development Report 1992*.

Household consumption consists largely of district heat and natural gas. The industrial sector uses heat, natural gas oil, and electricity. Agriculture and transportation largely use petroleum products. Latvia uses little coal, unlike many East European countries, and as a result has relatively clean air.

The northwest electric power grid that serves Latvia also serves the other Baltic countries, Belarus, and the St. Petersburg/Pskov area of Russia. Latvia has the largest hydroelectric generation component, which is especially needed for system peaking service (the other nearest peaking units in the region are 560 MW near St. Petersburg and 560 MW in Karelia). Although Latvia is a net importer of electricity, it distributes electric energy to Belarus. Energy balance figures for 1990 and 1991 are summarized in Table 7-3.

The common fuels for power and heat generation are heavy fuel oil and natural gas from the FSU. Some heavy fuel oil also comes from the Mazeikiai refinery in Lithuania. Natural gas makes up 70 percent of fuels used by Latvenergo for electricity and heat production, and its share has increased during the last five years. Total system losses, including both station and network losses, are 16 percent, a reasonable level given the large amount of electricity in transit.

Although the heavy fuel oil used has a high sulfur content (2.5 to 3.0 percent) and no effort has been made to minimize air emissions, the total amount of pollutants released is not large for a territory the size of Latvia. In 1990, of the estimated 53,500 tonnes per year of sulfur dioxide released in the country, only 14,090 tonnes per year, or 26 percent, originated from the power plants. Similarly, about 4,555 tonnes per year of nitrogen oxides were released by Latvenergo plants, compared with 14,190 tonnes per year from stationary sources and 37,817 tonnes per year from mobile sources. In other words, Latvenergo contributes only 8.8 percent to total nitrogen oxides emissions.

The capacity of the transmission system seems adequate for servicing domestic consumption. The system's high voltage lines use 330-kV and 110-kV lines and transformers. For handling power transmitted throughout the country, the lines reach their limits under certain circumstances, for example, cold weather and low hydroelectric output. Several 330-kV lines connect Latvia to neighboring countries: four to Lithuania, two to Estonia, and one to Russia.

The district heating system is widespread in Latvia. Several large cities have combined heat and power plants. Heat-only boilers were occasionally added at central plants, where they are owned by electricity generators, or in dispersed locations, where they are owned by local district heating companies. In Latvia, all these plants burn either heavy fuel oil or natural gas. Latvia's 1991 heat production is summarized in Table 7-4.

Table 7-4 indicates that heat-only boilers supply 77 percent of total heat consumed and that the co-generation heating power plant supplies nearly 23 percent. This imbalance negates the main advantage of the central district heating system, which is inexpensive, low-grade heat as a byproduct of power plants.

Latvia has some 8,000 boilers, of which 80 percent are used for heating purposes. About 50 percent of household consumers obtain their heat from central heating stations. In Riga the average is 80 percent. The total length of networks in the country is 1,000 kilometers (about 300 kilometers in Riga), which because of poor insulation, leakages, and so on results in high heat losses.

Table 7-3. Latvia's Electricity Balance, 1990 and 1991
(Gigawatt hour)

Type	1990	1991
Thermal Plant Generation	2,043	2,284
Hydroelectric Plant Generation	4,496	3,275
Industrial Plant Generation	108	86
Gross Domestic Generation	6,647	5,645
Imports (net)	3,583	4,225
Gross Electricity Available	10,230	9,870

Source: Latvian authorities.

Table 7-4. Heat Production, 1991

Heat Produced at	Heat Produced (Gcal thousand)
Central CHP Plant (Latvenergo)	3,704
Industrial CHP Boilers	4,000
Total in CHP Plants	7,704
Central HOB Plant (Latvenergo)	3,902
Industrial HOB Plants	15,000
Dispersed HOB Plants	6,800
Electric Heater Boilers	33
Total in HOB Plants	25,735
Total Gross Heat Produced	33,439
Station Own Use and Losses	1,435
Total Net Heat Usage	31,989

Notes: Gcal = gigacalories (billions of calories).
CHP = Co-generation heating/power.
HOB = Heat-only boiler plant.
Source: Latvian authorities.

Latvia has had considerable experience with hydropower, which supplies nearly half of its electricity. However, some of the works, especially Plavinas, were not implemented with due care paid to environmental issues, and damage to aquatic life and to the national historical heritage resulted. As a consequence, construction of new hydroelectric projects at Daugavpils (300 MW) and at Yekabpils (160 MW) was halted. Not only did these projects face strong environmental opposition, but they did not seem justified on economic grounds given the limited amount of energy to be generated.

Latvia has many small hydroelectric power stations. Before 1940 about 300 small hydroelectric stations were in operation, each with a capacity of more than 10 MW. In 1948 an additional 550 small hydroelectric power stations were planned and many of them were constructed. Today no small hydroelectric power stations are operating although their civil works and water reservoirs exist.[1] The potential for small hydroelectric power station is not significant in Latvia's total electricity scheme (about 0.1 percent of demand), but further study could identify suitable sites and make important contributions to farms and small agricultural businesses.

Institutional and Policymaking Framework

Higher energy prices and economic restructuring would probable lead to a leveling off, or even a decline, of energy demand over the next few years. Nonetheless, Latvia will continue to import all its oil, natural gas, and coal needs and a significant part of its electricity needs.

The government's plan to ensure that energy needs are continuously met without disruption focuses on two areas:

- Spot-market imports of oil products through Ventspils and immediate short-term measures, such as negotiating with Moscow for a new agreement for oil and gas;

- Long-term measures, including constructing a large generating power plant, importing gas from the West, engaging in future developments in the Barents Sea, and relocating a second-hand refinery to Ventspils.

As of early 1992, the electricity company and other energy entities in gas and oil were supervised by the Ministry of Industry and Energy, and their general managers were appointed by the government. They did not pay their costs, collect revenues, optimize their operations, or plan their activities as independent corporations. If the government intends to make the energy utilities autonomous corporations, even though owned wholly or partly owned by the government, the proper legal framework should be established for a rapid, but effective, transition period. Under the PHARE program, the EC is financing a study on restructuring and privatization of the energy sector. This study aims at proposing appropriate changes in the legislation and institutional framework at the governmental and enterprise levels as well as in the regulatory authorities and privatized enterprises.

---

1.   In 1987, an expert team concluded that twenty-one of the old hydroelectric power stations could be reconstructed, and that each would afford a capacity of 7 MW.

Sectoral Policies and Issues

Declining production of crude oil in Russia has already had the following effects:

- Reduced exports of crude oil via Ventspils, from 13 million tons per year in 1990 to 8 million tons per year in 1991, and therefore reduced transit fees for Latvia.

- Reduced exports of refined products, primarily diesel, via Ventspils, from 10 million tons per year in 1990 to 6 million tons per year in 1991, and therefore reduced payments-in-kind received by Latvia (the fee averages 4 to 6 percent).

- Reduced supplies of crude oil to refineries in Russia, Belarus, and Lithuania, which traditionally supplied refined products to Latvia. In the case of the Mazeikiai refinery in Lithuania, the situation is complicated by the soft blockade on oil supplies to the Baltic states.

Two scenarios for energy trade in 1992 are presented in Table 7-5. In the first scenario, Latvia's energy trade deficit could be as high as USD 700 million if most trading took place in hard currency at world prices. This estimate accounts for fuel supplies received as fees for energy transit through Latvia. In the second scenario, the deficit could be as low as USD 400 million if preferential import arrangements remained in place until the end of 1992. This scenario assumes that Latvia secured half of its oil, gas, and coal supplies at ruble denominated prices equal to 50 percent of world prices, and that the price of imported electricity (kopeks 24/kWh in February 1992) remained in effect until the end of the year.

In order to assess the adequacy of energy prices in early 1992, the economic cost of energy was estimated (see Table 7-6). Dividing the price paid by households and industry by the economic cost, the exchange rate implicit in domestic prices could be estimated. Comparison of these implicit exchange rates with the market exchange rate (RUR 100 to RUR 200 per USD 1 in early February 1992) reveals that controlled energy prices were below economic costs. Although prices for some products, for example, fuel oil and gasoline, had begun to approach world prices, others remained highly subsidized, for example, coal and district heat prices for households.

The only explicit energy subsidy was that of district heat to household consumers. Yet prices clearly reflected complex cross-subsidies. Some cross-subsidies, for example, from industrial consumers to household consumers, are evident in Table 7-6. Other examples include the following:

- District heat producers were subsidized via artificially low prices for heavy fuel oil and gas.

- Household consumers of LPG received a large subsidy from the natural gas industry. Before the proposed February LPG price increase, this subsidy amounted to RUR 1.5 billion per year in January 1992 prices.

Table 7-5. Estimated Balance of Energy Trade, 1992

Imports	1st Quarter Qantity [a]	Price	Value [b] (USD millions)	2nd-4th Quarters Quantity	Price	Value (USD millions)	Total Value (USD millions)
Scenario 1: Quantities as in 1991, at negotiated ruble prices in the first quarter and world prices for the rest of the year							
Gasoline [c] (thousand tons)	150	58	8	450	230	101	110
Kerosene (thousand tons)	28	50	1	83	200	17	18
Diesel [c] (thousand tons)	250	50	8	750	200	96	104
Fuel Oil (thousand tons)	250	18	5	750	73	55	59
Natural Gas (bn.m³) [d]	0	5	0	2.9	100	290	290
Coal (thousand tons)	197	13	2	591	50	27	29
Electricity (TWh)	1.06	0.002	3	3.17	0.052	165	167
Total Imports			27			750	777
Less Re-Exports of Crude [e]			15			46	61
Net Imports			12			704	716
Scenario 2: As for scenario 1, but with some preferential import arrangements extended until the end of 1992							
Gasoline [c] (thousand tons)	150	58	8	450	170	76	85
Kerosene (thousand tons)	28	50	1	83	145	12	14
Diesel [c] (thousand tons)	250	50	8	750	96	72	80
Fuel Oil (thousand tons)	250	18	5	750	55	41	46
Natural Gas (bn.m3) [d]	0	5	0	2.9	75	218	218
Coal (thousand tons)	197	13	2	591	34	20	22
Electricity (TWh)	1.06	0.002	3	3.17	0.002	8	10
Total Imports			27			447	474
less Re-Exports of crude [e]			15			46	61
Net Imports			12			401	413
Transit Fees (6%)(both scenarios)							
Gasoline (thousand tons)	3	N.A.	N.A.	9	N.A.	N.A.	
Diesel (thousand tons)	90			270	N.A.	N.A.	
Crude Oil (thousand tons)	120	127	115	360	127	46	61
Coal (thousand tons)	20	N.A.	N.A.	59	N.A.	N.A.	

a.   Quantities in the first quarter are assumed to be 25 percent of the whole year's quantities.

b.   Prices in the first quarter are assumed to be 25 percent of world market prices for oil and coal, prices in the 2nd-4th quarters are assumed to be equal to world prices.

c.   Total costs of gasoline, diesel, and coal are reduced by volumes received as transit fees, that is, by 6 percent of transit trade in that fuel.

d.   Zero gas imports in first quarter: Latvia draws down gas in storage.

e.   Fees on transit of crude oil are taken in-kind (6 percent) and re-exported at world prices.

N.A. = not available.

Notes: During the 2nd-4th quarters, imports are at world prices except half of oil products, gas and coal, which are acquired at 50 percent of world prices, and all electricity imports, which remain at 24 kopeks/kWh. Prices in the first quarter are assumed to be 25 percent of world market prices for oil and coal, RUR 450 per thousand cubic meter for gas, and kopeks 24/kWh for electricity (at RUR 100 = USD 1).

Source: Latvian authorities.

Table 7-6. Energy Prices in Latvia, January 1992 a

Product	Producer Price	Consumer Price (RUR)		Economic Cost (USD)		Implicit Exchange Rate	
		Industry	Household	Industry	Household	Industry	Household
Coal (ton)	110	110	98	50	60	2.2	1.6
Firewood (ton)	100	100	69	20	20	5.0	3.4
Natural Gas (cum thousands)	1,187	1,187	1,050	140	180	8.5	5.8
Gasoline (ton)		5,400	5,400	300	300	18.0	18.0
Diesel		1,627	1,627	170	200	9.6	8.1
Fuel Oil (tons)	1,627	1,627	1,627	80		20.3	
CHP Heat (Gcal)	298	298	19	30	55	9.9	0.3
HOB Heat (Gcal)	350	350	19	40	70	8.8	0.3
Electricity (MWh)	440	440	300	52	60	8.5	5.0
LPG (ton)		3,077	1,555	250	350	12.3	4.4

Gcal = gigacalories (billions of calories).
MWh = megawatt hours (millions of watt-hours).
cum = cubic meter.
Note: Producer and consumer prices of energy increased substantially during 1992 and became similar for both household and industrial use except in the cases of gas, electricity, and LPG, where consumer prices were higher than producer prices.
Source: Latvian authorities.

Latvia's domestic coal market will probably change substantially. At the moment coal is used mainly in small boilers, furnaces, and stoves. Practically no steam coal is used in large boilers, used for electricity generation, large industry, and so on, although coal is likely to be more cost-effective than oil or gas at world prices even after meeting emission standards. For these reasons, the coal market should shrink initially as world energy prices are phased in. For the longer term, however, coal could receive a large boost if investing in new coal-fired electricity plants is found to be the least-cost way to supply electricity for Latvia. Even a modest coal-fired plant would consume 0.7 million tons per year.

The prospects for the coal trade are uncertain. In 1991, approximately 1.1 million tons of coal were imported from the East by rail for domestic consumption. In addition, 0.9 million tons were exported via the port in Riga and 0.4 million tons via Ventspils. Some of the mines are 4,000 kilometers away from the Latvian border. If economic restructuring in Russia increases rail freight rates from their present levels (about RUR 0.1 per ton kilometer) to world levels (US¢ 1-2 per ton kilometer), Russian coal may not remain competitive on the Latvian or on the world market.

The main problems with Latvia's extensive district heating systems are as follows:

- The equipment's age and the high degree of corrosion cause large water losses, with consequent losses of heat. Water losses are typically 2 percent compared to losses of 0.1 percent in systems that are operating well.

- The networks supplying steam to industry receive little or no return, which causes additional water losses. Supplying process steam is costly and inefficient. Cogeneration units or direct gas connections would be more efficient.

- The systems operate at constant flow and variable temperatures, which requires high pumping energy even when heating requirements are low. In addition, the temperatures tend to fall to low levels, for example, 70-80° C, which degrades the quality of service. The reason for using this method is simple: variable speed drives for the pumping stations do not exist.

- Other reasons for heat loss include low quality of piping insulation and lack of regular repairs.

- The system provides service through direct connections to customers, which leads to higher than normal losses and does not provide the separation between primary and secondary circulation systems needed for better control.

- The system has no dispatching capability that would allow the least-expensive source of heat to carry the load at any time.

- No regulation (other than temperature regulation at the plant) exists that would allow the flow to be adjusted. Metering is limited to a few large industrial consumers (2 percent of total consumers). Charges for small and residential consumers are either at a fixed rate or based on surface area, which does not provide any incentives for conservation.

The continued use of natural gas is unavoidable in the short term. The most efficient method for utilizing gas is the combustion turbine, combined cycle technology. Installing six combustion turbine combined cycle units of 50-MW each at six different locations is being considered. However, a smaller number of larger units, for example, two units at Daugavpils and Liepaja, might be more advantageous. The siting of the proposed units depends upon the need to satisfy the heat demand, but this may be supplied later by gas networks.

The prospects for increasing trade in natural gas seem relatively good. Underground storage facilities at Incukalns and the possible future facilities at Dobele appear to have no major competitors in the Baltic region or in Belarus. Based on the experience of neighboring countries, Russia could change tariffs from a constant price in rubles per thousand cubic meters to a winter price of USD 100 per thousand cubic meters and a summer price of USD 60 per thousand cubic meters. Such a price differential would provide a good basis for financing rehabilitation of the Incukalns facility, and perhaps the future expansion of gas storage facilities. Therefore, introducing suitable contractual arrangements with Russia and the gas utilities in the three neighboring countries should receive high priority.

Investment Program and Priorities

Restructuring district heating systems in Latvia could effect energy savings of 20 to 30 percent. A master plan is needed, at least for the systems' biggest consumers, that is, the cities of Riga, Daugavpils, Liepaja, and Olaine. The plan would collect information on the present condition of the systems and offer advice for restructuring the system. The World Bank's experience with similar projects, for example, in Poland, could provide a useful guide.

A new dispatch center is being established for the Russian part of the interconnected power system (IPS), which used to be regulated by the Riga Dispatch Center. Yet the Riga Dispatch Center still fills an essential role given the Baltic countries' interdependence for base and peaking capacity. Technical updating and increased automation with the use of modern computer hardware and software could greatly enhance the new role of this important center.

The nuclear option is also under consideration. If nuclear power is to be introduced, a multi-unit site rather than a single or two-unit plant would be practical. Unit capacity should not exceed 300 to 400 MW if the system is to remain reliable. The construction period for nuclear units of current design is seven to eight years, thus nuclear power by the year 2000 is not realistic. Cost considerations are paramount. Based on construction experience to date, the optimum unit size, and expected construction time, it is not realistic to consider nuclear units as a least-cost solution to Latvia's electricity supply problem. Although the government has provisionally selected three sites--Pavilosta, the northwestern side of the Gulf of Riga, and Ludza in the southeast--no site investigations to study seismic, climatic, hydrological, and geological conditions are under way. Also no provisions for low- and high-level radioactive wastes have been made. Experience indicates that this latter problem may pose an insurmountable difficulty.

Many of the current proposals for investment in the sector assume that the government will take responsibility for large amounts of sovereign debt in hard currency. A nuclear power station, for example, would cost USD 1,000 to USD 1,500 million. To service this level of debt, Latvenergo would have to charge high tariffs, perhaps higher than tariffs in most West European utilities, to domestic consumers as well as to neighboring countries in the event of an exportable surplus. Given that such tariff levels would probably not be achievable (or desirable) in the near future, the government would have to take full responsibility for debt service. It might be appropriate to invite foreign and local consortia to consider investments in such projects. Bilateral or multilateral technical assistance could be used to establish their feasibility. Although other proposals for energy investment would be less capital-intensive than nuclear power, they would encounter similar problems.

Latvian energy sector institutions are now making contact with Western technical assistance agencies (bilateral and multilateral), lending institutions (for example, the World Bank, the European Bank for Reconstruction and Development, the Nordic Investment Bank), consultants, and equipment vendors. The Ministry of Industry and Energy is aware of the need to focus aid on a few high-priority objectives. In this connection, the government should:

- Focus technical assistance on energy reform and investment programs that the government plans to promote for support by multilateral lenders;

- Avoid offers of technical assistance that are linked to future sales of equipment, which is a frequent problem in relation to high technology energy and environmental equipment;

- Use limited amounts of funds to hire international specialists to advise on major government decisions, for example, investments in refineries or oil and gas pipelines, on oil product procurement, and so on.

The highest priorities for technical assistance in the sector would be to:

- Define a strategy for energy pricing and metering to bring domestic energy prices up to market-based levels as rapidly as possible, to move away from price controls to a mix of free and regulated prices, and to extend metering progressively from large to small energy consumers (such studies are already in progress with support from the US Agency for International Development).

- Prepare industrial energy audits to help enterprises adjust their energy consumption to world price levels and to changes in relative fuel prices (some audits have been initiated, with support from the US Agency for International Development). The EC-PHARE program would also address issues related to preparing proposals for energy restructuring

- Establish a basis for normal contractual relationships at world prices and in hard currency with energy exporters and importers. Top priority would go to tariffs that reflect the value of underground gas storage in Latvia.

- Prepare a strategy for oil and gas trade with Eastern and Western partners, focusing on contractual arrangements and direct foreign investment or joint ventures in ports, pipelines, storage, or refining.

- Prepare proposals for energy sector restructuring to separate budget (ministry) activities from commercial (enterprise) activities; set up transfer pricing and contractual relationships between independent energy supply enterprises; and develop these enterprises into commercial, joint stock companies capable of entering into ventures with private partners.

- Prepare an electric power master plan to define the least-cost way to supply Latvia with the electricity it needs (the EC is planning to finance such a study).

- Prepare pre-feasibility studies of investment options to be considered in the electric power master plan, including site identification; environmental assessment; and costs of associated infrastructure, such as ports, pipelines, railways, storage, and waste management.

- Prepare district heating master plans for the main urban networks, focusing on issues that need resolution, for example, metering and energy efficiency in buildings, competition between natural gas and district heating in the residential space heating market, loss reduction in the district heating networks and more efficient dispatch of cogenerated heat through the larger networks, and reorganization of district heating into commercial companies. (A master plan for power and heating is under preparation with assistance from Swedish and Finnish power companies.) The EBRD is also assisting the government in various energy subsectors.

Recommendations

All industrial energy prices should be gradually adjusted to reach economic costs. At the same time, a medium-term program to eliminate household energy subsidies should be introduced (in the interim, all subsidies should be covered by an explicit line item in the central government budget). Prices of coal and fuelwood should be decontrolled as soon as sufficient competition exists among suppliers and satisfactory forest management and environmental arrangements can be devised and put in place. However, the supply of electricity, district heat, and natural gas are natural monopolies, therefore a mechanism for regular adjustment of their prices should be established.

The most actively debated issue in Latvia is the expansion of the electricity generation system. The plans prepared to date do not have adequate analytical backing, have not considered realistic prices and implementation schedules, and have not been based on quantified national objectives, namely, environmental and economic targets or reasonable domestic and regional demand projections. A more rigorous plan should be undertaken in the framework of a national electricity master plan that will use the information and analyses developed to date. The ranking of the scenarios should be done on the basis of the lifetime costs of each option.

Top priority should be given to **energy conservation**, which is a cost-effective investment with great potential given the amount of energy consumed per unit of economic output. Industry offers great savings: obsolete or uneconomic enterprises can be phased out and advanced processing methods and efficient practices can be introduced.

Latvia's ability to service hard currency debt will gradually increase as exports are directed to Western markets. For this reason, the following approach to evaluating investment proposals by state-owned energy enterprises is recommended:

- Improve the efficiency of energy consumption in industrial enterprises;

- Rehabilitate and modernize existing energy supply systems, for example, hydroelectric plants, district heating networks, before committing resources to new projects;

- Compare all investment options to find the least-cost solution when selecting new generation plant;

- Adopt a commercial approach to borrowing by state-owned enterprises, that is, the enterprises would borrow only if tariff revenues were large enough to service the debt fully.

The heating companies should be owned by the municipalities they serve and should maintain business links with centralized fuel procurement and construction and repair companies. Regional distribution companies should also become independent and buy electricity from Latvenergo, the main generator, or from smaller industrial cogenerators, and sell it to the consumers. Such an arrangement would provide accountability, improve efficiency, lower costs, and improve service. However, such restructuring requires unified and rational tariffs and metering equipment.

The plan to introduce imported coal to the generation system is sound, considering the following: (a) the need to diversify the supply of fuel, now heavily dependent on natural gas and heavy fuel oil; (b) the lower price of coal per unit of heat content as well as the expected stability of coal prices compared to other fuels; (c) the availability of coal; and (d) the relatively short time required to implement the coal units. The coal units are planned for the port of Liepaja (300 MW), where an unloading facility would be required, and for Daugavpils (300 MW), where coal would be transported by rail.

Pre-feasibility studies should be initiated soon to address the issues related to a future coal-burning plant, including environmental issues of coal storage, air emissions, and liquid effluents and ash disposal problems. The proximity of the proposed plants to major cities could pose special problems. The studies should also examine options for meeting environmental standards, that is, the cost of fuel gas desulfurization equipment compared to the use of low-sulfur coal, to arrive at the least-cost solution.

Renewable energy resources are being advocated for their environmentally benign nature. Encouraging private parties to enter this field of power development on a modest scale would be appropriate. They include solar, wind, geothermal, and biomass resources. Their contributions to total demand may be small, but they may be worth pursuing on a modest scale. Solar is not an abundant resource in Latvia because of the country's location, but it may have some potential in providing hot water, especially in summer homes, and in drying agricultural products. Small units to tap wind energy have been installed, but their cost and the intermittent nature of wind make them suitable only on a small scale in special locations and for special applications, such as pumping water. Geothermal power may be possible in certain locations if conditions of temperature and pressure warrant it. Biomass depends on woodchips, forest debris, and other agricultural products for gas production or burning. This form of energy may have some application in local small boilers for heat production.

A strategy for attracting private investment capital to Latvia's energy sector could include:

- A complete liberalization of oil and coal imports, that is, open encouragement of private imports at uncontrolled prices in anticipation of the transition to world prices;

- A systematic approach to hard currency pricing of Latvia's natural gas storage services for neighboring countries as a basis for private participation in investment in expanded storage;

- A rapid transition to full cost recovery (investment and operating costs) for electricity and heat producers as a basis for negotiating with foreign investors who may be interested in becoming independent power producers selling electricity or heat to the Latvian networks;

- A rapid introduction of the planned legislation, tax codes, and contracts needed for licensing petroleum exploration to international oil companies;

- A continued effort to secure East-West energy trade by bringing enterprises from Eastern neighbors into joint venture arrangements at Ventspils, Riga, or Liepaja to bolster oil and coal transit trade and involving Western partners in future oil, gas, and coal trade in both directions through Latvia.

CHAPTER 8

Transport

Like its neighboring Baltic countries, Latvia performs an important transit function: 97 percent of its port traffic and 50 percent of its rail traffic is in transit, mainly to and from Belarus, Russia, and Ukraine. Most domestic transport is by road. The basic transport infrastructure is adequate, although parts of the road system have been neglected. The Riga airport needs some modernization, and several port and rail facilities should be renovated. Trucks and cars are obsolete in terms of their fuel efficiency and payload/weight ratio. However, Soviet designed vehicles are better adapted to local road conditions than their Western counterparts, and should therefore be retained for some time.

The restructuring of Latvia's economy and the economies of its neighbors for whom it performs such an important transit function has major implications for transport. The demand for heavy bulk movements, well-suited for rail transport, is likely to decline, partly as a result of the down-sizing of heavy industries, but also because the introduction of economic and world prices for energy and transport is likely to eliminate many existing irrational movements. However, the demand for higher quality (more timely and flexible) transport services for light industrial and consumer goods is likely to increase. These services are usually best provided by trucking, and it is important that Latvia develop a competitive trucking industry. The railways can participate in this growing element of the market via combined transport (containers or trailers), but only if they are converted into a commercial, market-oriented, and flexible enterprise. This requires a substantial change in management attitudes compared with those prevailing under a command economy, where much traffic was directed to rail, regardless of its performance. Similar considerations apply to the state shipping and airline enterprises if they are to help Latvia fulfill its transit potential in a highly competitive world. The government correctly sees privatization as the best way of commercializing shipping and airlines. While this is also immediately feasible for some ancillary parts of the railways, it seems likely that the core railway operation will remain a state enterprise, at least for some time. The challenge is thus to restructure the railway into a more market-responsive enterprise, which will require flexible arrangements with shippers and adjacent railways.

Structure and Recent Performance

Latvia has a public road network of 20,600 kilometer. In relation to area, the density of the public road network (0.32 kilometers per square kilometer) is comparable with Scandinavian countries (0.22 to 0.27 kilometers per square kilometer). In relation to population, road density is about half the level of that in Scandinavia, but considering that per capita car ownership is only one-quarter as high, the overall road density is adequate. Even on major inter-city routes, the volume of traffic is relatively modest, with a maximum of 4,000 to 6,000 vehicles per day. However, traffic levels have been growing at 4 to 6 percent a year.

The 2,400-kilometer long railroad network, is well used: 7.7 million net ton-kilometers per kilometer of track compared with 9.6 in Lithuania, 7.6 in Estonia, 5 in Poland, and 2 to 3 in the former Federal Republic of Germany, Hungary, and the former Yugoslavia. Rail is responsible for most freight, for example, oil and chemical products to Ventspils and grain imports for Russia.

Trucks are responsible for most domestic freight. In total terms, that is, transit plus domestic freight, trucks account for 90 percent of tons loaded. Yet they account for only about 45 percent of ton-kilometer because of the short average length of haul (about 28 kilometer).[1] Commercial or professional trucking enterprises own 20 percent of the national fleet of 65,000 trucks, and non-transport enterprises own 80 percent of the fleet.[2] The commercial fleet performs about 40 percent of the total ton-kilometer by road. About 25 percent of the trucks are more than ten years old, and 14 percent are more than thirteen years old. Compared with fleets in market economies, there is a high proportion (31 percent) of dump trucks and a low proportion of small delivery vehicles (18 percent).

As far as passenger transport is concerned, rail and buses are each responsible for 5 to 6 billion passenger-kilometer per year and represent the dominant means of commuting. No figures are available for passenger-kilometer by car, but the car fleet has been growing at twice the rate of the bus fleet in recent years.

Latvia has two major ports, Riga and Ventspils. Riga is the main commercial port and lies some 15 kilometer up the Daugava River from the Gulf of Riga. In 1990, the port of Riga handled 5.8 million tons of cargo, compared with 7 million tons in 1989 and 9.8 million tons in 1984. Imports made up 3.7 million tons, of which 2.7 million tons was corn; exports accounted for 1.6 million tons (about 1 million ton of coal and 75,000 cars); and cargo to other FSU republics came to 0.4 million tons. Containerized cargo amounted to about 0.6 million tons.

Latvia's other major port, Ventspils, some 200 kilometer to the west on the Baltic coast, is primarily an oil exporting port. It handles 85 percent of Soviet oil exports by sea. In 1990 Ventspils was responsible for 31.2 million tons of cargo. Exports of crude oil and diesel amounted to 24.6 million tons. Other exports included potash chloride (2.6 million tons), liquid chemicals (1.6 million tons), coal (0.4 million tons), and grain imports (0.7 million tons). Both ports are presently used far below capacity, and planned improvements are directed at increasing efficiency.

In September 1991 the Latvian Shipping Company, which has a fleet of forty tankers, thirty refrigerated cargo vessels, and six roll on/roll off (RORO) vessels, formally separated from the former Soviet Union Maritime Ministry and is now undergoing commercialization in preparation for privatization. The vessels are fully employed and the company reportedly operates profitably, though this may be based on inappropriate treatment of capital costs. The Maras Line, a small private company that is a joint venture with U.K. interests, started operations in early 1991 and is trading successfully between Riga/St. Petersburg and West European ports and plans to expand.

Civil aviation activities separated from Moscow in late 1991 (although the airline's accounting and payment system is still in Moscow. Latvian Airlines was established from the former regional Aeroflot fleet, and civil airports and airspace have been placed under the control of the Civil

---

1.   In 1990, truck ton-kms were 5.8 billion. Rail ton-kms were 18.5 billion, implying an average length of haul of more than 1,000 km. The maximum possible distance within Latvia is only 450 km. The figure obviously includes that part of the trip that traverses other republics, and therefore needs to be adjusted when comparing with road transport, which is mostly domestic.

2.   Most of the commercial or professional trucking enterprises are large state enterprises with an average fleet of 300 trucks, although some have as many as 1,000 trucks. Only 3,000 of the national fleet of trucks are privately owned by farmers and small enterprises.

Aviation Department of the Ministry of Transport and Communications. Most of Latvian Airlines' flights (90 percent) are still to the East because it lacks the hard currency, parts, and fuel to fly to Western Europe.   Flights to and from the East are expected to drop by 50 percent because of declining demand and resources.   The airline would like to lease aircraft to operate flights to the West.   The passenger terminal at the Riga airport needs to be expanded because of the increased numbers of international passengers.   Work started in early 1991 on a separate international terminal that was designed in Moscow, but was later halted. Proposals are now being examined for a modest extension of the existing terminal.

Institutional and Policymaking Framework

With the exception of roads and road transport, Latvia's transport sector was administered from Moscow, and the country now faces the formidable task of establishing virtually overnight its own policy and administrative capacity to succeed the previous regional branches of All-Union enterprises in the aviation, maritime, and railways subsectors.[3] A Ministry of Transport and Communications has been established, with responsibility for all modes of transport except maritime, which comes under the Ministry of Maritime Affairs, whose responsibilities also include the fishing industry. This is an unusual arrangement, especially in view of the importance of ensuring integrated development and operation of the port/land transport interface. Latvia would be better served by having all transport modes under the same ministry, which would also facilitate prioritization of public expenditures within the sector. Fisheries, as in most other countries, could be placed with agriculture, for example, under a ministry of primary industries.

Transport Policies and Issues

Commercializing and Privatizing State Transport Enterprises

As far as aviation, maritime transport, and railways are concerned, Latvia initially focused on appropriating assets and establishing a separate administration for these areas. Now that this phase has been largely completed, even though much remains to be done in terms of adopting appropriate legislation and of institutional development, Latvia needs to move quickly to establish commercially-oriented firms and to privatize some of them so that these activities do not become a burden on the public budget. Given that the past accounts of these enterprises were distorted, little is known of their inherent viability. However, rail tariffs appear particularly low, and most transport enterprises seem heavily overstaffed. Considering the rapid changes in transport volumes and the high rate of inflation, measures to contain costs and enhance revenues should be taken during the next few months.

Commercialization of the Latvian Shipping Company is under way, and it may eventually be privatized. To help with commercialization efforts, the government should address deficiencies in mortgage laws and the maritime code, and needs to obtain the Council of Ministers' approval to dispose of vessels. Ports, which should operate as commercial entities, may also be suitable for privatization. Further development of specialized facilities, for example, for grain or coal, should be undertaken by

---

3.   Even for roads, the principal funding decisions were made in Moscow, and the Latvian road authority was responsible mostly for implementing annual works programs within parameters set by Moscow.

joint ventures when possible. Efforts to improve operations at the Riga container terminal would also benefit from a joint venture or management contract.

In aviation, it is common to split airline operations, airports, and air traffic control into separate entities. All three can be operated as commercial enterprises without government subsidies. According to the Civil Aviation Department, foreign expertise will be necessary to help develop and implement a corporate strategy for Latvian Airlines, and joint venture possibilities should be actively pursued. In the meantime, Latvian Airlines should exercise caution in leasing aircraft and should explore possibilities for retrofitting its fleet, including replacing engines. It should also look for low-cost ways to participate in the growing air travel to and from the West, for example, by providing agency and ground services for foreign airlines. The air traffic control system should pay for itself with navigation charges. Investments to upgrade the system should await the outcome of the Swedavia study and should consider potential economies from a shared Baltic system, at least for upper air space.

The railways should also be operated as a commercial enterprise. Many railways have lost business, and in the process incurred heavy financial losses, which the taxpayers will have to cover, as a result of not adapting to changing market conditions or focusing their resources on the tasks for which they are best suited. A contributing factor is often political interference, that is, the imposition of vaguely defined social obligations. In such cases the responsibilities of the government and the railway management are not specified, and railway management is not held responsible for performance. Increasingly, governments are recognizing that they cannot afford to perpetuate such a situation. Latvia should follow this lead and take the following actions:

- The government should make it clear that Latvian Railways is a commercial enterprise and that railway management has the freedom to pursue commercial objectives as it sees fit.[4] Social obligations should be kept to a minimum, and when necessary, they should be clearly specified along with a formula for compensating the railway, that is related to the output of services, and not determined based on underwriting losses or subsidizing inputs.

- A contract should be made between the government and Latvian Railways defining the responsibilities of each party and the operating and financial targets the railway is expected to attain in return for specific government support, such as financing modernization requirements.

- Latvian Railways should develop a commercially-oriented strategic corporate plan that identifies its role in the market, the types of traffic it will and will not pursue, and its operating and financial goals consistent with market objectives.

- Latvian Railways should reorganize into business units and should become a business-led rather than an engineering-led railway, that is, no expenditure should be incurred unless one or more of the business units agrees to pay for it out of revenues.

---

4.   For example, railway management should be free to set and negotiate all freight rates and should not have to adhere to a government-approved tariff schedule. The only exception would be some government supervision to prevent abuse of monopoly power. In most situations, however, railways will be operating in a competitive environment.

- Latvian Railways should develop an action plan that assigns responsibility to individual managers for each of the needed measures to fulfill its corporate plan.

In road transport, the large and highly diversified enterprises should be broken up for privatization into separate components (tourism, urban and inter-urban buses, taxis, trucks, maintenance facilities, and so on).[5] The large truck fleets should also be split into smaller, more efficient units to ensure an adequate degree of competition and to provide opportunities for small investors. Road freight firms are subject to rate of return regulations, which should be retained until the regional monopolies are broken up. The Ministry of Transport and Communications needs to establish a transparent and equitable system for distributing quotas for international trucking under bilateral agreements so that all qualified carriers have an equal opportunity to participate in this business. In addition, the ministry should take up the following matters with other government authorities:

- Regulation of non-transport prices is creating distortions in transport markets and posing problems for trucking privatization, for example, regulation of food distribution margins means that distributors and retailers may not be able to pay market-determined commercial transport charges, raising the possibility of food distribution problems if trucking is privatized.[6]

- Many non-transport firms own fleets for their own use, which restricts market opportunities for the commercial trucking companies. These non-transport companies should be subjected to hard budget constraints and privatized as soon as possible.

Good opportunities exist for privatizing construction, maintenance, materials suppliers (for example, asphalt plants), spare parts manufacturers, and repair services. The Ministry of Transport and Communications should take a more assertive role in promoting privatization and will need technical assistance for this purpose. If the initiative for privatization is left with the management and staff of the existing state enterprises, it will probably not occur quickly enough or in an appropriate form.[7] If partial privatization occurs, the Ministry of Transport and Communications needs to take a strong ownership interest in the remaining state company, for example, by having representatives on the board to ensure that the equity is not raided by uneconomic transfer prices for services, for example, repairs and fuel supply, that the state company might provide to the newly privatized unit(s). The Ministry of Transport and Communications also needs to create market opportunities, for example, carrying out periodic road maintenance by competitively awarded contracts. The remaining state-owned construction and maintenance firms should not be precluded from competing for these contracts, but the Ministry of Transport and Communications will need to ensure that they do not enjoy unfair advantages, such as lower costs for capital, equipment, and supplies.

---

5.   Urban bus companies will be taken over by the municipalities.

6.   Distribution and retail margins were eliminated in 1992.

7.   Management and staff tend to preserve the enterprise and its staffing in its present form, which would rarely be appropriate.

Transport Pricing

All transport prices need to reflect costs so that the correct market signals are conveyed. While the government seems to accept this principle for the maritime and aviation sectors, its intentions are less clear regarding rail and road. Its position is particularly important, given that about half of Latvian Railways' freight traffic is in transit to other countries. The common argument is that railways should be subsidized because of the environmental or energy-saving advantages of rail. For users to make informed choices they should face the full cost of each alternative. The best approach is to ensure that both rail and road users pay their full costs, including their external costs (the costs of accidents, pollution, and congestion). Although a start was made with road users by introducing a fuel excise tax, road users, especially heavy vehicles, are a long way from paying their full costs.[8] Increasing the fuel excise tax would improve cost recovery from road users, and it is administratively efficient. Given that it does not recover a sufficient contribution from heavy vehicles, the government should introduce a substantial annual tax on heavy vehicles.

Transit Role

As mentioned earlier, transit traffic to and from Belarus, Russia, Ukraine, and other former Soviet republics accounts for about 97 percent of port traffic and about 50 percent of rail traffic. Ventspils will probably remain as the major oil and chemical port of the Baltic countries and Riga as the major container port. However, the outlook for the other major commodities, grain and coal, is less clear, both in terms of the Latvian ports' competitive position and of the commodities themselves. The coal facility at old Tallinn, while somewhat antiquated, functions better than those at Riga and Ventspils.[9] There are also doubts regarding the continuity of grain imports once agricultural reform is implemented in the other former Soviet republics, and of coal exports once true costs are charged for the rail transport from mine to port (rail tariffs for coal may be only one-third of their true economic cost).

If grain and coal flows are to continue for some time, Latvia could improve its competitive position for this traffic either by renovating the port at Riga or by converting the military port of Liepaja to commercial use. The proposed port master planning study might help weigh these considerations. The study should also assess the feasibility of shifting other functions, for example, container, RORO, and general cargo, from Riga to Liepaja. The study should take a total systems approach, for example, taking into account the costs of upgrading the rail link to Liepaja and the additional operating costs of the longer land transport link. The study should also examine the desirability of establishing a free port or foreign trade zone where duty free inventories could be held closer to the point of final delivery.

To reach its potential as a transit country, Latvia needs a comprehensive approach to reforming its entire trade logistics system in cooperation with its neighbors. The reliability and quality of transport services will be as important as the direct transport costs because trading partners will be evaluating the total cost of trade, including inventories (a direct function of the quality of transport

---

8.   It is important to distinguish between a broadly applied tax (e.g., profits tax, value added tax, import or sales tax applied at uniform rates throughout the economy) and a tax (or higher rate of taxation) applied specifically to road users. Only the latter is a genuine user charge to reflect the costs of road use. Moreover, when fuel prices are below world parity, there is no road user charge in economic terms, regardless of the underlying tax structure.

9.   A few years ago, a start was made on new coal berths at Riga, but the work was suspended for lack of funds.

services), customs procedures, documentation and related information processes, insurance, and financial services. Latvia and its neighbors need to implement the international conventions and codes relating to these matters.[10] According to trade sources, customs clearance between the Baltic republics is not a problem, although it is at the borders with Belarus and Russia.

Improved rail service would enhance Latvia's prospects as a gateway, particularly for combined transport. The practice of driving containers by truck as far as 1,000 kilometer or more into the republics of the former Soviet Union indicates the quality of rail service (and its deficiencies beyond Latvia). Latvian Railways should consider establishing a joint venture with a major international multimodal company to market and operate these services, as is being done with the Trans-Siberian Railway.

The principle of joint ventures, that is, incorporating the major operating partners and customers, should be extended to leasing berths and joint ownership of equipment. It is an excellent way of "locking in" transit traffic. Latvia is open to Russian participation in the oil exporting port of Ventspils, but is seeking reciprocal participation in the pipeline and in a Russian refinery.

Setting transit fees will need careful consideration. Transit traffic should pay for its costs. Beyond that, Latvia should charge what the traffic will bear, which will be a function of the quality of the service Latvia can provide. However, most transit traffic has alternative routes, and there are limits to what the traffic will bear in terms of charges and their administrative complexity or uncertainties created by frequent changes in the level or format of transit fees. For example, Latvia is contemplating a truck transit fee on a ton-kilometer basis, which would be administratively cumbersome and would probably create delays at borders. Levying an approximated fee based on truck type regardless of load or kilometer would be more reasonable.

Efficient Public Administration

A principal difference between a command economy and a well-managed market economy lies in the approach to determining expenditure priorities and allocating funds. To get the maximum benefit from scarce resources, all major items of public expenditure should be subjected to a comparison of alternatives using discounted cash flow analysis. This applies to ongoing projects, new commitments, recurrent (operating and maintenance) expenditures and capital expenditures. One of the distinctive features of socialist economies has been the tendency to initiate many major projects, then take five years or longer to complete them compared with one to two years to complete similar projects in market economies. The Ministry of Transport and Communications and Ministry of Maritime Affairs should, with technical assistance, review all major outstanding projects to determine how to focus the limited available funds on completing higher priority works, which may entail abandoning some ongoing projects for the time being.

The same sort of benefit-cost analysis should be applied to the military facilities that Latvia inherits, such as airfields and Liepaja port. Although Latvia should consider using them in an economically viable way, these facilities should not become a burden on the budget nor should they be maintained and staffed simply because they are there. Latvia should obtain assistance to inventory these facilities and assess the prospects for their commercial use.

---

10.   For more on this issue, see World Bank (1991, pp. 22-25).

The National Roads Administration is responsible for the public road network and is being pressured to develop other roads (39,000 kilometer), that to date have been the responsibility of collective farms and other entities. This added responsibility would overtax the capacity of this organization, and such roads are more efficiently administered at the local government level. Priority needs to be given to developing the necessary financial and institutional capacity at this level.

There is substantial room to improve the effectiveness of road expenditures by taking the following measures:

- Introducing pavement and bridge management systems, benefit-cost analysis, and other modern decisionmaking tools.[11]

- Using more cost-conscious designs for new construction and making more use of stage construction techniques.

- Focusing the limited funds available for new construction on a small number of projects so they can be completed quickly and the benefits can start to accrue. The National Roads Administration has already taken steps in this direction.

- Using better technology and increasing the use of local materials.

- Pursuing aggressively the process of privatizing maintenance and construction enterprises. For example, in other reforming economies when contracts for periodic maintenance were awarded after competitive bidding, they resulted in savings of as much as 20 percent.

The National Roads Administration should evaluate its internal operations and consider scaling down its administration and staffing. Compared with Finland, for example, Latvia employs almost twice as many staff per kilometer of road.

A program to alleviate the pending crisis in construction material supply and equipment maintenance should be devised jointly with the other Baltic nations. Reliance on the combined resources and production facilities already available in each country is clearly necessary for the rational management of road works. (For example, Latvia would be better off drawing its bitumen supplies from Estonia and Lithuania than attempting to develop its own production capacity. Equally, Estonia and Lithuania should source their road signs and paint supplies from Latvia rather than develop their own capacity.) Indeed, this principle of jointly addressing requirements should be extended into other areas. Latvia and its neighbors should avoid attempting to be completely autonomous in such matters as port dredging, ice breaking, air traffic control, and facilities for heavy maintenance of rail and aviation equipment, where it is more economic to have common facilities and equipment. Adequate access can be assured through joint ownership arrangements.

---

11.   Pavement management systems use computerized data, models (for example, of road inventories, deterioration relationships, traffic), and costs of alternatives to identify optimum design and maintenance standards for each road section and optimum allocation of funds between different road sections, thereby allowing the decisionmaker to consider the implications of alternative budgets and allocations.

Investment Program and Priorities

Spare parts and other supplies are urgently needed to restore operations in urban public transport, road maintenance, trucking, railways, aviation and ports. In some cases, Latvia has the capability to make the spare parts itself (and indeed, Latvia is the sole supplier to other former Soviet republics), but it lacks the materials to make them. The lack of spare parts meant, for example, that in early 1992 Riga was able to operate only 160 of its 320 buses. External agencies could help by providing hard currency so that existing equipment can be used. Eventually, Latvia will want to upgrade to more modern and efficient equipment, but existing fleets must be operated for some time to come. In the case of trucking, the practical approach would be to continue to operate the more robust Soviet vehicles, despite their lower fuel efficiency and poorer payload/gross weight ratios, until the roads have been improved.

Donations of equipment from Western sources may be a useful means of upgrading technology, but it could create undue diversity in equipment fleets, greatly complicating the future management of inventory and maintenance. To minimize this diversity and give the new private sector enterprises an opportunity to participate, a clearing house could be established, preferably at the all-Baltic level, where agencies and enterprises could bid on equipment, thereby maximizing opportunities for standardization.

As concerns infrastructure, the most pressing requirements are to decrease the backlog of road maintenance and unbalanced development of the road network, and to modernize and renovate the Riga airport. The major public roads are basically sound, but the structural integrity of the rest of the system is suspect. Almost half of the total public road length is subject to vehicle weight restrictions during the spring thaw. The National Roads Administration should analyze the economic impact of these restrictions to determine whether investments should be made to strengthen some of these roads. At the same time, a maintenance backlog is building up for roads and bridges as a result of reduced maintenance budgets over the past several years.[12] It would be in the interests of road users to pay more in order to finance a justifiable increase in road expenditure. The government is considering earmarking the proceeds of transport turnover and fuel taxes for roads. Any such earmarking should be for maintenance only, and new construction projects should compete with other projects for government funds on the basis of comparative benefit-cost analyses.[13] Regarding the Via Baltica, no major investments need to be made until there has been a thorough review of the whole route, and even then, staged improvements are likely to be the appropriate approach, rather than significant lengths of motorway.[14]

At the Riga airport, the terminal building needs to be renovated to accommodate the increasing flows of international passengers. The runway lighting needs to be replaced, local navigation aids installed, and an adequate hangar constructed for aircraft servicing and maintenance. In the medium

---

12. The volume of all road repair work declined from 2,230 km in 1989 to 950 km in 1991. One-quarter of the bridges are more than thirty years old, which is the age when major repairs are usually needed. Moreover, in the next eight years this backlog will grow rapidly to include nearly two thirds of the bridges.

13. For more on this, see the World Bank (1991, pp.31-32).

14. See, for example, World Bank (1991, pp. 38-39).

term, air traffic control equipment throughout the country may need to be replaced. This is currently being assessed by Swedavia.

In the medium term, Latvian Railways will need equipment for track maintenance and renewal, and a Riga bypass should be studied to avoid routing hazardous cargo through passenger stations. At Riga and Ventspils ports, operations would be improved by better rail yard layouts (the responsibility of the port authorities). Substantial upgrading of the line from Liepaja would be required if that port is to be reactivated for civilian use.

In overall terms, the two existing ports of Riga and Ventspils provide adequate capacity for the moment; both are handling substantially less cargo than in the past. Thus, there appears little immediate need to convert the military port of Liepaja back to commercial use.[15] For the medium term, the authorities should study the economics of using Liepaja for new traffic resulting from possible future developments in the pulp, paper, and cement industries. These issues should be addressed in the EC PHARE port master plan study, which should also assess the need to modernize the coal, grain, and container operations and the best site for any improved facilities. It should be noted, however, that there is considerable scope for improving the operational efficiency of the existing container terminal at Riga with better management and relatively modest investments in equipment, and by increasing the bearing capacity of the yard to allow higher stacking. If it is decided to retain that terminal, improved rail and road access would be needed, but again the expenditures required are relatively modest.

Recommendations

Short-Term Measures

In the immediate future, the government should:

- Undertake a review of public expenditure in the sector and develop a plan for focusing available funds on priority projects. This should include a review of ongoing projects to assess whether they should be completed, modified, or abandoned, and a study of the Via Baltica route to determine an appropriate program of phased improvements.

- Monitor closely the financial results of newly established aviation, maritime, and rail enterprises, and make cost and revenue adjustments to prevent them from incurring deficits and becoming a burden on the public budget.

- Pursue more aggressively the commercialization and privatization of state transport enterprises.

- Obtain independent advice to develop a corporate strategy for Latvian Airlines and for the management of its fleet.

- Revise the maritime code and introduce appropriate mortgage and guarantee mechanisms throughout the sector.

---

15.   Liepaja was Latvia's principal commercial port in the 1920s and 1930s.

- Increase taxes on road users to generate funds for road maintenance and development.

- Review the economics of improving the strength of the lower national road network to reduce the need for weight restrictions during the spring thaw.

- Begin developing local government capacity to assume responsibility for much of the road network not covered by the National Roads Administration.

- Pursue cooperation with other countries, especially the other Baltic countries, on such matters as material supplies for construction, spare parts manufacture, equipment maintenance, transit services, air traffic control, and dredging.

Medium-term Measures

In the medium term the authorities should:

- Conclude a performance contract and corporate plan for Latvian Railways.

- Introduce improved decisionmaking tools for budgeting throughout the sector.

- Develop and implement a strategy for promoting multimodal transport, which should include a ports master plan on a total systems basis, the improvement of rail services, and the adoption of international codes and conventions governing trade documentation, customs procedures, and financial services.

- Introduce periodic road maintenance by competitive contracts.

- Promote private investment in roadside services (service stations, restaurants, motels) along major routes.

CHAPTER 9

Telecommunications

Latvia's telecommunications network is obsolete, provides only a moderate quality of service, requires labor-intensive maintenance, and uses spare parts that are scarce and can only be purchased in Eastern Europe and former Soviet republics for hard currency. In the past year and a half, the Latvian government has begun to commercialize, modernize, and expand the telecommunications infrastructure and has sought foreign assistance to help its efforts.

The main reform issues confronting the government and Lattelecom management in the short and medium term are the following:

- Establishing institutional structures and functions that enable the Ministry of Transport and Communications to manage the sector effectively;
- Establishing a sound regulatory framework that includes economically and financially viable tariffs;
- Commercializing the sector;
- Restructuring Lattelecom along more commercially-oriented lines;
- Reviewing the development and modernization plan;
- Improving the existing network and developing a new digital telecommunications network;
- Re-establishing supply ties with the East for critical spare parts.

Reliable and good quality telecommunications services are essential for successful economic development, particularly in information technology, transport, tourism, services, and export-oriented industries. Telecommunication services provide timely and cost-effective voice and data communication, reduce transportation costs, and create new economic opportunities. They can also be a large source of revenue for the government and provide social benefits, particularly to pensioners and the handicapped. The European Commission estimates that the telecommunications industry will represent 7 percent of EC GDP by 2000, compared with 2 percent in 1990. Information management and processing represents 20 to 25 percent of GDP in the industrialized countries. Telecommunications, as a carrier of that information, is becoming a major ingredient in the overall viability of a country's economy. The average economic and financial returns on World Bank telecommunications projects in the 1980s were 30 percent and 20 percent, respectively.

Structure

Lattelecom is responsible for providing local, long distance, and international telephone, data transfer, telex, and telegraph services to business and residential subscribers in Latvia. It is accountable for the day-to-day operations of the existing network and facilities and for planning and implementing future developments. It is also responsible for radio and television broadcasting services.

Organizational Structure

A board of directors, approved by the government, is responsible for Lattelecom's performance. The board's primary roles are to assist in defining the company's strategy, review annual financial and planning proposals, and approve extraordinary activities. A director general, selected by the board is responsible for all day-to-day activities. The number of staff reporting to the director general is relatively high. The directors of engineering, economy and finance, marketing and administration, and personnel and training, as well as the principal bookkeeper and the head of the Foreign Economic Relations Department, report directly to the director general, as do the heads of thirty-five regional exchanges.

The organizational structure and culture of Lattelecom must be suitable for a commercially-oriented firm. To establish this orientation, Lattelecom should review activities carried out by the marketing, economy and finance, and personnel and training groups to ensure that appropriate functions are performed. In addition, corporate planning and customer service functions should be established.

Planning

Historically, most planning directives were set up by Moscow, and some activities were conducted by the Economics and Finance Department. As an independent firm in a competitive market, Lattelecom must establish a corporate planning function to develop short- (one-year) and long-term (five-year) strategic plans for the corporation.

Personnel and Training

The personnel and training group works with management to determine the corporate human resource strategy and to oversee management development, career development, and compensation. Recruitment is typically done from within. A new human resource policy is needed as well as procedures that reflect the new organizational goals and strategy.

From an efficiency standpoint, Lattelecom's staff ratio per 1,000 direct exchange lines is 12, in the middle range of all countries. Tanzania, for instance, has 76 employees per 1,000 direct exchange lines, while most Western European and U.S. firms have a ratio between 15 and 10. The ratio in Lattelecom is due in part to the older analog network, which requires higher levels of maintenance than modern digital networks. Modernizing the exchanges and expanding network capacity while keeping staffing levels constant, and introducing new management techniques to enhance productivity would improve the overall efficiency of the organization.

Lattelecom employs 7,200 people. Engineers and technical specialists account for 2,400 to 2,700 positions, managers for 120, and economists for 100. The remaining staff are technicians, operators, and clerical staff. The staff is relatively well educated: more than 55 percent of the technical and administrative staff have university degrees, and virtually all the economic staff have university degrees or specialized training. However, the majority have little or no education in international business concepts, and although most of the high-level technical staff have engineering degrees from well-respected universities, they have had little exposure to the more advanced telecommunication concepts used internationally.

To move effectively to a free market economy, a major staff retraining program will be required. The quality of the retraining effort will be a major determinant of the success of the commercialization effort. The training group has developed initial plans for retraining, which should be reviewed to ensure that they mesh with other organizational changes.

Financial and Accounting Systems

Financial statements are prepared annually on a calendar year basis according to standards developed by the former communist regime. As part of its shift to a market orientation, Lattelecom is beginning to prepare its financial statements according to international accounting practices. Computer systems may need to be modified to support the new accounting practices and should be a priority.

Audits are done by the Ministry of Finance for tax and budget purposes. The Department of Telecommunications will audit financial statements. Audits should ensure that these statements reflect Lattelecom's financial position, results from operations, and cash flows in an accurate, consistent, and reasonable manner and should be done by an auditor familiar with international accounting practices.

Computerized bills are sent monthly to customers for telephone services. Collections rates average 95 to 100 percent. Late fees and disconnection policies are rigid so that the vast majority of subscribers pay on time.

Marketing and the Customer Profile

In a commercially-driven firm, marketing and sales are essential functions. They help a firm identify what markets to operate in, who the customers are, what products it should provide, and how best to provide them. Establishing effective marketing and sales groups and developing a marketing strategy should be a priority for Lattelecom.

Lattelecom provides service to 700,000 telephone subscribers, of which 51 percent are in Riga. Government or business clients represent 16 percent of subscribers, and they have no waiting list. The official unmet demand for residential clients is 190,000 (154,000 are urban). Some of these subscribers have been on the waiting list for more than twenty years. Technical limitations often prevent them from obtaining service. The unofficial unmet demand (people who would like service, but are not on a waiting list) may be as much as twice the number on the official waiting list. Price elasticity for services is strong. A few subscribers, particularly residential subscribers, have discontinued telephone service as the cost has risen.

Facilities

Lattelecom has installed capacity of approximately 694,000 telephone lines, of which 624,000 lines are used to provide services to subscribers. In other words, average capacity utilization is 90 percent. In urban areas utilization reaches 95 percent, which is high, and in rural areas utilization is about 67 percent. The world average is between 75 and 85 percent.

Of Lattelecom's exchanges, 31 percent are step-by-step, 60 percent are cross-bar, and 8 percent are electronic. Of the step-by-step exchanges, 20 percent are forty years old; and of the cross-bar exchanges 10 percent are fifteen to twenty years old. These exchanges should clearly be replaced. The remaining exchanges are adequate, but spare parts are needed. The semi-electronic exchanges are no longer produced so it is impossible to get spare parts.

Metal symmetrical cable is widely used in the local and long distance network. In the 1970s plastic began to be used in the local network. Two fiber optic cables were recently installed in Jurmula and one from Riga to Sigulda.

As of early 1992, the long distance network consisted of one automatic long distance exchange in Riga that connected to the Russian long distance network and the international gateway in Moscow. It is a cross-bar exchange. Analog transmission systems are used, although 2 to 8 percent of the transmission channels are digital. International calls go through thirteen channels in Moscow. The number of calls in 1990 was 193,000, with an average duration of nine minutes.

The Riga public network consists of seven nodes connected to thirty-four exchanges and a PABX with a capacity of 54,300 subscribers. Of these exchanges, 50 percent are cross-bar and the remainder step-by-step. Technical problems exist within the network that are difficult to overcome. Thus, modernization of the network is a priority.

Recent Performance

Technical and Operational Performance

Plans by Moscow to develop the network resulted in an analog network that has gradually become obsolete and provides only basic telephone services. Certain materials for the system are only available from Eastern European and former Soviet republics and are difficult to obtain, and frequently the quality of these materials is poor. As a consequence, the quality of service provided by the network is quite low, with approximately 40 faults per 1,000 direct exchange lines per year (the U.S. average is less than 1). Congestion on the line--occurrence is 20 percent on the long distance network--and old equipment cause most of the faults. From 6 to 10 percent of the connected lines do not work.

The telecommunications infrastructure in Latvia provides telephone services to 624,000 subscribers or 23 out of every 100 people in the country. This density is comparable to the other Baltic states and is in the middle range of densities compared to other countries (Table 9-1). One development report estimated that 80 percent of the demand for trunk calls and 50 percent of international traffic demand is satisfied. Virtually all the urban subscribers are connected to an automatic exchange for local calls, and 94 percent of national and regional (former Soviet republics) calls are automatic. In rural areas, however, only 30 percent of subscribers have automatic dialing for local calls. All urban and rural international traffic is manual.

Table 9-1. International Comparison of Telephone Density (number of subscribers per 100 people)

Country	Density
Denmark	54.0
Estonia	22.0
Lithuania	28.0
Latvia	23.0
Portugal	17.0
Romania	10.0
Russia	14.0
Poland	8.0
China	0.8
India	0.5
Indonesia	0.5
Tanzania	0.2

Currently, the only means of making international telephone calls are an NMT 450 mobile system with limited coverage and thirteen incoming and outgoing channels from Moscow. Latvia receives 60 percent of the revenue from outgoing calls and none of the incoming revenue for traffic through Moscow.

Financial Performance

Indicators of Lattelecom's financial performance (Table 9-2) should be treated with caution given the distortions in input and output price structures and the differences in accounting principles and practices compared with international systems. Nevertheless, the available data highlight past performance trends. Figures are shown in current ruble values.

Table 9-2. Financial Performance Summary, Lattelcom, 1987-92
(RUR Million)

Costs and Profits	1987	1988	1989	1990	1991	1992 [a]
Total Revenue	124.5	135.1	141.7	149.4	317.8	384.5
Total Operating Costs	67.9	67.0	70.9	76.8	217.7	271.5
Operating Profit	56.6	68.1	70.8	72.6	100.1	113.2
Taxes	42.6	48.6	49.6	51.4	34.7	45.2
Net Profit (Loss) after Tax	14.0	19.5	21.2	21.2	65.4	68.0
Depreciation	5.8	12.5	13.4	14.3	15.7	40.2
Cash Generated	19.8	32.0	34.6	35.5	82.1	N.A.
Social Tax (part of operating costs)			2.6	4.0	40.7	38.3

a. Estimated.
N.A. = Not available.
Source: Latvian authorities.

The old Ministry of Posts and Telecommunications was reasonably profitable on a ruble basis. In current ruble terms, the operating profit in 1991 rose 38 percent from the previous year. In real terms, however, the operating profit actually fell by 50 percent. Cash generated increased by 80 percent between 1987 and 1990 and 130 percent in 1991. This rate, however, is still well below the 1991 inflation rate. In dollar terms, the cash generated in 1991 could support an investment program of USD 4 million. If the currency appreciates, it could support an investment program of USD 8 to 14 million, well below the USD 65 million required to fund the proposed investment program.

Another problem confronting Lattelecom in funding an investment program is the level of taxes it pays to the government. In 1990 the effective tax rate as a percentage of operating profits was 70 percent (71 percent if wage taxes are included). Although Lattelecom had a healthy operating profit, it had to obtain a subsidy from the government to finance bare-bones capital investments for the year. In response, in 1991 the government lowered its effective tax rate to 35 percent of operating profit. If wage taxes are taken into account, however, the tax rate was 54 percent. Clearly, tariffs will need to be raised substantially in real terms, particularly for international traffic, to support a moderate expansion program funded in hard currency. In addition, Lattelecom's investment program will need to be scaled back and a resource mobilization program established.

Operating revenues, which rose 112 percent in 1991, did not keep pace with inflation. Operating expenses as a percentage of total revenue increased from 52 percent in 1990 to 68 percent in 1991. Although it could be inferred that Lattelecom's efficiency worsened during the year, in real terms operating expenses declined only slightly, indicating an efficiency gain. Net income for 1991 in real terms was about the same as for 1990 due to a decline in the tax rate.

Institutional and Policymaking Framework

In 1991, the Ministry of Posts and Telecommunications was dissolved and responsibility for telecommunications was transferred to a new Ministry of Transport and Communications. This ministry has broad responsibilities for telephone, telex, data, radio, and broadcasting equipment and services in the country. As part of the restructuring, the ministry established a Communications Department to carry out regulatory functions and created Lattelecom, a legally separate enterprise.

As part of the Soviet network, all policy and regulatory functions for Latvian telecommunications were centrally managed by Moscow. Since independence, Latvia has begun to establish its own policy and regulatory functions. The minister of transport and communications is responsible for overall management of the telecommunications sector. A special advisor for telecommunications appraises the minister of matters related to the sector and coordinates with the Communications Department, Lattelecom, and other branches of the government. Specific functions to be carried out by the ministry have not yet been defined.

The Communications Department was established within the Ministry of Transport and Communications to carry out regulatory functions. Such functions include determining competitive practices, reviewing proposals for tariff changes, drafting telecommunications legislation for the government, recommending telecommunications laws (for example, on competition), establishing technical standards, and issuing licenses. The first deputy director for telecommunications, radio, and television and deputy directors for posts and economic and foreign relations report to the director of the Communications Department; making a total of five staff reporting to the director.

Lattelecom is the principal telecommunications firm operating within the country, and is wholly state owned. However, competition in telecommunications services is legal and encouraged by the government. Lattelecom is currently negotiating with Swedish Telecom to establish a joint venture that would take over most or all of its functions. The precise details of the venture have yet to be determined, but the government would probably retain a controlling interest. In addition, a separate joint venture has been established between the Latvian government (51.0 percent ownership), Swedish Telecom (24.5 percent), and Finnish Telecom (24.5 percent) to provide mobile telephone services. Other firms are expected to enter the market, particularly in value added services.

Sectoral Policies and Issues

Ministerial Functions

One of the first activities to be done is to identify clear objectives for the sector, develop a strategic plan to fulfill these objectives, map out priorities, and create an appropriate environment to achieve them. The objectives and the regulatory framework are the government's primary tools to influence the sector's development for the next thirty years. It is essential that they be carefully defined to ensure that they promote and protect the government's short- and long-term interests. The ministry would benefit from assistance from international experts in this area.

Regulatory Framework

Ideally, a regulatory body would promote an environment conducive to foreign investors, that is, with appropriate laws on property ownership, repatriation of profits, tariff setting policies, nationalization, and related matters. If this kind of environment is not established, foreign entities (joint venture partners, investment partners, development and commercial banks) are unlikely to invest in the sector. This body should also help guide the activities of the independent telecommunications firm(s) through such mechanisms as licensing, frequency allocation, tariff and taxation policy, and laws on competition. Licensing policy now appears to be ad hoc and frequency allocation is established by Moscow, although a team is in the process of dividing frequencies among the former Soviet republics. International standards for cables, switches, and radios should be established to be compatible with international equipment.

To establish the appropriate regulatory environment effectively, the Communications Department should have the authority to approve sectoral policies, for example, tariff setting, licensing, and frequency allocation. The department should make recommendations to other governmental agencies on such national issues as rules for repatriation of profits or taxation policy. To carry out these activities successfully, the Communications Department will need to do detailed economic, financial, and policy analyses that may not have been required under the previous system. Lattelecom, as an operating entity with experience in the day-to-day implications of such policies, should be encouraged to make recommendations to the Communications Department. The staff in the Communications Department may also need to be expanded and may require additional training.

Telecommunications regulations create a framework within which firms can operate in a market economy. However, Latvia has few telecommunications regulations. The entire regulatory structure should be reviewed with particular emphasis on the following areas:

- Tariff policy, including levels and currency;
- Telecommunication laws, for example, clarifying current competition laws;
- Licensing for basic and value added services;
- Technical standards and membership in international standards groups);
- Frequency allocation.

Since many of these functions are new to the Communications Department, it should retain an independent international consultant for assistance. The consultant could also advise on organizational, staffing, and training changes that may be required.

Commercialization of the Sector

Lattelecom was established as an autonomous entity operated with a commercial perspective, that is, with an efficient, high-quality, low-cost, customer-driven orientation on a sound financial basis. Eventually, Lattelecom should be able to compete with other firms in the market. Therefore, a commercial perspective is critical to Lattelecom's success. Lattelecom will probably require international assistance in this effort either from a joint venture partner, an investment partner, a development bank, or a consulting firm. Securing this assistance should be an important component of an investment agreement.

Lattelecom's efforts to solicit alternative investment proposals appear more rigorous than those of other Eastern European and FSU countries. However, Lattelecom must work with the Communications Department and the ministry to establish selection criteria. These groups should be kept well informed of the process, given that the partner is subject to approval by the government.

A joint venture partner would typically be interested in investing in Latvia in exchange for such things as a percentage of the physical assets of Lattelecom, access to a franchise in an untapped market, access to a well-educated and diligent work force, Lattelecom's knowledge of the customer profile, and the company's experience with operating in Latvia's political and economic environment. In exchange, Lattelecom should be looking for a substantial financial investment, improved access to suppliers, knowledge of how to negotiate a lower price for equipment, access to people with experience in market-oriented management and training techniques, advanced technical expertise, experience operating internationally and access to new markets, and the backing of a well-respected, low-risk firm that would help Lattelecom obtain less expensive funding in the international capital markets. An investment partner, usually with a shorter term perspective on financial assistance, would most likely seek a return on investment commensurate with the level of investment risk. This partner may also be willing to provide training and technical assistance to Lattelecom, depending upon the terms of the agreement.

In choosing a partner, Lattelecom should ensure that the arrangement will achieve its objectives. An impartial lawyer and a financial analyst with international experience in telecommunications partnerships should advise Lattelecom when an agreement is being worked out. An international lawyer could offer advice on the reasonableness of the proposed terms and on appropriate legal terminology. Valuation of the current and future earning potential of a partnership will largely determine the amount the government and Lattelecom would receive from a foreign partner. A financial analyst could provide a second opinion on the methods and assumptions used in a valuation exercise. Such experts are available internationally, either through a consulting firm or on a freelance basis.

Tariff Policy and Procedures

Inflation in Latvia has spiraled since independence, but increases in tariffs have not kept pace with inflation.[1] Consequently, Lattelecom's financial position worsened as expenses rose faster than revenues. As a result, Lattelecom had less available cash than expected and could not fund the capital investments planned for the existing network. Lattelecom was forced to request tax rebates from the government to finance these activities.

The Communications Department and Lattelecom recognize that the tariff levels do not reflect the true economic cost of the service. Tariffs will need to rise substantially simply to maintain

---

1.   During 1991, monthly rental tariffs for business subscribers more than doubled (from RUR 22.5 to RUR 60.0). Installation charges increased by fivefold (from RUR 400 to RUR 2,000). Business subscribers, however, account for only 25 percent of total subscribers in Latvia. Monthly rental fees for residential subscribers doubled (from RUR 7.5 to RUR 15.0) and installation charges tripled (from RUR 150 to RUR 500). The average rate of inflation from December 1990 to December 1991 was 263 percent.

the existing network. In the past, no one was given the responsibility for establishing tariff levels. Although this responsibility was recently handed over to Lattelecom and the Communications Department, precise roles and accountability are unclear. Consequently, no coherent tariff policy exists that takes into account the true economic cost of providing a service, the impact of inflation and devaluation, and factors to encourage efficiency. For example, levels of international tariffs are set arbitrarily at levels somewhat higher than those Moscow charges Lattelecom.

A study of the tariff structure would help determine the optimal levels to achieve the objectives for the sector. In conjunction with a tariff study, a thorough demand analysis should be done to identify market segments to target according to type of customer (business, residential, or government), calling patterns, geographical location, financial capacity, and so on. An 80/20 analysis of high-revenue-generating customers should be included in this study.[2]

The role of the Communications Department and Lattelecom in tariff setting should be specifically defined. Ideally, Lattelecom would have the authority to raise tariffs automatically to cover domestic inflation and devaluation on a monthly or quarterly basis. Real increases in tariffs, however, may need the approval of the Communications Department and the ministry.

Investment Program and Priorities

The ministry's role and the functions needed to manage the sector effectively should be carefully studied. Particular attention should be given to strategic and policymaking activities and to the organization and staffing of these functions. The ministry should seek external assistance from persons experienced in these areas to work on the study.

The Latvian government has made a commitment to expanding and modernizing the telecommunications services provided to business and residential subscribers. To facilitate this, it has begun to reorganize the sector and taken initial steps to establish a regulatory framework. A comprehensive framework to regulate competition and commercialize the sector has yet to be established, however.

A study of regulatory issues in the sector should be carried out and should include an assessment of the following:

- Consultative services for developing and assisting in the implementation of an appropriate regulatory framework for the sector, including tariff and demand analysis, rules for competition, standards, and licensing;

- Functions, organization, and staffing of a regulatory group;

- Implementation of management improvements to enable commercialization of the sector and Lattelecom.

---

2.   Typically, 80 percent of a firms' revenues come from 20 percent of its customers. In an 80/20 analysis, the customer base is classified by the amount of revenue it generates so that the top 20 percent of clients can be targeted for special services. This type of analysis is also used to help classify customers into market segments.

During its transition to a commercial enterprise, Lattelecom should seek technical assistance to assist in reviewing the existing structure, identifying an optimal structure and culture for a market-oriented firm, and implementing changes accordingly. New or expanded departments or functions might include corporate planning, marketing, sales, customer service, and financial planning and control. Lattelecom should obtain technical assistance from independent international consultants experienced in these areas to assist in the reorganization process, particularly in developing the strategic plan.

International financial and accounting standards and practices will need to be introduced as part of the commercialization effort, and supporting financial and accounting systems will need to be modified. Effective implementation of these systems will be critical to transforming Lattelecom to a profit-oriented firm and should be given priority in an investment plan. Consulting expertise should be obtained as required.

A new human resource policy and strategy will need to be established to support the commercialization effort. Lattelecom should seek international assistance in developing this plan. Most Lattelecom staff have had little or no exposure to international business concepts or to the latest technical advances. Successful application of such knowledge and skills will be essential to compete effectively with other providers of domestic and international telecommunications services. If not available from other sources, financial assistance to improve managerial, financial, and accounting skills and technical retraining should be sought from multilateral donors.

Under Latvia's plans for modernization and development of the sector Lattelecom will be transformed to a joint stock company with foreign partners. An independent council for tariffs will be established and the telecommunications functions of the Ministry of Transport and Communications will be more clearly defined. Lattelecom's short-term (two-year) development plan includes installation of the following:

- A new digital transit exchange in Riga with a capacity of 4,500 trunk lines;

- New digital local exchange equipment in Riga with capacity to connect 50,000 subscriber lines including local cables if needed;

- A fiber optic submarine cable across the Baltic sea to Sweden, plus a fiber optic cable from Ventspils to Riga for high-quality international traffic;

- The Latvian part of a fiber optic cable between Riga and Tallinn as part of the Baltic fiber optic concept;

- The installation of approximately 600 kilometers of fiber optic cables in the national trunk network from Riga to Cesis, Dougavpils, and Liepaja;

- The provision of equipment and tools required in connection with the development of support systems.

The long-term development plan includes:

- Creating a fully digitalized network by the year 2012;

- Eliminating the current high number of waiting subscribers to a reasonable level before the end of the year 2000.

The estimated cost for the two-year plan would be USD 110 million, and approximately USD 65 million would be required each year thereafter. Lattelecom should review its development plan in light of the technical, financial, and managerial capabilities and priorities available internally and externally.

A likely priority in a development plan will be to begin to introduce digital telephone services to a small group of customers who are able to pay the true economic cost of the service, preferably in hard currency. The revenue generated from a new digital line will need to cover the total costs of the service. The annual revenue on a per line basis should therefore equal operating costs plus a percentage of the initial investment (with a five- to fifteen-year payback period) plus taxes, financing costs, and a profit margin. As a rough estimate, assuming an optimal installation cost per line is USD 1,200, operating costs are USD 10 per line, and the payback period is ten years, then the average subscriber to the digital exchange would pay USD 120 per year. On average, in 1991 a subscriber spent less than USD 4 per year. According to financial estimates, the average subscriber will spend less than USD 10 in 1992. Thus, it appears likely that in the near future only a small portion of the population will be able to afford the true economic cost of a telephone connected to a new digital exchange.

A possible development strategy for Lattelecom, therefore, would be to supply digital telephones initially to the high revenue generating subscribers. In exchange for high quality service and automatic local, national, and international access, these customers would pay a fee sufficient to pay for the true cost of the line and would provide funds for future investment. Analog lines no longer used by these subscribers would be made available to other business or residential subscribers. In addition, the quality of service to analog subscribers could be improved. Tariff charges for the analog lines would be gradually raised to cover the operating costs of the lines at world market prices. Digital services would be expanded as necessitated by demand.

As Lattelecom and the government are well aware, re-establishing supply ties with traditional suppliers, often monopoly producers, for spare parts that are vital to operation of the analog network is essential. It is recognized, however, that the situation in the FSU is fluid, and that without hard currency it is extremely difficult to obtain reliable supply agreements. If hard currency cannot be secured from other sources, the possibility of a critical imports loan that would allow procurement in the FSU should be sought.

In the event that the Latvian government is interested in obtaining multilateral financial assistance, the World Bank could provide funds to help revitalize the telecommunications sector.

Recommendations

Short-Term Measures

In the immediate future, the following measures should be taken.

- The Latvian government should clearly identify and prioritize its objectives for the telecommunications sector.

- The government needs to develop a strategic plan and an organizational design with assistance from independent international experts.

- The government ought to review its commercialization and privatization policies, specifically, the implications of current laws on competition and their impact on Lattelecom.

- The government must begin a regulatory review process that would look, in particular, at tariff and demand policy, legislative and contractual issues, technical standards, and taxation policy. A consultant with international experience in establishing telecommunications regulatory policy should assist in this process.

- Lattelecom and the government must work in cooperation to re-establish supply ties with the East and to investigate the possibility of obtaining a critical imports loan that would allow purchases from the former Soviet republics.

- Lattelecom should secure legal and advisory services from international experts when negotiating cooperative or joint venture arrangements.

- Lattelecom needs to review its development plan in light of the technical, financial, and managerial capabilities available internally and externally and its priorities.

Medium-Term Measures

In the medium term:

- The government should obtain consulting assistance to study tariffs to determine the optimal levels to achieve the objectives for the sector. The consultant should have international experience in setting tariff rates and tariff policy.

- The government, in conjunction with the tariff study, should obtain a consultant to perform a thorough, but realistic, demand analysis.

- The government needs to clarify its own role and that of Lattelecom in setting tariff rates, and tariff regulations should be expanded to cover all competitors.

- Lattelecom must develop a detailed reorganization plan. This should include identifying an optimal structure; studying its existing structure, culture, and capabilities; and designing a strategic plan and a detailed action plan on how to achieve the strategy.

- Lattelecom needs to identify and implement a new human resource policy in line with organizational changes, including a new staffing policy, new management techniques, and employee incentive programs that will improve operational efficiency.

- Lattelecom should complete a detailed staff retraining plan that would ensure that its staff obtain international business and technical training.

- Lattelecom needs to introduce new financial and accounting policies and practices in accordance with internationally accepted standards and develop and implement a computerization plan for its financial and accounting systems.

CHAPTER 10

Housing and Municipal Services

The housing sector is important in Latvia currently, since housing is one of the sectors where price relations have been most distorted, and the building industry will be an important factor in the economy's overall performance and improvement. Since annexation by the former Soviet Union, most housing has been provided by the state and housing conditions rank below those in many other Eastern European countries. As Latvia implements market reforms, dramatic changes in the sector are expected, particularly as private households play the main role in housing provision, and this will lead to major shifts in the provision of housing services and the financing of housing. The government has recently begun the process of implementing market reforms for housing. While the direction of current housing policy is correct, the pace of the reform program is not moving quickly enough. Assistance is recommended for speeding up the reform process and for studying and evaluating the impact of reforms in a number of areas.

The government has already decentralized urban services, for example, water, sewerage, rental housing, street lighting, refuse collection, and urban transport, for which municipalities are now responsible. These services are generally of adequate quality, although facilities were inadequately maintained and now require new investments. With responsibility for these services came the authority to set tariffs, which must be increased to ensure adequate maintenance, replacement, and new investment. Water supplies and sewerage treatment are priority areas for improvements.

Structure and Recent Performance

Housing

The housing stock in Latvia is characterized by a large state rental sector and a relatively small private sector, typical of centrally planned economies. A private rental sector is practically non-existent, and privately-owned houses are concentrated in the countryside. As shown in Table 10-1, among the Eastern European countries for which statistics are available, Latvia ranks highest in terms of size of the public rental sector. Table 10-2 shows the distribution of the housing stock among urban and rural areas.

Latvia ranks below many other Eastern European countries in terms of housing conditions, although it ranks higher than most of the former Soviet Union. Floor area is an important indicator: the average for Latvia was 17.6 square meters per person in 1991, while the average in Estonia was 21.6 square meters per person in 1990, and the average in the former Soviet Union was 15.5 square meters per person in 1990. Only in the private sector was the floor area considerably larger.

Table 10-1. International Comparison of Housing Stock by Tenure Form and Floor Area
(percent)

Country	Rental Sector, 1991			Owner		
	Private	Public	Other	Coops.	Occupied	Year
Albania	-	40.0	-	-	60.0	1989
Bulgaria	2.8	15.2	1.1	-	80.9	1985
Czechoslovakia	0.3	34.1	-	18.8	46.9	1988
Estonia	-	56.5	8.5	5.6	29.4	1991
Hungary	2.0	24.0	-	-	74.0	1987
Latvia	-	61.7	8.2	4.5	25.6	1989
Lithuania	-	56.4	6.3	11.1	26.3	1990
Poland	4.1	27.2	11.9	35.4	21.4	1987
Romania	-	33.0	-	-	67.0	1989
Yugoslavia	5.4	20.5	4.6	-	69.4	1984

- = not available.
Source: Latvian authorities.

The average floor space in urban areas is smaller than in rural areas. Even though the floor area per person has increased since 1965, floor area per person is still smaller than it was in 1939. This deviates from the experience of Western Europe, where housing losses due to World War II have long since been overcome. The Latvian level of floor area consumption is considered to be worse than in other countries at similar levels of development and incomes. Table 10-3 compares floor area per person in Latvia with that in a number of other countries.

With respect to the quality of housing-related services, Latvia is on a par with the other Baltic republics. The proportion of housing units receiving these services is as follows: piped water, 91.7 percent; sewerage services, 91.2 percent; baths, 74.5 percent; central heating, 74.4 percent; and hot water, 70.6 percent.

One indicator of the level of crowding is the number of individuals or households that live in communal dwellings or in hostels. The share of households living in hostels and communal dwellings ranges from 11 to 18 percent for the country as a whole. In Riga the share is up to 23 percent, depending on ethnic origin. These levels of crowding are considered to be high. Non-Latvian households (predominantly Russian-speaking) live in the worst conditions, with a high share of households living in hostels and the

Table 10-2: Housing Stock by Tenure Form and Location, 1991
(millions of square meters)

Area, Type	Total	Urban	Rural
Total Floor Area	51.5	32.6	18.8
Public Sector	38.3	27.5	10.7
of which Cooperatives	2.3	2.2	0.1
Privately-Owned	13.2	5.1	8.1
(as percentage of total)	(26%)	(16%)	(43%)

Source: Latvian Ministry of Architecture and Construction.

Table 10-3. International Comparison of Total Floor Area per Person
(square meters per person)

Country	Floor Area	Year
Bulgaria	25.3	1988
Czechoslovakia	30.9	1989
Estonia	21.6	1990
Hungary	31.9	1988
Latvia	19.9	1991
Lithuania	19.3	1991
Poland	21.1	1988
Federal Republic of Germany	44.9	1988
Yugoslavia	21.9	1987

Source: Latvian authorities.

highest share of households living in communal flats. The most striking feature is the high proportion of communal households in Riga, which range from 14 to 17 percent (Table 10-4).

Table 10-4. Tenure Form by Ethnic Group and Location, 1989
(percent)

Tenure Form	Latvia			Riga		
	Latvian Household	Mixed Latvian/ Other	Other	Latvian Household	Mixed Latvian/ Other	Other
Owned Single Family House	24.3	15.5	7.4	5.0	2.6	0.8
Flat in Single Family House	7.4	3.9	2.4	4.2	1.6	0.8
Separate Flat	56.9	70.0	72.6	69.2	77.7	75.6
Communal Flat	6.9	7.5	9.7	17.1	15.0	14.4
Hostel	4.5	3.1	7.9	4.5	3.1	8.4

Source: Krastins (1990).

Given that a large number of households live in shared or communal flats, it is not surprising that there is a large variation in space consumption across households. This is not only a result of differences in tenure forms, but also the result of a state-controlled allocation process. Table 10-5 shows the space distribution in terms of living space across tenure forms. The table measures living space per person excluding hallways, kitchens, and bathrooms, which is about 65 percent of total floor area per person as shown in Table 10-3.

Table 10-5. Average Living Space Area by Tenure Form, 1989
(percent)

Tenure Form	Living Space (square meters/person)					
	<5	5-8	9-12	13-16	>16	Total
Owned Single Family House	1.8	14.6	25.2	20.8	37.6	100.0
Flat in Single Family House	8.2	29.8	24.3	17.1	21.7	100.0
Separate Flat	3.7	30.2	35.6	19.0	11.5	100.0
Communal Flat	13.0	39.1	22.9	13.5	12.5	100.0
Hostel	23.5	55.8	14.8	2.1	3.8	100.0
Total	6.0	31.6	31.6	17.4	13.5	100.0

Source: Latvian Ministry of Architecture and Construction.

Table 10-5 shows that 6 percent of all households have less than five square meters of living space per person. Nearly 24 percent of households living in hostels and 13 percent of households living in communal flats also have less than five square meters of living space per person. By contrast, more than 37 percent of the households in owned houses have more than sixteen square meters per person. Thus, space consumption is unevenly spread, with a substantial share of households living in crowded conditions. The situation seems to be worse than in most countries in Eastern Europe, but is probably similar to that in the rest of the former Soviet Union.

The state-owned dwellings have been inadequately maintained because rents, which have remained the same since 1940, do not generate enough revenue. This lack of maintenance and renovation is apparent in towns of all sizes, but is particularly bad in Cesis. In 1989, maintenance expenditures were only RUR 21.6 million, while renovation expenditures were RUR 42.8 million. Together these expenditures equaled only about 8 percent of expenditures for new housing construction in 1989.

Housing production has decreased rapidly during the past several years, due partly to the slowdown in the economy and the limited availability of construction finance and building materials. In 1985, 20,000 dwelling units were constructed; in 1986, 21,000 units were produced; and in 1987, 23,000 units were produced. Decreases in production began in 1988 with only 18,400 units produced, in 1989 only 17,400 were produced, and 1990 saw only 13,100 units. The total production in 1991 was estimated to be no more than 10,000 units. During this period of decreasing production, housing costs have escalated in line with inflation. In 1980, one square meter cost approximately RUR 190 to produce. By 1989 the cost had increased to RUR 250. Thereafter, inflation pushed up building costs substantially. In December 1991, costs increased to RUR 1,800 to RUR 2,500 per square meter, and in January 1992, costs jumped to about RUR 5,500 to RUR 6,000 per square meter.

Municipal Services

Water Supply. Water supplies in most of Latvia come from groundwater sources. In Riga about 45 percent of water comes from surface water, including the River Daugava. Over the medium term plans call for substituting the surface water sources with groundwater. Riga has a shortage of chemicals for water purification, which is considered very serious. In order to improve the water purification process in Riga, a French company is planning to introduce ozone purification. Another problem in Riga is the drinking water distribution system. The capacity of many water pumping stations is insufficient. As a result top floor apartments, particularly in the center of Riga, are sometimes without water. Several projects were initiated to improve the water pressure, including constructing a new water tower and replacing equipment in existing pumping stations. However, due to the lack of funds, equipment, and technology these projects have not been completed.

Sewerage/Drainage. Latvian urban areas are well served with sewerage facilities: more than 90 percent of households are connected to piped sewerage systems. Separate systems for sewerage and drainage were introduced in the 1960s, but in some older sections of towns drainage systems are lacking, putting an additional burden on the sewage treatment plants, which have low capacity. Industrial pollutants are also present in the sewage system. Projects were begun to increase the capacity and efficiency of the Riga sewage treatment plant and to connect the entire sewerage system to the treatment plant, but again due to the current economic situation and the lack of funding it is not clear when these projects can be completed. Improving and installing sewage treatment plants in Latvian towns is a high priority. In order to replace the outdated Soviet standards, exchanging experiences with other countries is encouraged, particularly those surrounding the Baltic Sea.

Refuse Collection. The collection of refuse in Latvian towns is satisfactory. Typically, garbage is collected and transported to the city landfill site. Future problems with leakage into groundwater could result, which could seriously affect the water supply sources, especially in Riga, given that the landfill site is close to the Daugava River. A study should be undertaken to assess the extent of the problem and provide recommendations for future action.

Central Heating. About 75 percent of all Latvian households are connected to central heating systems. In Riga the coverage is more than 95 percent. A program for energy saving is to be undertaken, for example, to identify methods of thermal insulation and automatic heat control. According to a preliminary study, about 35 percent of heating consumption could be saved by such methods. Tariffs for central heating should be increased to levels that would fully cover costs and provide incentives for consumers to reduce their high levels of energy consumption. Other economic incentives such as investment tax credits could be provided to households to stimulate investments in energy saving devices.

Urban Transport Systems. Most Latvian towns are responsible for operating and maintaining their urban transport systems, primarily buses. The average age of the bus fleets is high, which will necessitate replacement of vehicles over the short and medium term. In Riga, the municipality is also responsible for operating the trams and trolley buses, which are in a similar condition as the buses. The municipality is considering improving the utilization of the existing railway lines by adding stations to the existing double track lines. In a second phase a new line might be added to connect the two parts of the town divided by the river. A company in Riga has the capability to produce cars for the railway lines, and an experimental wagon has already been produced.

Institutional and Policymaking Framework

The Ministry of Architecture and Construction is responsible for coordinating building activities, planning major construction projects, and setting housing and construction policies, including policies for building standards.

Management, maintenance, and construction of state housing have been carried out by state-owned housing management companies, which have now been transferred into municipal ownership along with the state-owned houses. The housing management companies are responsible for collecting rents and utility charges, but currently rents are estimated to cover only a small fraction of maintenance and management expenses due to the low rents and the poor collection performance resulting from the lack of sanctions for non-payment. Funding for state housing was provided from the state budget in the past, but is now being phased out.

In 1991, the government began the process of legally re-establishing local authorities: regions, municipalities, and districts. Some analysts question whether regional and district levels of government are needed and how revenues should be divided among the budgets of regions, municipalities, and districts. Due to the municipalities' uneven levels of development, the regions are expected to remain over the short term to help solve problems of a regional nature, for example, water supplies. However, regional and district levels of government are expected to disappear in the future.

Sectoral Policies, Issues, and Reform Measures

Housing

Policies. Since 1940 when the Soviet Union annexed Latvia, housing policies were based on the Soviet laws and were directed from Moscow. All land and houses larger than 220 square meters in the major towns and 130 square meters in rural areas were nationalized, placing most housing in government hands. Of the 11.7 million square meters of private dwelling space in 1939, only about 2.0 million square meters remained in private hands after nationalization. Since that period, public provision of rental housing has dominated the sector, although private individuals with the means and ability to obtain building materials were permitted to construct their own dwellings. Public rental housing consisted mostly of unattractive, high rise, prefabricated buildings containing standardized, small flats. The buildings often lacked adequate community facilities. Rents were fixed at the same unit price per square meter of living space, regardless of location and amenities, and were not permitted to increase since 1940, resulting in inadequate revenues for proper maintenance. Since few housing options existed, most households did not move, and the demand for housing services remained unsatisfied. In summary, these command-driven policies resulted in a public sector-dominated, rigid housing market that impeded household mobility.

The government has already taken a number of steps to move toward a market-based housing sector. Reforms under preparation would effectively eliminate the burden on the state budget for housing provision. Key elements of current thinking on Latvian housing policy include the following:

- Reducing public sector involvement in housing except for fulfilling the government's social welfare role and for establishing housing policies;

- Providing new housing through the private sector;

- Returning nationalized housing to the former owners or their legal successors with some exceptions, in which case compensation will be provided;

- Selling (privatizing) the government-owned rental housing stock to shift responsibility for maintenance into private hands;

- Shifting the responsibility for government-owned rental housing not sold from the state to municipalities;

- Increasing rents gradually to cover costs and introducing differentiated rent levels by location and building features as determined by municipalities, but within a government ceiling for the next seven years;

- Establishing more appropriate building standards and introducing energy-saving technologies.

Subsidies. Subsidies in the housing sector are very high. Most subsidies are not visible in state or municipal budgets, and take many forms: direct subsidies for maintaining housing and providing utility services, interest rate subsidies, and rent subsidies. A rough calculation indicates that in 1991 subsidies for maintenance could have been as much as RUR 96 million.[1] Subsidies for renovation, heating, water, sewerage, and electricity services are also substantial, but no information is available on which to base an accurate assessment. According to some sources, central heating is a prime target for subsidies; charges reportedly cover only 10 percent of costs. Reforms would reduce state subsidies when implemented.

The limited housing finance provided through state institutions was given at highly subsidized interest rates of 0.5 to 4.0 percent. Loans to private house builders were no more than

---

1.   The difference between actual maintenance costs, estimated to be RUR 2.60 per square meter, and rents of RUR 0.10 per square meter multiplied by 38.3 million square meters in the public and cooperative housing stock.

RUR 5,000 to RUR 20,000 with a loan maturity of five to twenty years. Commercial banks will be expected to provide the bulk of housing finance under a market-based housing system. As far as housing for the poor and vulnerable groups is concerned, municipalities are expected to provide it.

Some government subsidy may be justified in the short term to sustain investment in the sector, given the difficulty households may have in carrying the full cost of housing through mortgage loans. However, it is not advisable to continue subsidizing interest rates, particularly because this creates the need for subsidies over the life of the mortgage (ten to twenty years). One alternative is to provide a one-time, up-front, capital grant to home purchasers to reduce construction costs. These grants would have several advantages: they are transparent, explicit, controllable within fiscal constraints, easier to target to those in need, and easier to reduce. Another alternative is to use indexed loan schemes, whereby mortgage payments are set low initially, but increase in line with inflation, which would reduce subsidies over the life of the loan.

The municipality of Riga and other cities have started to buy out (subsidize), some families who are considering leaving state rental flats. The subsidy is approximately RUR 800 per square meter depending on the condition of the dwelling and the municipality. The subsidy is intended to give an incentive to those who will either build a house of their own or who might consider leaving the republic, for example, those who were part of the military. This military population is estimated to be about 300,000 persons, including family members, or 11 percent of the population. Many in this group reputedly occupy attractive dwellings. Freeing up these attractive highly subsidized rental flats and allocating them to those willing to pay more than RUR 800 per square meter would reduce the pressure for constructing expensive new housing. The net subsidy effect may be negligible.

Restitution. The restitution process for nationalized properties has been initiated under the Restitution Law and the Denationalization Law (October 30, 1991). The two laws have the same content, but cover different methods for nationalizing properties. The Restitution Law refers to property that was taken by force, while the Denationalization Law refers to nationalization carried out by legal means.

For legitimate claims, properties will be returned to the former owners or their legal successors free of charge. The deadline for claims is October 30, 1994. A significant number of claims has been filed, but due to the length of time of the process, it is too early to predict the outcome.

Limitations on legitimate claims include houses that no longer exist or that were legally purchased from the state after 1940. In these cases compensation will be given, although the compensation system has not yet been worked out. The need to compensate claimants for properties that cannot be returned has slowed down new construction and planning, since the cities are forced to save land for future compensation to claimants.

The restitution process has affected the housing market in a number of ways. Renovation activities have ceased because municipalities cannot make alterations to houses unless their legal status has been established. A number of vacant houses undergoing renovation are the subject of claims; however, the former owners in many cases find it too expensive to complete the renovation, and the buildings are too dilapidated to continue renting. In Riga about 400 to 500 houses are in this category, which has resulted in an underutilization of older houses.

Some local authorities are trying to speed up the process, since they do not have the resources to maintain a housing stock that in many cases is in a severe state of disrepair. The government should take initiatives to support local governments to speed up the restitution process. Revising the two restitution laws to reduce the three-year claim period to a six-month period is recommended.

Rent Reform. Steps toward rent reform have already been taken in Latvia. In November 1991, municipalities became responsible for setting rents for properties under their jurisdiction under a government ceiling that would be in effect for seven years. The first increase would permit rents to increase from RUR 0.10 per square meter of living space to an average of RUR 0.40 per square meter of total space. Current proposals call for rents to be raised in three steps to cover the full costs of management, maintenance, and capital repairs by the end of 1993. After seven years, rents would be set at a market level for private rental property, but would remain at a cost-covering level in the public sector.

The government is in the process of introducing market rents on office space and living areas in prime locations, particularly in the center of Riga. Present plans are to charge USD 200 per square meter for office space. Rents will also be differentiated by location and by building features and amenities. An appropriate rent structure is vital to avoid future imbalances in the housing market.

To stimulate future privatization of government-owned rental apartments, it is particularly important that the remaining steps for rent reform take place as soon as possible, so that the rental apartments will be more attractive for purchase. Given the present situation where most household income goes to buy food, the mission supports a more gradual increase in rents if the circumstances should warrant it.

As it is expected that most of the reclaimed multi-family houses will remain as rental units, the restitution process will create a private rental sector in Latvia. A number of households, however, will have to find alternative accommodation. Tenant security applies strictly to the seven-year period, after which landlords will be free to evict tenants. The cities are expected to assist those tenants that cannot afford alternative accommodation.

As rental apartments are privatized, high-rise apartments buildings will contain a mixture of private and government-owned flats. During this period municipalities will be required to maintain common areas in buildings. However, no clear guidelines have been developed yet for the maintenance of common areas. In Lithuania, cities are proposing a temporary rent or charge on private flats in buildings of mixed ownership to cover the costs of management and maintenance until the buildings are completely privately owned. Latvian cities might consider introducing a similar charge.

Privatization of Publicly Owned Housing. After restitution, the government plans to sell off the majority of the remaining stock of state rental properties (approximately 38.3 million square meters). Only 10 percent of the stock is expected to remain in public hands. The privatization process has already been initiated for cooperative stock, which consists of 2.3 million square meters of floor area. According to the 1991 law on privatizing cooperative housing, cooperative tenants are given the right to purchase their flat by taking over responsibility for their remaining portion of the cooperative's loans. The offer is attractive: older cooperatives were funded by a loan with a 0.5 percent rate of interest.

For the majority of housing remaining in the state rental sector, a privatization law has not yet been enacted, but the government is expected to introduce a combined voucher/cash system similar to the model used in Lithuania. Current proposals would link the distribution of vouchers to the number of years the prospective buyer has worked in Latvia. A voucher system would have a profound effect on income distribution. Eligible households are expected to buy their flats at a low nominal price (as in Lithuania) as compared with the free market value of privatized flats, which is estimated at USD 200 per square meter of total floor area.

Residential mobility is almost nonexistent in Latvia. A sound housing finance system with a positive borrowing rate in real terms may contribute to improving mobility because households would be better able to afford alternative housing options. The Latvian government should develop financing systems that stimulate mobility in the housing market. Development of a housing finance system will also be important for facilitating the privatization process, which is expected to require some cash payments, as well as for upgrading the deteriorated housing stock.

Social Safety Net. The privatization of houses and rent reform will probably have detrimental effects on the poorer and vulnerable groups, since rent increases will be sharp and expenditures for food are expected to consume most of people's monthly incomes. Municipalities are planning to use some of the flats remaining in public hands for allocation to vulnerable households. Latvia should investigate the experiences of other countries that have used housing allowances as part of the social safety net. Studies may be needed to construct income registers and other databases that are important in administering a social safety net.

Development of a Building Materials Industry. The building materials industry in Latvia has largely been dependent upon other republics in the former Soviet Union for importing raw materials and equipment and for exporting Latvian-produced goods. Existing building equipment and technologies are outdated and energy intensive. Joint ventures could help achieve the required modernization and technical development. Building materials such as cement, gypsum, and wood products have export potential, but investments in new equipment and technology are required to develop them. Investments of USD 200 million are needed to renew the Broceni cement plant, for example. Other investments are required for the Liepaja steel plant to expand its product mix and meet existing domestic demand.

Both the construction industry and the building materials industry still exist in the form of state- and cooperative-owned enterprises. To increase productivity, many of the state and cooperative firms, which specialize in different activities and operate as monopolies, should be restructured into smaller companies. Competition would probably achieve higher productivity and efficiency, and companies would have to respond to market demand for products in the future.

As energy prices increase, construction companies will have opportunities to install higher quality thermal insulation. In addition, opportunities exist for renovating poorly maintained housing units. As the reform process proceeds, demand for new housing construction and renovation will likely increase.

Municipal Services

The transfer of urban services to local authorities is well advanced. Water supplies, sewerage, street and drainage maintenance, refuse collection, street lighting, urban transport systems, central heating, and rental housing as well as education, public health, and cultural activities are now the responsibility of municipalities, as are user charges for these services (some user charges are the responsibility of districts as in the case of Riga). Tariffs will need to be raised, and strategies for financing the replacement and rehabilitation of old equipment and facilities should be explored. Although tariffs were raised for water, sewerage, and urban transport services, they are still inadequate to permit proper maintenance of infrastructure or investment in new assets. Borrowing by local authorities for capital investment, within prudent limits and within the overall framework of credit to the government, should be considered along with a program of gradual tariff increases.

Investment Programs and Priorities

Housing. The volume of housing construction had depended mainly upon the levels of state budget allocations. Little private construction (mainly through private housing cooperatives) took place by using formal loans. The limited housing finance was provided through state institutions on highly subsidized terms. As the private sector takes on the responsibility for the majority of housing production in the future, contributions from private household savings will need to take on a larger role in housing construction. However, a functioning banking system must be in place to mobilize savings.

Development of a housing finance system is key to the transition to a market-based housing system. It will be important for supporting the privatization effort and for upgrading and construction requirements. Macroeconomic stabilization and long-term structural adjustment in Latvia require that subsidies to housing be minimized. Housing finance should be part of a general financial system that helps channel resources into priority sectors. Such a system requires financial institutions that can mobilize resources from both the household and enterprise sectors and make loans to private or commercial investors for housing at market interest rates with long maturities. Mortgage lending should not distort resource allocation by offering below market interest rates. Advisory services should be sought to establish and manage a housing finance system and to design lending instruments that are both affordable to the borrower and profitable to the lender.

Municipal Services. Most urban services have been poorly maintained because tariff levels have been inadequate. New investments are needed in all areas, particularly water supply and sewerage services. Although several tariffs have been raised recently, they are still inadequate to properly maintain infrastructure or invest in new assets.

Recommendations

As concerns short-term measures, it is recommended that the government:

- Support local authorities in speeding up the restitution process;

- Ensure that rents are raised so that the remaining government-owned rental apartments will be more attractive for sale;

- Introduce a differentiated rent structure to avoid future imbalances in the housing market;

- Investigate the experience of a social safety net in other countries;

- Study the requirements for a housing finance system and the design of appropriate lending instruments;

- Consider the introduction of tax credits, on a temporary basis, to stimulate private house construction;

- Clarify the formula whereby municipalities divide revenues from personal income taxes.

As concerns medium-term measures, it is recommended that the government:

- Encourage Latvian cities to consider introducing a charge for maintaining flats in buildings of mixed ownership during the privatization process;

- Restructure the construction industry into smaller companies to increase competition, productivity, and efficiency;

- Establish a database of housing indicators for monitoring performance in the sector;

- Consider giving local governments the authority to collect local taxes;

- Plan for high priority urban investments, particularly in water supply, sewerage, sanitation, and urban transport;

- Encourage more exchanges of experiences among countries and municipalities on sewage treatment methods in order to create new standards;

- Undertake a study of leakage into the groundwater at the Riga landfill site;

- Raise energy tariffs to cover the full costs of providing the service to reduce energy consumption;

- Provide economic incentives to households to stimulate investment in energy-saving technology.

CHAPTER 11

Health

Over the last twenty years, life expectancy has been decreasing for men, but has remained stable for women. Life expectancy is sixty-four years for men and seventy-five years for women, which is four to five years lower than in most European countries and the lowest among the Baltic countries (Tables 11-1 and 11-2). Latvia has about 35,000 newborns and about 45,000 legal abortions per year. This extraordinarily high number of abortions may in part reflect birth control traditions, but reportedly it is due more to a lack of contraceptives and family planning.

Table 11-1. Health Indicators, Selected Years

Indicator	1960	1970	1980	1990
Life Expectancy at Birth (years)	69.1	70.2	68.9	69.5
Male	65.2	65.5	63.6	64.2
Female	72.4	74.4	73.9	74.6
Life Expectancy at Age 40 (years)				
Male	N.A.	N.A.	N.A.	29
Female	N.A.	N.A.	N.A.	37
Crude Mortality Rate per 1,000 Population (number)	10.0	11.2	12.7	13.0
Infant Mortality per 1,000 Newborns (number)	27.0	17.9	15.4	13.7
Perinatal Mortality per 1,000 Newborns (number)	N.A.	11.8	10.2	12.1
Maternal Mortality per 1,000 Newborns (number)	N.A.	0.7	0.2	0.2

N.A. = not available.
Source: Ministry of Welfare, Labor, and Health.

Table 11-2. Health Indicators, Selected Countries and Years

Country	Year	Life Expectancy at Birth (years)		Life Expectancy at age 40 (years)		Infant Mortality per 1,000 Live Births (number)	Crude Mortality rate per 1,000 Population (number)
		Male	Female	Male	Female		
Czechoslovakia	1989	67	75	-	-	11.3	11.9
Denmark	1987	71	77	34	39	8.2	11.3
Estonia	1990	66	75	30	37	12.3	12.3
France	1987	72	80	33	41	8.0	9.5
Hungary	1989	65	73	-	-	15.7	13.4
Latvia	1990	64	74	29	37	13.5	13.0
Lithuania	1990	67	76	31	38	10.2	10.6
Netherlands	1987	73	80	35	41	6.4	8.3
Poland	1989	66	75	-	-	15.9	9.9
Spain	1987	74	80	37	42	8.7	7.9
Sweden	1987	74	80	36	41	6.1	11.1
United Kingdom	1987	71	77	34	39	9.1	11.3

Source: Ministry of Welfare, Labor, and Health.

Although infant mortality has decreased considerably during the last thirty years, the recent increase in the number of stillbirths calls for epidemiological analysis of the causes. However, given the limited value of research data in social medicine and the absence of reliable data, determining the real causes seems unlikely.

The past thirty years have also witnessed significant increases in hypertensive-related diseases, such as stroke and myocardial infarction, which are commonly related to social stress, and increases in bronchial asthma, bronchitis, emphysema, and lung cancer, which are frequently related to smoking and environmental pollution. Not surprisingly, residents of those parts of the country that are heavily industrialized and polluted have a lower life expectancy.

Structure and Recent Performance

Latvia has about 11,500 physicians and 18,600 nurses (Tables 11-3 and 11-4). The majority of physicians (75 percent) are women. Salaries are traditionally low, at the level of the average industrial worker. The number of physicians in relation to population (43 per 10,000 inhabitants) is high from an international perspective, but the ratio of physicians to nurses and to other paramedical personnel is low. In short, Latvia has too many doctors and too few nurses.

Table 11-3. Number of Physicians, Dentists, Nurses, and Paramedical Personnel, Selected Years

Medical Personnel	1960	1970	1980	1990
Physicians	4,743	7,020	9,515	11,527
Dentists	925	1,467	1,551	1,713
Nurses	7,055	11,424	15,221	18,610
Other Paramedical Personnel	8,347	10,673	14,006	12,724

Source: Ministry of Welfare, Labor, and Health.

Table 11-4. Physicians and Dentists per 10,000 Population, Selected Countries and Selected Years

Country	Year	Physicians	Dentists
Denmark	1987	26	9
France	1987	25	N.A.
Latvia	1990	43	6
Lithuania	1991	45	6
Netherlands	1987	24	5
Spain	1986	34	1
Sweden	1987	26	10
United Kingdom	1987	14	4

N.A. = not available.
Source: OECD (1990); Ministry of Welfare, Department of Health, and Medical Statistics Bureau, Riga, Latvia; National Center of Statistics, Vilnius, Lithuania.

Latvia has more than 200 hospitals. Most of them are concentrated in urban areas, and most are old and in need of maintenance, renovation, or replacement. Together these hospitals have nearly 40,000 beds, far too many for a population of 2.7 million (Tables 11-5 and 11-6). Although the number of hospitals and sanatoriums or rehabilitation centers has decreased during the last few decades, the number of beds has increased from 108 to 147 per 10,000 inhabitants, a ratio much higher than in the other two Baltic countries.

Table 11-5. Administrative Responsibility for Health Resources 1990

Health Resource	Administered by	
	Ministry of Welfare	City and District Councils
Hospitals	176	28
Beds	35,800	3,700
Outpatient Institutions	343	47
Sanatoriums	15	0
Infant Homes	6	0
Physicians	11,400	1,800
Paramedical Personnel	25,700	5,600

Source: Ministry of Welfare, Labor, and Health.

Table 11-6. Health Facilities and their Utilization, Selected Years

Unit	1960	1970	1980	1990
Number of Hospitals	269.0	211.0	183.0	204
Number of Beds	22,990.0	28,140.0	34,490.0	39,500
Beds per 10,000 Population	108.0	119.0	136.0	147
Average Length of Stay in Short-Term Hospitals (days)	18.0	19.0	19.0	17
Occupancy Rate (percent)	89.0	95.0	94.0	76
Number of Outpatient Facilities	524.0	405.0	346.0	389
Number of Visits to Doctors (millions)	14.5	21.7	29.2	25.6
Number of Visits per Population per Year	6.7	9.4	11.7	9.5
Number of Pharmacies	854.0	1,056.0	1,061.0	1,010
Number of Sanitary Stations	N.A.	N.A.	46.0	N.A.
Number of Sanatoriums	52.0	48.0	47.0	42

Source: Ministry of Welfare, Labor, and Health.

Outpatient care is rendered at about 375 clinics. Huge, free-standing outpatient clinics exist in the cities, each staffed with 30 to 100 physicians. In the countryside, a network of outpatient services exists for prevention and primary health care in the form of ambulatory centers, usually staffed by three to five physicians, or by district stations staffed by physician assistants and/or midwives.

No special facilities exist for the elderly, chronically ill, mentally ill, mentally retarded, or physically handicapped. Reportedly, relatively few beds are occupied by long-term patients. They are generally cared for at home by relatives. However, no financial support exists for this type of care.

Investment plans for new facilities amounted to 30 percent of the health care budget in 1991. Yet none of the planned construction could be completed because of the lack of building materials. Investments in the 1992 state budget amount to only 0.5 percent of the health care budget.

Institutional and Policymaking Framework

Latvia's health care system remains highly centralized and administered by rigid rules and standards. Few changes have occurred during the last fifty years. The Ministry of Welfare administers the specialized hospitals and educational and scientific institutions as well as most other hospitals and hospital-related outpatient departments for psychiatry, oncology, infectious diseases, and special programs for the treatment of tuberculosis, drug dependency, and AIDS.

Local governments, that is, city and district councils, administer general hospitals, outpatient clinics, and other parts of the primary health services. Patients typically enter the system through any of the outpatient services and are then referred to specialists or hospital care as deemed necessary. Patients have no free choice of doctor or institution, and each citizen is assigned a certain clinic or hospital. In principle, health care is free of charge. However, an estimated 2.5 percent of the health care budget is paid for out-of-pocket by patients for extra services and medical supplies.

Total health care resources, measured in terms of the number of hospitals, beds, and physicians, are high by international comparison, as is the rate of hospitalization (210 per 1,000 population) and the number of visits (9.5 per inhabitant a year). There seems to be an oversupply of hospitals and beds, yet there is a very low rate of bed utilization, particularly for pediatrics, obstetrics, dermatology (65 percent occupancy for all three), neurology, and infectious disease (50 percent occupancy for both).

Physician training has focused on quantity and specialization. As a result of this policy, there are not only too many physicians, but too many specialists and too few generalists. Family or general practitioners do not exist in Latvia; however, initiatives were recently taken to promote the development of this specialty.

The principle of centralized authority still applies to the provision and distribution of pharmaceuticals. Farmacija, an agency linked to the Ministry of Welfare, Labor, and Health coordinates all pharmaceutical imports and exports and the distribution of drugs, vaccines, and medical supplies through 400 special pharmacies, which in turn supply both hospitals and other pharmacies. As part of the restructuring process, Farmacija is being decentralized, and it will become more of a regulatory and monitoring agency than a supply and distribution giant.

Until 1991 more than 90 percent of Latvia's total pharmaceutical production was exported to the republics of the former Soviet Union. The export system has collapsed, however, because of economic and political problems and because of difficulties created by customs barriers in Russia and Ukraine.

Production, import, and distribution of medical equipment is handled by the trade firm Latvmedtechnica, whose central office is located within the Ministry of Welfare, Labor, and Health. This agency supervises wholesale and retail trade enterprises as well as a few small factories that produce minor medical equipment. Given the scarcity of hard currency, Latvmedtechnica's current focus is to maintain existing equipment to the extent possible.

Sectoral Policies and Issues

In 1990, Latvia spent 3.4 percent of its GDP on health services, or about RUR 150 per capita (Table 11-7). The state budget financed approximately 30 percent, and local governments contributed 70 percent. By 1992 the state's share of expenditures on health care had increased to 40 percent.

Table 11-7. *Total Expenditures on Health Care, Selected Years*

Expenditures	1960	1970	1980	1990	1991
Total Expenditures on Health Care (RUR millions)	49.0	97.0	202.0	410.0	700.0
Expenditures as Percentage of GNP	2.5	2.6	2.6	3.4	2.4
Expenditures per capita (RUR)	23.0	40.0	80.0	154.0	263.0
Percentage of Expenditures on:					
Inpatient Care Including Sanatoriums and Infant Homes					76.0
Outpatient Care Including Prevention and District Care					13.0
Investments					3.0
Other					8.0

Source: The Ministry of Welfare, Labor, and Health.

About 35 percent of the state budget for health in 1991 went toward salaries, 16 percent for pharmaceuticals and medical supplies, 5 percent for medical equipment, and 3 percent for investments, although only one new facility, a maternal home in Riga, came close to completion. About 3 percent of the state budget was spent on AIDS prevention and care, a respectable amount considering the relatively low frequency of known AIDS patients (one AIDS patient and thirteen HIV positives). The rest of the budget was allocated to hospital care.

Local budgets for health care, which include expenditures for education, and social welfare, totaled almost twice the amount of state expenditures. Distribution followed essentially the same pattern as the state health budget.

The government of Latvia has developed a five-year plan for restructuring the health care system. The major components of this plan include privatizing the pharmaceuticals market and implementing a national health insurance plan.

Private initiatives and competition in the pharmaceutical field are, in principle, viewed as positive. However, financial or other direct governmental support--tax exemptions, for example--is lacking. Such initiatives might help alleviate the critical shortage of drugs in the country. A few privatized pharmacies exist, but only one accepts rubles.

An important issue is eliminating the sources of preventable disease. Outbreaks of bacterial and viral diseases caused by contaminated food and polluted water are common. Several epidemics have already surfaced: waterborne hepatitis A, typhus, and leptospirosis. Gastrointestinal diseases, particularly among children, are rampant. Such diseases now place a heavy burden on the health care system. If they persist, they may render a national health insurance plan financially untenable for citizens and employers.

The quality of service seems visibly low by Western standards. There is a shortage of basic medical supplies, equipment, and pharmaceuticals and a lack of maintenance and repair of old facilities. Only 3 of the 200 hospitals are deemed modern.

The supply of drugs is reportedly bordering on catastrophe. According to estimates by the Ministry of Welfare, Labor, and Health only 25 percent of the drugs and medical supplies needed are currently available. Shortages include life-saving drugs, analgesics, sedatives, vaccines, syringes, sutures, anesthetics, sterilants, and disinfectants. Reportedly, such shortages have periodically led to epidemics of infectious disease, to increased mortality among infants and children, and to curtailment of elective surgery.

The current ad hoc delivery system for drugs and vaccines encourages hoarding, which in turn increases the shortages and prevents an adequate build-up of inventories. The optimal stock of drugs is said to be about 150 days, but inventories now average about 90 days, and many drugs are completely out of stock.

Sufficient experience and skills exist to increase domestic production of both pharmaceuticals and medical devices. Humanitarian aid and international assistance is a short-term solution to help realize capabilities in this area. In the long run, the government should consider tax exemptions to encourage private initiatives and secure the supply of raw materials.

Maternal and child health care seems to be structurally developed, but the real content of these programs is unsatisfactory. The rate of abortion is higher than the number of births. The rate of premature birth, stillbirth, and spontaneous abortions is extraordinarily high in certain parts of the country. Only 35 percent of deliveries are normal, far below the incidence of complicated deliveries. Complications during pregnancy commonly require medical/surgical attention and place a heavy burden on the health care system. Gastrointestinal problems among children account for about 35,000 admissions and visits to outpatient care per year.

Medical services, particularly for elective surgery, are very limited. Advanced medical technology, such as lithotripsy, CT-scans, and magnetic resonance imaging, and such surgery as artificial hip and lens operations are rare or non-existent.

An early emphasis on quantity and specialization of physicians resulted in too little attention directed to the sources of preventable disease and death in the population. However, resources are increasingly going toward treatment of illnesses caused by sanitary and nutritional conditions, by bacterial and viral contamination of food and water, and by environmental pollution.

The availability of beds has little relation to the incidence of hospital admissions, reflected by the low rate of occupancy, as low as 50 percent for some specialties. However, the large number of physicians in relation to the number of inhabitants seems to increase admissions. The average length of stay for short-term cases is twice as long as in many European countries.

Recommendations

The system urgently needs to be restructured to achieve internal efficiency and effectiveness. Key elements for reform should include decentralized decisionmaking, budget responsibility, and consumer satisfaction.

The principle of allocating health care funds should be changed. Instead of basing allocations on the number of beds and personnel, the ministry could base it on the number of patients treated related to population served. An alternative would be to allocate funds on a per capita basis and allow payment for services to stimulate competition among health institutions.

Primary health care and sanitary stations must be reoriented toward, and given the responsibility for, a more active role in health protection and reduction of preventable death and disease. The government must secure a supply of coagulants to purify drinking water and take measures to prevent the negligent disposal of hazardous waste. Reallocating the resources away from hospital services, which are notoriously oversupplied and overspecialized, would make reform possible.

The government should give high priority to developing a comprehensive maternal and child health care program. Such a program could include appropriate nutrition for school children, school health programs, nutritional support during pregnancy, provision of less hazardous working conditions for pregnant women, health education, services for children with vision problems (which are reportedly prevalent), and dental care services for children.

Plans are under way to reorganize medical education, including reducing the number of students admitted to medical schools and reducing the number of positions for doctors. Within the next few years the government also plans to alter the medical school curriculum in accordance with standards in Western countries. Some contacts have already been made with professionals in other countries to help revise basic and postgraduate training, research, and clinical practices.

The government should intensify its efforts to obtain urgent humanitarian aid for purchasing pharmaceutical raw materials, medical supplies, and critical drugs and vaccines. The price of drugs should be raised. Drug prices are low compared with international prices and compared to production costs.

CHAPTER 12

Education, Training, and Research

Latvia has a rich history of educational development. A religious school system was started in the thirteenth century and the first secular school was established in 1353. The network of Latvian schools expanded toward the latter part of the eighteenth century. During the second half of the nineteenth century and at the beginning of the twentieth century advanced educational establishments, such as, trade schools and naval colleges, were started.

The system of education flourished during the period of independence (1918-40), including the establishment of elementary education for children ages eight to fourteen, classical secondary schools, technical training institutions, and universities (the University of Latvia was established in 1919). The system of Latvian education was subordinated to the authoritarian Soviet education system after Latvia's incorporation into the USSR. This period saw extensive development of highly specialized vocational and technical training.

In 1990 extensive reforms were introduced to bring the system more in line with educational systems in Western Europe. Latvia's longstanding emphasis on education has resulted in a strong system of general and university education. Enrollment indicators compare favorably with most Western countries at all levels. Quality is reportedly high in terms of academic achievement, especially in sciences, mathematics, and the arts. Almost all teachers have been trained at the level of higher education. Textbooks are in ample supply, the majority having been produced locally in the Latvian language. Completion rates of entering students are also high. Research in the basic and applied sciences is noted for its excellence.

Despite these achievements, the Latvian system of education, training, and research is not well positioned to serve current national development needs. The system as a whole does not have the capacity to produce the kinds of skills or retraining needed in a market economy. It is not up-to-date with developments in advanced economies. Academic achievements have been fact oriented in narrow fields, with insufficient emphasis on synthesis, evaluation, and generalization. There seem to be more teachers in the system than are required for efficient teaching. Necessary improvements in relevance and quality probably cannot be financed without major adjustments in the use of resources or without sharing costs with beneficiaries.

Too many youth are probably enrolled in vocational and technical training, including 70 percent of enrollment at the upper secondary level. The structure of technical and vocational training is needlessly complex and specialized. Technician training is insufficient in both scope and orientation to meet the demands of a modern technological economy. Too little attention has been paid to upgrading the skills of those employed. Virtually no system exists for retraining unemployed adults.

Structure and Recent Performance

Education is provided to a relatively advanced age. Education has been compulsory for more than a decade in Latvian schools, beginning at age six. Russian-speaking schools start at age seven and continue for eleven years, consistent with education in the Russian Republic. Virtually all children are enrolled in school through grade 9.

After grade 9, based on national examinations, students may choose university preparation in upper secondary schools (grades 10 through 12) or preparation for vocational schools or technical colleges. About 70 percent of the students enrolled in grades 10 through 12 enroll in vocational and technical courses and 28 percent in academic programs (Table 12-1). About 80 percent of seventeen- and eighteen-year-olds are enrolled in the secondary schools. About 27 percent of the group age twenty to twenty-four, or 46,000 students, is enrolled in ten institutions of higher education.

Table 12-1. Enrollments at the Upper Secondary Level (Grades 10-12), 1991-92

Type of Education	Number of Students	No. of Students as a Percentage of Total
Academic	28,000	28.3
Vocational	33,000	33.3
Technical	38,000	38.4
Total	99,000	100.0

Source: Latvian authorities.

General Education (Grades 1-12)

Under Soviet rule, every step in the educational process was controlled. School directors were responsible to local party committees; the school staff was told what to teach and how to teach it.[1] Inspection visits were frequent. About three years ago, local party committees were abolished and local government councils took over direct supervision of schools. Representatives of the local government may visit schools twice annually, but usually they visit to identify problems or to ask advice on how to deal with issues.

General education is divided into three stages: elementary (grades 1-4), lower secondary (grades 5-9), and upper secondary (grades 10-12). A school may offer only the elementary grades (in rural areas 69 schools enroll 4,400 pupils); grades 1-9 (444 schools enroll 67,000 students), or grades 1-12 (380 schools enroll 260,000 students). In addition, 7,700 students are enrolled in 54 special schools for handicapped children. All schools are coeducational. The language distribution of enrollments was 54 percent Latvian and 46 percent Russian, as shown in Table 12-2.

Table 12-2. Language Distribution of General Education, 1991-92
(number of schools and students)

Type of Schools	Latvian		Russian	
	Schools	Students	Schools	Students
Primary Schools (grades 1-4)	47	2,730	10	1,570
Basic Schools (grades 1-9)	337	52,940	53	13,930
Comprehensive Schools (grades 1-12)	170	122,570	145	138,530
Total	554	178,240	152	152,030

Source: Latvian authorities.

---

1.   For example, schools and teachers were told to introduce an "ideological moment" in every class.

In elementary education, a single teacher instructs the class for the full four years. No formal assessment is made of student performance in grades 1 through 3. Pupils in grades 1 through 2 take four classes; in grades 3 through 4 they take five classes. The school year lasts about 180 days. In 1991 the government permitted the establishment of private schools, which also receive public subsidies.

In lower secondary education, subject-specialist teachers instruct in six classes. Each class is preserved as a unit until grade 9. Instruction in the Russian language is obligatory from grade 3 to grade 9. Dropouts are virtually non-existent and repetition is rare. Two examinations are administered nationally at the end of grade 9: one in mathematics and one in the native language. Performance on these examinations governs entry to upper secondary (academic) education. No private schools exist at this level yet, although in principle they are permitted.

About half the children who complete grade 9 continue their studies, usually in the same school. Proportionally more girls choose university preparation, while more boys elect vocational education. The school year is longer and more intensive: about 200 days a year and seven classes a day. Ability streaming is common, for example, schools may emphasize languages or physics and mathematics. Successful completion of upper secondary schooling requires satisfactory performance on five examinations: an essay in the native language and four examinations in subjects of the student's choice. According to school directors, graduates from Latvian-speaking schools at grade 9 typically have no difficulties in reading, comprehending, or speaking the Russian language; however, most graduates (90 percent) from Russian-speaking schools can read Latvian, but few can write or speak it.

About 32,000 teachers worked in general schools in 1991-92, or a ratio of 1.0 teacher to every 10.6 students (compared with 1.0 to 12.4 in 1986-87). A full-time teaching load is about twenty-one hours weekly. Teachers are trained, depending on the grades they will teach, in three teacher training colleges in Riga, two pedagogical institutes outside Riga, or at the University of Latvia. About 80 percent of teachers go through higher education.

In 1991 a new system of teacher pay was introduced that differentiates teacher pay according to qualifications and experience. The system works on the basis of multiples of the minimum wage. For example, a starting teacher in the upper grades with a university degree receives 2.8 times the minimum wage per month; a qualified, well-experienced teacher receives 4.4 times the minimum wage, and an experienced school director gets 5.7 times the minimum wage. Teachers receive periodic retraining at the Institute for Education Advancement and other specialized institutions.

Curricula traditionally emphasized the teaching of facts, and rote memorization prevailed. Choice of subjects was not permitted. Moscow determined, at every point, which subjects should be taught for how many hours and covering which topics. The authority of the teacher was not to be challenged by students, and classroom discussion was not encouraged. The strengths of such a system were the mastery of facts and a good knowledge of science and mathematics. The consequences were a weak ability to integrate and see relationships across subjects, analyze, and think creatively.

These restrictions are being removed, and elective subjects are being introduced in upper secondary education (seven of twelve subjects will be electives). New subjects such as psychology, the history of Latvian culture, and additional foreign languages are being introduced. An attempt is being made in the lower grades to focus on useful, everyday topics, such as health and civics. However, one legacy of prior central control is the lack of local experience in curriculum development.

Textbooks were developed in Moscow to be translated locally into Latvian and printed by the monopoly publisher in Riga. These readily available books were heavily subsidized by the state, and ideological content was emphasized. For example, 75 percent of the first textbook was devoted to ideology and propaganda. Local governments paid less than RUR 1 per copy. Such centralization of control and content translates into a lack of local experience in writing textbooks. Sufficiently trained or experienced authors do not exist for most subjects, excluding Latvian language, Latvian history, and foreign languages. In 1991 the Ministry of Education gradually began to diversify its sources for textbooks. However, book production was stopped for lack of imported paper.

Recognizing that not everyone has an aptitude for formal schooling, in 1992 the length of compulsory education was reduced from twelve years to nine years. Compulsory education had led teachers to pass students without much regard for learning achievements. The intention is to stimulate vocational schooling.

Vocational and Technical Training

About 35 percent of the graduates from grade 9 enter vocational schools.[2] There are about 100 vocational schools: 62 under the Ministry of Education, 25 under the Ministry of Agriculture, 4 under the Ministry of Industry, and the rest within firms. Total enrollment is an estimated 33,000 students, of whom 19,200 are in vocational schools under the Ministry of Education and 9,000 are under the Ministry of Agriculture (Table 12-3).

Table 12-3. Vocational and Technical Training, 1991-92

Type of Training	Number of Schools	Number of Students
Vocational Total	100	33,000
of which: MOE	62	19,200
MOA	25	9,000
Technical Total	53	38,000
of which: MOE	16	9,500
MOA	16	6,500

MOE = Ministry of Education.
MOA = Ministry of Agriculture.
Note: Technical includes both technikums and specialized secondary schools.
Source: Latvian authorities.

Vocational and technical schools offer different teaching programs, but are often located in the same institution. Most programs last three years, with additional training for the more difficult professions. The range of occupations covered is wide, for example, agricultural vocational schools teach thirty-five different occupations. For some key occupations, six different levels of qualifications exist, from level 1 (beginner) to 6 (master).

During the first year, teachers usually identify the most able students and encourage them to take upper secondary classes along with vocational specialization, which usually takes four years. Practical work occupies from 40 to 75 percent of the student's time, depending on the year of study and field of specialization. In the past, schools were linked with firms, which subsidized some of the costs. The teaching staff is drawn from universities for theoretical work and from factories for practical work. There are about eight students per teacher.

Technical schools, technikums, or specialized secondary schools focus on industrial specializations to prepare technicians. Specialized secondary schools include medicine (for nurses), pedagogy (for pre-school teachers), and the arts. In 1990 there were fifty-three technical institutions in

---

2.   Statistics about vocational schools are particularly weak; records were kept in Moscow and not reported locally. No comprehensive data exist on all types of schools. No data are available on enrollments or outputs by field of specialization.

Latvia enrolling about 38,000 students.   About 25 percent of the students were studying by correspondence and 6 percent in evening courses. The Ministry of Agriculture operates sixteen of these technikums, enrolling about 6,500 students. There were 3,850 full-time teachers; the ratio of students per teacher was less than ten to one. The length of study depends on the specialization, for example, electromechanics requires 3.0 years, computer programming 3.5 years, and agriculture and telecommunications 4.0 years (Table 12-4).

Table 12-4. Existing Vocational Programs

Type of School	Entry	Length of Program (years)	Qualifications Obtained
Basic School	Grade 9	2	Trade certificate
Vocational School	Grade 9	3	Basic secondary + trade certificate
Vocational Secondary School	Grade 9	4	Secondary diploma + trade certificate

Source: Latvian authorities.

The teaching content is more theoretical than in trade schools. In one school visited, for example, the curriculum was almost exclusively theoretical in the first year, about 20 percent in the second year, 40 percent in the third year, and 75 percent in the fourth year. The class sizes are about thirty students. Students receive stipends depending on their performance in examinations. A high proportion of entering students complete the program successfully. At one radio-electronic technikum visited in Riga, the completion rate was 87 percent. About 20 percent of graduates go on to engineering studies at the university level, and 80 percent go to work as technicians or highly specialized workers.

Despite the large number of students enrolled, vocational training is one of the weakest points in the current system. Curricula have been overly specialized, and little experience exists locally to develop programs more relevant to Latvian needs because teaching programs were developed centrally in Moscow. Teaching materials are often lacking. Firms, which had provided places for on-the-job training, are no longer willing to play that role because of pressing financial problems.

Four types of teaching programs had been introduced by fall 1992 (Table 12-5). Some adult training has taken place in the past at vocational centers, usually in the evening. The main responsibility for retraining unemployed adults rests with the Ministry of Welfare.

Table 12-5. Teaching Programs, 1992

Type of Teaching Program	Entry	Length (years)	Qualification
Basic Vocational	Grade 9	2	Trade Certificate
Vocational School and Gymnasium	Grade 9	3-5	Diploma of Secondary Education or Vocational Education
Vocational School	Grade 12	1-2	Trade Certificate

Source: Latvian authorities.

Higher Education

Higher education consists of three types of institutions: universities, academies, and institutes. Ten such institutions exist at present (Table 12-6).

Table 12-6. Higher Education Institutions

Institutes	Year established	Number of Faculties	Number of Students	Number of Lecturers
Riga Technical University	1862	10	13,000	1,000
University of Latvia	1919	13	12,600	820
Latvian Academy of Agriculture	1939	9	6,200	470
Latvian Academy of Medicine	1950	4	2,500	400
Civil Aviation Institute	1960	4	4,100	460
Pedagogical Institute, Daugavpils	1952	5	2,800	210
Pedagogical Institute, Liepaja	1954	3	2,700	140

Note: The above list excludes the three academies of arts, music, and physical culture. Enrollments include evening and correspondence students.

Source: Latvian authorities.

Of the 46,300 students enrolled, 61.5 percent are in full-time studies, 30.8 percent are in correspondence courses, and 7.7 percent are in evening classes. Total enrollment has increased 7 percent since 1986-87. Currently there are 17 students in higher education per 1,000 population. No data were available on enrollments by discipline or faculty.

Each university administers its own entrance examination, and students must sit for the examination of the particular faculty they wish to join. Students are able to take the examination in Latvian or Russian. About half the upper secondary graduates enter higher education. At the Technical University, 50 percent of new admissions are in Russian and 50 percent in Latvian. The applicant to acceptance ratio is about 2.5 to 1.0 in Russian and 1.5 to 1.0 in Latvian (there are actually more available places than there are Latvian-speaking applicants).

Industrial management, computer science, and automotive engineering are the most popular fields, while civil engineering is the least popular. Russian-speaking entrants are equally divided by gender; almost 90 percent of Latvian-speaking entrants are male. At the University of Latvia, about 80 percent of the students are Latvian-speaking and 20 percent Russian-speaking. The overall applicant to entrant ratio is 3:1. The most popular fields of study are psychology, English, finance, history, and law. Natural sciences are the least popular. In the absence of more complete statistics, table 12-7 indicates the distribution of enrollments by field of study at the Technical University. Completion rates have averaged 75 percent of entering students for the diploma (for example, first degree) after five years of study at the University of Latvia and 60 to 70 percent at the Technical University.

Institutions are now free to decide on their teaching programs and to set academic standards, although the government retains the right to approve the types of degrees awarded and the total annual budget. In the past, the State Planning Commission in Moscow determined the number of entering students per field of study (as well as output requirements). Entrants were assigned to five years of study in a specialized area with no possibility of taking subjects in other departments. Moreover, about 20 percent of the teaching content was ideology, for example, history of the Communist Party, philosophy, or Marxism/Leninism. At the Technical University the number of specializations has been reduced from seventy to fifty organized into six general fields. Students will take common studies the first year before choosing a more specialized study course. In addition to compulsory subjects, students will, for the first time, be allowed to take elective subjects, amounting to 12 to 35 percent of total class time.

In the past, students were taught exclusively by lectures which took about forty to fifty hours per week. Little outside preparation was required, and virtually no discussion was permitted in class. Plans are being formulated to reduce class hours to about twenty-five per week. Students will be required to do homework and library work and only the basics will be taught in

Table 12-7. Student Intake by Field, Technical University, 1991-92

Field of Study	Intake (no. of students)
Electrical Engineering	250
Radio/Telecommunications	200
Mechanical Engineering	200
Automation	200
Civil Engineering	200
Computer Science	150
Chemical Engineering	100
Building Services	100
Engineering Economics/Management	100
Naval Engineering	50
Architecture	30
Total	1,580

Source: Latvian authorities.

class. All these changes are designed to promote an interest in learning; make students responsible for their own work; and promote analysis, thought, and discussion. One of the main problems in achieving these changes is how to change the thinking of teaching staff, both in terms of content and teaching methods.

New degrees are planned that conform with those in many Western countries, for example, a bachelor's degree after four years of study and a master's degree after a further two years of study. The process of changing curricula has involved conflicts between deans and teachers and between teachers and students, and has involved questions on the correct balance among common, basic, and specialized study or among compulsory and elective subjects.

The main priorities for new programs at the Technical University are management, computer science, ecology, telecommunications, and efficient energy use. Overall, there are about eight students in higher education for each teacher. In certain universities, such as the Technical University, the ratio is five to one. Reportedly, staff are required to teach 25 hours per week and a total of 1,000 hours per year. At the Technical University it was reported that 90 percent of professors held the rank of doctor of science, 80 percent of the associate professors held at least a candidate of science (roughly equal to a Western Ph.D.). Among assistant professors and senior lecturers, however, the qualifications were much lower: only about 25 percent held candidate of science degrees.

There is no shortage of qualified staff, except possibly in Western languages and business subjects. Layoffs from research institutes contributed to a surplus of job seekers in teaching institutions, particularly in science and technology. Teaching salaries have been increased recently, with coefficients ranging from 4.00 to 5.96 depending on rank and experience. At the Technical University, if the department has funds available, it can, at the discretion of the chairman, increase teaching staff salaries up to 50 percent. These incentives will undoubtedly help retain staff, but rectors report that many good staff are going to the private sector or abroad. These are mainly younger staff members, which has obvious implications for the vitality of the teaching staff. The average age is over fifty.

Complaints are almost universal about teaching equipment in higher education. Most is badly out of date and there is little modern technology, such as computers. In an inflationary environment, virtually all budgeted amounts are taken up by salaries, social security taxes, and operation and maintenance of buildings. Modern laboratories require hard currency, both for equipment and supplies, and almost none is available.

Each institution of higher education is governed by its own statutes. Currently, only the constitution of the University of Latvia has been adopted by parliament. Internal decisions are taken by a senate, composed of eighty elected persons. Teaching staff elect half the members, students one-quarter, and administrators (for example, deans) one-quarter. The rector is elected by the senate, but must be approved by the parliament. In addition, a Council of Rectors coordinates procedures among the institutions and negotiates with the government.

Overall, about 95 percent of the budget for higher education comes from the state and 5 percent from outside contracts. (This varies by institution. The Technical University has a larger share from research.) The parliament votes a single line for the budget of higher education institutions, with one stipulation: the proportion that must be spent on salaries. The senate allocates the overall funds to the various departments. Some institutions are now admitting fee-paying students. For example, about 300 (2.5 percent) of the students enrolled at the University of Latvia pay fees amounting to RUR 4,000 a year. The Technical University is considering charging fees for some of the students in post-degree courses.

Scientific Research

Science research in Latvia dates back to 1775 with the foundation of the Academia Petrina in Jelgava. The establishment of the Riga Polytechnic in 1862 facilitated the expansion of research in engineering, biology, and chemistry. During the period of Latvian independence, Latvia carried out research in such fields as Baltic philology, medicine, chemistry, biology, and agriculture. However, after Latvia was incorporated into the USSR in 1940, the organization, leadership, and development of research was subordinated to the corresponding institutions of the Soviet Union. A wide network of scientific research organizations was established, much of it serving the needs of the Soviet military.

Research has been divided into three categories: (a) the Academy of Sciences network of sixteen research institutes that employ about 7,500 staff, (b) higher education establishments, and (c) departmental research institutes belonging to various ministries and enterprises. Latvia has a total of 108 research institutes that together employ more than 10,000 scientists.

Universities generally did not play a major role in research, with a few exceptions, such as the Technical University. One of the reasons was the heavy teaching load expected of staff, averaging 100 hours of teaching per month and 1,000 per year. This averages to twenty-five hours per week, compared with nine to twelve hours in Western universities. Teachers simply do not have the time for research. The Technical University historically received 80 percent of its research funds from contracts and 20 percent from the state budget. These contracts have declined sharply since independence: in 1992 the proportion was just 27 percent (RUR 1.3 million) from contracts. As a result 200 to 300 research staff have been shed from the university's payroll. Only about 60 percent of the scientists employed in the research complex three years ago currently remain.

The Latvian Science Council, established in 1990, prepares the research budgets, develops projects for financing, and drafts laws aimed at the reorganization and development of science in Latvia. It has a total of twenty-eight members, thirteen of whom are elected representatives of various fields of science, eleven are elected to represent the various leading research organizations (for example, the academy and the universities), and the remaining four occupy key positions, for example, the president of the Academy of Sciences. The Science Council reviews applications for research and recommends financing to government. In 1991, for example, 1,400 applications were received and 900 were deemed acceptable to recommend for financing (RUR 70 million). Criteria for assessing proposals were whether the research would be useful for Latvia and whether it involved important new knowledge generation. As an interested party in research, the Science Council cannot be expected to set overall government policy on research and chart new directions. Consequently, the administration established a Science Department within the Ministry of Education for these purposes. The department has only five staff members.

The principal problems for research in Latvia include the need to consolidate research on fields relevant to Latvia, to achieve an affordable system, and to retain the quality that has been built in the system. The tendency is for the brightest minds in science to leave the field, and for those who remain to be handicapped by the lack of hard currency to buy research equipment and materials.

Institutional and Policymaking Framework

In 1991, a new education law gave the Ministry of Education authority for all levels and types of education and training. The ministry, which employs about 105 staff in Riga, sets overall policy as well as curricula and standards, and directly controls vocational schools and technical colleges. About 500 local municipalities organized into 38 districts are responsible for the operations of general schools, including upper secondary academic education. Thirty-eight district inspectors hired by the ministry liaise with local governments and control application of the education law. Each general school has its own board elected by parents (51 percent of the vote), teachers, and students.

Higher education institutions are semi-autonomous, and each is governed by its own statutes. However, the ministry oversees the budget for these institutions and the ministry's Science Department coordinates matters at the level of government and oversees government policy on research. Parliament has a Commission on Education, Science, and Culture. Together they set laws and overall regulations. The commission can replace the minister of education but cannot overrule the minister's decisions on policy, content, and standards for the system. A parliamentary decision is needed to open a new institution at the vocational and higher levels.

The state finances almost all education and training.[3] Only subsidies for agriculture absorb more public resources. As a rule, local authorities finance kindergartens and general schools,

---

3.   Expenditures amounted to RUR 570 million in 1990, or 4.7 percent of GDP and 15 percent of the state budget. Expenditure per student in 1991 was RUR 960 in general schools, RUR 1,220 in upper secondary schools, RUR 2,660 in vocational schools, and RUR 4,120 in universities.

while the central authorities finance vocational and technical schools and higher education. No tuition is charged in state schools. Students in vocational and technical schools and universities receive grants equal to 50 or 60 percent of the minimum wage.

Of total state expenditures for education and training, 45 percent is devoted to general schools, 25 percent to vocational and technical training, 15 percent to higher education, and about 15 percent to kindergartens. Research contracts supply about 5 percent of higher education expenditures. Maintenance absorbed only 2 percent of total expenditures in vocational schools, 3 percent in technical schools, and 5 percent in higher education. Spending on books and teaching materials amounted to just 1 or 2 percent in general schools and 0.4 to 2.0 percent in vocational schools.

Strengths, Weaknesses, and Issues

Thanks to its historical emphasis on education, Latvia has a strong system of general and university education. A good part of the traditional system remains in place. The challenge is determining what elements of this legacy to retain and what to discard. To help in the evaluation, this section presents the primary strengths, and weaknesses of the system and other relevant issues.

Latvia's educational and training system has a number of strengths on which to build. Latvia enrolls virtually all (95 percent) of its youth through age 16 in school, about 80 percent of youth age seventeen to eighteen at the upper secondary level, and almost 25 percent of the twenty to twenty-four age group in higher education. These enrollment rates compare favorably with the more economically advanced countries in the West.

Higher education is extensive for a country of Latvia's size, enrolling 46,300 students in ten institutions. Quality, defined in terms of academic achievement, is strong in many fields of general education. Textbooks, many locally produced, are readily available in general schools. Specialized education is available for gifted students. Theoretical subjects, such as mathematics and science, are well known for their excellence and rigor.

The system also has some weaknesses that will need attention. General education has stressed the learning of facts in compartmentalized subjects. Teaching programs were uniform by subject, allowing little individual choice. A modern democratic society and market economy needs people who can integrate, synthesize, analyze, and evaluate information and who can take responsibility for their own actions.

Enrollments and teaching programs for the various occupations were determined centrally by Soviet authorities in Moscow and were linked closely to local enterprises. However, the system is not well adapted to a market economy. It is overly rigid and cannot respond flexibly to the frequent changes in occupational demand typical of a market economy.

Too many youth are probably enrolled in vocational and technical training. At the upper secondary level about 70 percent of those enrolled are attending vocational or technical schools. Comparable figures range from 20 to 40 percent in the West. This is a problem for the following reasons: (a) a market economy needs trainable workers with transferable, general skills, not occupation-specific skills; and (b) technical and vocational training costs about 2.2 times as much per student than general education.

The types of training available in Latvia are not congruent with the skills likely to be needed in the market economy of the future. Enrollments in agricultural courses and in vocational and technical schools probably exceed future requirements. Fewer specialists will likely be needed in metal trades and electronics as employment drops sharply in the corresponding industries. Enrollments in business, commerce, and services, however, will likely need to be increased sharply.

The structure of technical and vocational training is needlessly complex, involving five different types of schools and six degrees of proficiency within each occupation. Specialization is excessive, involving hundreds of occupations. It starts early on in the training and little opportunity exists for switching subjects during training. Too much stress has been placed on acquiring specific skills before employment, while too little attention has been paid to upgrading skills as part of employment.

A major gap in the system is retraining adults for new occupations. No system exists for retraining unemployed adults, largely because the phenomenon of overstaffing typical of the Soviet economy did not permit unemployment.

University teaching and science research suffer from many of the same problems of rigidity, overspecialization, and gaps in coverage as vocational training. Virtually no possibility existed for general study, exploration of options, or transfer between specializations. As would be expected, important fields of study in a market economy either do not exist or are oriented in the wrong direction. Programs improperly oriented include economics, business, law, agriculture, and several fields of technology. Economics and management, in particular, need a complete overhaul. Moreover, owing to Latvia's isolation from outside development, university teaching and scientific research have become seriously outdated. Engineering, for example, uses a level of technology ten to twenty years behind that of developed countries. Lacking ready access to professional networks and literature, many teachers and researchers have fallen well behind developments by their colleagues in the West. Staff, teaching programs, libraries and textbooks, and laboratory equipment are not as up-to-date as they need to be in a competitive market economy. The scientific research complex, while extensive, has been tied to All-Union concerns, particularly the needs of the Soviet military. The agendas of research institutes were largely set in Moscow and were not relevant to national development priorities. The research complex needs to be consolidated and re-oriented to national concerns.

A better flow of information is required in both directions. Current statistics are poor in documenting trends and performance in the system, and do not conform to internationally accepted categories and standards. Greatly improved statistics are required to enable the Ministry of Education to manage the system. School directors, who previously were not made aware of the recurrent budgets of their institutions, also need complete information and better control over their own resources.

Teaching has tended to stress the acquisition of facts. Much time was devoted to ideology and indoctrination. Teachers throughout the system need to be retrained in teaching methods that stimulate inquiry, critical examination, and discussion. High completion rates have been the result of distorted incentives that valued high pass rates and satisfaction of graduation targets, regardless of learning achievements. The lack of modern teaching programs and equipment--only 1 to 2 percent of recurrent spending is devoted to teaching aids and equipment--is striking by international norms. Future production of textbooks depends on importing paper and ink at world prices in foreign exchange. Quality could be eroded if book supplies were cut sharply.

The quality of vocational and technical training needs to be improved. The mission observed an absence of written assignments and job sheets in the practical classes of vocational schools visited, teaching equipment tended to be antiquated, and the age profile of instructors was relatively high. In addition, the commercial production of goods for sale to supplement teachers' salaries and school budgets, while understandable, seems to occupy an inordinate amount of the learning time of advanced students.

University teaching is reportedly strong in mathematics, sciences, and some fields of engineering. However, the lack of modern teaching equipment contributes to low quality instruction.[4] Teaching methods rely excessively on lectures. Teaching staff usually were not involved in research activities and depended on published work (itself about five years behind) to keep up with research findings.

Latvian science research is at the level of world standards in several fields. Much of the scientific community is well qualified. Several of the existing research centers compare favorably with counterpart institutions in the West. However, quality varies widely. Departmental research institutions, in particular, are not known for quality. Without access to Western journals and literature, research staff have not been able to keep themselves up-to-date.

As with other public enterprises and government agencies, the state probably employs more teachers than needed for efficient teaching. This overstaffing is illustrated by small class sizes and relatively low teaching loads per week, for example, twenty-one in general schools. In general education, the overall ratio of about eight to ten students per teacher is between a half and a third that in other Western countries. Causes include the small sizes of schools in rural areas, specialized (teacher-intensive) forms of schooling, and the fact that teachers are trained to teach one subject only. This is an obstacle to flexible and efficient use of staff within schools. This leads to high recurrent costs per student. Reportedly, a few schools even have more teachers than students. Physical facilities do not appear to be used intensively, except possibly for general schools. Class sizes and use factors (the percentage of available time that teaching spaces are actually in use) appear low in vocational and technical schools and in universities. Many facilities are in a poor state of repair, the result of exceptionally low expenditures on maintenance.

At the university level, too many administrative and non-teaching staff exist.[5] Each institution had an average of seventy administrators, and this figure excludes rectors, vice rectors, heads of faculty, and deans. The present fragmentation of the research complex into many small institutions leads to needlessly high overhead costs. Improvements in relevance and quality will be expensive. Substantial investments are required to retrain staff and buy new equipment. Given that the government is almost the sole source of financing for education and training, the question arises of whether it can

---

4.   How, for example, can engineers be trained adequately in problem solving and applications without access to modern computing equipment?

5.   In 1991, only 2,775 of 8,150 staff were teachers.

afford to continue to provide such exclusive support and also find the money necessary to improve quality and relevance.

Another issue is whether the government can sustain the extensive and specialized network of research institutes. Previous sources of financing for research--contracts with the Union and with firms--have evaporated or will soon decline substantially. Quality is costly to sustain in research. Given likely constraints in future government budgets, how much of the current research network can be sustained and what parts should be preserved?

Recommendations

The essential challenges for Latvia are to adapt the former system to a democratic society, re-orient content to a free-market economy, bring obsolete programs up to date, maintain quality, and make better use of resources. In general, recent developments in general schools, universities, and research have been commendable. However, plans for vocational training seem overly complex and do not differentiate technician training adequately.

Short-Term Measures

An affordable, effective system should be developed to retrain adults expected to be displaced by structural adjustment of the economy. The new system of adult retraining should have sufficient capacity to assist many of the tens of thousands of workers expected to be shed by state enterprises and government service. Such a system of retraining cannot be a panacea for unemployment. Not all adults will be willing to undergo, or be capable of, retraining. Nor is retraining alone sufficient to ensure employment in a new occupation. It is merely one of several measures that must be taken to deal with the problem.

More specifically, the following measures are recommended:

- Trying various alternatives and evaluating the results;

- Stressing training for self-employment since wage employment is likely to become more difficult to find;

- Separating the financing of retraining from its provision, that is, the funding agency should not necessarily deliver the training;

- Using diverse providers of training, including private agencies;

- Having employers participate in financing retraining to the maximum extent possible.

In addition to retraining unemployed workers for new occupations, it is also necessary to upgrade the knowledge and skills of those presently employed, for example, training engineers to conduct feasibility studies and training bankers to analyze balance sheets and accounts. Short courses of this type should be organized on demand, particularly by institutions of higher education.

The government should define a comprehensive strategy to restructure vocational and technical training. This should encompass training for skilled workers and for technicians. The objective should be to make training more adaptable to changes in occupational demand. Such a strategy should include:

- Providing more general and transferable skills, including reducing specific vocational training in favor of broad technical or general secondary education;
- Upgrading technikums and specialized secondary schools to technical colleges exclusively at the post-grade 12 level;
- Strengthening management capacity, perhaps through alternative organizational structures (for example, a separate training agency);
- Taking steps to improve the quality of training, including raising the skills of instructors and improving teaching materials;
- Introducing measures to enhance upgrading within employment;
- Making routine use of studies to gather information on absorption of graduates into relevant employment.

Measures are immediately needed to reform existing market-oriented courses. Such fields include management and business administration, law, social sciences (for example, economics), technology, and languages. This should be done with a view to early expansion of enrollments and outputs. International expertise may be required to assess current programs. Study tours and fellowships abroad should be offered to Latvians to learn about the best existing programs.

Latvia needs to preserve the best parts of its scientific research complex. Despite efforts to restructure scientific research, the present complex remains too large for strictly Latvian (compared with former Soviet) purposes. Fragmentation into many institutions entails needlessly high overhead expenditures. Excellent, perhaps world class, research capacity exists in several fields potentially important for Latvian development (for example, microelectronics and microbiology), yet this could be lost if the government does not identify priority fields and reinforce support for them. Following completion of the evaluation of research by the Danish Academy of Sciences, the government should develop a comprehensive program to rationalize the research complex.

Medium-Term Measures

A management information system should be established, including vastly improved data on inputs to the system (for example, expenditures, enrollments, and teachers) as well as outputs (learning achievements and employment of graduates). The recent decentralization of authority risks a loss of central contact with local trends and control over developments. The challenge is for the ministry to guide the system indirectly and to establish accountability for results.

The government should prepare a strategy for financing the costs of needed system improvements by making more efficient use of resources spent on education and training. Improvements in relevance and quality will be costly. The number of students taught per teacher, very low by international standards, could be increased substantially. More efficient use should be made of existing teaching space. Larger class sizes would not mean reductions in quality of instruction, but could lead to lower recurrent costs per student. The government, as a matter of policy, may wish to exempt parts of the system, such as small rural schools or centers of excellence in certain fields. Such exceptions would not invalidate the substantial savings that could accrue from more efficient use of teaching staff.

The government should undertake a massive program to bring teaching content in all fields up-to-date with modern developments. Modernization requires staff training, teaching materials, programs, equipment and permanent access to networks and literature from abroad. Changes are already under way, but need to be intensified. Integration of research with teaching should be given high priority, as should the modernization of libraries.

The government should preserve and enhance the quality of teaching in general schools. First, more intensive programs should be developed to retrain school directors to become leaders of change and innovation. They are the key actors in implementing classroom reforms. Second, the program of textbook development should be strengthened, even in the face of difficulties in importing paper with scarce foreign exchange. Third, a continuous view of student achievement throughout the system is needed. Standardized diagnostic tests should be developed and administered at various key stages of the education process. The purpose would be to give students, parents, and teachers an incentive to improve performance as well as to identify weaknesses for remedial action. Fourth, consideration should be given to selective enhancement of teacher salaries in exchange for improvements in productivity, for example, ability to handle multiple subjects, thus enabling the teacher to handle more students.

CHAPTER 13

Environment

As a major importer of electricity and natural gas with significant domestic sources of hydropower, Latvia has a considerably lower level of air pollution than most other countries in Central and Eastern Europe. Most environmental problems in Latvia are concentrated in the major urban and industrial areas, at selected industrial sites in secondary towns, at intensive livestock enterprises, and at storage areas for agricultural chemicals. The heavy pollution of the Daugava and Lielupe rivers from point and non-point sources has serious impacts on water quality in the rivers and the Gulf of Riga. Localized groundwater pollution is occurring in areas adjacent to solid and hazardous waste disposal sites and major agricultural facilities. Many problems are the result of inadequate attention given to environmental issues in the development of urban areas and siting of industrial facilities and disposal locations for solid wastes, hazardous materials, and sludge.

Environmental Status and Health Effects

Air quality data suggest that problems are most evident in (a) Daugavpils, Jelgava, Liepaja, Olaine, Riga, and Ventspils, where industries are concentrated and vehicle traffic is heavy; and (b) a series of industrial facilities that are point sources of air pollution, including the Riga power plant complex, the Broceni asbestos cement and construction materials plant, the milk cannery in Rezekne, and the Liepaja ferrous metallurgical plant. In addition, there are problems of transboundary pollution from Mazeikiai (a petroleum refinery) and Naujoji Akmene (a cement plant) in Lithuania. The total discharge of pollutants into the atmosphere from all air pollution sources in Latvia was 584,780 tons in 1989, of which 427,000 tons (73 percent of the total) was from motor vehicles. Limited inspections of vehicles found 29 percent to be in violation of state emission standards. Small heating plants are a common point source of pollution in most urban areas and contribute to ambient air quality problems due to the use of low grade oil and short stacks.[1]

Few human health studies have been carried out in relation to air pollution in Latvia. There seem to be three principal reasons for this. First, the sanitary and epidemiology stations have been confined, almost exclusively, to infectious disease control and have not become very involved in air pollution issues. Second, expertise in the design and execution of valid environmental health studies is largely lacking. Third, there has been a long tradition of secrecy surrounding investigations into environmental contamination and its impact on human health.[2] The following are the documented health effects:

- In Brocenai, the cement plant's workers are heavily exposed to asbestos in the work room air, and the plant emits over 5,000 tons of asbestos laden dust into the atmosphere each

---

1.   It is important to note that most emission data in Latvia is calculated, rather than measured, with all the validity problems that this implies.

2.   One notable example of this is in Liepaja, where approximately six investigations into human health problems associated with electromagnetic radiation and industrial pollution have been carried out in recent years. The results of these studies are scattered around different agencies in the country with no agency having a complete overview of them.

year. Local clinic records show that a high proportion of plant workers has obstructive lung disease.

- Two studies have been done in Olaine of workers at the pharmaceutical firms and of residents. The first study demonstrated increased rates of allergic sensitization and immunosuppression among the workers at Biolar and residents of Olaine compared to the control group. The second study showed higher rates of unhealthy newborns and of acute respiratory and allergic diseases among children in Olaine than in the control area.

Groundwater resources are increasingly being exploited in the major urban and industrial areas due to the widespread pollution of surface and shallow groundwater from point and non-point sources. Overextraction of groundwater has caused the water table to drop in both Riga and Liepaja, leading to salt water intrusion into Liepaja's groundwater. Groundwater quality is negatively affected by leachates from combined municipal and industrial waste disposal sites; sludge disposal sites contaminated by heavy metals; and manure, fertilizers, pesticides, and oil storage facilities. Documented cases of groundwater pollution include: Cesis (disposal site leachate), Daugavpils (biological oxygen demand, chemical oxygen demand, ammonia, caprolactam), Iecava (ammonia, nitrates, chlorides, organic matter), Incukalns (oil products), Jelgava (hydrocarbons, chlorides, organic compounds), Jurmala (chemical wastes from pulp and paper mill), Olaine (piridine, chlorides, phenols, and so on), Riga (detergents, oil products), and Ulbroke (nitrogen compounds, chlorides, phenols). Groundwater pollution also contributes to the pollution of surface waters, as in the case of the Getlini dump in Riga, where groundwater contaminated by hydrocarbons and chlorides is directed to the Daugava River. A special risk is associated with the presence of approximately 500 tons of dated and banned pesticides stored at a series of facilities.

Surface Waters. Most major cities in Latvia discharge their wastewaters to the Daugava River (Daugavpils, Riga), the Lielupe and its tributaries (Jelgava, Olaine), or directly to the Baltic Sea (Jurmala, Liepaja, Ventspils). Management of water quality in the Daugava and Lielupe river basins is complicated by the international nature of the rivers. Latvian rivers discharge either to the Gulf of Riga or directly into the Baltic Sea. The Gulf of Riga is under severe stress from heavy loads of organic material and nutrients. The coastal areas of the bay, especially in the vicinity of river mouths and wastewater discharge points, have high levels of bacteriological pollution. There are concentrations of heavy metals and hydrocarbons in the ports of Liepaja, Riga, and Ventspils. Eutrophication is occurring as the result of heavy loading of nutrients and seasonally extensive algae blooms can be observed in a number of areas. This has resulted in damage to fish habitats, significant declines in fish production, a reduction in fish species, losses of recreational use, aesthetic problems from strong odors, and pollution of the Baltic Sea.

Beaches. Contamination of the Daugava and Lielupe rivers from sewage and local emissions from the Sloka pulp and paper mill have contributed to beach closures in Jurmala, one of the prime summer recreation areas on the Baltic Sea coast. During the pre-independence period, stop swimming orders were rarely issued. Water samples were rarely taken at the beaches, and public health officials were reluctant to take actions that might affect the summer vacationers there. However, over the last three summers such orders have become common in Jurmala, and in 1991 lasted for the whole season. Cases of skin rash have been reported among some who ignored the stop swimming orders. Bathing has also been frequently prohibited in the Venta River (Ventspils region and Kuldiga), the Daugava River (Jekabpils and Plavinas), and the Gauja River (Cesis region).

The annual discharge of wastewater in Latvia is 367,210 million cubic meters, of which 65 percent is treated and 35 percent untreated. The untreated wastewater load across the country was recently reduced from 70 percent to 35 percent following the completion of phase I of the Riga municipal wastewater treatment plant in late 1991. However, many of the existing plants are moderately to severely overloaded, resulting in portions of their flow being discharged after partial treatment. Approximately 50 percent of the municipal discharge is from industries connected to the municipal sewers, of which it is estimated that only 10 percent receives pre-treatment. Large loads of heavy metals are discharged into the sewage systems from industrial users (galvanic industries in Daugavpils and Riga are the most important sources). The large Sloka pulp and paper plant in Jurmala is a major point source of pollution on the Gulf of Riga. Threats to surface waters also come from accidents due to negligence in the handling of industrial waste discharges into rivers.

In Latvia, 386,000 cubic meters of sludge are produced per year by combined municipal and industrial wastewater treatment plants. In addition, an undetermined amount of sludge and slime is produced by pre-treatment at a limited number of industrial plants. Sludge management is hampered by a lack of dewatering technology, while its disposal and reuse is often constrained by high concentrations of heavy metals. Most sludge is dried in land-extensive facilities that are not lined or monitored, then disposed of in landfills, which presents a major risk of groundwater contamination. The completion of new municipal wastewater treatment plants and an expansion of industrial pre-treatment facilities will increase the scope of this problem in the future.

Agricultural runoff is estimated to contribute approximately 40 to 50 percent of the nutrient load in Latvian rivers and the Bay of Riga. This runoff results from the application and storage of natural and chemical fertilizers, and from large-scale intensive livestock and poultry operations located throughout the country. Groundwater pollution has occurred in the vicinity of ten large regional storehouses for agricultural chemicals, with the most serious conditions developing at Grobina, Iecava, Skrunda, Stende, and Ventspils. Large amounts of fertilizers are regularly found in runoff, which pollutes surface and groundwater resources. The excessive fertilizer runoff is due to (a) poor application technology, (b) problems with the fertilizer balance for specific fields, (c) poor tillage practices that fail to incorporate the fertilizer into the soil, and (d) open and unsealed storage facilities. However, a twentytwo fold increase in fertilizer prices and the sale of pesticides for hard currency only (as of the beginning of 1992) have resulted in a massive decline in their use.

Other major sources of pollution are 200 large pig breeding complexes, 14 large poultry farms, 230 cattle breeding complexes, 90 meat and milk processing plants, 10 large agrochemical storehouses, and 20 fur-bearing animal farms that create locally severe pollution of surface waters and groundwaters. Often the storage capacity for manure at these facilities is inadequate, resulting in manure application at inappropriate times. With the re-privatization of land and a decrease in supplies of grain imported from the former Soviet Union, many Latvian experts believe that a restructuring of the livestock industry will occur over the next five years, including reduced pig production and increased small-scale cattle production.

The most important and well-documented human health problems from water pollution in Latvia are due to contamination of drinking water. Unlike other countries in Eastern Europe, Latvia relies more extensively on surface waters for its drinking water needs. Shortages of alum, an agent used for water disinfection, are common in Latvia, and sporadic waterborne cases of hepatitis A and typhoid occur. During the winter of 1988-89, the city of Riga ran low on alum, which resulted in a two-month long epidemic of hepatitis A, with about 1,000 cases recorded. Surface water contaminated through negligence by food handlers has also contributed to foodborne infectious disease problems. Leptospirosis has become more frequent in Latvia, a serious concern because 18 to 25 percent of cases are fatal. Other threats to safe surface water come from accidents due to negligence in the handling of industrial wastewater discharges into rivers. In the last two years three major incidents have affected the Daugava River, and required emergency action to prevent toxic chemicals, including cyanide, from entering the water supply systems of Daugavpils and other towns.

Nearly 250,000 tons of hazardous industrial waste and 265,000 tons of non-toxic industrial solid waste are generated each year, mostly in Riga and Liepaja. The generation of household waste also varies greatly depending on location and living patterns: from 100 to 150 kilograms per capita per year in rural areas to 300 kilograms per capita per year in cities (Jurmala). The city of Riga generates the largest amount by far—205,500 tons—plus another 33,000 tons from the surrounding district. Of Riga's waste, the largest share (65 percent) consists of paper and cardboard and food wastes in roughly equal amounts. The next largest share (3 to 4 percent each) consists of textiles, plastics, ferrous metals, and glass.

Most of the waste generated in Latvia, of whatever character, is deposited in landfills or on waste piles. Excavated, lined, hydrogeologically safe landfills are virtually unknown. Existing landfills were designed without subsurface investigation, groundwater protection measures, or, until recently, monitoring protocols. Medical waste and hazardous industrial waste of all kinds are routinely deposited with household solid waste in these landfills. While environmental officials are now aware of the extensive groundwater contamination that this has caused, the practice of combining these wastes continues unabated.[3]

Less than 500 tons of the nearly 250,000 tons of hazardous waste generated are incinerated. In Olaine, Latbiofarm incinerates about 300 tons of solvents in its gas incinerator, and Biolar burns about 30 tons of organic waste and solvents in its small incinerator. In Riga, the harbor facility has converted two Norwegian ship boilers into an incinerator for waste oils and oil-containing solids, burning about 150 tons per year. None of these incineration units has air pollution controls nor are data on emission content available. As in Estonia and Lithuania, an effort is being made to recycle mercury bulbs, about 50,000 per year in Liepaja. In addition, for the use of sludge in brick production is being investigated.

Forests cover 2,803,000 hectares, or approximately 43 percent, of Latvia's territory, and are administered by the Ministry of Forests and the Ministry of Agriculture, which is responsible for forests on land controlled by agricultural cooperatives. It is anticipated that the forest lands held by the agricultural cooperatives will be returned to private ownership. The composition of the forests is pine (38 percent), spruce (20 percent), birch (31 percent), and other deciduous species (10 percent). The status of forests is generally satisfactory, although some damage to pine trees has been reported from both transboundary air pollution in the form of acid rain and from air pollution from the oil refinery at Mazeikiai and cement plant at Naujoji Akmene along the southwestern border with Lithuania.

Nature protection areas cover 407,496 hectares, or 6.4 percent of Latvian territory. However, these include only one national park (Gauja) and five strictly protected reserves. The national

---

3.   The Nordic Project Fund, in its May 1991 environmental report on Latvia, identified 450 dumps in Latvia, covering some 517 hectares, and classified them as follows: satisfactory, 168; bad, 166; and disastrous, 116.

park is managed by the Ministry of Forestry and includes a mixture of cultural and natural elements. A system of protected areas and nature reserves is managed by the Environmental Protection Committee. Limited budget resources restrict staffing, management, and development programs. Management problems in protected areas include the control of building activities (especially recreational cottages near the seashore and lakes), the maintenance of approved land use patterns, and the impact of agricultural runoff. Authorities consider the basic system of protected areas satisfactory, however, there are increasing concerns about the effects of land restitution and privatization.

Wetlands. Large-scale investments have been made in Latvia for agricultural drainage, which agronomists consider necessary for 70 percent of all agricultural land. It is estimated that 60 percent of agricultural land has been provided with drainage. In addition, channel straightening programs were conducted during the 1960s and 1970s in older agricultural areas. These programs have had a major influence on the status and distribution of natural areas of wetland habitat. The clearance of floodplain forests has also been practiced to increase the cultivable area. Recently, efforts have been made to conserve the remaining wetlands, with many areas being placed under a variety of forms of protection. Most wetland areas—particularly those with large drainage areas—are being adversely effected by agricultural runoff. Farmers' strong interest in obtaining additional agricultural land through drainage improvements remains a potential threat to Latvian wetlands.

Environmental Laws

The legislation governing environmental protection in Latvia is changing. Since 1990, the Supreme Council has enacted the following environmental laws:

- The Law on the Environmental Protection Committee (June 1990): establishes the Environmental Protection Committee as the central state executive and oversight organ for all environmental protection and natural resource use in Latvia.

- The Law on State Environmental Impact Assessments (October 1990): establishes and regulates the environmental impact assessment process in Latvia.

- The Environmental Protection Committee Inspectorate Regulation (October 1990): vests enforcement power in inspectors to halt activities that violate the law and to punish violators.

- The Law on Environmental Protection (August 1991): omnibus environmental protection law that delegates responsibility regarding environmental protection, natural resource use, Environmental Impact Assessment procedures, standards, permits, and public information and sets out goals for the protection of the environment and the rational utilization of natural resources.

- The Law on Natural Resource and Pollution Charges (December 1990): establishes charges for the use of natural resources and the release of effluents within standards and enforces sanctions against those whose use exceeds permitted levels or whose releases exceed the standards.

•   The Baltic Sea and Gulf of Riga Coastal Protection Regime (June 1990): establishes a coastal protection belt by resolution of the Council of Ministers.

A transition is required from a system in which environmental laws represent a statement of goals to a system in which those laws provide operative requirements for the control of potential sources of environmental risk. The Environmental Protection Committee and the Supreme Council are both considering a range of new legislation, including a hazardous waste law, an air act, and a forest resources law. The first step in such an effort is to design a national strategy of environmental protection that is closely linked to the strategy guiding the economic reform process. It will not be possible to address all environmental problems at once, and care must be exercised to apply the limited regulatory resources to sources of pollution that are likely to survive economic restructuring.

A leading example of the clash in reform values is found in the movement for land use reform, particularly the restitution of land to former owners on the one hand, and the laws (beginning in 1987) that extend state protection to special lands as nature reserves on the other. The legal and policy question being debated is whether such lands belong to former owners or to the state. Because of the past, there is a reluctance to interpose the state in a priority position over equitable claimants. The Ministry of Forestry and the Environmental Protection Committee have recognized the potential problem; however, an adequate way to protect the status of these lands has not been developed. An important obstacle is the present inability of the government to pay adequate compensation to landowners for the maintenance of private lands for conservation purposes. Procedures need to be developed that provide proper compensation to private owners and enforceable restrictions on land use in conservation areas. The issue should be addressed as an element of the new land ownership and nature protection legislation. In the medium term, environmental education programs should be implemented for private landowners.

Latvia participated in the Ronneby Conference, endorsed the Baltic Sea Environmental Declaration (1990), and has been active in the Baltic Sea Task Force. Latvia plans to become a signatory to the Helsinki Convention in the future and also plans to sign the various environmental protocols sponsored by the United Nations Economic Commission for Europe. In December 1991, the Latvian parliament ratified the Basel convention on the transport of hazardous waste. The Environmental Protection Committee is presently coordinating Latvia's application for membership in United Nations Environment Programme and ratification of the Ramsar Convention.

The government of Latvia has entered into bilateral agreements on environmental cooperation with Denmark, Finland, and Ukraine and agreements with Belarus, Germany, and Sweden are under discussion. Representatives of the United States Agency for International Development and United States Environmental Protection Agency have initiated discussions concerning potential cooperation. Denmark and Sweden funded preparation of the pre-feasibility study of the Daugava River basin and the Gulf of Riga under the Baltic Sea Environmental Program. Denmark has also supported the preparation of a preliminary evaluation of hazardous waste. Assistance to date from other countries has been limited to technical assistance, training, and study tours. Latvia is also involved in a variety of twinning agreements on a cooperative basis with sister cities in other Baltic countries. The World Wide Fund for Nature has supported the development of the Latvian Fund for Nature. To date, the role of the foreign private sector has been limited to the establishment of a series of joint ventures for consulting services and the production and distribution of pollution control equipment.

Institutions

The Environmental Protection Committee was created by the Supreme Council on June 2, 1990 (after the declaration of Latvian independence). Because of the strong public interest generated by the election in addressing Latvia's environmental situation, the Environmental Protection Committee was placed on a level equal to but outside the Council of Ministers structure. The rationale for this arrangement was that environmental concerns would otherwise be lost amid economic priorities and a yet-to-be reformed Soviet-style bureaucracy.

The Environmental Protection Committee is responsible for formulating and implementing Latvia's policy for environmental protection and natural resource use; performing state environmental impact assessments; establishing environmental standards; and administering and enforcing environmental protection and natural resource use throughout Latvia, the continental shelf, and the nation's Baltic Sea economic zone. The Environmental Protection Committee is divided into two major subdivisions: technical expertise, generally overseen by the first vice chairman; and enforcement, generally overseen by the chief inspector. The technical expertise section works out overall policy and standards, while the enforcement section is the implementation arm of the agency, carrying out legal mandates in the field, including levying pollution taxes and penalties, principally through nine regional committees and, where appropriate, the Marine Inspection Agency. The headquarters group numbers some eighty-nine staff members, while the regions generally have seventeen to twenty staff each. A sizeable number of additional staff is also found in the so-called subordinated organizations, which contain a Research Center, an Analytic and Information Center, a Forest and Hunting Inspection Agency, a Water Resource Use and Inspectorate, a Water Reservoirs and Mineral Resources Inspectorate, and several nature reserves. The Hydrogeological and Meteorological Institute, a large group formed under the Soviet system, performs independent environmental monitoring and maintains a database. Coordination is often effected with this group, but the Environmental Protection Committee has no administrative control over it.

The Environmental Protection Committee also drafts and submits to the Supreme Council proposals for new environmental legislation. These proposals are submitted to the Environmental Protection Commission, which is also chaired by an elected member of the Council of Ministers. Commission members may change the proposed legislation, return it to the Environmental Protection Committee for further work, or approve it and forward it to the Legislative Commission before submission to the full Supreme Council for its first reading.

Ultimately, the Latvian environmental agenda will best be served by the inclusion of the Environmental Protection Committee in the Cabinet as a full-fledged ministry, where there is likely to be greater political accountability. The Environmental Protection Committee's scientific, monitoring, and laboratory capabilities need to be better integrated, especially in a time of scarce resources. These capabilities are presently scattered among such agencies as the Environmental Protection Committee, the Republic Hygiene Center, and the Hydrogeology Institute. Therefore, consideration should be given to a structural arrangement that allows the resources and expertise of the Hydrogeology Institute to be more effectively deployed in support of the Environmental Protection Committee's regulatory mandates.

Nine regional environmental protection committees are responsible for enforcing environmental regulations, issuing permits for projects, and providing public information services. Latvia has twenty-six local government administrative units, so each regional committee supervises about three local government units. Each regional committee has five subdivisions: (a) an inspectorate, the largest group; (b) a laboratory for sampling and testing; (c) an expert group that performs environmental impact assessments preparatory to the issuance of permits for new or expanded facilities; (d) a cadastre that catalogs statistics on emission discharges, natural resource use, volumes, and so on; and (e) support services. The principal function of the regional committees is to determine the pollution charge level, to inspect for compliance, to impose penalties for exceeding limits, and to negotiate a compliance schedule to achieve the necessary reductions in emissions. The ultimate sanction, closing down an enterprise, is as yet unexercised.

Coordination between the environment protection and hygiene networks is hampered by the fact that the Environmental Protection Committee is organized on the basis of nine regions, while the hygiene centers are organized on the basis of twenty-six districts and six cities. In the Ventspils and Liepaja areas, cooperation between municipal environmental authorities and their respective regional environmental protection committee representatives seemed quite close. However, cooperation between environmental and sanitary epidemiology officials was much less evident. In Ventspils there was sharp disagreement about the interpretation of health data between sanitary epidemiology and municipal specialists. In Liepaja, the knowledge bases of environment and health officials were quite different from one another. This seemed to be due to a lack of information sharing between agencies and a lack of understanding of how inter-agency teamwork might improve environmental management. By contrast, relations between sanitary epidemiology officials and the medical community concerned with environmental health (pediatricians, oncologists, and respirologists) seem to be stronger in Latvia than elsewhere in Central and Eastern Europe. To improve coordination between the environmental and hygiene networks, nine lead hygiene centers should be appointed and, after a period of transition, consolidated in a way that is consistent with both the structure of governance and the structure of environmental protection.

Environmental Standards

Currently, Latvia uses the air and water standards of the former Soviet Union and has added a limited number of its own national standards. The Soviet standards are more stringent than European Community or United States standards; however, their use as a basis for enforcing compliance was limited in the former Soviet Union. The standards were most frequently used as a reference point for the description of air and water quality at a specific location. The practice of setting unrealistic standards that cannot be enforced contributed to the general disregard for environmental laws and regulations.

Soviet ambient air quality standards (AAQS) apply to over 543 pollutants. The current standards specify twenty-minute and twenty-four-hour averages for maximum allowable concentrations. Annual average standards are desirable because the twenty-four-hour maximum allowable concentrations are not related to long-time exposures. Annual AAQS should be promulgated for compounds that (a) tend to bioaccumulate in the environment, or (b) are determined to produce adverse public health impacts after chronic low-level exposures. The adoption of EC AAQS appears a realistic solution for pollutants that have corresponding EC standards, since, based on reported measurements of actual air quality, Latvia may reasonably aim at the achievement of ambient air quality that meets EC standards in all areas of the country within a relatively short time. The adoption of EC annual AAQS implies the rolling back of current twenty-four-hour air quality standards. The adoption of AAQS for too many pollutants makes it difficult to focus on the most significant air quality problems. Even more important, it is practically impossible to establish monitoring and enforcement programs for all the proposed pollutants. Therefore standards should be limited to those pollutants that have been identified in Latvia.

Currently, plant-specific emission limits are based on manual calculations using the simplified dispersion algorithms applied in the former Soviet Union. After AAQS are revised, the same formulas may be used to recalculate the emission limits for each polluter. However, in the medium term, computerized dispersion models should be developed and applied in areas most affected by air pollution.

An All-Union regulation of less than 1.5 percent carbon monoxide emissions exists for automobiles, but 3 percent is allowed when testing randomly selected automobiles on the road. Officials estimate that 30 percent of all vehicles tested fail the carbon monoxide test. There is no regulation for nitrogen oxides emissions. Two-cycle engines and older vehicles, both of which contribute significantly to automobile emissions, are not banned. Hydrocarbon exhaust emissions are specified for automobiles and vary with the number of cylinders. A regulation defining the level of pollutants in smoke from diesel engines exists. Lead is used at a level of 0.15 milligram per liter in 92-octane fuel, but 76-octane fuel is currently available in both leaded and unleaded formulations. The exact quantity of unleaded fuel available is unknown. Current thinking about motor vehicle pollution abatement appears to be centered on catalytic converters. However, until unleaded fuel is available in greater quantity no abatement of motor exhaust emissions is planned.

More than 2,000 water quality indicators were applied in the former Soviet Union. Water quality requirements were defined in terms of these indicators for household and service sector water use, for recreational use, and for use in fisheries. As with ambient air quality standards, water quality standards were too strict, too large in number, and impossible to monitor and analyze. Therefore, a revised set of standards should be developed.

Individual effluent limits are based on manual calculations using dispersion algorithms that take into account the characteristics of the particular river receiving the effluent. Short-term achievement of the water quality objective cannot realistically be expected. Continuous improvement of water quality assumes the development of water quality management programs for the Daugava and Lielupe river basins, other minor drainage basins, and the Gulf of Riga. With the aim of achieving the targeted water quality in the medium term, interim effluent limits and compliance schedules should be established for each major polluter.

Enforcement

Latvia relies on a blend of command and control and market-based instruments in the enforcement of environmental regulations, with greater emphasis given to the latter. In a market economy, if enterprises are required to pay environmental charges that take account of the social costs of extraction and pollution of natural resources, they will have powerful incentives to modify their operations to make more efficient use of resources and to reduce the volume and potential toxicity of any wastes that are produced. In Latvia, the institutional framework of a market economy will develop over an extended period and it will take time before market rules become effective. If state industry continues to experience limited accountability and soft budget constraints, the economic incentives provided by market-based instruments will be rendered less effective. Therefore, the government should take steps to increase the use and effectiveness of command and control instruments (permits, civil penalties, and closure of plants and processes).

Enforcement is the operational responsibility of inspectors from the nine regional environmental protection committees (Daugavpils, Jelgava, Liepaja, Madona, Ogre, Rezekne, Riga, Valmiera, and Ventspils) and the recently established municipal environmental units in selected cities. The Republican Hygiene Center, in cooperation with local sanitary-epidemiological centers, is primarily responsible for the enforcement of drinking and recreational water standards and handles occupational health issues. These organizations are authorized to review and approve permits for the construction, expansion, and operation of municipal, industrial, and agro-industrial facilities. They participate in the land use planning and zoning process, including the identification of land tracts suitable for residential development. Their field personnel are dispersed throughout the country and have the authority to conduct site visits, collect and analyze samples, and take enforcement actions.

Permits are issued by the regional environment protection committees. The permits stipulate limits on the emission and discharge of major pollutants into the air and water bodies and on waste generation. The limits are subject to revision every year. When a factory has no equipment to meet emission limits calculated on the basis of ambient standards, temporary limits are established on the basis of the best possible utilization of the technology installed at the plant.

Natural resource and pollution taxes and fines were introduced in January 1991 under the Law on Natural Resource Taxes. The taxes are intended to promote the efficient use of resources and encourage their conservation. Natural resource taxes (fees) are levied for the use of surface water, groundwater, sand, gravel, clay, dolomite, limestone, gypsum, peat, sapropel, and medicinal mud according to the number of cubic meters used. All funds collected for the use of these resources are retained for use in environmental protection programs by the municipal government where the activity is carried out. Environmental taxes are levied on air pollution and water pollution per ton of pollutants on the basis of four hazard classification categories (non-toxic substances, medium hazard substances, hazardous substances, and very hazardous substances). Taxes are also collected for waste disposal per cubic meter on the basis of five hazard classification categories (non-toxic substances, medium hazard substances, hazardous substances, very hazardous substances, and extremely toxic substances). The fees were designed to reflect the harmful effects of pollutants. The law provides that 75 percent of collected fees go to local governments and 25 percent to the state budget; however, these funds are specifically earmarked for environmental protection. The real (inflation adjusted) level of the fees was seriously eroded during 1991 and was adjusted by the introduction of indexing by the Latvian parliament, which was effective January 1, 1992.

Fines have to be paid by enterprises if emissions are above the permitted amount. Fines are equal to three times the fees and paid from the (after taxes) profit. Fines accrue to the State Environment Protection Fund, which allocates 30 percent for use by the National Committee and 70 percent for use by regional committees. The fund is administered by the Environmental Protection Committee and is used to finance environment-related expenditures, including investments. In 1991, about RUR 6 million accrued to the fund.

Since the purpose of fines is to ensure compliance with permits rather than revenue generation, the use of fines as the sole source of revenues for the State Environmental Protection Fund appears inappropriate. Also, the level of fines is inadequate to cause significant changes in polluters' behavior, therefore the relationship between fees and fines should be modified. Natural resource taxes (royalties) should be revised to reflect the relationship between extraction costs and market prices more fully.

The earmarked taxes on natural resource use have often been used for general budget support by the municipal governments. This has been further complicated by the fact that the municipalities have not been provided with guidelines for the use of the taxes and fees or criteria for the selection of project activities. In light of these problems, priority should be given to the development of detailed guidelines, financing criteria, operational procedures, and accounting systems for the use of natural resource and environmental taxes by the Environmental Protection Committee and municipal governments. Criteria should be based on the principles of polluter pays (that is, the funds should finance only part of the abatement costs) and cost-effectiveness (measures with the highest benefits per unit of investment costs should have priority). It is important that the environment protection funds at the national and local level be operated in a transparent way, fully disclosed to the public.

The monitoring capacity of the Environmental Protection Committee needs to be strengthened at the national and regional level to improve enforcement activities. A special problem exists with industrial facilities, which often attempt to avoid paying environmental taxes and fines through a wide variety of techniques. The Environmental Protection Committee has initiated action to reduce the evasion of such charges through the practice of diluting industrial wastewater with groundwater to reduce concentrations of wastes to discharge limits.

The extensive lack of infrastructure itself creates the conditions for many dischargers simply to be overlooked, for example, Riga is justly proud of its recently commissioned wastewater treatment plant (phase I), but there is no escaping the fact that the system will not be able to extend its coverage to a large portion of Riga's inhabitants, nor to many of its industries, which will continue to discharge directly to the River Daugava, in many cases without any treatment at all. That this is the condition in many of Latvia's cities underscores the likelihood that many dischargers are not yet included in the pollution tax system nor are they subject to any regulatory management of any kind. The success of the Environmental Protection Committee as an institution is directly linked to its success in creating a level playing field where the regulated community perceives that its members are being treated fairly and even-handedly. Militating against achieving that goal is the significant fraction of enterprises still outside the regulatory net. It is recommended that priority should be given to reducing that number.

Monitoring

The Hydrometeorological Agency in Riga is responsible for the collection, analysis, and dissemination of all types of basic environmental, meteorological, and hydrological data at the national level. It maintains a central laboratory and a system of six regional laboratories. It conducts its work program in coordination with the Environmental Protection Committee, which establishes the environmental standards and the broad objectives of monitoring programs. The Hydrometeorological Agency publishes annual reports on freshwater and coastal waters. The agency is in the process of developing a series of key databases. A complementary central laboratory is maintained by the Environmental Protection Committee in Riga that provides support for the nine laboratories maintained by the regional environmental protection committees. These laboratories focus on the analysis of samples collected during environmental control activities and special studies. The State Geological Service monitors the quantity and quality of groundwaters. The Republican Hygiene Center is responsible for bacteriological monitoring of drinking and bathing waters, monitoring occupational environmental quality, and conducting spot measurements of ambient air quality.

Air quality monitoring is carried out by the Environmental Protection Committee, the Hydrometeorological Service, and the Sanitary Epidemiological Stations. The program of the sanitary epidemiology stations is mostly concentrated on the occupational environment. The management programs of all agencies are hampered by a lack of equipment and continuous automated monitoring. Regional and municipal environmental authorities generally rely on calculations of emissions for regulatory purposes and rarely use ambient air quality information in their work.

The Hydrometeorological Service has the capacity to monitor twenty-two gases and volatile organics as well as eight metals and benzo(a)pyrene. The national air quality monitoring system includes twenty-two stations for ambient measurements and emission data is collected for approximately 200 point sources. Data is routinely collected in eight principal locations: Daugavpils (two locations), Jekabpils (two locations), Jurmala (two locations), Liepaja (two locations), Olaine (one location), Riga (five locations), Valmiera (two locations), and Ventspils (two locations). Episodic measurements are also collected for Jelgava, Kuldiga, Liepaja, and Riga. Although summaries of this data do exist, they are not published in an easily accessible form. Regional environmental protection authorities did not appear to be fully aware of the results of their own monitoring activities or have access to the data in a format that would be useful for environmental management actions.

The national water quality monitoring system includes sixty-nine monitoring stations for receiving water quality, and is supplemented by measurements at major discharge points made by the regional environmental protection committees. A monitoring program also exists for coastal (ten stations) and marine waters (forty-four stations). The parameters examined include temperature, pH, color, suspended solids, chemical oxygen demand, biological oxygen demand (5 days), salinity, dry material, ammonia, nitrates, nitrites, sulfates, chlorides, calcium, heavy metals (chromium, copper, iron, manganese, nickel, lead), oil, detergents, phenol, and pesticides. Monitoring stations have been selected on the basis of their position in the drainage basins, the existence of known pollution sources, and their importance as sources of drinking water. Monitoring is conducted at major locations on a monthly basis, bimonthly at secondary stations, and special monitoring programs are conducted in areas that have special water quality management problems, such as Olaine.

Even though emission data are collected on 200 sources in Latvia, there is a limited amount of systematic emissions monitoring. Regulated industries appear to lack self-monitoring equipment. Emissions testing is conducted sporadically. Although there are protocols for monitoring and analytical methods, industrial laboratories largely ignore or are unaware of them. Integrating point source emission data into areawide pollution patterns is performed sporadically. Modeling and incorporating meteorological data with emission and air quality testing is planned, but is not presently practiced to any significant extent. Submission of source emission data to regional environment boards is required from all industrial pollution sources on a routine basis; however, it is either calculated using emission factors or sporadically gathered, which at best can only approximate actual emission levels. Unlike wastewater monitoring, which is generally based on intermittent samples taken from the source, air source sampling is best undertaken by continuous monitoring. Processes, even those assumed to operate under steady conditions, are subject to variations, and a true picture of emissions is generally achievable only by integrating data over long time periods. Unfortunately, instruments required for air source emissions monitoring are generally not available. There is also a lack of trained personnel at industrial sites.

Many countries apply a system whereby major enterprises monitor their own emissions on a continuous basis, subject to review by the government. This system saves scarce administrative resources; however, it assumes that the government has the capability to control the monitoring activities of the enterprises and that enforcement is carried out uncompromisingly. Regulations should be introduced that require self-monitoring and reporting by the enterprises and makes the reporting of false information a criminal violation. The purchase of necessary equipment may not be such a burden. The application of stack gas analysis instruments usually provides productive opportunities for improving energy efficiency for many enterprises.

In Latvia, effective air and water monitoring is inhibited by dated equipment, a proliferation of small analytical laboratories, problems with the standardization of procedures, inter-calibration between laboratories, and the limited development of data management systems. The large number of laboratories exacerbates the problem by spreading scarce resources available for the purchase and maintenance of equipment and replacement of reagents between a great number of competing parties. Quality control and inter-calibration can most effectively be done with a comparatively small number of laboratories. In addition to the central and six regional laboratories of the Hydrometeorological Agency, the central and the nine regional environmental laboratories of the Environmental Protection Committee, the laboratories maintained by the Republican Hygiene Center, and the academic laboratories, there are also additional water testing laboratories operated by industrial enterprises. A significant reduction in the number of laboratories, especially those dealing with water, is a necessary precondition for rehabilitating and upgrading the system as a whole.

The organization of the public health system, particularly with respect to its efforts in environmental health, is undergoing review at the present time. It has been recognized that the present network of sanitary epidemiology stations is not providing adequate environmental health monitoring and is not taking leadership in identifying, evaluating, and controlling pollution situations of potential threat to human health. There is disagreement as to why this is so. One reason given is a lack of budgetary resources. Another is a lack of appropriate training among the sanitary epidemiology staff. A reorganization was recently proposed to integrate all activities that are directly related to preventive aspects of health.[4] The current activities of the sanitary epidemiology stations would be reported to parliament through a newly created National Control Service. So far, the proposal has not undergone an extensive consultation process and runs the risk of being attacked by people who might have accepted it if they had helped develop it.

Investment Priorities for Pollution Abatement

National Environmental Strategy

A key constraint to addressing priority environmental problems in Latvia successfully is the lack of a national environmental strategy. This strategy should support a shift in approach from one of reactive environmental control to one of proactive environmental management with a balanced focus

---

4.   A new deputy director of the Department of Health would be appointed as the chief of Human Ecology and Public Health Services. Reporting to the chief would be the heads of Statistics, Emergency Services, and a newly formed Institute of Human Ecology and Public Health. This latter would be composed of a team of epidemiologists and national specialists in medical disciplines relevant to disease prevention.

on preventive and curative actions. The strategy could provide a framework for the allocation of scarce domestic resources and give direction for the use of grants and loans from international sources. The development of the national environmental strategy would benefit from the concurrent development of local environmental strategies for a limited number of key areas.

Environmental Planning and Management

Many of Latvia's environmental problems have been made significantly more difficult to manage as the result of inadequate attention being given to environmental issues in the development of urban areas; siting of industrial facilities; and selection of sites for the disposal of solid wastes, hazardous materials, and sludge. The process of administrative and economic restructuring currently occurring in Latvia provides the opportunity to take a new approach to spatial planning that fully incorporates environmental concerns. Priority should be given to strengthening the capabilities of institutions and professionals, from both the public and private sectors, in environmental planning. In addition, environmental planning issues should be a major factor in the preparation of environmental impact assessments.

Technical solutions are available for most of the environmental problems caused by industry. Key measures should include the expanded use of modern equipment for industrial pollution control, waste utilization, and environmental monitoring. However, substantial investments are required in pollution abatement technology, and most of the enterprises do not have the funds to finance these investments. There is danger of using support from the government to invest in pollution abatement for industries that will prove themselves uneconomic and will have to be closed down in the near future. Also, investments have to be cost-effective, that is, there should not be any other option that can achieve the pollution reduction goals at a lower cost. Therefore, two basic conditions should be met before providing government support to an enterprise: (a) the enterprise should have a restructuring or privatization plan approved by the ministries of Economy and Finance, and (b) the enterprise should have an environmental protection action plan based on a completed environmental audit approved by the Environmental Protection Committee.

Industrial Environmental Audits

Industrial environmental audits can produce many benefits. Used in conjunction with air quality monitoring data, industrywide emission inventories can be instrumental in guiding programs for remedial development and assisting in the preparation of remediation priorities. The geographical identification of pollutants, together with meteorological modeling, can contribute to an understanding of the transport of contaminants that air quality measurement alone cannot account for. One of the most important benefits of plantwide environmental audits is to identify processes and operational practices that are habitual polluters. This internalization of pollution problems assists plant operators in making changes that reduce emissions rather than focusing on control, which can be costly and sometimes ineffective. The process change route often brings other benefits, such as reducing operating costs, making better use of raw materials, and smoothing out plant operations. It is also necessary to provide for auditing as an ongoing activity. Industrial activity is dynamic. Processes are changed, added, and discontinued; technology changes, fuel patterns change, and population changes occur. These changes will often require a re-evaluation of permissible industrial pollution emissions based on the need to meet ambient air and water quality requirements.

Air Pollution

The relatively high concentration of particulates in the air of certain cities is mostly due to point source emissions from the stacks of power plants and large factories. The solution is the installation and/or proper maintenance of appropriate particulate control equipment, such as electrostatic precipitators or fabric filters. Most large boilers have no control equipment of any kind. Fabric filtration equipment (dustbags) may be a feasible low-cost method of particulate emission control for small and medium-sized industrial operations. Enterprises that do not implement these measures should be heavily fined. The cost implications of these measures appear modest and could be financed by the enterprises themselves (with a few exceptions).

Based on reported air quality measurements, the health hazards caused by the ambient sulphur dioxide concentrations do not justify the installation of expensive control equipment. However, the ecological impact of emitted sulphur dioxide cannot be denied and may be considerable in Latvia and in neighboring countries. However, in view of the current economic situation, the country cannot afford the cost of sulphur dioxide control investments that would produce little economic benefits in the short and medium term. The appropriate short- and medium-term objective should be to import fuels with a reduced sulphur content and to switch selectively from heavy oil to natural gas at critical locations.

Water Pollution

The highest priority should be given to the protection of the domestic drinking water supply, which is a serious health concern. On an immediate basis, this requires that measures be taken to assure adequate treatment of domestic water supplies, particularly in Daugavpils and Riga. This involves the reliable provision of water supply treatment chemicals and close monitoring of the water supply. Steps should be taken to obtain analytical equipment that would permit measuring key water quality indicators within hours of sampling rather than after a period of days. Measures should also be taken to increase the monitoring of groundwater resources used for domestic consumption.

Problems are emerging with the continued operation of the water supply and wastewater systems due to a severe shortage of replacement units and spare parts from the former Soviet Union. Key types of potentially required materials include submersible pumps for groundwater wells, pumps for water and wastewater pumping stations, and aerators for wastewater treatment plants. Unless this problem is addressed in the near future through a properly planned and managed program to provide such materials, considerable difficulties could occur in maintaining the operation of certain water supply and wastewater facilities.

A major cause of environmental health problems is the use of surface water for domestic consumption. Industrial users, where technically feasible and cost-effective, should be made to use surface water sources to increase the availability of higher quality groundwater for domestic consumption. In addition, water conservation programs should be initiated for both domestic and industrial users to reduce the total demand for water and the associated increased costs for the supply and treatment of this water. To implement a water conservation program effectively, the use of economic measures (metering, increased user fees, and so on) should be combined with technical interventions (leak detection and repair, process modification in industry, and so on).

To improve water quality, partially completed wastewater treatment plants need to be finished on the basis of established priorities reflecting their level of completion and potential health, ecological, and economic benefits. First priority should be assigned to the completion of the Liepaja and Riga phase II (USD 75 million) systems. Construction should be started on the proposed new plant for Daugavpils (USD 46.5 million) only when full domestic and foreign funding is available for a phased program of construction. In these locations concurrent programs should be conducted to promote water conservation in industries and to promote pre-treatment of industrial wastewaters prior to their discharge to the sewer system. The existing wastewater treatment plant at Olaine should be considered for rehabilitation and expansion. A second priority in wastewater management would be the rehabilitation of existing municipal treatment plants in other locations, facilities at livestock complexes, and facilities at selected industrial plants to assure their proper performance until adequate funding becomes available for their upgrading and/or expansion. The long-term goal should be for all cities to construct their own sewage treatment plants. For smaller towns, consideration should be given to simpler and lower-cost alternatives to activated sludge technology, such as trickling filters and lagoons.

Significant improvement in water pollution control, however, will depend on the availability of large amounts of funding. The completion of plants is proceeding slowly due to a funding strategy that focused on the construction of a large number of plants simultaneously and a design approach that focused on construction of complete plants rather than phased construction of facilities. Historically, civil works have proceeded, subject to the availability of funds, while concurrent efforts were made to obtain scarce mechanical and electrical equipment. Plants have also been designed to accept very large wastewater flows that in many cases could be significantly reduced by water conservation programs, use of economic incentives to reduce water use, and the more cost-effective expenditure of funds in activities to reduce leakage into the sewer systems. Funds for municipal and industrial wastewater treatment have traditionally come from the state budget. The operation and maintenance of facilities is to be provided by user charges that are collected and retained by the operators of the municipal plants. However, these charges have not been set to reflect real costs.

Primary funding for the program should come from bank loans, but these will not materialize unless borrowers are creditworthy and generate enough revenue to service debt. That requires, in turn, that (a) the economic restructuring process leads to solvent, profitable companies; (b) there is an adequate local tax base provided to the municipalities; and (c) the municipal water and sewerage enterprises set user charges at a level that includes the cost of capital. Supplementary funding to finance cost-effective pollution control investments may come from the central and local environmental protection funds. However, water and sewerage enterprises should not be eligible for grants unless they move toward charging fees that are based on the economic cost of their services.

An international meeting on funding the Baltic Sea Environmental Program was held in late 1992. This meeting sought to mobilize public and private sector support for projects included in the program from multilateral institutions, bilateral donors, export credit agencies, commercial banks, and private companies and through sister city cooperation. Support provided under the program would be predicated on significant local participation in the funding of local expenditures required for project implementation and on the capability of water enterprises to service debt.

Non-Point Source Pollution

Non-point source pollution should be addressed as a long-term problem through changes in the pricing of inputs; agronomic practices; investments in controls, application equipment, and storage facilities; applied research; and agricultural extension. Control interventions could include the construction of low-cost weirs and artificial wetlands and plant covers along watercourses and reservoirs.

For example, meadows and shelterbelts of trees can minimize chemical runoff from agriculture by forming biological barriers.

In view of the widespread and serious problems associated with chemical fertilizer and manure management in Latvia, a plan should be developed jointly by the Environmental Protection Committee and the Ministry of Agriculture to identify actions that should be taken to improve fertilizer selection, application, and storage. This program should be designed to meet the needs of a restructured agricultural sector and include specific provisions for agricultural extension services and farmer training. Given the significance of runoff from large-scale livestock and poultry complexes, an evaluation should be prepared to assess their future realistically and develop a strategy to address pollution from these facilities.

Waste Management

A waste strategy should be put in place that addresses and integrates all dimensions of the problem: solid, industrial, sludge, and hazardous wastes. It needs to be based on accurate information. Therefore, a study should be performed that identifies solid and hazardous waste sites throughout Latvia (they are often the same) by reviewing permits, records, and any other information that may bear on waste disposal problems. After a full inventory exists, risk-based screening and site ranking techniques should be used to set priorities and to evaluate the need for remedial action. The waste strategy should include a detailed plan for the cradle-to-grave management of the nation's hazardous wastes. The system must include hazardous waste definitions; a way to inventory sources; a foolproof tracking system; rules governing transport and labeling; monitoring protocols; minimum technology requirements for all treatment, storage, and disposal facilities; recordkeeping and reporting requirements; and enforceable sanctions for violations of the law. The strategy should also contain well thought out programs of source reduction, recycling, and re-use for both solid and hazardous wastes. Source separation of solid wastes should be especially encouraged together with a strategy for opening up secondary markets. If this is pursued aggressively, it should be possible to reduce solid waste volumes for land disposal by 25 percent or more.

Finally, an investment program should be agreed upon that focuses on the future management of currently generated waste in all categories. For hazardous waste, a central processing facility seems well advised. It is cost-effective, reduces environmental exposures, offers the convenience of selecting and training a limited number of qualified personnel, centralizes capacity with a variety of processing methods, and provides research opportunities. For solid waste, a limited number of well-designed regional facilities should be considered, with the first criterion being appropriate hydrogeology. Although privatization should be promoted for construction and operation of these facilities, the government should not hesitate to employ its power to appropriate land at a fair price to the owner. Investment funds will likely be a mix of public and private funds, including user charges, environment funds (both local and state), government budget, and international donor agencies.

Technical Assistance

There are several high priority areas where technical assistance will be needed:

- Developing a national environment strategy;
- Revising ambient air and water quality standards;

- Developing a management strategy for the Daugava and Lielupe river basins (based on the findings of recent studies);
- Developing detailed guidelines, financing criteria, operational procedures, and an accounting system for the use of environmental taxes and fines by the Environmental Protection Committee and municipal governments;
- Strengthening institutions and human resources development for environmental planning and management;
- Reviewing the environmental monitoring and information system, including national, regional, and local laboratories;
- Training in the planning, conduct, and implementation of environmental audits of industrial enterprises;
- Designing, operating, and managing modern sludge disposal systems;
- Designing waste management technologies (landfill and combustion) and recycling and re-use technologies, practices, and secondary markets.

ANNEX 1

The Current Budgetary System and
Financing Local Government

The Current Budgetary System

The general government budget is composed of (a) the central government; (b) the local government budgets (municipalities, towns, and villages); and (c) the four extrabudgetary funds: the Social Security Fund, the Environment Fund, the Privatization Fund, and the Foreign Exchange Budget.[1] In 1991, the revenues of the central government budget accounted for 53 percent of general government revenues, the local budgets for 16 percent, and the extrabudgetary funds for 31 percent.

Revenue sharing between the central and local governments is as follows: The central government receives the revenues from the profit tax, the personal income tax, the taxes on goods and services, and import tariffs, whereas local governments receive the revenues from property and land taxes, as well as fees and user charges on public utilities and services provided at the local level. In addition, depending on local needs, each year the central government shares a portion of its revenues with local authorities.[2] In 1991 transfers from the central government accounted for 27 percent of local governments' revenues.

The Social Security Fund is the largest extrabudgetary fund, accounting for 28 percent of general government revenues. It is administered by the Ministry of Social Welfare, Labor, and Health, and is financed by a new payroll tax. Its expenditures include pension payments, sick pay, maternity pay, and family allowances. Beginning in January 1992, the Social Security Fund also covers unemployment benefits, which are financed by an allocation of 1.5 percentage points of the social security contribution rate. The operations of the Environment Fund, and the Privatization Fund, which are about 8 percent of the extrabudgetary funds are financed from a natural resource tax and from sales of government property, respectively. The small foreign exchange budget, which until March 1992 was funded from retention of enterprises' foreign exchange receipts, financed various foreign exchange expenditures of the government (payments for goods and services and embassy personnel). The government intended to abolish this budget by the end of 1992.

---

1.   Control of expenditures and the audit functions of the budget are carried out by the State Financial Inspectorate, established in 1990. The inspectorate is also responsible for revenue collection on behalf of both the central government and local authorities.

2.   The Ministry of Finance prepares the state budget while the budget authorities at the local level prepare the local budgets. This system contrasts with the former one, abandoned after independence, in which the Soviet Supreme Council determined the revenues and expenditures of the state budget and the Latvian Supreme Council determined the revenues and expenditures of the local budgets. The fiscal year is the calendar year, and the budget must be approved by the parliament three months before the budget year begins.

Composition of Budgetary Revenues

The fiscal reforms implemented since 1990 have changed the structure of budgetary revenues considerably and narrowed the differences between the structure of Latvia's revenues and those in Western Europe. More specifically, the share of income tax revenues in total revenues increased from 7 percent in 1989 to 9.4 percent in 1991 and 12 percent in the 1992 budget, gradually approaching Western European levels. At the same time, the shares of the tax on enterprises and the tax on domestic goods and services have declined considerably, and now approach EC averages. The share of social security contributions in total revenues rose dramatically, from 6 percent in 1989 to 27 percent in 1991, which is almost equal to the EC average. The principal features of the new tax system are described below.

Taxes on profits are levied on the net earnings of enterprises, cooperatives, and private entities. The tax rate ranges from 15 to 35 percent, depending on the amount of net earnings. The concept of net earnings differs somewhat from internationally accepted standards, with numerous deductions being permitted. As of early 1992, tax rules allow enterprises to reduce taxable income through depreciation allowances, but the adjustments of the value of fixed assets for inflation have been infrequent, and do not follow clear rules.

The *personal income tax* is levied on individuals' wage income, including bonuses, and the income of legal entities formed by individuals. The tax is progressive, with tax rates ranging from 15 to 35 percent, and the tax brackets defined as multiples of the minimum wage. *Social security contributions* amount to 38 percent of wages and salaries, with employers contributing 37 percent and employees 1 percent.

The taxes on goods and services are composed of the turnover tax, excise tax, and custom duties. The turnover tax is levied on the sales of all goods, although some exemptions apply, particularly for goods related to agriculture. A base rate of 10 percent is imposed at the manufacturing and wholesale levels, with an additional surcharge of 2 percent imposed at the retail level. *The excise tax* is levied on luxury items and some other commodities, such as alcohol and tobacco. Tax rates range from 10 to 90 percent, with the lowest rate applied to petroleum products and the highest rate applied to alcoholic beverages. However, exports to hard currency areas are exempted. *Customs duties* are imposed on all imports from outside the former Soviet Union. Imports from the former Soviet Union are exempted mainly because of the absence of border controls.

Other taxes include a property tax, a land tax, and a natural resource tax. The *property tax* is imposed on fixed assets of state enterprises and on unfinished buildings. The *land tax* amounts to a leasing fee individuals and enterprises are charged for the use of land (for example, for farming and housing). The rates differ for rural and urban centers and across locations. The *natural resource tax* was introduced to discourage excessive use of natural resources and accrues to the Environment Fund.

Non-tax revenues include *fees* collected on documents and official services performed by the state, and *user charges* on the provision of various public services, such as water and sewerage. Some of these charges have already been raised (water and transport), and other increases are under consideration.

Composition of Budgetary Expenditures

The structure of expenditures has also changed considerably since 1990. Subsidies and transfers accounted for 60 percent of government expenditures in the late 1980s, but have been significantly reduced since then. Subsidies alone were reduced from an average of 12.0 percent of GDP in the late 1980s to 1.3 percent of GDP in 1991. Subsidies on food accounted for nearly 90 percent of total subsidies, with meat and dairy products receiving the largest share of total subsidies. Other food-related subsidies included price support for agricultural producers, subsidies to agro-industries, and direct transfers to low-profit farms. Subsidy expenditures also included housing maintenance, heating, and other housing-related expenditures. The government intended to reduce the share of subsidies further in the 1992 budget.

Whereas subsidies and transfers have declined, some expenditures related to defense and administration, which were previously included in the All-Union budget, have been introduced in the general budget. For example, social security expenditures have been a growing item in the general government budget, with a share in total expenditures that rose to 29 percent in 1991. Over two-thirds of the expenditures of the Social Security Fund have been pension benefits.

Financing Local Government

Local governments in Latvia are responsible for a wide variety of services. Those directly funded by the municipalities include urban and rural infrastructure, primary and secondary education, and outpatient and inpatient health care. Other services such as housing maintenance, transport, and water supply are the responsibility of council-owned enterprises. Typically they rely on council financing for their capital budgets, but they are financially autonomous in their day-to-day operations, although they sometimes receive subsidies from the budget.[3] In addition, the councils have under their jurisdiction a large number of state-owned enterprises, such as shops and transport companies, that are not directly related to the services they provide to the community. Current government policy is to give greater responsibility to the local councils to increase the accountability of the public sector. Thus, the central government recently transferred a number of specialized secondary schools to the local governments.

There are a total of twenty-six regional councils and seven municipal councils. Under these are lower tiers of elected town councils, of which there are 70, and village councils, of which there are 475. With the exception of Riga, these lower tiers do not have their own independent budget resources.

Local government is financed from two main sources. First, almost one-third of the state budget is allocated as subsidies and grants to the councils.[4] Second, the councils receive revenues

---

3.   For example, an operational subsidy for transport services of RUR 39 million was included in the budget of the Riga City Council for the first half of 1992.

4.   This assistance, which amounted to RUR 2.1 billion for the first half of 1992, is divided between targeted subsidies (RUR 1.1 billion) covering investment expenses (with rural infrastructure specified separately), rural road construction and maintenance, education, and some social welfare expenses and block grants (RUR 970 million) that are intended to equalize the differences in the local revenue base.

earmarked from the tax system that are collected within their areas.[5] The main sources are the turnover tax (the central government receives the standard 10 percent turnover tax and the local government an additional 2 percent tax on retail sales), profit tax (30 percent of the tax collected), personal income tax (30 percent of total tax collected in Riga, 80 percent elsewhere), property tax (100 percent of tax collected), and land tax (100 percent of tax collected). Table A1-1 gives the budgeted revenues to local government for the first six months of 1992.

The parliament determines the proportion of taxes allocated to local governments as well as the rates of the main taxes, except for the property and land taxes. Tax collection is the responsibility of the regional offices of the Supreme State Financial Inspectorate, which divides the revenues collected and transfers them to the central government and the councils. The result is that the councils have relatively little control over their revenues at a time when they are under pressure to identify additional revenue sources.[6]

Financial allocations are seen as increasingly inadequate for the councils' needs. Generally, the councils appear to respond to these financing constraints with service cutbacks, increases in user charges, and the sale of assets. They see little prospects of obtaining additional resources from the state budget. In the case of the Riga City Council, the investment budget covered only 4 percent of the capital investment requirements for the first half of 1992.

The central government imposes relatively few restrictions over the budgets of local government.[7] The targeted subsidies and block grants are determined based on norms that take into account the adequacy of the local revenue base to meet the needs of the population.

Given the present high tax burdens, there is little prospect for immediate improvement in the overall financing position of local government. The municipal councils will have to reduce expenditures through further cutbacks in their activities. The emphasis should be on identifying the key services provided by the councils and ensuring that these are financed as adequately as possible. It is likely that this process will require much greater guidance from the central government in elaborating national and sectoral policies and their implication for council activities than is currently the case. Privatization of services and enterprises, particularly in the housing sector, also offers prospects of considerable financial saving, while helping to clarify and simplify the role of local government.

---

5.   These were estimated at RUR 1.8 billion for the first half of 1992.

6.   The Riga City Council recently introduced a charge for the use of council property at levels "agreed to" with individual enterprises. It emphasized that this levy was a user charge and not a tax (which would have to have been legislated by parliament and collected by the Supreme State Financial Inspectorate).

7.   The Budget Law of June 1990 gives the councils the right to formulate their budgets without interference from state authorities.

Table A1-1. Local Government Budgetary Revenues, January-June 1992

Source of Revenue	Projected 1992 Revenue (RUR millions)	Percentage of Total Revenues	Comment
Turnover Tax	202.4	10.0	2% tax on retail sales
Profit Tax	482.1	23.8	30% of tax collected-In Riga two-thirds of this amount goes to the district councils and one-third to the City Council.
Property Tax	100.9	5.0	100% of tax collected
Personal Income Tax	606.1	29.9	80% of tax collected, except for Riga, which receives 30% of tax collected
Environment/Pollution Tax	24.4	1.2	75% of tax collected
Forest Income	44.2	2.2	
Local Duty Payments	10.3	0.5	
Other Fees	14.8	0.7	
Income from Leasing Property	39.6	2.0	
Sale of Shares	230.9	11.4	
Land Tax	269.9	13.3	
Surplus from Previous Year	0.7	0.0	
Total	2,026.3	100.0	

Source: Latvian authorities.

ANNEX 2

The Foreign Exchange Market

Institutional Framework

Based on the laissez-faire policy stance, Latvia's foreign exchange market has organized around private foreign exchange dealers and a couple of commercial banks. The Central Bank does not intervene in the foreign exchange market. However, the central government levies a hard currency tax on foreign exchange earners. As of early 1992, apart from the Riga Commerce Bank, which is responsible for much of Latvia's trade-related payments with the West, and the Land Bank, which provides some short-term lending, few commercial banks participate in foreign currency transactions, and the introduction of auctions at the Riga and Latvia stock exchanges did not attract much participation. The dominant agents participating in the system are private foreign exchange dealers, principally the private company PAREX, which by its own account covers almost three-quarters of the market and maintains a significant presence throughout the ruble area.

Private Dealers

While there are no barriers to entry into the market and many new, small firms are beginning to participate, the system currently consists of a small number of players. A small sample of some of the foreign exchange outlets has generally revealed high spreads of 10 to 15 percent between the buying and selling rates. PAREX still maintains a competitive advantage over other players or entrants due to its scale, ability to deliver quickly, and network of connections throughout the ruble zone. PAREX has a beneficial position in relation to the commercial banks due to its special unregulated status as a private company rather than as a financial institution. Originally a travel agency, since late 1991 PAREX has been organized as a private company concentrating exclusively on trading and lending foreign currencies.

PAREX represents the central clearinghouse for most cash-related foreign exchange transactions in Latvia and many of the other republics as evidenced by its daily turnover volume, which rivals that of the Moscow inter-bank market. Certainly the inter-republic arbitrage, much of which is carried out by this Latvian-based firm, goes across the ruble zone. PAREX price setting rules take into account the Moscow market, along with the various restrictions and taxation policies across the countries in the ruble zone, in an effort to capture a large proportion of the ruble zone market. There are indications that PAREX may be somewhat of a price leader in the setting of the daily exchange rate.

With its current competitive advantage in attracting customers to its financial services, PAREX is likely to become a private commercial bank in Latvia and has recently received a license from the Central Bank. PAREX has already offered a limited volume of short-term loans in foreign currency based on collateral and bank guarantees, and has therefore attracted a large number of regular customers.

Commercial Banks

There are about thirty commercial banks operating in Latvia, of which most are also licensed to engage in foreign exchange transactions. The largest commercial operation is carried out by the commercial arm of the Bank of Latvia (BOL), which holds 85 percent of all outstanding credit in the economy, but is burdened with a high percentage of doubtful loans and non-performing assets. The international department at the BOL is a clearinghouse for all foreign transactions for the commercial branches, but does not yet provide international payments for its customers using basic techniques such as letters of credit. BOL clients obtain foreign exchange through the market or through their own export earnings.

Of the other commercial banks in Latvia, only the Riga Commerce Bank, the Land Bank, the Baltia Bank, and the Riga Bank represent a significant share of the remaining banking sector. Only two of these banks currently engage in foreign exchange transactions for their customers, but they rarely engage in regular buying and selling on the foreign exchange market. The Riga Commerce Bank, which is responsible for a large proportion of foreign trade-related transactions, currently has enough foreign currency in its own accounts to satisfy the needs of its customers. The Land Bank, currently offering a limited number of short term foreign exchange loans due the prominence of import/export companies among its clients, did make an unsuccessful attempt to auction foreign currency on the auction market. Other commercial banks have not yet begun to engage in foreign trade-related services, but have stated plans to begin using letters of credit and foreign currency loans to serve their customers better.

Foreign trade servicing, both on the export and the import side, is a major area that is lacking in the commercial banks' service package for their growing number of private sector clients. Some commercial banks are even trying to form a consortium to block the PAREX monopoly in foreign currency exchange. Yet the numerous deficiencies in the payments system, the inexperience with international trade transactions, and the use of the Russian ruble will continue to hinder, for the short term, the commercial banking system's ability to attract customers away from PAREX. In the medium term, the lack of commercial bank experience in international transactions will also place Latvian producers at a competitive disadvantage, since imports to Latvia are normally pre-paid, a costly method compared to the standard payment arrangements in world trade. The commercial banks have a dire need for technical assistance in basic international banking services, with training in the use of letters of credit and in currency management is of high priority.

The Auction Mechanism

The Riga Stock Exchange (a commodity exchange) held its first weekly auction on April 9, 1992. The stock exchange does not auction its own resources, but only attempts to bring together buyers and sellers once a week. As would be expected in the Latvian system where the inter-bank market has been doing the same job, the volume of transactions for the first two auctions has been insignificant.[1] The minimum price for sellers was far above the maximum price for buyers and offers seemed to be motivated by an attempt to capture a windfall during the auction. The price at which the limited amount of sold currency was actually traded turned out to be precisely the rate offered by PAREX.[2] The first auction at the Latvia Stock Exchange was held on April 24, 1992. Given the dominance of the private system of exchange outlets, it is unlikely that auctions held at the two stock exchanges will capture a significant proportion of the foreign currency transactions.

---

1.   During the first auction, twelve sellers and five buyers expressed interest. Sellers offered USD 156,000 for sale, but only USD 1,000 were sold to the public library. The second auction involved fewer buyers and sellers, but again more than USD 250,000 was offered and only USD 4,000 were sold.

2.   Even if information distortions did exist, windfalls were made impossible by handouts during the auction that provided rates in other foreign currency outlets throughout the ruble zone.

Recent Developments

Replacement of Surrender Requirement with Taxation

Until March 1992, the government imposed a surrender requirement that required exporters to sell between 18 and 40 percent of foreign their exchange earnings at the official rate of RUR 1.8 per dollar. The system naturally induced exporters to avoid the surrender requirement by keeping foreign currency earnings in foreign accounts. Recognizing the distortive effects of the surrender system, its inefficiency as a revenue tax, and its detrimental effects on the incentive to export, the government eliminated the surrender system. Instead, a multiple system of foreign currency taxes was imposed.

Although export taxes are superior to the old system of licensing, Latvian officials recognize that export taxes still result in an unacceptable, direct anti-export bias and consider them to be a temporary measure designed to enhance badly needed hard currency resources at the government level. Despite its fluidity, the foreign exchange market contains segmentation that impedes the government from buying and selling foreign currency either directly or through accounts held in the Central Bank. The authorities also recognize the need to move to a more transparent consolidated budget in domestic currency where the Central Bank provides foreign exchange for government imports.

Introduction of the Latvian Ruble

On May 7, 1992, the Central Bank introduced the Latvian ruble at a par rate of one to one with the Russian ruble. The introduction of the Latvian ruble was intended to relieve some of the cash shortage that has prevented the timely payment of wages and pensions. On July 20, 1992, the government declared the Latvian ruble to be the only legal tender in Latvia.

While the cash shortage may have been eased, the banking system itself has not been affected to a great extent, as the restrictions on access to deposits and the reluctance to place money in the banks persists. The new liquidity has perhaps even enhanced the cash orientation of transactions, increasing the commercial banks' competitive disadvantage in the foreign exchange market. The continued monopoly position of PAREX is sustained by its exchange outlets throughout Latvia and its connections throughout the ruble zone. Existing commercial banks continue to remain outside the market, with only one or two banks able to provide foreign currency to their customers, while smaller banks must send customers to private dealers for their foreign currency needs.

Short Run Factors

Temporary Relaxation of Liquidity Shortage

Until the recent introduction of the Latvian ruble, the payments system was facing a severe crisis in terms of the amount of cash ruble liquidity available to the economy. The shortage of ruble cash became acute in recent months due to the simultaneous rise in demand for cash balances and the fall in supply of ruble notes, which in turn led to a premium on cash (over deposits) that ranged from 35 percent to as much as 100 percent.[3]

Causes behind the shortage of Russian rubles include a dramatic decline in cash ruble inflows from Russia resulting from (a) a significant volume of ruble deposits frozen in Vneshekonombank in Moscow, (b) severely disrupted trade payments with Russia, and (c) a lack of new rubles from the Russian Central Bank. On the demand side, the inadequacies in the bank-related payments system has led many payments to take the form of cash. The additional cash requirement, along with the rapid rise in prices, simultaneously increased the demand for ruble cash balances, intensifying the cash shortage and forcing officials to introduce a parallel Latvian ruble.

Incipient Demand for Foreign Currency

The relaxation of the ruble liquidity crisis does not seem to have impeded factors that have in the past escalated the shift from rubles to hard currency. Continued expectations of inflation (along with the negative interest rates on ruble-denominated assets) have intensified the asset demand for foreign currency, causing an accelerating dollarization of the country. In addition, at the current exchange rate (USD 1=RUR 120), it is generally not attractive to export to the ruble zone if a significant portion of costs are paid for in foreign currency. This lack of a transaction demand for foreign exchange has enhanced its current demand as an indexed asset. The uncertainty surrounding the introduction of the new domestic currency and the debate over the policy on Latvian citizenship have created a turbulent environment and severe uncertainty concerning the protection of the value of ruble assets and reinforced the asset demand for foreign currency.

These psychological factors, along with the principal economic forces such as the negative interest rates and the highly depreciated exchange rate, have led agents to move increasingly into foreign currency for protection of wealth. As the need for cash rubles arises, agents can convert to ruble cash instantly through the private exchange dealers. Such flexible portfolio management would likely be easiest though cash transactions, which may be one of the reasons that commercial banks are not yet the primary players in the currency market.

Proposed Changes in Market Organization

The government is currently considering a number of changes in the organization of the foreign exchange market that aim to broaden the participants in the market, particularly the Central Bank. Two notable proposed changes are:

- Re-introducing a surrender requirement for a portion of export earnings, but this time the foreign exchange earnings would be sold to the Central Bank at the market rate.

- Eliminating the foreign currency budget and unifying it with the budget. For its import needs, the government would be required to purchase foreign exchange from the Central Bank at the market rate. The question is whether the commercial banks in Latvia would be able to fulfill their normal role as a channel for injecting foreign exchange back into

---

3.   The premium was revealed through the dual exchange rate for cash and for ruble deposits. It was also possible to observe the premium directly as PAREX was prepared to sell ruble cash for ruble deposits.

the market and begin to provide a more service-oriented product to their customers engaging in foreign transactions.

Foreign Exchange Market Issues

The Introduction of a Domestic Convertible Currency

There is much discussion regarding the necessary conditions for the prudent introduction of a new domestic currency with current account convertibility, if not full convertibility. Generally, the conditions cited for sustainable current account convertibility include an independent Central Bank that has developed efficient instruments for monetary control and accumulated a sufficient volume of international reserves,[4] a relatively competitive and principally private financial sector, an accurate assessment of fiscal deficit financing needs, a strong degree of financial discipline in the banks and enterprises, a organized and non-inflationary method for financing public sector loss makers, and a commitment to interest and exchange rate policies that will prevent capital flight.

Current account convertibility, where domestic currency is freely exchanged for imports, is just the counterpart to the elimination of trade restrictions in the pursuit of a liberal trade regime. In other words, a lack of current account convertibility implies some form of administered allocation of foreign exchange, and therefore distortions in the trade regime that are analogous to, and perhaps even more distortive (due to the lack of transparency) than, explicit import and/or export restrictions. Similar to arguments for liberalizing trade, arguments for introducing current account convertibility focus on the benefits of importing a world price structure into domestic production and consumption decisions, the competitive force of imports on monopolies, and the unbiased incentives for investment and production choices.

The sustainability of full convertibility, where domestic residents are allowed to hold foreign assets, depends on the strength of forces within the domestic economy that would lead to capital flight. If exchange and interest rate policies are sufficient to make domestic assets attractive and government policies are credible enough to minimize the perceived risk of holding domestic assets, then full convertibility can be achieved. The benefits, particularly in a country like Latvia, are most important in the effect of full convertibility on private foreign investment. Without full convertibility, private investors are likely to be reluctant without offsetting guarantees, tax advantages, and other incentives that can be costly and can bias the investment regime against domestic investors.

Definitional differences between current account and capital account convertibility should not be overstated, particularly in Latvia, where many residents hold foreign exchange accounts abroad. Appropriate interest rate and exchange rate policies are becoming increasingly critical to the sustainability of even current account convertibility as capital flight has become easier as the world economy becomes more globalized through the introduction of electronic transfers.

---

4.   More accurately, international liquidity, which includes foreign exchange reserves, access to foreign financing, and private foreign currency assets. The requisite volume of liquidity depends on the type of exchange regime (fixed versus floating), the underlying pressures on the balance of payments, and the degree of exchange rate flexibility desired under the particular conditions.

The Exchange Rate Regime

Another policy choice in the design of an exchange rate regime is the type of market organization used in the setting of the rate and the allocation of purchased foreign exchange. In the first case, the choice is between a fixed versus a floating rate. Naturally, under a fixed rate all balance of payments adjustment occurs using the stock of international reserves. An inflow of reserves under a trade surplus will inflate prices and make imports more attractive and exports less so, while an outflow of reserves will do the opposite. A pre-requisite therefore, to a fixed regime is a stock of international reserves sufficient to accept the burden of adjustment, which in the case of Latvia may be heavy in the short run.

In the case of a floating regime, some of the adjustment can take place in the form of exchange rate movements, though it is normally undesirable for full adjustment be filtered to the exchange rate and interest rate, particularly if the adjustment process is to be quite extensive and volatile. However, as pointed out by Greene and Isard (1991), for economies in transition, the real exchange rate at which domestic production is competitive in the short run may differ considerably from the rate at which they are competitive in the long run. There is, therefore, the problem of finding the appropriate exchange rate not only at the initial stages, but at a given point in time in the transition. The possible need for frequent exchange rate adjustments during the transition along with the fact that the initial equilibrium rate is unknown and international reserves are likely at a low level, means that there are strong arguments for the introduction of a flexible rate regime (of which a floating rate is one form), at least in the initial stages of convertibility.

A more technical issue in the organization of the market for foreign exchange concerns the mechanism for rate setting in a floating regime. The choices in a floating regime are normally between frequent and regular auction markets, organized and sometimes fed by the Central Bank, and an inter-bank market, where the commercial banks meet to discuss individual supplies and demands and set the rate for the next period. While an inter-bank market is in most cases superior to the auction market for customer service and efficiency of information, the ability of Latvia to organize an inter-bank market depends on the speed of development in the financial sector, particularly in the privatization of banks, and the improvement in the payments system. Alternatively, in a flexible regime the Central Bank can change the official rate administratively and/or support the rate with intervention through the commercial banks based on regular financial information and perceived changes in internal and external economic conditions.

Finally, with regard to surrender, the choice has to be made whether to allow or disallow foreign exchange holdings and side trading. The extent to which internal convertibility is allowed (domestic holding of foreign exchange) depends on large part on the probability officials place on capital flight possibilities. There is, therefore, particularly in the initial stages, scope for organizing the market under conditions of full surrender of foreign exchange, which can then be repurchased on demand through the market. In this way, some possibility exists for ensuring that only current account transactions receive foreign exchange, and the rate that emerges from the market will embody information on the full supply of and demand for foreign exchange, not just the portion that enters the market.

ANNEX 3

Public Investment Program

Investment under Central Planning

Under central planning, the State Planning Committee was responsible for coordinating the investment programs of the state administration and non-Union enterprises. Prior to 1985 state-owned enterprises had no investment resources of their own, their surpluses were transferred to the state, and their investment requirements were then reflected in the state budget. Thereafter, state-owned enterprises were allowed to retain their surpluses and were required to invest using their own resources, although they still had to get State Planning Committee approval. Investment allocations under the state budget became limited to financing the requirements of (a) central government ministries and agencies, (b) local councils, and (c) state-owned enterprises that were either non-commercial or did not generate sufficient surpluses to meet their investment requirements.

Investment by the state sector accounted for around 80 percent of total investment during 1985-90. Of this nearly one-quarter was allocated through the state budget. The remainder represented investment by state-owned enterprises, of which around one-third was undertaken by All-Union enterprises.

The Present Situation

Currently, the main sources of public sector investment are the state and local governments, the latter comprising twenty-six rural regional councils and seven municipal councils. Local governments are financed almost equally by (a) grants and subsidies from the state budget, and (b) earmarked tax revenues. Since investment by state enterprises out of their own funds no longer requires sanction by the government, this category of investment can no longer be considered as the state-financed investment program.[1]

The state and local government budgets only provide information on planned expenditures for a single time period, and therefore give little indication of future investment needs and plans. (A first attempt at identifying future investment requirements was made by preparing a list of projects for implementation during 1992-94.)

Institutional Arrangements for Public Investment Management

The planning and management of public sector investment are presently divided between the Ministry of Economic Reform, which is responsible for aggregating and appraising investment proposals from the different sectors, and the Ministry of Finance, which makes the necessary resources available from the state budget. Thus, a basic framework for public sector investment planning exists,

---

1. From a planning perspective it would be impractical to classify state-owned enterprises' own funds as part of the public investment program (PIP) because information on such investments is only available *ex-post* from the returns submitted by the enterprises to the State Statistics Committee. The most recent year for which investment statistics for state-owned enterprises are available is 1990.

with the Ministry of Economic Reform responsible for the detailed planning of the program within a resource framework agreed to with the Ministry of Finance. This effective collaboration between the two ministries stands in marked contrast to the situation in some other former centrally planned economies and many developing countries, where the planning ministries have, by failing to plan within realistic resource constraints, become marginalized in allocating resources to meet investment needs. However, the system lacks both the personnel and professional expertise to function effectively. The number of staff in the MER's Public Investment Department has been reduced from forty under the former State Planning Committee to five. A further problem is that familiarity with economic planning and appraisal techniques in market economies is limited.

An aid coordination unit, which is currently located in the Ministry of Foreign Affairs, coordinates the program of external technical assistance to Latvia and is being assisted by a two-person technical assistance team under the EC/PHARE Program. Technical assistance is also to be provided for the establishment of investment planning and foreign assistance management units in key sectoral ministries (agriculture, industry, and energy and a joint unit covering transport and maritime affairs).

The 1992 Budget for PIP

The present fiscal pressure has led to a substantial fall in the level of investment funded through state and local budgets. Budgeted investment expenditures for the first six months of 1992 (Table A3-1), represent 10.5 percent of the total state and local council budgets. Over 40 percent of the total allocations are for the Ministry of Agriculture, primarily to finance rural infrastructure requirements. A further 45 percent of expenditures is budgeted under the local councils.

Budgeted investment allocations understate the level of government investment in at least two ways. First, some investment expenditures in infrastructure are included under recurrent expenditures, for example, the Ministry of Transport and Communications allocation includes RUR 185 million to maintain roads. Second, the hard currency budget includes some capital expenditures, principally for the renovation of the Riga Opera House, for which USD 1.0 million was allocated. Nevertheless, it is clear that overall public sector investment has fallen to levels that fail to meet even capital replacement needs, which are themselves growing because of inadequate maintenance. The result has been large numbers of uncompleted construction projects, an increasingly out-of-date infrastructure, and inadequate facilities in the social service sectors, such as health and education.[2]

Table A3-1. Budgetary Investment Allocations, January–June 1992

Levels of Government	Allocation (RUR millions)
Central Government	
Agriculture and Forestry	383.8
Industry and Energy	10.9
Transport and Maritime Affairs	20.0
Construction	8.1
Education, Health, and Welfare	35.2
Other	49.4
Subtotal	507.4
Local Government	
Grants from Central Government	
Rural Social Infrastructure	100.0
Other	48.5
Investment from Own Funds	261.2
Subtotal	409.7
Total	917.1

Source: Latvian authorities.

---

2.   In Riga, the shortage of school classroom facilities was reported to have led many schools to teach on a shift system.

The investment program lacks both transparency and a multi-year perspective. The government operates no separate capital budget, and the state and local government budgets show planned investment expenditures as state investments against each of the major budget categories. The classification is highly aggregated, and no information is provided about the investment to be carried out.[3]

Proposed Investment Projects

In early 1992, the government prepared an initial list of around fifty priority investment projects to be financed either (a) directly by the government, (b) through government guaranteed foreign credits, or (c) by joint venture capital. This list, which represents a first step in identifying future capital investment priorities, details projects scheduled to start in 1992-94 and their total lifetime financing requirements. The program is dominated by investments in the energy and industrial sectors, and includes some essential import programs. The total costs of the program are estimated at USD 13.0 billion, of which USD 2.6 billion is scheduled to be incurred during 1992 and 1993. Funding is divided between foreign credits supported by government guarantee (USD 3.2 billion), joint venture credits from foreign companies (USD 9.6 billion), and locally financed projects (USD 46 million).

There are a number of shortcomings in the list of proposed projects if it is to serve as the basis for planning future public sector investment: the list overestimates by a substantial margin the likely level of investment resources; it includes a number of projects that are more suited to implementation after privatization of the industries concerned and for which government investment resources or guarantees are inappropriate, for example, the Riga Electric Light Bulb Plant and the Riga Paint and Varnish Plant; and it pays relatively little attention to infrastructure or the social service sectors.

A Framework for Public Investment

To provide a framework within which investment priorities can be elaborated, it is recommended that the following measures be implemented without delay:

- *A series of sectoral and local government reviews.* These would seek to identify the key functions of a ministry or council and the minimum structure of departments and agencies (including non-commercial state-owned enterprises) necessary to perform these functions.[4] This exercise would provide an agenda for both (a) reform of the ministry or council, and (b) identification of future public investment requirements.

- *Commercialization of state-owned enterprises.* Preparation of a PIP is being held back by the slow pace of privatization, which has resulted in ministries and councils retaining a residual responsibility for large numbers of these enterprises. To address this problem,

---

3.   A more detailed list of investment projects is prepared by the MER in support of the annual budget. However, it only gives the expenditures to be incurred during a particular financial year and does not indicate the total cost of the project or the required future commitments.

4.   In practice, not all councils need to be reviewed. Two or three samples would provide a sufficient basis for developing effective guidelines covering functions, structure, and staffing and for identifying major demands for the investment program.

a list of commercial state-owned enterprises for which direct government support is no longer required should be prepared for each ministry and council. Typically, all trading enterprises that do not have a strategically important role within their sector would be on the list. These enterprises should then be barred from receiving financial assistance from their sponsoring ministries or local councils pending privatization.

- ***Elaborating a general policy for enterprise investment.*** In general, the government should seek to establish an enabling framework for enterprise investment through the financial sector. This task would involve ensuring that the financial institutions, such as the newly established Latvia Investment Bank, have adequate access to capital resources for investing in and on-lending to enterprises, rather than having the government identify and promote individual investment projects directly.

- ***Establishing ongoing training in public investment planning and appraisal for government staff.*** This training would be for staff in units in the core resource planning ministries, such as the Public Investment Department in the MER, the Aid Coordination Unit in the Ministry of Foreign Affairs, and the Budget Department in the Ministry of Finance as well as in the sectoral ministries and local councils. It should be linked to the identification of suitable candidates currently within the government as well as new recruits.

The technical assistance being provided to the core resource ministries and sectoral ministries should provide an appropriate framework for supporting these initiatives.

Statistical Appendix

Statistical Appendix - Contents

Table 1.1 - Latvia: Population and Demographic Indicators

	1980	1981	1982	1983	1984	1985	1986	1987	1988	1989	1990	1991
Thousands of Persons as of End of Year												
TOTAL	2514.6	2524.2	2538.0	2554.0	2570.0	2587.7	2612.1	2641.1	2665.8	2673.5	2667.9	2657.0
Male	1157.9	1163.1	1170.2	1178.7	1187.1	1196.3	1209.5	1224.8	1238.4	1243.8	1242.4	1237.2
Female	1356.7	1361.1	1367.8	1375.3	1382.9	1391.4	1402.6	1416.3	1427.4	1429.7	1425.5	1419.8
Urban	1701.2	1717.8	1735.5	1753.3	1769.8	1787.5	1809.8	1835.5	1855.9	1863.5	1858.0	1846.9
Rural	813.4	806.4	802.5	800.7	800.2	800.2	802.3	805.6	809.9	810.0	809.9	810.1
Latvian [a]	1344.0	NA	NA	NA	NA	NA	NA	NA	1387.3	1393.2	1395.3	1396.1
Russian	821.0	NA	NA	NA	NA	NA	NA	NA	905.3	909.9	908.2	902.3
Other	349.6	NA	NA	NA	NA	NA	NA	NA	373.2	370.4	364.4	358.6
Working Age [b]	1464.6	1464.2	1466.2	1467.6	1471.8	1477.1	1486.3	1498.1	1507.8	1507.8	1498.7	1486.9
NonWorking Age	1050.0	1060.0	1071.8	1086.4	1098.2	1110.6	1125.8	1143.0	1158.0	1165.7	1169.2	1170.1
Labor Force (LF)	1440.4	1441.3	1442.2	1443.6	1446.5	1450.7	1457.8	1468.3	1478.8	1481.8	1476.4	1461.9
Pension Recipients	NA	NA	NA	NA	NA	592.0	601.0	612.0	622.0	631.0	635.0	641.0
Percent of Total Population												
TOTAL	100.0	100.0	100.0	100.0	100.0	100.0	100.0	100.0	100.0	100.0	100.0	100.0
Male	46.0	46.1	46.1	46.2	46.2	46.2	46.3	46.4	46.5	46.5	46.6	46.6
Female	54.0	53.9	53.9	53.8	53.8	53.8	53.7	53.6	53.5	53.5	53.4	53.4
Urban	67.7	68.1	68.4	68.6	68.9	69.1	69.3	69.5	69.6	69.7	69.6	69.5
Rural	32.3	31.9	31.6	31.4	31.1	30.9	30.7	30.5	30.4	30.3	30.4	30.5
Latvian [a]	53.7	NA	NA	NA	NA	NA	NA	NA	52.0	52.1	52.3	52.5
Russian	32.8	NA	NA	NA	NA	NA	NA	NA	34.0	34.0	34.0	34.0
Other	13.5	NA	NA	NA	NA	NA	NA	NA	14.0	13.9	13.7	13.5
Working Age [b]	58.2	58.0	57.8	57.5	57.3	57.1	56.9	56.7	56.6	56.4	56.2	56.0
NonWorking Age	41.8	42.0	42.2	42.5	42.7	42.9	43.1	43.3	43.4	43.6	43.8	44.0
Labor Force (LF)	57.3	57.1	56.8	56.5	56.3	56.1	55.8	55.6	55.5	55.4	55.3	55.0
Pension Recipients	NA	NA	NA	NA	NA	22.9	23.0	23.2	23.3	23.6	23.8	24.1
Crude Birth Rate	14.1	14.2	14.8	15.9	15.9	15.4	16.1	16.0	15.6	14.6	14.2	13.0
Crude Death Rate	12.8	12.7	12.3	12.7	13.0	13.2	12.0	12.2	12.2	12.2	13.0	13.1
Rate of Natural Increase	1.3	1.5	2.5	3.2	2.9	2.2	4.1	3.8	3.4	2.4	1.2	-0.1

a. Data for 1980 refer to 1979 Census data.
b. Working age is 16-59 for men and 16-54 for women.
Source: State Committee for Statistics.

Table 1.2 - Latvia: Employment Distribution by Sector and Enterprise Type

	1980	1981	1982	1983	1984	1985	1986	1987	1988	1989	1990	1991
(Thousands of Persons)												
TOTAL	1364.4	1367.6	1371.9	1382.6	1389.6	1394.8	1403.7	1412.6	1413.1	1406.9	1408.7	1396.8
By Economic Sectors												
Material Sector	1012.8	1014.7	1018.7	1020.3	1024.8	1027.7	1029.9	1027.8	1021.1	1008.3	1018.0	1026.1
NonMaterial Sector	351.6	352.9	353.2	362.3	364.8	367.1	373.8	384.8	392.0	398.6	390.7	370.7
By Type of Enterprise												
State Sector	1218.5	1222.6	1228.4	1240.4	1244.8	1248.8	1255.0	1259.2	1252.9	1211.4	1139.3	1083.2
Industry	418.8	418.8	420.4	421.7	421.6	420.7	419.2	413.4	406.7	388.5	367.1	351.4
Agriculture	107.6	108.9	114.8	109.8	110.8	112.8	112.7	118.9	101.6	95.6	86.8	83.0
Construction	103.2	103.1	98.3	102.4	103.2	103.5	105.2	107.5	109.0	104.8	100.9	82.2
Transport & Communications	128.9	128.0	128.9	129.6	128.6	128.3	126.2	122.9	118.3	115.9	101.3	103.7
Trade & Public Catering	119.6	121.7	122.8	122.8	123.3	123.7	125.2	124.9	129.6	126.5	121.9	119.6
Health & Related Activities	71.5	72.2	73.3	74.2	75.1	75.5	76.1	79.6	81.4	82.6	80.0	76.7
Education, Culture & Arts	108.1	109.0	109.8	111.2	112.8	114.3	117.0	121.5	128.5	129.1	126.6	117.3
Other Branches	160.8	160.9	160.1	168.7	169.4	170.0	173.4	170.5	177.8	168.4	154.7	149.3
Cooperative Farms	132.7	132.5	133.0	134.6	136.6	137.6	138.8	140.3	141.0	145.6	152.1	143.6
Cooperative Production and Services	0.0	0.0	0.0	0.0	0.0	0.0	0.0	0.4	3.5	29.0	88.3	131.5
Self-Employed	0.5	0.5	0.6	0.8	0.6	0.7	0.8	3.0	4.4	7.7	11.6	18.2
Private Employment	12.7	12.0	9.9	6.8	7.6	7.7	9.1	9.7	11.3	13.2	17.4	20.3
(Percent of Total)												
TOTAL	100.0	100.0	100.0	100.0	100.0	100.0	100.0	100.0	100.0	100.0	100.0	100.0
By Economic Sectors												
Material Sector	74.2	74.2	74.3	73.8	73.7	73.7	73.4	72.8	72.3	71.7	72.3	73.5
NonMaterial Sector	25.8	25.8	25.7	26.2	26.3	26.3	26.6	27.2	27.7	28.3	27.7	26.5
By Type of Enterprise												
State Sector	89.3	89.4	89.5	89.7	89.6	89.5	89.4	89.1	88.7	86.1	80.9	77.5
Industry	30.7	30.6	30.6	30.5	30.3	30.2	29.9	29.3	28.8	27.6	26.1	25.2
Agriculture	7.9	8.0	8.4	7.9	8.0	8.1	8.0	8.4	7.2	6.8	6.2	5.9
Construction	7.6	7.5	7.2	7.4	7.4	7.4	7.5	7.6	7.7	7.4	7.2	5.9
Transport & Communications	9.4	9.4	9.4	9.4	9.3	9.2	9.0	8.7	8.4	8.2	7.2	7.4
Trade & Public Catering	8.8	8.9	9.0	8.9	8.9	8.9	8.9	8.8	9.2	9.0	8.7	8.6
Health and Related Activitie	5.2	5.3	5.3	5.4	5.4	5.4	5.4	5.6	5.8	5.9	5.7	5.5
Education	7.9	8.0	8.0	8.0	8.1	8.2	8.3	8.6	9.1	9.2	9.0	8.4
Other Branches	11.8	11.8	11.7	12.2	12.2	12.2	12.4	12.1	12.6	12.0	11.0	10.7
Cooperative Farms	9.7	9.7	9.7	9.7	9.8	9.9	9.9	9.9	10.0	10.3	10.8	10.3
Cooperative Production and Services	0.0	0.0	0.0	0.0	0.0	0.0	0.0	0.0	0.2	2.1	6.3	9.4
Self-Employed	0.0	0.0	0.0	0.1	0.0	0.1	0.1	0.2	0.3	0.5	0.8	1.3
Private Employment	0.9	0.9	0.7	0.5	0.5	0.6	0.6	0.7	0.8	0.9	1.2	1.5

Source: State Committee for Statistics.

Table 2.1 - Latvia: Gross Domestic Product at Current Prices

	1980	1981	1982	1983	1984	1985	1986	1987	1988	1989	1990	1991
					(Mln of Current Rubles)							
By Industrial Origin:												
Agriculture	892.0	1111.0	1347.0	1600.0	1862.0	1882.0	1823.0	1649.0	2086.0	2098.0	2233.0	5739.0
Net Value-Added	697.0	903.0	1130.0	1369.0	1620.0	1629.0	1559.0	1372.0	1802.0	1805.0	1931.0	NA
Depreciation	195.0	208.0	217.0	231.0	242.0	253.0	264.0	277.0	284.0	293.0	302.0	NA
Industry	3613.0	3790.0	3715.0	3326.0	3260.0	3348.0	3617.0	3774.0	3657.0	4043.0	5178.0	12303.0
Net Value-Added	3254.0	3409.0	3306.0	2887.0	2796.0	2855.0	3109.0	3241.0	3099.0	3436.0	4534.0	NA
Depreciation	359.0	381.0	409.0	439.0	464.0	493.0	508.0	533.0	558.0	607.0	644.0	NA
Construction	464.0	495.0	505.0	523.0	588.0	613.0	576.0	636.0	726.0	833.0	807.0	1604.0
Net Value-Added	412.0	440.0	449.0	463.0	526.0	548.0	513.0	559.0	640.0	744.0	717.0	NA
Depreciation	52.0	55.0	56.0	60.0	62.0	65.0	63.0	77.0	86.0	89.0	90.0	NA
Transport & Communications	538.0	568.0	609.0	656.0	715.0	733.0	772.0	794.0	862.0	884.0	1009.0	NA
Net Value-Added	321.0	343.0	373.0	410.0	447.0	459.0	466.0	475.0	526.0	551.0	668.0	NA
Depreciation	217.0	225.0	236.0	246.0	268.0	274.0	306.0	319.0	336.0	333.0	341.0	NA
Other Material Services	1132.0	1232.0	1315.0	1355.0	1387.0	893.0	933.0	934.0	990.0	1133.0	1043.0	7710.0
Net Value-Added	1106.0	1205.0	1286.0	1325.0	1354.0	859.0	898.0	896.0	954.0	1094.0	1004.0	NA
Depreciation	26.0	27.0	29.0	30.0	33.0	34.0	35.0	38.0	36.0	39.0	39.0	NA
NonMaterial Services *	1265.6	1267.8	1369.9	1463.6	1480.2	1561.0	1604.0	1675.3	1635.1	1937.2	1931.0	1309.0
Net Value-Added *	1041.6	1035.8	1128.9	1209.6	1215.2	1284.0	1318.0	1370.3	1302.1	1585.2	1563.0	NA
Depreciation	224.0	232.0	241.0	254.0	265.0	277.0	286.0	305.0	333.0	352.0	368.0	NA
Gross Domestic Product at mp	7904.6	8463.8	8860.9	8923.6	9292.2	9030.0	9325.0	9462.3	9956.1	10928.2	12201.0	28665.0
Net Value-Added	6831.6	7335.8	7672.9	7663.6	7958.2	7634.0	7863.0	7913.3	8323.1	9215.2	10417.0	NA
Depreciation	1073.0	1128.0	1188.0	1260.0	1334.0	1396.0	1462.0	1549.0	1633.0	1713.0	1784.0	NA
By Expenditure Category:												
Consumption	5322.6	5521.8	5804.9	5964.6	6085.2	5839.0	5972.0	6148.3	6210.1	6789.2	8226.0	16198.0
Private Consumption	4539.8	4705.8	4936.7	5050.5	5125.3	4811.1	4891.9	4990.7	5009.8	5546.2	6888.5	13249.6
Government Consumption	782.8	816.0	868.2	914.1	959.9	1027.9	1080.1	1157.6	1200.3	1243.0	1337.5	2948.4
Gross Domestic Investment	2029.0	2532.0	2710.0	2798.0	3069.0	3194.0	3396.0	3505.0	3616.0	3892.0	4057.0	9669.5
Gross Fixed Investment	2003.8	2013.1	2205.3	2307.5	2498.1	2910.1	3192.6	3285.8	3420.4	3493.0	3337.9	NA
Increase in Stocks	25.2	518.9	504.7	490.5	570.9	283.9	203.4	219.2	195.6	399.0	719.1	NA
Net Exports (GNFS)	553.0	410.0	346.0	161.0	138.0	-3.0	-43.0	-191.0	130.0	247.0	-82.0	2797.5
Percentage Shares of GDP												
By Industrial Origin:												
Agriculture	11.3	13.1	15.2	17.9	20.0	20.8	19.5	17.4	21.0	19.2	18.3	20.0
Net Value-Added	8.8	10.7	12.8	15.3	17.4	18.0	16.7	14.5	18.1	16.5	15.8	NA
Depreciation	2.5	2.5	2.4	2.6	2.6	2.8	2.8	2.9	2.9	2.7	2.5	NA
Industry	45.7	44.8	41.9	37.3	35.1	37.1	38.8	39.9	36.7	37.0	42.4	42.9
Net Value-Added	41.2	40.3	37.3	32.4	30.1	31.6	33.3	34.3	31.1	31.4	37.2	NA
Depreciation	4.5	4.5	4.6	4.9	5.0	5.5	5.4	5.6	5.6	5.6	5.3	NA
Construction	5.9	5.8	5.7	5.9	6.3	6.8	6.2	6.7	7.3	7.6	6.6	5.6
Net Value-Added	5.2	5.2	5.1	5.2	5.7	6.1	5.5	5.9	6.4	6.8	5.9	NA
Depreciation	0.7	0.6	0.6	0.7	0.7	0.7	0.7	0.8	0.9	0.8	0.7	NA
Transport & Communications	6.8	6.7	6.9	7.4	7.7	8.1	8.3	8.4	8.7	8.1	8.3	NA
Net Value-Added	4.1	4.1	4.2	4.6	4.8	5.1	5.0	5.0	5.3	5.0	5.5	NA
Depreciation	2.7	2.7	2.7	2.8	2.9	3.0	3.3	3.4	3.4	3.0	2.8	NA
Other Material Services	14.3	14.6	14.8	15.2	14.9	9.9	10.0	9.9	9.9	10.4	8.5	26.9
Net Value-Added	14.0	14.2	14.5	14.8	14.6	9.5	9.6	9.5	9.6	10.0	8.2	NA
Depreciation	0.3	0.3	0.3	0.3	0.4	0.4	0.4	0.4	0.4	0.4	0.3	NA
NonMaterial Services *	16.0	15.0	15.5	16.4	15.9	17.3	17.2	17.7	16.4	17.7	15.8	4.6
Net Value-Added *	13.2	12.2	12.7	13.6	13.1	14.2	14.1	14.5	13.1	14.5	12.8	NA
Depreciation	2.8	2.7	2.7	2.8	2.9	3.1	3.1	3.2	3.3	3.2	3.0	NA
GDP at mp	100.0	100.0	100.0	100.0	100.0	100.0	100.0	100.0	100.0	100.0	100.0	100.0
Net Value-Added	86.4	86.7	86.6	85.9	85.6	84.5	84.3	83.6	83.6	84.3	85.4	NA
Depreciation	13.6	13.3	13.4	14.1	14.4	15.5	15.7	16.4	16.4	15.7	14.6	NA
By Expenditure Category:												
Consumption	67.3	65.2	65.5	66.8	65.5	64.7	64.0	65.0	62.4	62.1	67.4	56.5
Private Consumption	57.4	55.6	55.7	56.6	55.2	53.3	52.5	52.7	50.3	50.8	56.5	46.2
Government Consumption	9.9	9.6	9.8	10.2	10.3	11.4	11.6	12.2	12.1	11.4	11.0	10.3
Gross Domestic Investment	25.7	29.9	30.6	31.4	33.0	35.4	36.4	37.0	36.3	35.6	33.3	33.7
Gross Fixed Investment	25.3	23.8	24.9	25.9	26.9	32.2	34.2	34.7	34.4	32.0	27.4	NA
Increase in Stocks	0.3	6.1	5.7	5.5	6.1	3.1	2.2	2.3	2.0	3.7	5.9	NA
Net Exports (GNFS)	7.0	4.8	3.9	1.8	1.5	0.0	-0.5	-2.0	1.3	2.3	-0.7	9.8

* Excludes expenditure on social and cultural services furnished by enterprises of the material sphere to their employees.
Note: GDP methodology changed in 1991. The 1991 GDP data were calculated on the basis of the European System of Integrated Economic Accounts (ESA) and the International Standard Industrial Classification (ISIC, Revised 3).
Sources: State Committee for Statistics and Bank staff estimates.

Table 2.2 - Latvia: GDP by Industrial Origin at Constant 1990 Prices

	1980	1981	1982	1983	1984	1985	1986	1987	1988	1989	1990	1991
						(Mln of Rubles)						
Agriculture	2033.6	2209.7	2256.9	2454.2	2754.8	2541.9	2697.8	2554.2	2553.7	2675.4	2233.0	2306.0
Net Value-Added	1821.5	1990.7	2030.1	2199.9	2487.8	2246.1	2384.6	2220.5	2215.1	2330.2	1931.0	NA
Depreciation	212.1	219.0	226.7	254.3	266.9	295.8	313.2	333.6	338.6	345.2	302.0	NA
Industry	3359.9	3494.3	3601.7	3728.0	3807.5	3885.9	4134.2	4388.7	4662.9	4937.1	5178.0	5461.0
Net Value-Added	2969.4	3093.3	3174.3	3244.8	3295.7	3309.5	3531.6	3746.7	3997.7	4222.0	4534.0	NA
Depreciation	390.5	401.1	427.4	483.2	511.8	576.3	602.6	642.0	665.2	715.1	644.0	NA
Construction	517.6	544.3	539.0	559.2	619.9	621.7	618.8	636.2	731.6	807.8	807.0	693.0
Net Value-Added	461.1	486.4	480.5	493.2	551.5	545.7	544.0	543.5	629.0	702.9	717.0	NA
Depreciation	56.6	57.9	58.5	66.0	68.4	76.0	74.7	92.7	102.5	104.9	90.0	NA
Transport & Communications	705.2	730.8	749.7	823.5	899.3	914.8	968.0	1005.5	1086.0	1094.7	1009.0	NA
Net Value-Added	469.1	493.9	503.1	552.7	603.7	594.5	605.0	621.3	685.4	702.4	668.0	NA
Depreciation	236.0	236.8	246.6	270.8	295.6	320.3	363.0	384.2	400.5	392.3	341.0	NA
Other Material Services	655.0	696.5	749.4	796.9	846.3	879.1	884.5	888.2	932.8	1092.3	1043.0	2612.0
Net Value-Added	626.7	668.1	719.1	763.8	809.9	839.4	843.0	842.4	889.9	1046.3	1004.0	NA
Depreciation	28.3	28.4	30.3	33.0	36.4	39.7	41.5	45.8	42.9	45.9	39.0	NA
NonMaterial Services *	1714.5	1688.2	1677.9	1716.2	1739.4	1768.0	1809.9	1908.4	1990.5	2029.8	1931.0	383.0
Net Value-Added *	1470.5	1444.2	1425.9	1436.2	1447.4	1444.0	1470.9	1541.4	1593.5	1614.8	1563.0	NA
Depreciation	244.0	244.0	252.0	280.0	292.0	324.0	339.0	367.0	397.0	415.0	368.0	NA
GDP at mp	8985.8	9363.8	9574.5	10077.9	10667.2	10611.4	11113.1	11381.1	11957.4	12637.1	12201.0	11455.0
Net Value-Added	7818.3	8176.6	8333.0	8690.6	9196.1	8979.3	9379.1	9515.8	10010.6	10618.7	10417.0	NA
Depreciation	1167.5	1187.2	1241.5	1387.3	1471.1	1632.1	1734.0	1865.4	1946.7	2018.4	1784.0	NA
						Growth Rates (%)						
Agriculture		8.7	2.1	8.7	12.2	-7.7	6.1	-5.3	0.0	4.8	-16.5	-2.1
Net Value-Added		9.3	2.0	8.4	13.1	-9.7	6.2	-6.9	-0.2	5.2	-17.1	NA
Depreciation		3.2	3.6	12.1	5.0	10.8	5.9	6.5	1.5	2.0	-12.5	NA
Industry		4.0	3.1	3.5	2.1	2.1	6.4	6.2	6.2	5.9	4.9	0.0
Net Value-Added		4.2	2.6	2.2	1.6	0.4	6.7	6.1	6.7	5.6	7.4	NA
Depreciation		2.7	6.6	13.1	5.9	12.6	4.6	6.5	3.6	7.5	-9.9	NA
Construction		5.1	-1.0	3.7	10.9	0.3	-0.5	2.8	15.0	10.4	-0.1	-40.6
Net Value-Added		5.5	-1.2	2.6	11.8	-1.1	-0.3	-0.1	15.7	11.8	2.0	NA
Depreciation		2.4	1.1	12.9	3.5	11.1	-1.6	24.1	10.5	2.3	-14.2	NA
Transport & Communications		3.6	2.6	9.8	9.2	1.7	5.8	3.9	8.0	0.8	-7.8	NA
Net Value-Added		5.3	1.9	9.9	9.2	-1.5	1.8	2.7	10.3	2.5	-4.9	NA
Depreciation		0.3	4.1	9.8	9.2	8.4	13.3	5.8	4.2	-2.1	-13.1	NA
Other Material Services		6.3	7.6	6.3	6.2	3.9	0.6	0.4	5.0	17.1	-4.5	-15.8
Net Value-Added		6.6	7.6	6.2	6.0	3.6	0.4	-0.1	5.6	17.6	-4.0	NA
Depreciation		0.5	6.6	9.0	10.2	9.2	4.5	10.2	-6.2	7.1	-15.1	NA
NonMaterial Services *		-1.5	-0.6	2.3	1.4	1.6	2.4	5.4	4.3	2.0	-4.9	-5.0
Net Value-Added *		-1.8	-1.3	0.7	0.8	-0.2	1.9	4.8	3.4	1.3	-3.2	NA
Depreciation		0.0	3.3	11.1	4.3	11.0	4.6	8.3	8.2	4.5	-11.3	NA
GDP at mp		4.2	2.2	5.3	5.8	-0.5	4.7	2.4	5.1	5.7	-3.5	-8.3
Net		4.6	1.9	4.3	5.8	-2.4	4.5	1.5	5.2	6.1	-1.9	NA
Depreciation		1.7	4.6	11.7	6.0	10.9	6.2	7.6	4.4	3.7	-11.6	NA

* Excludes expenditure on social and cultural services furnished by enterprises of the material sphere to their employees.

Note: GDP methodology changed in 1991. The 1991 GDP data were calculated on the basis of the European System of Integrated Economic Accounts (ESA) and the International Standard Industrial Classification (ISIC, Revised 3).

Sources: State Committee for Statistics and Bank staff estimates.

Table 2.3 - Latvia: GDP Implicit Price Deflators
(1990 = 100.0)

	1980	1981	1982	1983	1984	1985	1986	1987	1988	1989	1990	1991
Agriculture	43.9	50.3	59.7	65.2	67.6	74.0	67.6	64.6	81.7	78.4	100.0	248.9
Net Value-Added	38.3	45.4	55.7	62.2	65.1	72.5	65.4	61.8	81.3	77.5	100.0	NA
Depreciation	91.9	95.0	95.7	90.9	90.7	85.5	84.3	83.0	83.9	84.9	100.0	NA
Industry	107.5	108.5	103.1	89.2	85.6	86.2	87.5	86.0	78.4	81.9	100.0	225.3
Net Value-Added	109.6	110.2	104.1	89.0	84.8	86.3	88.0	86.5	77.5	81.4	100.0	NA
Depreciation	91.9	95.0	95.7	90.9	90.7	85.5	84.3	83.0	83.9	84.9	100.0	NA
Construction	89.6	90.9	93.7	93.5	94.9	98.6	93.1	100.0	99.2	103.1	100.0	231.5
Net Value-Added	89.4	90.5	93.4	93.9	95.4	100.4	94.3	102.9	101.7	105.8	100.0	NA
Depreciation	91.9	95.0	95.7	90.9	90.7	85.5	84.3	83.0	83.9	84.9	100.0	NA
Transport & Communications	76.3	77.7	81.2	79.7	79.5	80.1	79.8	79.0	79.4	80.8	100.0	NA
Net Value-Added	68.4	69.4	74.1	74.2	74.0	77.2	77.0	76.5	76.7	78.4	100.0	NA
Depreciation	91.9	95.0	95.7	90.9	90.7	85.5	84.3	83.0	83.9	84.9	100.0	NA
Other Material Services	172.8	176.9	175.5	170.0	163.9	101.6	105.5	105.2	106.1	103.7	100.0	295.2
Net Value-Added	176.5	180.4	178.8	173.5	167.2	102.3	106.5	106.4	107.2	104.6	100.0	NA
Depreciation	91.9	95.0	95.7	90.9	90.7	85.5	84.3	83.0	83.9	84.9	100.0	NA
NonMaterial Services *	73.8	75.1	81.6	85.3	85.1	88.3	88.6	87.8	82.1	95.4	100.0	341.8
Net Value-Added *	70.8	71.7	79.2	84.2	84.0	88.9	89.6	88.9	81.7	98.2	100.0	NA
Depreciation	91.8	95.1	95.6	90.7	90.8	85.5	84.4	83.1	83.9	84.8	100.0	NA
GDP at mp	88.0	90.4	92.5	88.5	87.1	85.1	83.9	83.1	83.3	86.5	100.0	250.2
Net Value-Added	87.4	89.7	92.1	88.2	86.5	85.0	83.8	83.2	83.1	86.8	100.0	NA
Depreciation	91.9	95.0	95.7	90.8	90.7	85.5	84.3	83.0	83.9	84.9	100.0	NA

* Excludes expenditure on social and cultural services furnished by enterprises of the material sphere to their employees.

Note: GDP methodology changed in 1991. The 1991 GDP data were calculated on the basis of the European System of Integrated Economic Accounts (ESA) and the International Standard Industrial Classification (ISIC, Revised 3).

Sources: State Committee for Statistics and Bank staff estimates.

Table 2.4 - Latvia: National Income and Gross Domestic Product

		1980	1981	1982	1983	1984	1985	1986	1987	1988	1989
		(Mln of Current Rubles)									
Net Material Product	1	5790.3	6299.8	6543.9	6454.5	6743.6	6349.6	6545.3	6542.3	7021.1	7629.5
Wages & Salaries, NonMaterial Sphere	2	992.2	1007.1	1093.5	1128.2	1138.0	1200.1	1254.7	1286.3	1427.3	1701.2
Social Security Contributions in the NonMaterial Sphere	3	59.7	59.8	64.6	65.9	73.9	71.3	75.3	86.2	76.8	65.2
Insurance Compensation received by Material Sphere	4	44.0	37.3	17.6	11.9	6.1	21.1	14.3	33.9	60.2	50.2
Profit, NonMaterial Sphere	5	89.3	100.6	123.3	197.0	199.0	223.3	205.6	224.2	39.8	65.4
Losses in Reserves in the Material Sphere	6	29.6	46.2	47.3	52.2	34.1	63.5	56.8	59.6	57.6	60.3
Insurance Premiums Paid, Material Sphere	7	32.3	32.7	31.9	51.7	72.3	77.0	80.7	83.7	89.9	64.6
Social/Cultural Expenditures of Material Sphere for Employees	8	84.9	95.0	98.1	104.8	112.1	117.2	120.7	142.3	185.8	200.8
Imputed Gross Output of Financial Institutions	9	0.0	0.0	0.0	0.0	0.0	0.0	0.0	0.0	0.0	0.0
Net Factor Income from Abroad	10	0.0	0.0	0.0	0.0	0.0	0.0	0.00.0	0.0	0.0	
National Income at Market Prices (Net National Product) = (1+2+3+4+5-6-7-8-9+10)	11	6828.7	7330.7	7665.6	7648.8	7942.1	7607.7	7837.0	7887.3	8291.9	9185.8
Consumption of Fixed Capital	12	1075.9	1133.1	1195.3	1274.8	1350.1	1422.3	1488.0	1575.0	1664.2	1742.4
Gross Domestic Product at mp = (11+12)	13	7904.6	8463.8	8860.9	8923.6	9292.2	9030.0	9325.0	9462.3	9956.1	10928.2

Note: The NMP figure in this table used as the 'true' NMP figure.
Source: State Committee of Statistics.

Table 2.5 - Latvia: Net Material Product at Current Prices

	1970	1975	1980	1981	1982	1983	1984	1985	1986	1987	1988	1989	1990	1991
						(Mln of Current Rubles)								
Net Material Product *	3737.8	4751.8	5790.3	6299.8	6543.9	6454.5	6743.6	6349.6	6545.3	6542.3	7021.1	7629.5	8848.5	17283.0
By Origin:														
Industry	1976.0	2593.0	3254.0	3409.0	3306.0	2887.0	2796.0	2855.0	3109.0	3241.0	3099.0	3436.0	4534.0	10565.0
Agriculture	873.8	812.8	697.1	902.7	1130.2	1369.3	1620.4	1628.8	1559.3	1371.7	1802.0	1804.9	1930.5	2835.0
Construction	281.0	429.0	412.0	440.0	449.0	463.0	526.0	548.0	513.0	559.0	640.0	744.0	717.0	1585.0
Transport & Communications	166.0	260.0	321.0	343.0	373.0	410.0	447.0	459.0	466.0	475.0	526.0	551.0	668.0	680.0
Other Material Services *	441.0	657.0	1106.2	1205.1	1285.7	1325.2	1354.2	858.8	898.0	895.6	954.1	1093.6	999.0	1618.0
By Final Use:														
Consumption	2762.0	3507.0	4540.0	4761.0	4857.0	4911.0	5041.0	5222.0	5367.0	5511.0	5803.0	6109.0	6990.0	15221.0
Personal Consumption	2497.0	3105.0	4045.0	4245.0	4308.0	4333.0	4434.0	4572.0	4684.0	4779.0	5044.0	5323.0	5996.0	13391.0
Social Consumption	265.0	402.0	495.0	516.0	549.0	578.0	607.0	650.0	683.0	732.0	759.0	786.0	994.0	1830.0
Investment (Accumulation)	893.0	957.0	732.0	1172.0	1281.0	1284.0	1470.0	1521.0	1648.0	1651.0	1650.0	1827.0	1774.0	506.0
Net Fixed Investment	425.0	575.0	492.0	529.0	622.0	582.0	690.0	864.0	933.0	1007.0	800.0	803.0	799.0	-965.0
Others (w/ Change in Stock)	468.0	382.0	240.0	643.0	659.0	702.0	780.0	657.0	715.0	644.0	850.0	1024.0	975.0	1471.0
Losses on Fixed Capital end Stocks (Discrepancy)	18.0	30.0	38.0	50.0	53.0	57.0	43.0	69.0	62.0	70.0	66.0	73.0	137.0	160.0
Foreign (Resource) Balance	65.0	258.0	480.0	317.0	353.0	202.0	189.0	-462.0	-532.0	-689.0	-498.0	-379.0	-52.0	1396.0
Exports, GNFS	NA	NA	NA	NA	NA	NA	NA	NA	NA	NA	NA	NA	NA	NA
Imports, GNFS	NA	NA	NA	NA	NA	NA	NA	NA	NA	NA	NA	NA	NA	NA
						As Percentage of Net Material Product								
Net Material Product *	100.0	100.0	100.0	100.0	100.0	100.0	100.0	100.0	100.0	100.0	100.0	100.0	100.0	100.0
By Origin:														
Industry	52.9	54.6	56.2	54.1	50.5	44.7	41.5	45.0	47.5	49.5	44.1	45.0	51.2	61.1
Agriculture	23.4	17.1	12.0	14.3	17.3	21.2	24.0	25.7	23.8	21.0	25.7	23.7	21.8	16.4
Construction	7.5	9.0	7.1	7.0	6.9	7.2	7.8	8.6	7.8	8.5	9.1	9.8	8.1	9.2
Transport & Communications	4.4	5.5	5.5	5.4	5.7	6.4	6.6	7.2	7.1	7.3	7.5	7.2	7.5	3.9
Other Material Services *	11.8	13.8	19.1	19.1	19.6	20.5	20.1	13.5	13.7	13.7	13.6	14.3	11.3	9.4
By Final Use:														
Consumption	73.9	73.8	78.4	75.6	74.2	76.1	74.8	82.2	82.0	84.2	82.7	80.1	79.0	88.1
Personal Consumption	66.8	65.3	69.9	67.4	65.8	67.1	65.8	72.0	71.6	73.0	71.8	69.8	67.8	77.5
Social Consumption	7.1	8.5	8.5	8.2	8.4	9.0	9.0	10.2	10.4	11.2	10.8	10.3	11.2	10.6
Investment (Accumulation)	23.9	20.1	12.6	18.6	19.6	19.9	21.8	24.0	25.2	25.2	23.5	23.9	20.0	2.9
Net Fixed Investment	11.4	12.1	8.5	8.4	9.5	9.0	10.2	13.6	14.3	15.4	11.4	10.5	9.0	-5.6
Others (w/ Change in Stock)	12.5	8.0	4.1	10.2	10.1	10.9	11.6	10.3	10.9	9.8	12.1	13.4	11.0	8.5
Losses on Fixed Capital end Stocks (Discrepancy)	0.5	0.6	0.7	0.8	0.8	0.9	0.6	1.1	0.9	1.1	0.9	1.0	1.5	0.9
Foreign (Resource) Balance	1.7	5.4	8.3	5.0	5.4	3.1	2.8	-7.3	-8.1	-10.5	-7.1	-5.0	-0.6	8.1
Exports, GNFS	NA	NA	NA	NA	NA	NA	NA	NA	NA	NA	NA	NA	NA	NA
Imports, GNFS	NA	NA	NA	NA	NA	NA	NA	NA	NA	NA	NA	NA	NA	NA

* Adjusted to match figures from the State Committee of Statistics.
Source: State Committee for Statistics.

Table 2.6 - Latvia: Net Material Product at Constant 1990 Prices

	1980	1981	1982	1983	1984	1985	1986	1987	1988	1989	1990	1991
					(Mln of 1990 Rubles)							
Net Material Product	6293.4	6626.9	6833.0	7098.8	7432.5	7418.4	7758.9	7875.2	8364.3	8983.2	8848.5	8513.1
By Origin:												
Industry	2969.4	3093.3	3174.3	3244.8	3295.7	3309.5	3531.6	3746.7	3997.7	4222.0	4534.0	4638.3
Agriculture	1821.7	1990.1	2030.5	2200.4	2488.5	2245.8	2385.1	2220.0	2215.1	2330.1	1930.5	1861.0
Construction	461.1	486.4	480.5	493.2	551.5	545.7	544.0	543.5	629.0	702.9	717.0	595.1
Transport & Communications	469.1	493.9	503.1	552.7	603.7	594.5	605.0	621.3	685.4	702.4	668.0	563.1
Trade & Others	626.8	668.2	718.9	764.0	810.0	839.2	843.0	842.0	890.0	1046.0	999.0	853.1
Statistical Discrepancy	-54.8	-104.9	-74.2	-156.2	-316.9	-116.4	-149.8	-98.3	-53.0	-20.2	0.0	2.5
By Final Use:												
Consumption	5597.5	5786.9	5654.0	5739.8	5956.2	6150.6	6214.2	6322.7	6626.3	6788.2	6990.0	5630.6
Personal Consumption	5047.8	5214.4	5052.2	5103.2	5287.0	5445.6	5473.3	5527.5	5803.9	5948.4	5996.0	4958.7
Social Consumption	549.7	572.5	601.8	636.6	669.2	705.1	740.9	795.2	822.4	839.7	994.0	671.9
Investment (Accumulation)	1072.2	1656.8	1738.4	1692.2	1773.3	1889.8	2138.8	2145.4	2105.7	2020.4	1774.0	NA
Net Fixed Investment	694.9	757.3	867.4	791.0	798.5	964.7	1031.5	1066.5	820.7	653.3	799.0	NA
Others (w/ Change in Stock)	377.3	899.5	871.0	901.1	974.8	925.1	1107.4	1078.9	1285.0	1367.1	975.0	NA
Foreign (Resource) Balance	-446.3	-916.1	-664.9	-451.5	-388.2	-714.5	-681.6	-692.9	-454.0	97.8	-52.5	NA
Exports, GNFS	NA	NA	NA	NA	NA	NA	NA	NA	NA	NA	NA	NA
Imports, GNFS	NA	NA	NA	NA	NA	NA	NA	NA	NA	NA	NA	NA
Losses on Fixed Capital end Stocks	70.0	99.4	105.5	118.4	91.3	92.4	87.4	100.0	86.3	76.9	137.0	NA
					Growth Rates (Percent)							
Net Material Product		5.3	3.1	3.9	4.7	-0.2	4.6	1.5	6.2	7.4	-1.5	-3.8
By Origin:												
Industry		4.2	2.6	2.2	1.6	0.4	6.7	6.1	6.7	5.6	7.4	2.3
Agriculture		9.2	2.0	8.4	13.1	-9.8	6.2	-6.9	-0.2	5.2	-17.2	-3.6
Construction		5.5	-1.2	2.6	11.8	-1.1	-0.3	-0.1	15.7	11.8	2.0	-17.0
Transport & Communications		5.3	1.9	9.9	9.2	-1.5	1.8	2.7	10.3	2.5	-4.9	-15.7
Trade & Others		6.6	7.6	6.3	6.0	3.6	0.5	-0.1	5.7	17.5	-4.5	-14.6
By Final Use:												
Consumption		3.4	-2.3	1.5	3.8	3.3	1.0	1.7	4.8	2.4	3.0	-19.4
Personal Consumption		3.3	-3.1	1.0	3.6	3.0	0.5	1.0	5.0	2.5	0.8	-17.3
Social Consumption		4.2	5.1	5.8	5.1	5.4	5.1	7.3	3.4	2.1	18.4	-32.4
Investment (Accumulation)		54.5	4.9	-2.7	4.8	6.6	13.2	0.3	-1.8	-4.1	-12.2	NA
Net Fixed Investment		9.0	14.5	-8.8	0.9	20.8	6.9	3.4	-23.0	-20.4	22.3	NA
Others (w/ Change in Stock)		138.4	-3.2	3.5	8.2	-5.1	19.7	-2.6	19.1	6.4	-28.7	NA
Foreign (Resource) Balance		105.3	-27.4	-32.1	-14.0	84.0	-4.6	1.7	-34.5	-121.5	153.7	NA
Losses on Fixed Capital end Stocks		42.0	6.2	12.2	-22.9	1.2	-5.4	14.5	-13.7	-10.9	78.1	NA

Sources: State Committee for Statistics and Bank staff estimates.

Table 2.7 - Latvia: Net Material Product Implicit Price Deflators
(1990 = 100.0)

	1980	1981	1982	1983	1984	1985	1986	1987	1988	1989	1990	1991
Net Material Product	92.0	95.1	95.8	90.9	90.7	85.6	84.4	83.1	83.9	84.9	100.0	203.0
By Origin:												
Industry	109.6	110.2	104.1	89.0	84.8	86.3	88.0	86.5	77.5	81.4	100.0	227.8
Agriculture	38.3	45.4	55.7	62.2	65.1	72.5	65.4	61.8	81.3	77.5	100.0	152.3
Construction	89.4	90.5	93.4	93.9	95.4	100.4	94.3	102.9	101.7	105.8	100.0	266.3
Transport & Communications	68.4	69.4	74.1	74.2	74.0	77.2	77.0	76.5	76.7	78.4	100.0	120.8
Trade & Others	176.5	180.4	178.8	173.5	167.2	102.3	106.5	106.4	107.2	104.6	100.0	189.7
By Final Use:												
Consumption	81.1	82.3	85.9	85.6	84.6	84.9	86.4	87.2	87.6	90.0	100.0	270.3
Personal Consumption	80.1	81.4	85.3	84.9	83.9	84.0	85.6	86.5	86.9	89.5	100.0	270.1
Social Consumption	90.1	90.1	91.2	90.8	90.7	92.2	92.2	92.1	92.3	93.6	100.0	272.3
Investment (Accumulation)	68.3	70.7	73.7	75.9	82.9	80.5	77.1	77.0	78.4	90.4	100.0	NA
Net Fixed Investment	70.8	69.9	71.7	73.6	86.4	89.6	90.5	94.4	97.5	122.9	100.0	NA
Others (w/ Change in Stock)	63.6	71.5	75.7	77.9	80.0	71.0	64.6	59.7	66.1	74.9	100.0	NA
Losses on Fixed Capital end Stocks	54.3	50.3	50.2	48.2	47.1	74.7	71.0	70.0	76.4	94.9	100.0	NA

Sources: State Committee for Statistics and Bank staff estimates.

Table 2.8 - Latvia: Gross Output at Current Prices

	1980	1981	1982	1983	1984	1985	1986	1987	1988	1989	1990	1991
						(Mln of Rubles)						
Industry												
Gross Output	9060.0	9367.0	9752.0	9433.0	9625.0	9968.0	10394.0	10773.0	10835.0	11540.0	12639.0	28798.0
Material Input	5806.0	5958.0	6446.0	6546.0	6829.0	7113.0	7285.0	7532.0	7736.0	8104.0	8105.0	18233.0
Net Product	3254.0	3409.0	3306.0	2887.0	2796.0	2855.0	3109.0	3241.0	3099.0	3436.0	4534.0	10565.0
Agriculture												
Gross Output	2053.1	2307.7	2568.2	2974.3	3285.4	3355.8	3338.3	3210.7	3752.0	3842.9	4131.5	5431.0
Material Input	1356.0	1405.0	1438.0	1605.0	1665.0	1727.0	1779.0	1839.0	1950.0	2038.0	2201.0	2596.0
Net Product	697.1	902.7	1130.2	1369.3	1620.4	1628.8	1559.3	1371.7	1802.0	1804.9	1930.5	2835.0
Construction												
Gross Output	845.0	928.0	942.0	1009.0	1110.0	1134.0	1166.0	1256.0	1331.0	1526.0	1404.0	3091.0
Material Input	433.0	488.0	493.0	546.0	584.0	586.0	653.0	697.0	691.0	782.0	687.0	1506.0
Net Product	412.0	440.0	449.0	463.0	526.0	548.0	513.0	559.0	640.0	744.0	717.0	1585.0
Transport and Communication												
Gross Output	600.0	633.0	696.0	756.0	798.0	907.0	943.0	953.0	1003.0	1022.0	1157.0	1168.0
Material Input	279.0	290.0	323.0	346.0	351.0	448.0	477.0	478.0	477.0	471.0	489.0	488.0
Net Product	321.0	343.0	373.0	410.0	447.0	459.0	466.0	475.0	526.0	551.0	668.0	680.0
Trade												
Gross Output	1210.2	1314.1	1404.7	1455.2	1489.2	1031.8	1068.0	1076.6	1176.1	1334.6	1330.0	2117.0
Material Input	104.0	109.0	119.0	130.0	135.0	173.0	170.0	181.0	222.0	241.0	331.0	499.0
Net Product	1106.2	1205.1	1285.7	1325.2	1354.2	858.8	898.0	895.6	954.1	1093.6	999.0	1618.0
Total Economy												
Gross Output	13768.3	14549.8	15362.9	15627.5	16307.6	16396.6	16909.3	17269.3	18097.1	19265.5	20661.5	40605.0
Material Input	7978.0	8250.0	8819.0	9173.0	9564.0	10047.0	10364.0	10727.0	11076.0	11636.0	11813.0	23322.0
Net Product	5790.3	6299.8	6543.9	6454.5	6743.6	6349.6	6545.3	6542.3	7021.1	7629.5	8848.5	17283.0
Memorandum Item:												
Income received from Foreign Trade	556.0	638.0	686.0	721.0	743.0	243.0	224.0	211.0	197.0	238.0	47.0	NA

Source: State Committee for Statistics.

Table 2.9 - Latvia: Capital Investment by State Enterprises and Organizations
(Mln of Current Rubles)

	1980	1985	1986	1987	1988	1989	1990	1991
TOTAL of which in:	887.0	950.0	1029.0	1120.0	1259.0	1360.0	1324.0	1581.0
Industry	248.0	282.0	256.0	290.0	363.0	511.0	438.0	410.0
Agriculture	233.0	238.0	230.0	269.0	261.0	250.0	253.0	324.0
Construction	25.0	27.0	32.0	31.0	47.0	48.0	30.0	31.0
Transport	85.0	90.0	97.0	132.0	107.0	129.0	135.0	138.0
Communications	12.0	18.0	15.0	16.0	18.0	38.0	34.0	23.0
Trade and Catering	20.0	10.0	14.0	12.0	13.0	13.0	20.0	18.0
Housing	132.0	143.0	151.0	162.0	170.0	182.0	184.0	309.0
Municipal Services	47.0	58.0	66.0	78.0	83.0	92.0	102.0	161.0
Health Protection and Social Maintenance	17.0	18.0	20.0	16.0	18.0	38.0	33.0	58.0
Public Education	20.0	26.0	29.0	30.0	38.0	40.0	39.0	70.0
Culture and Art	10.0	9.0	8.0	12.0	11.0	9.0	14.0	29.0

Source: State Committee for Statistics.

Table 3.1 - Latvia: Balance of Payments - Consolidated
(Mln of Rubles)

	1980	1981	1982	1983	1984	1985	1986	1987	1988	1989	1990	1991
Current Account	-1185.0	-1469.0	-1412.0	-1488.0	-1260.0	-1297.0	-1283.0	-1567.0	-996.0	-1092.0	-647.0	1578.0
Trade Balance	255.0	96.0	-86.0	-314.0	-317.0	-469.0	-588.0	-672.0	-635.0	-515.0	-827.0	762.0
Exports [a]	4252.0	4449.0	4562.0	4639.0	4710.0	4991.0	5091.0	4617.0	4602.0	5107.0	4881.0	6895.0
Imports [b]	3997.0	4353.0	4648.0	4953.0	5027.0	5460.0	5679.0	5289.0	5237.0	5622.0	5708.0	6133.0
Services Balance	298.0	314.0	432.0	475.0	455.0	466.0	545.0	481.0	765.0	762.0	745.0	1070.0
Receipts	599.0	620.0	814.0	879.0	904.0	909.0	983.0	890.0	1081.0	1076.0	1053.0	1391.0
Shipment/Transport	332.0	354.0	399.0	540.0	486.0	505.0	532.0	472.0	572.0	589.0	589.0	787.0
Travel	47.0	43.0	46.0	43.0	44.0	44.0	60.0	59.0	78.0	50.0	27.0	41.0
Other [c]	220.0	223.0	369.0	296.0	374.0	360.0	391.0	359.0	431.0	437.0	437.0	563.0
Payments	301.0	306.0	382.0	404.0	449.0	443.0	438.0	409.0	316.0	314.0	308.0	321.0
Shipment/Transport	115.0	108.0	88.0	103.0	114.0	111.0	113.0	176.0	132.0	135.0	135.0	138.0
Other incl Travel	186.0	198.0	294.0	301.0	335.0	332.0	325.0	233.0	184.0	179.0	173.0	183.0
Unrequited Transfers, Net [d]	-1738.0	-1879.0	-1758.0	-1649.0	-1398.0	-1294.0	-1240.0	-1376.0	-1126.0	-1339.0	-565.0	-254.0
Capital Account	502.0	259.0	241.0	-225.0	-429.0	471.0	-482.0	-787.0	-1502.0	-284.0	-506.0	-106.0
Medium & Long-Term, Net	38.0	-20.0	0.0	-36.0	-2.0	17.0	84.0	5.0	-57.0	43.0	9.0	0.0
Short-Term Capital, Net [e]	464.0	279.0	241.0	-189.0	-427.0	454.0	-566.0	-792.0	-1445.0	-327.0	-515.0	-106.0
Over-all Balance [f]	-683.0	1210.0	1171.0	-1713.0	-1689.0	-826.0	-1765.0	-2354.0	-2498.0	-1376.0	-1153.0	1472.0

a. Includes goods bought by tourists and other visiting populations from other Soviet Republics.
b. Includes goods purchased by Latvians out of Latvia and supplies for the USSR Armed Forces, State Committee of Security and other Soviet organizations.
c. Mainly port services, trade and related services.
d. Mainly taxes, profit of Latvian enterprises and the central budget transfers.
e. Includes transfers. For 1991, includes cash position of Latvian enterprises vis-a-vis enterpises in other Soviet Republics, transfers from foreign trade bank for negative trade and services balance, and ruble transfer (mainly for circulation).
f. Latvia did not have its own national currency until 1992 and thus balancing position has been excluded.
Source: State Committee for Statistics.

Table 3.2 - Latvia: Exports and Imports of Goods [a]
(Mln of Foreign Currency Rubles) [b]

	1968	1970	1975	1976	1977	1978	1979	1980	1981	1982	1983	1984	1985	1986	1987	1988	1989	1990
Total Exports	131	124	138	146	157	150	144	138	138	131	190	222	201	228	275	302	264	189
Socialist Countries	93	88	107	116	129	124	119	116	117	112	161	186	166	187	223	215	162	97
Developed Countries	25	24	21	20	19	18	18	17	17	17	25	30	28	32	40	71	86	79
Developing Countries	13	12	10	10	9	8	7	5	4	2	4	6	7	9	12	16	16	13
Total Imports	250	363	481	470	472	540	595	634	691	751	836	898	897	979	589	621	893	929
Socialist Countries	181	263	354	348	351	394	425	443	473	502	560	603	603	659	399	382	495	459
Developed Countries	45	65	89	88	90	110	129	146	168	194	212	225	221	239	142	182	310	371
Developing Countries	24	35	38	34	31	36	41	45	50	55	64	70	73	81	48	57	88	99

a. Excluding former Soviet Republics.

b. Foreign currency rubles (also known as devisa rubles) refer to the valuation of trade at world prices.

Source: State Committee for Statistics.

Table 3.3 - Latvia: Commodity Composition of Trade
(Mln of Rubles)

	1987	1988	1989	1990	1991
TOTAL EXPORTS	4693	4896	5413	5283	7705
Electricity	90	75	81	88	121
Fuel	10	8	6	6	18
Ferrous Metals	108	116	117	100	92
NonFerrous Metals	14	14	14	13	11
Chemicals	634	668	693	653	630
Machinery & Equipment	1344	1403	1518	1474	1912
Forest Products	162	168	148	136	414
Building Materials	62	65	83	73	190
Textiles	896	813	875	915	994
Food Products	1101	1099	1196	1140	1583
Agricultural Products	102	113	143	109	87
Others	170	354	539	576	1653
TOTAL IMPORTS	5594	5591	6030	6327	6309
Electricity	128	134	122	111	352
Fuel	515	517	513	482	558
Ferrous Metals	399	411	347	355	205
NonFerrous Metals	127	136	138	140	73
Chemicals	694	718	701	733	908
Machinery & Equipment	1626	1677	1823	1980	864
Forest Products	156	160	159	155	256
Building Materials	76	79	93	72	69
Textiles	851	762	873	1033	1385
Food Products	623	596	693	626	523
Agricultural Products	268	263	356	288	334
Others	131	138	212	352	782

Source: State Committee for Statistics.

Table 3.4 - Latvia: Geographical Distribution of Trade
(Mln of Rubles)

	1987	1989	1990	1991	I Qtr 1992	1987	1989	1990	1991	I Qtr 1992
	Exports					Imports				
TOTAL	4693	5413	5283	7705	7342	5594	6030	6327	6309	4423
Soviet Republics	4309	5039	5028	7459	6579	4618	4520	4711	5500	4191
Slavic Republics	3176	3768	3810	5649	5359	3433	3347	3542	3733	2335
Russia	2153	2717	2680	4193	3659	2469	2363	2652	2810	1341
Ukraine	691	731	762	925	1025	534	563	520	550	707
Belarus	332	320	368	531	675	430	421	370	373	287
Baltic Republics	422	411	437	662	754	685	627	668	963	1639
Lithuania	244	246	244	416	553	490	456	488	635	1177
Estonia	178	165	193	246	201	195	171	180	328	462
Central Asian Republics	421	502	468	678	292	181	178	209	531	75
Kazakhstan	203	246	224	293	122	83	109	96	280	56
Uzbekistan	128	162	141	205	76	34	29	53	86	10
Tajikistan	33	29	35	58	34	10	11	9	23	1
Kyrghyzstan	28	36	32	56	34	31	20	36	128	4
Turkmenistan	29	29	36	66	26	23	9	15	14	4
Southern Republics	290	358	313	470	174	318	368	292	273	142
Georgia	98	143	106	104	36	95	88	87	62	14
Moldova	72	85	78	159	87	152	183	134	100	82
Azerbaijan	65	75	71	92	31	38	47	40	56	36
Armenia	55	55	58	115	20	33	50	31	55	10
CMEA Countries	343	230	255	25	76	654	837	1616	106	33
Other Countries	80	144	a	221	687	312	673	a	703	199
Statistical Discrepancy	-43	0	0	0	0	2	0	0	0	0

a. In 1990, trade data for Other countries are included in CMEA countries.
Source: State Committee for Statistics.

Table 3.5 - Latvia: Trade Data Reconciliation
(Mln of Rubles)

		1987	1988	1989	1990	1987	1988	1989	1990
		Exports				Imports			
Trade Data in Tables 3.3 and 3.4 (Domestic Prices)	(1)	4693.0	4896.0	5413.0	5283.0	5594.0	5591.0	6030.0	6327.0
Trade with CMEA and Other Countries (Domestic Prices)	(2)	423.0	380.8	374.0	255.0	966.0	958.2	1510.0	1616.0
Statistical Discrepancy	(3)	-42.5	0.0	0.0	0.0	1.7	0.0	0.0	0.0
Trade with CMEA and Other Countries (World Prices)	(4)	275.0	302.0	264.0	178.0	589.0	621.0	893.0	960.0
Goods Bought by Residents of other USSR Republics into Latvia or by Residents of Latvia in other USSR Republics	(5)	584.0	788.0	647.0	352.0	189.0	278.0	327.0	178.0
Services (from Table 3.1) less NonMaterial Services	(6)	848.0	1025.0	1039.0	1026.0	409.0	316.0	314.0	301.0
Other Differences	(7)	293.2	21.7	195.6	338.0	293.4	21.0	195.8	191.0
Trade (from Table 3.1) [(1)-(2)-(3)+(4)+(5)-(6)+(7)]		4617.0	4602.0	5107.0	4881.0	5289.0	5237.0	5622.0	5708.0

Source: State Committee for Statistics.

Table 3.6 - Latvia: Foreign Trade in Domestic and World Prices in 1989
(million rubles)

| | Interrepublic Trade | | | | | | Extrarepublic Trade | | | | | | Total Trade | | | | | |
| | Domestic Prices | | | World Prices | | | Domestic Prices | | | World Prices | | | Domestic Prices | | | World Prices | | |
	Export	Import	Net	Export	Import	Net	Export	Import	Net	Export	Import	Net	Export	Import	Net	Export	Import	Net
Industry	4,590	4,324	266	3,769	4,602	(834)	311	1,275	(964)	226	772	(546)	4,901	5,598	(698)	3,995	5,375	(1,380)
Power	81	122	(41)	122	184	(62)	0	0	0	0	0	0	81	122	(41)	122	184	(62)
Oil and Gas	6	486	(480)	10	808	(799)	0	1	(1)	0	1	(1)	6	487	(481)	10	810	(800)
Oil Products	0	0	0	0	0	0	0	0	0	0	0	0	0	0	0	0	0	0
Refineries	6	445	(439)	10	721	(711)	0	1	(1)	0	1	(1)	6	446	(440)	10	722	(713)
Gas Products	0	41	(41)	0	87	(87)	0	0	0	0	0	0	0	41	(41)	0	87	(87)
COAL	0	3	(3)	0	2	(2)	0	24	(24)	0	36	(36)	0	26	(26)	0	39	(39)
Other Fuel	0	0	(0)	0	0	(0)	0	0	0	0	0	0	0	0	(0)	0	0	(0)
Combustible Shales	0	0	(0)	0	0	(0)	0	0	0	0	0	0	0	0	(0)	0	0	(0)
Peat	0	0	0	0	0	0	0	0	0	0	0	0	0	0	0	0	0	0
Ferrous Metallurgy	102	333	(231)	123	388	(265)	15	14	1	14	19	(4)	117	347	(230)	137	406	(269)
Ferrous Ores	0	1	(1)	0	1	(1)	0	0	0	0	0	0	0	1	(1)	0	1	(1)
Ferrous Metals	98	290	(192)	121	357	(236)	9	9	(1)	11	11	0	108	299	(191)	132	368	(236)
Coking Products	0	5	(5)	0	6	(6)	0	4	(4)	0	6	(6)	0	9	(9)	0	12	(12)
Fire Resistant	0	4	(4)	0	7	(7)	0	0	0	0	0	0	0	4	(4)	0	7	(7)
Metal Products	4	35	(31)	2	18	(16)	6	1	4	3	1	2	10	36	(26)	5	19	(14)
Non-Ferrous Metallurgy	14	136	(122)	21	210	(188)	0	2	(2)	1	2	(1)	14	138	(124)	22	212	(190)
Non-ferrous Ores	0	0	(0)	0	0	(0)	0	0	(0)	0	0	(0)	0	0	(0)	0	0	(0)
Non-ferrous Metals	14	135	(121)	21	210	(188)	0	2	(2)	1	2	(1)	14	137	(123)	22	211	(189)
Chemical & Petroleum	683	618	64	517	438	78	11	83	(72)	9	60	(51)	693	701	(8)	525	498	28
Mineral Chemistry	0	9	(9)	0	12	(12)	1	0	1	1	0	1	1	9	(8)	1	12	(11)
Basic Chemicals	74	134	(60)	49	88	(40)	1	7	(6)	1	5	(5)	75	141	(66)	49	94	(44)
Chemical Fibers	156	72	84	92	43	49	2	1	1	1	0	0	158	73	85	93	43	50
Synthetic Resins	2	146	(144)	1	91	(89)	0	9	(9)	0	6	(6)	3	155	(153)	2	97	(95)
Plastic Products	107	47	60	87	39	49	0	2	(2)	0	1	(1)	107	49	58	88	40	48
Paints & Laquers	42	36	6	33	28	5	0	12	(11)	0	10	(10)	42	47	(5)	33	38	(5)
Synthetic Paints	0	10	(10)	0	6	(6)	0	0	(0)	0	0	(0)	0	10	(10)	0	6	(6)
Synthetic Rubber	0	12	(12)	0	9	(9)	0	1	(1)	0	1	(1)	0	13	(13)	0	10	(10)
Organic Chemicals	1	37	(36)	0	21	(21)	0	4	(4)	0	3	(3)	1	41	(40)	0	24	(23)
Tires	0	37	(37)	0	36	(36)	0	0	(0)	0	0	(0)	0	37	(37)	0	36	(36)
Rubber & Asbestos	102	28	74	91	25	66	2	7	(5)	2	4	(2)	104	35	68	93	29	64
Other Products	117	18	99	99	15	84	2	10	(8)	2	5	(3)	119	28	90	101	20	81
Pharmaceuticals	83	32	50	63	25	38	3	30	(27)	2	24	(22)	85	62	23	65	49	16

Table 3.6 - Latvia: Foreign Trade in Domestic and World Prices in 1989
(million rubles)

| | Interrepublic Trade | | | | | | Extrarepublic Trade | | | | | | Total Trade | | | | | |
| | Domestic Prices | | | World Prices | | | Domestic Prices | | | World Prices | | | Domestic Prices | | | World Prices | | |
	Export	Import	Net	Export	Import	Net	Export	Import	Net	Export	Import	Net	Export	Import	Net	Export	Import	Net
Machinery & Metal Work	1,404	1,502	(98)	1,829	2,023	(194)	115	321	(207)	114	271	(157)	1,518	1,823	(304)	1,943	2,294	(351)
Energy & power	27	22	6	30	23	6	4	4	(0)	4	4	0	31	26	6	34	27	6
Technology	11	4	7	24	9	15	0	1	(1)	0	1	(1)	11	5	6	24	9	14
Mining	0	0	(0)	0	1	(1)	0	0	0	0	0	0	0	0	(0)	0	1	(1)
Transportation	25	13	12	33	18	16	0	11	(11)	0	11	(11)	25	25	0	33	29	4
Railway Equipment	50	7	43	34	5	29	4	7	(3)	3	8	(5)	54	14	40	36	13	24
Electro-technical	130	142	(11)	150	163	(13)	6	7	(1)	7	6	1	137	149	(12)	157	169	(12)
Cables	0	44	(44)	0	50	(50)	0	0	(0)	0	0	0	0	45	(45)	0	50	(50)
Pumps &Chemical Equipm	19	27	(8)	20	29	(8)	1	13	(12)	1	11	(10)	20	40	(20)	22	40	(18)
Machine Tools	21	11	9	24	13	11	0	7	(7)	0	7	(7)	21	19	2	24	20	4
Forging/Pressing	0	8	(8)	0	9	(9)	0	5	(5)	0	4	(4)	0	13	(13)	0	13	(13)
Casting Equipment	0	1	(1)	0	2	(2)	0	0	(0)	0	0	(0)	0	1	(1)	0	2	(2)
Precision Instruments	21	10	11	18	8	10	1	2	(1)	1	2	(2)	22	12	10	18	11	8
Synthetic Diamonds	3	8	(5)	5	1	4	0	0	(0)	0	12	(12)	3	8	(5)	5	13	(8)
Tools and Dies	43	175	(133)	36	150	(114)	1	23	(21)	1	20	(19)	44	198	(154)	38	170	(132)
Autos & Parts	330	167	163	559	172	387	13	25	(12)	20	26	(6)	343	192	150	579	198	381
Bearings	0	12	(12)	0	12	(12)	0	0	0	0	0	0	0	12	(12)	0	12	(12)
Tractors & Agri.Equipm	160	139	21	246	214	32	9	31	(22)	14	31	(17)	169	170	(1)	260	245	15
Construction M&E	56	27	29	84	40	43	0	4	(3)	1	3	(3)	57	31	26	84	44	40
Communal-Everyday M&E	6	5	1	8	7	1	0	1	(1)	0	1	(1)	6	7	(1)	8	8	(0)
Light Industry M&E	4	14	(9)	6	19	(13)	0	69	(69)	0	53	(53)	4	82	(78)	6	71	(65)
Processed Food & Feed	8	23	(15)	11	33	(22)	1	4	(4)	1	4	(3)	8	27	(19)	12	36	(25)
Trade and Dining M&E	10	6	4	13	8	5	0	0	0	0	0	0	10	6	4	13	8	5
Printing M&E	0	2	(2)	0	2	(2)	0	9	(9)	0	8	(8)	0	11	(11)	0	11	(11)
Household Appliances	40	34	6	21	11	10	5	4	2	3	1	2	45	38	8	24	12	12
Sanitary Engineering	13	19	(7)	7	11	(4)	1	1	(1)	0	1	(1)	13	20	(7)	7	12	(5)
Shipbuilding	6	10	(4)	7	12	(4)	1	8	(7)	1	8	(7)	7	18	(11)	9	19	(11)
Radio Electronics	322	203	119	321	193	128	63	31	32	50	21	29	385	234	151	371	214	157
Other Industries M&E	27	304	(277)	65	735	(670)	2	6	(4)	5	6	(1)	29	310	(281)	70	741	(671)
Metal Construction	1	7	(6)	1	6	(5)	0	0	(0)	0	0	(0)	1	7	(6)	1	7	(6)
Metal Products	35	42	(6)	25	30	(5)	3	15	(13)	2	3	(1)	38	57	(19)	27	33	(5)
M&E Repair	36	8	28	82	18	63	0	26	(26)	0	25	(25)	36	34	2	82	43	38
Medical Equipment	0	8	(8)	0	9	(9)	0	5	(5)	0	5	(5)	0	13	(13)	0	14	(13)
Sawmill & Lumber Ind.	119	140	(21)	78	99	(21)	28	20	9	16	13	3	148	159	(12)	94	112	(18)
Logging	2	17	(15)	1	10	(9)	5	0	5	3	0	3	7	17	(10)	4	10	(6)
Sawmill	12	17	(5)	7	10	(3)	7	3	5	4	2	2	19	20	(1)	11	12	(1)
Plywood	10	2	9	7	1	6	6	2	5	4	1	3	17	3	13	11	2	9
Furniture	35	5	30	15	2	13	8	9	(1)	4	5	(1)	43	14	29	18	7	11
Paper & Pulp	59	92	(32)	48	74	(26)	2	6	(5)	1	5	(4)	61	98	(37)	49	79	(30)
Wood Chemistry Product	1	8	(7)	0	2	(2)	0	0	0	0	0	0	1	8	(7)	0	2	(2)

Table 3.6 - Latvia: Foreign Trade in Domestic and World Prices in 1989
(million rubles)

	Interrepublic Trade						Extrarepublic Trade						Total Trade					
	Domestic Prices			World Prices			Domestic Prices			World Prices			Domestic Prices			World Prices		
	Export	Import	Net	Export	Import	Net	Export	Import	Net	Export	Import	Net	Export	Import	Net	Export	Import	Net
Building Materials	80	88	(8)	62	86	(24)	3	6	(3)	3	2	1	83	93	(10)	65	88	(23)
Cement	21	25	(4)	16	20	(4)	1	0	1	1	0	1	22	25	(3)	17	20	(3)
Asbestos Products	3	4	(1)	4	5	(1)	0	0	0	0	0	0	3	4	(1)	4	5	(1)
Roofing & Insulation	0	5	(5)	0	5	(5)	0	0	0	0	0	0	0	5	(5)	0	5	(5)
Precast Concrete	4	4	0	5	4	0	0	0	0	0	0	0	4	4	0	5	4	0
Wall Materials	0	0	0	0	0	0	0	0	0	0	0	0	0	0	0	0	0	0
Construction Ceramics	0	3	(3)	0	7	(7)	0	0	(0)	0	0	(0)	0	4	(4)	1	7	(7)
Construction Products	14	2	12	8	1	7	0	1	(1)	1	1	(1)	14	3	11	8	2	6
Other	2	15	(13)	2	19	(17)	1	0	1	1	1	1	3	15	(12)	4	19	(16)
Glass & Porcelain	36	24	11	26	20	6	1	4	(3)	1	1	(0)	37	28	8	27	21	6
Medical Products	0	4	(4)	0	4	(4)	0	0	(0)	0	0	(0)	0	4	(4)	0	4	(4)
Light Industry	852	456	396	281	131	149	24	417	(394)	10	105	(94)	875	873	3	291	236	55
Cotton Products	62	138	(76)	16	41	(25)	9	19	(10)	3	7	(4)	71	157	(86)	19	48	(29)
Flax Products	19	6	13	7	2	4	1	1	(1)	0	1	(1)	20	8	12	7	3	4
Wool Products	103	99	5	27	20	7	1	91	(90)	0	24	(24)	104	189	(86)	27	44	(17)
Silk Products	57	74	(17)	10	13	(3)	4	6	(2)	2	1	1	61	80	(19)	12	15	(3)
Hosiery/Knitwear	286	38	248	74	10	64	1	68	(66)	1	13	(12)	287	106	182	75	22	52
Other Textile Products	152	26	126	66	13	53	0	10	(10)	0	2	(2)	152	36	116	66	15	51
Sewn Goods	58	5	53	31	3	28	6	140	(134)	3	33	(30)	64	145	(81)	34	36	(2)
Leather	115	70	45	51	29	21	2	83	(81)	1	24	(22)	117	153	(36)	52	53	(1)
Food Production	1,089	313	776	567	112	455	107	380	(273)	51	261	(209)	1,196	693	503	619	373	246
Sugar	88	9	79	27	3	25	0	161	(161)	0	194	(194)	88	170	(81)	27	197	(169)
Bread & Baked Products	1	0	1	0	0	0	0	0	0	0	0	0	1	0	1	0	0	0
Confections	18	0	18	7	0	7	0	0	0	0	0	0	18	0	18	7	0	7
Vegetable Oils	1	36	(35)	1	20	(19)	1	28	(27)	1	21	(20)	2	64	(62)	1	41	(40)
Perfume Oils	385	20	365	250	13	237	3	96	(94)	3	24	(21)	387	116	271	253	37	216
Distilleries	2	1	1	0	0	0	3	0	3	2	0	2	5	1	4	2	0	2
Wines	18	98	(80)	3	15	(12)	1	9	(8)	1	3	(2)	19	107	(88)	4	17	(14)
Fruit/Vegetables	7	21	(14)	3	6	(3)	0	9	(9)	0	6	(6)	7	30	(23)	3	12	(9)
Tabacco	10	15	(6)	3	5	(3)	0	5	(5)	0	2	(2)	10	20	(11)	3	7	(5)
Other Food	40	59	(20)	14	20	(6)	1	68	(68)	1	9	(9)	40	127	(87)	14	29	(15)
Meat Products	122	1	121	58	1	58	13	1	12	6	0	5	134	2	133	64	1	63
Dairy Products	125	0	124	69	0	68	14	0	13	8	0	7	139	1	138	76	0	76
Fish Products	250	24	226	116	11	105	72	2	71	32	1	31	323	26	297	148	12	136
Flour & Cereals	24	28	(4)	17	18	(1)	0	1	(1)	0	4	(0)	24	28	(5)	17	18	(2)
Other Industries	161	129	32	159	120	38	8	8	0	8	4	4	169	137	32	167	125	42
Microbiology	4	36	(32)	3	28	(25)	0	0	0	0	0	0	4	36	(32)	3	28	(25)
Animal Feed	4	2	1	2	1	1	0	0	0	0	0	0	4	2	1	2	1	1
Other Products	154	91	63	154	91	63	8	8	0	8	4	4	162	99	63	162	95	67

Table 3.6 - Latvia: Foreign Trade in Domestic and World Prices in 1989
(million rubles)

| | Interrepublic Trade | | | | | | Extrarepublic Trade | | | | | | Total Trade | | | | | |
| | Domestic Prices | | | World Prices | | | Domestic Prices | | | World Prices | | | Domestic Prices | | | World Prices | | |
	Export	Import	Net	Export	Import	Net	Export	Import	Net	Export	Import	Net	Export	Import	Net	Export	Import	Net
AGRICULTURE	102	124	(22)	31	70	(38)	41	232	(191)	16	118	(102)	143	356	(213)	47	188	(141)
Crops	22	78	(55)	6	55	(49)	0	214	(214)	0	108	(108)	23	292	(269)	6	163	(157)
Animal Husbandry	80	46	33	25	15	10	41	18	23	15	10	6	120	64	56	41	25	16
Other Material Product	348	73	275	348	75	273	22	3	20	23	3	20	370	76	294	371	78	293
Information Services	0	0	0	0	0	0	0	0	0	0	0	0	0	0	0	0	0	0
Other Services	4	9	(5)	5	11	(7)	0	3	(3)	0	3	(2)	4	12	(8)	5	14	(9)
Transportation Expense	344	64	280	344	64	280	22	0	22	22	0	22	366	64	302	366	64	302
TOTAL	5,039	4,520	519	4,149	4,747	(599)	374	1,510	(1,136)	264	893	(629)	5,413	6,030	(617)	4,413	5,640	(1,228)

Source: Intelligent Decision Systems (IDS).

Table 3.7 - Latvia: Foreign Trade in Domestic and World Prices in 1989
(million rubles)

	Interrepublic Trade — Domestic Prices			Interrepublic Trade — World Prices			Extrarepublic Trade — Domestic Prices			Extrarepublic Trade — World Prices			Total Trade — Domestic Prices			Total Trade — World Prices		
	Export	Import	Net	Export	Import	Net	Export	Import	Net	Export	Import	Net	Export	Import	Net	Export	Import	Net
INDUSTRY	4,590	4,324	266	3,769	4,602	(834)	311	1,275	(964)	226	772	(546)	4,901	5,598	(698)	3,995	5,375	(1,380)
Power	81	122	(41)	122	184	(62)	0	0	0	0	0	0	81	122	(41)	122	184	(62)
Oil and Gas	6	486	(480)	10	808	(799)	0	1	(1)	0	1	(1)	6	487	(481)	10	810	(800)
Coal	0	3	(3)	0	2	(2)	0	24	(24)	0	36	(36)	0	26	(26)	0	39	(39)
Other Fuels	0	0	(0)	0	0	(0)	0	0	0	0	0	0	0	0	(0)	0	0	(0)
Ferrous Metallurgy	102	333	(231)	123	388	(265)	15	14	1	14	19	(4)	117	347	(230)	137	406	(269)
Non-Ferrous Metallurgy	14	136	(122)	21	210	(188)	0	2	(2)	1	2	(1)	14	138	(124)	22	212	(190)
Chemical & Petroleum	683	618	64	517	438	78	11	83	(72)	9	60	(51)	693	701	(8)	525	498	28
Machinery	1,404	1,502	(98)	1,829	2,023	(194)	115	321	(207)	114	271	(157)	1,518	1,823	(304)	1,943	2,294	(351)
Sawmill & Lumber	119	140	(21)	78	99	(21)	28	20	9	16	13	3	148	159	(12)	94	112	(18)
Building Materials	80	88	(8)	62	86	(24)	3	6	(3)	3	2	1	83	93	(10)	65	88	(23)
Light Industry	852	456	396	281	131	149	24	417	(394)	10	105	(94)	875	873	3	291	236	55
Food Production	1,089	313	776	567	112	455	107	380	(273)	51	261	(209)	1,196	693	503	619	373	246
Other Industries	161	129	32	159	120	38	8	8	0	8	4	4	169	137	32	167	125	42
Agriculture	102	124	(22)	31	70	(38)	41	232	(191)	16	118	(102)	143	356	(213)	47	188	(141)
Other Prod Sectors	348	73	275	348	75	273	22	3	20	23	3	20	370	76	294	371	78	293
TOTAL	5,039	4,520	519	4,149	4,747	(599)	374	1,510	(1,136)	264	893	(629)	5,413	6,030	(617)	4,413	5,640	(1,228)

Source: Intelligent Decision Systems (IDS).

Table 3.8 - Latvia: Unrequited Transfers, Net
(Mln of Rubles)

	1970	1975	1976	1977	1978	1979	1980	1981	1982	1983	1984	1985	1986	1987	1988	1989	1990
Unrequited Transfers, Net	-893	-1290	-1263	-1366	-1343	-1542	-1738	-1879	-1758	-1649	-1398	-1294	-1240	-1376	-1126	-1339	-565
Mutual Accounts Between State Budget of Latvia and USSR Central Budget	126	86	75	98	63	52	45	84	291	311	148	132	157	16	91	54	17
Turnover Tax Transfer to USSR Central Budget	-599	-654	-733	-832	-885	-942	-1006	-1058	-1163	-1063	-783	-629	-570	-582	-587	-887	0
Profit of Latvian Enterprises Transfer to USSR Central Budget	-256	-452	-325	-367	-340	-459	-502	-544	-514	-555	-607	-602	-661	-753	-771	-674	-319
Tax Transfer to USSR Central Budget	-125	-169	-187	-176	-184	-189	-210	-235	-284	-247	-242	-289	-273	-263	-278	-130	0
Subsidies Received from USSR Central Budget for Milk, Cattle, etc	30	31	32	35	52	51	53	57	128	145	310	315	313	152	177	229	0
Subsidies Received from USSR Central Budget for Maintenance of the Social Sphere, Science, etc	65	29	30	31	34	35	37	40	45	45	41	49	71	354	428	503	100
USSR Central Budget Incomes from Latvian Foreign Trade	-43	-76	-96	-107	-112	-132	-170	-195	-210	-220	-227	-243	-224	-272	-258	-507	-508
Turnover Tax from Other USSR Republics	31	56	85	100	181	198	175	135	116	106	137	152	129	170	263	253	262
Latvian Enterprise Accounts with USSR Central Ministries	-127	-147	-151	-155	-159	-163	-167	-171	-175	-179	-183	-187	-191	-195	-199	-175	-116
Latvian Trade Union Budget and Social Maintenance Budget Accounts with Corresponding Central Budgets of USSR	5	6	6	7	7	7	7	8	8	8	8	8	9	-3	8	-5	-1

Source: State Committee for Statistics.

Table 3.9 - Latvia: Exchange Rates
(Kopeks per USD)

	1980	1981	1982	1983	1984	1985	1986	1987	1988	1989	1990	1991
Official Rates:												
January 1	64.40	67.50	70.80	71.05	79.10	87.00	75.85	67.00	58.43	60.67	60.88	56.40
April 1	65.75	70.90	72.55	73.15	78.05	86.55	72.75	63.60	59.38	62.56	61.20	58.38
July 1	64.35	74.00	73.50	73.50	81.45	85.30	70.40	63.83	62.06	64.30	59.76	60.44
October 1	64.40	72.50	74.10	76.30	84.55	78.80	67.68	63.37	63.16	63.30	56.91	58.48
Annual Rate	64.94	71.98	72.53	74.33	81.61	83.70	68.65	63.31	59.59	63.00	58.43	58.21
Memorandum Items:												
Commercial Exchange Rate (USSR State Committee of Statistics)	161.00	152.00	157.00	156.00	148.00	149.00	152.00	156.00	150.00	157.00	N.A.	N.A.

	Market Exchange Rates (Rubles per US$)			Quoted by Bank of Latvia	Currency Exchange ("Dienas Bizness")	
1991	**Buying**	**Selling**	**1992**		**Buying**	**Selling**
May	31.17	35.76	April 6	125.00	120	133
June	29.83	34.26	May 4	125.00	124	135
July	29.31	33.53	June 1	119.35	124	131
August	30.82	37.25	July 6	129.20	131	142
September	37.20	43.94	August 3	136.00	140	151
October	47.06	54.76	September 7	159.05	176	189
November	69.28	81.13	October 6	160.07	180	191
December	103.50	120.55				

100 Kopeks = Rb 1.
Since November 1990 the USSR State Bank determined also commercial rate which was three times the official rate.
Source: Bank of Latvia.

Table 4.1 - Latvia: Consolidated General Government Operations - Economic Classification
(Mln of Rubles)

	1980	1981	1982	1983	1984	1985	1986	1987	1988	1989	1990	1991	Budget 1992
Total Revenues	**3847.3**	**4069.9**	**4347.5**	**4616.2**	**4673.5**	**4657.5**	**4843.6**	**4950.5**	**5388.1**	**5659.0**	**5490.0**	**10995.1**	**44350.5**
Tax Revenues	3327.1	3477.8	3547.8	3654.8	3742.1	3627.7	3789.5	3897.4	4128.2	4360.0	4475.4	10168.2	41757.9
Taxes on Income and Profits	1441.0	1496.4	1449.4	1577.5	1656.5	1649.3	1750.4	1882.7	1895.6	1970.2	1881.8	3121.4	12087.6
Taxes on Enterprises	1174.0	1222.6	1164.7	1284.1	1349.8	1329.0	1417.0	1533.3	1514.6	1554.2	1419.8	2086.6	7269.0
Taxes on Individuals	267.0	273.8	284.7	293.4	306.7	320.3	333.4	349.4	381.0	416.0	462.0	1034.8	4818.6
Social security contributions	138.9	158.7	243.9	250.3	265.6	210.4	279.1	288.7	309.6	329.2	442.0	2962.4	15869.1
Domestic Taxes on Goods and Services	1747.2	1822.7	1854.5	1827.0	1820.0	1768.0	1760.0	1726.0	1923.0	2053.0	2124.0	2891.0	10487.4
Turnover Tax, Excises and VAT	1747.2	1822.6	1854.5	1826.9	1820.0	1718.0	1712.0	1726.0	1923.0	2053.0	2124.0	2723.1	10487.4
Taxes on Foreign Trade	0.0	0.0	0.0	0.0	0.0	0.0	0.0	0.0	0.0	0.0	0.0	11.4	797.0
Other Taxes	0.0	0.0	0.0	0.0	0.0	0.0	0.0	0.0	0.0	7.627.6	1182.0	2516.8	
Non-Tax Revenues	503.2	574.6	781.7	943.4	913.3	1010.9	1033.4	1031.8	1238.1	1275.8	988.3	553.1	2570.4
Transfers from the USSR budget	381.6	446.6	613.5	702.5	510.1	566.9	599.4	451.8	595.1	543.8	540.3	0.0	0.0
Other [a]	121.6	128.0	168.2	240.9	403.2	444.0	434.0	580.0	643.0	732.0	448.0	553.1	2570.4
Other Funds [b]	17.0	17.5	18.0	18.0	18.1	18.9	20.7	21.3	21.8	23.2	26.3	273.8	22.2
Total Expenditures	**3834.7**	**4070.9**	**4315.5**	**4626.2**	**4611.0**	**4629.8**	**4805.6**	**4916.9**	**5333.4**	**5572.5**	**5241.6**	**9154.4**	**46182.4**
Current Expenditures	3132.9	3313.3	3533.4	3773.6	3726.3	3737.8	3880.8	3920.2	4249.6	4408.5	3899.3	8063.7	43067.2
Wages and Salaries	248.7	255.7	260.5	262.0	268.5	279.6	291.2	307.2	311.6	328.0	379.2	1307.9	NA
Supplies and Maintenance	214.3	223.9	240.5	242.5	260.3	276.6	294.8	315.8	310.6	386.7	448.1	1595.6	NA
Subsidies	471.5	478.9	523.9	757.4	1001.2	1115.2	1115.2	1005.5	1229.6	1265.6	1677.1	375.1	NA
Transfers to Enterprises & Individuals	239.1	255.6	273.5	279.5	280.4	298.2	322.9	343.8	369.5	398.6	448.3	3275.6	NA
Transfers to USSR budget	1664.9	1766.2	1846.8	1837.1	1576.2	1411.6	1462.0	1554.9	1634.8	1623.9	36.3	0.0	0.0
Other current expenditures	294.4	333.0	388.2	395.1	339.7	356.6	394.7	393.0	393.5	405.7	910.3	1509.5	NA
Capital Expenditures	238.8	255.4	255.5	282.5	282.1	259.8	257.6	299.9	344.3	410.8	477.2	858.5	3115.2
Gross Fixed Capital Formation	94.6	95.0	97.8	100.1	111.8	119.5	122.4	131.2	159.9	162.4	217.0	858.5	2551.2
Loans to Enterprises	144.2	160.4	157.7	182.4	170.3	140.3	135.2	168.7	184.4	248.4	260.2	0.0	564.0
Loans to Households													
Other Funds [b]	463.0	502.2	526.6	570.1	602.6	632.2	667.2	696.8	739.5	753.2	865.1	232.2	0.0
General Budget Balance	**12.6**	**-1.0**	**32.0**	**-10.0**	**62.5**	**27.7**	**38.0**	**33.6**	**54.7**	**86.5**	**248.4**	**1840.7**	**-1831.9**

a. Includes revenue from the foreign currency budget in 1991 and 1992.
b. Includes the following Funds: Social Insurance, Environmental Protection, Privatization, and Agricultural Stabilization Funds.
Note: Consolidated General Government Operations include: Central (Republican) Government, Local Governments, and the following Funds: Social Insurance, Environmental Protection, Privatization, Agricultural Stabilization, and the Foreign Currency.
Source: Ministry of Finance.

Table 4.2 - Latvia: Consolidated General Government Operations - Economic Classification
(Percent Share of Total)

	1980	1981	1982	1983	1984	1985	1986	1987	1988	1989	1990	1991	Budget 1992
Total Revenues	**100.0**	**100.0**	**100.0**	**100.0**	**100.0**	**100.0**	**100.0**	**100.0**	**100.0**	**100.0**	**100.0**	**100.0**	**100.0**
Tax Revenues	86.5	85.5	81.6	79.2	80.1	77.9	78.2	78.7	76.6	77.0	81.5	92.5	94.2
Taxes on Income and Profits	37.5	36.8	33.3	34.2	35.4	35.4	36.1	38.0	35.2	34.8	34.3	28.4	27.3
Taxes on Enterprises	30.5	30.0	26.8	27.8	28.9	28.5	29.3	31.0	28.1	27.5	25.9	19.0	16.4
Taxes on Individuals	6.9	6.7	6.5	6.4	6.6	6.9	6.9	7.1	7.1	7.4	8.4	9.4	10.9
Social Security Contributions	3.6	3.9	5.6	5.4	5.7	4.5	5.8	5.8	5.7	5.8	8.1	26.9	35.8
Domestic Taxes on Goods and Services	45.4	44.8	42.7	39.6	38.9	38.0	36.3	34.9	35.7	36.3	38.7	26.3	23.6
Turnover Tax, Excises and VAT	45.4	44.8	42.7	39.6	38.9	36.9	35.3	34.9	35.7	36.3	38.7	24.8	23.6
Taxes on Foreign Trade	0.0	0.0	0.0	0.0	0.0	0.0	0.0	0.0	0.0	0.0	0.0	0.1	1.8
Other Taxes	0.0	0.0	0.0	0.0	0.0	0.0	0.0	0.0	0.0	0.1	0.5	10.8	5.7
Non-Tax Revenues	13.1	14.1	18.0	20.4	19.5	21.7	21.3	20.8	23.0	22.5	18.0	5.0	5.8
Transfers from the USSR Budget	9.9	11.0	14.1	15.2	10.9	12.2	12.4	9.1	11.0	9.6	9.8	0.0	0.0
Other [a]	3.2	3.1	3.9	5.2	8.6	9.5	9.0	11.7	11.9	12.9	8.2	5.0	5.8
Other Funds [b]	0.4	0.4	0.4	0.4	0.4	0.4	0.4	0.4	0.4	0.4	0.5	2.5	0.1
Total Expenditures	**100.0**	**100.0**	**100.0**	**100.0**	**100.0**	**100.0**	**100.0**	**100.0**	**100.0**	**100.0**	**100.0**	**100.0**	**100.0**
Current Expenditures	81.7	81.4	81.9	81.6	80.8	80.7	80.8	79.7	79.7	79.1	74.4	88.1	93.3
Wages and Salaries	6.5	6.3	6.0	5.7	5.8	6.0	6.1	6.2	5.8	5.9	7.2	14.3	NA
Supplies and Maintenance	5.6	5.5	5.6	5.2	5.6	6.0	6.1	6.4	5.8	6.9	8.5	17.4	NA
Subsidies	12.3	11.8	12.1	16.4	21.7	24.1	23.2	20.4	23.1	22.7	32.0	4.1	NA
Transfers to Enterprises & Individuals	6.2	6.3	6.3	6.0	6.1	6.4	6.7	7.0	6.9	7.2	8.6	35.8	NA
Transfers to USSR budget	43.4	43.4	42.8	39.7	34.2	30.5	30.4	31.6	30.7	29.1	0.7	0.0	0.0
Other Current Expenditures	7.7	8.2	9.0	8.5	7.4	7.7	8.2	8.0	7.4	7.3	17.4	16.5	NA
Capital Expenditures	6.2	6.3	5.9	6.1	6.1	5.6	5.4	6.1	6.5	7.4	9.1	9.4	6.7
Gross Fixed Capital Formation	2.5	2.3	2.3	2.2	2.4	2.6	2.5	2.7	3.0	2.9	4.1	9.4	5.5
Loans to Enterprises	3.8	3.9	3.7	3.9	3.7	3.0	2.8	3.4	3.5	4.5	5.0	0.0	1.2
Other Funds [b]	12.1	12.3	12.2	12.3	13.1	13.7	13.9	14.2	13.9	13.5	16.5	2.5	0.0

a. Includes revenue from the foreign currency budget in 1991 and 1992.
b. Includes the following Funds: Social Insurance, Environmental Protection, Privatization, and Agricultural Stabilization Funds.
Note: Consolidated General Government Operations include: Central (Republican) Government, Local Governments, and the following Funds: Social Insurance, Environmental Protection, Privatization, Agricultural Stabilization, and the Foreign Currency.
Source: Ministry of Finance.

Table 4.3 - Latvia: Consolidated General Government Operations - Economic Classification
(Percent)

	1980	1981	1982	1983	1984	1985	1986	1987	1988	1989	1990	1991
Total Revenues	**48.7**	**48.1**	**49.1**	**51.7**	**50.3**	**51.6**	**51.9**	**52.3**	**54.1**	**51.8**	**45.0**	**38.4**
Tax Revenues	42.1	41.1	40.0	41.0	40.3	40.2	40.6	41.2	41.5	39.9	36.7	35.5
Taxes on Income and Profits	18.2	17.7	16.4	17.7	17.8	18.3	18.8	19.9	19.0	18.0	15.4	10.9
Taxes on Enterprises	14.9	14.4	13.1	14.4	14.5	14.7	15.2	16.2	15.2	14.2	11.6	7.3
Taxes on Individuals	3.4	3.2	3.2	3.3	3.3	3.5	3.6	3.7	3.8	3.8	3.8	3.6
Social Security Contributions	1.8	1.9	2.8	2.8	2.9	2.3	3.0	3.1	3.1	3.0	3.6	10.3
Domestic Taxes on Goods and Services	22.1	21.5	20.9	20.5	19.6	19.6	18.9	18.2	19.3	18.8	17.4	10.1
Turnover Tax, Excises and VAT	22.1	21.5	20.9	20.5	19.6	19.0	18.4	18.2	19.3	18.8	17.4	9.5
Taxes on Foreign Trade	0.0	0.0	0.0	0.0	0.0	0.0	0.0	0.0	0.0	0.0	0.0	0.0
Other Taxes	0.0	0.0	0.0	0.0	0.0	0.0	0.0	0.0	0.0	0.1	0.2	4.1
Non-Tax Revenues	6.4	6.8	8.8	10.6	9.8	11.2	11.1	10.9	12.4	11.7	8.1	1.9
Transfers from the USSR Budget	4.8	5.3	6.9	7.9	5.5	6.3	6.4	4.8	6.0	5.0	4.4	0.0
Other [a]	1.5	1.5	1.9	2.7	4.3	4.9	4.7	6.1	6.5	6.7	3.7	1.9
Other Funds [b]	0.2	0.2	0.2	0.2	0.2	0.2	0.2	0.2	0.2	0.2	0.2	1.0
Total Expenditures	**48.5**	**48.1**	**48.7**	**51.8**	**49.6**	**51.3**	**51.5**	**52.0**	**53.6**	**51.0**	**43.0**	**31.9**
Current Expenditures	39.6	39.1	39.9	42.3	40.1	41.4	41.6	41.4	42.7	40.3	32.0	28.1
Wages and Salaries	3.1	3.0	2.9	2.9	2.9	3.1	3.1	3.2	3.1	3.0	3.1	4.6
Supplies and Maintenance	2.7	2.6	2.7	2.7	2.8	3.1	3.2	3.3	3.1	3.5	3.7	5.6
Subsidies	6.0	5.7	5.9	8.5	10.8	12.3	12.0	10.6	12.4	11.6	13.7	1.3
Transfers to Enterprises & Individuals	3.0	3.0	3.1	3.1	3.0	3.3	3.5	3.6	3.7	3.6	3.7	11.4
Transfers to USSR budget	21.1	20.9	20.8	20.6	17.0	15.6	15.7	16.4	16.4	14.9	0.3	0.0
Other Current Expenditures	3.7	3.9	4.4	4.4	3.7	3.9	4.2	4.2	4.0	3.7	7.5	5.3
Capital Expenditures	3.0	3.0	2.9	3.2	3.0	2.9	2.8	3.2	3.5	3.8	3.9	3.0
Gross Fixed Capital Formation	1.2	1.1	1.1	1.1	1.2	1.3	1.3	1.4	1.6	1.5	1.8	3.0
Loans to Enterprises	1.8	1.9	1.8	2.0	1.8	1.6	1.4	1.8	1.9	2.3	2.1	0.0
Other Funds [b]	5.9	5.9	5.9	6.4	6.5	7.0	7.2	7.4	7.4	6.9	7.1	0.8
General Budget Balance	**0.2**	**0.0**	**0.4**	**-0.1**	**0.7**	**0.3**	**0.4**	**0.4**	**0.5**	**0.8**	**2.0**	**6.4**

a. Includes revenue from the foreign currency budget in 1991 and 1992.
b. Includes the following Funds: Social Insurance, Environmental Protection, Privatization, and Agricultural Stabilization Funds.
Note: Consolidated General Government Operations include: Central (Republican) Government, Local Governments, and the following Funds: Social Insurance, Environmental Protection, Privatization, Agricultural Stabilization, and the Foreign Currency.
Source: Ministry of Finance.

Table 4.4 - Latvia: Consolidated General Government Operations - Economic Classification
(Mln of Rubles)

	1980	1981	1982	1983	1984	1985	1986	1987	1988	1989	1990	1991	Budget 1992
Total Revenues	**3289.0**	**3480.9**	**3735.3**	**3998.8**	**4004.3**	**3878.3**	**4015.4**	**3863.4**	**3910.0**	**4213.0**	**3931.0**	**5993.9**	**22494.3**
Tax Revenues	3109.2	3243.7	3246.2	3342.0	3408.6	3294.3	3393.4	3534.4	3680.0	3749.0	3652.0	5526.5	20009.2
Taxes on Income and Profits	1362.0	1421.1	1391.7	1515.1	1588.6	1576.3	1681.4	1808.4	1757.0	1696.0	1528.0	1894.5	7812.7
Taxes on Enterprises	1095.0	1147.3	1107.0	1221.7	1281.9	1256.0	1348.0	1459.0	1376.0	1280.0	1066.0	1417.5	5333.9
Taxes on Individuals	267.0	273.8	284.7	293.4	306.7	320.3	333.4	349.4	381.0	416.0	462.0	477.0	2478.8
Domestic Taxes on Goods and Services	1747.2	1822.6	1854.5	1826.9	1820.0	1718.0	1712.0	1726.0	1923.0	2053.0	2124.0	2891.0	9960.3
Turnover Tax and Excises	1747.2	1822.6	1854.5	1826.9	1820.0	1718.0	1712.0	1726.0	1923.0	2053.0	2124.0	2723.1	9960.3
Other	0.0	0.0	0.0	0.0	0.0	0.0	0.0	0.0	0.0	0.0	0.0	167.9	0.0
Taxes on Foreign Trade	0.0	0.0	0.0	0.0	0.0	0.0	0.0	0.0	0.0	0.0	0.0	11.4	797.0
Property Taxes	0.0	0.0	0.0	0.0	0.0	0.0	0.0	0.0	0.0	0.0	0.0	77.0	0.0
Other	0.0	0.0	0.0	0.0	0.0	0.0	0.0	0.0	0.0	0.0	0.0	0.0	0.0
Other Taxes [a]	0.0	0.0	0.0	0.0	0.0	0.0	0.0	0.0	0.0	0.0	0.0	652.6	1439.2
Non-Tax Revenues	179.8	237.2	489.1	656.8	595.7	584.0	622.0	329.0	230.0	464.0	279.0	467.4	2485.1
Transfers from the USSR budget	74.5	120.6	329.0	394.5	191.2	164.0	232.0	65.0	187.0	113.0	53.0	0.0	0.0
Other [b]	105.3	116.6	160.1	262.3	404.5	420.0	390.0	264.0	43.0	351.0	226.0	467.4	2485.1
Total Expenditures	**3238.6**	**3452.9**	**3675.8**	**3910.5**	**3864.7**	**3806.5**	**3926.7**	**3960.5**	**4339.8**	**4492.1**	**3793.9**	**4878.5**	**23678.0**
Current Expenditures	3077.3	3272.1	3491.0	3700.5	3655.2	3631.5	3758.5	3765.6	4113.5	4214.8	3493.6	4321.7	21621.5
Wages and Salaries	96.6	99.2	100.6	101.6	102.8	104.6	108.3	107.6	99.6	101.4	118.9	525.4	4249.1
Supplies and Maintenance	94.0	99.2	105.7	110.5	125.2	128.6	131.7	138.9	115.8	146.8	170.6	897.5	3804.0
Subsidies	461.6	477.6	523.2	756.4	1000.3	1114.3	1114.2	1004.9	1228.6	1264.9	1649.7	295.0	456.0
Interest	0.0	0.0	0.0	0.0	0.0	0.0	0.0	0.0	0.0	0.0	0.0	0.0	140.3
Transfers to Local Budgets	294.4	313.9	337.9	355.5	351.3	346.0	356.9	360.0	394.5	408.3	344.9	653.3	5402.4
Transfers to USSR budget	1664.9	1766.2	1846.8	1837.1	1576.2	1411.6	1462.0	1554.9	1634.8	1623.9	36.3	0.0	0.0
Other Transfers	231.3	247.8	265.8	270.0	272.3	288.6	314.6	333.9	356.4	383.0	439.8	625.4	304.4
Transfers to Individuals	222.7	232.2	246.8	253.2	267.6	283.0	310.4	330.5	353.9	379.0	425.4	610.7	224.0
Transfers to Enterprises	8.6	15.6	19.0	16.8	4.7	5.6	4.2	3.4	2.5	4.0	14.4	14.7	80.4
Other Current Expenditures [c]	234.5	268.2	311.0	269.4	227.1	237.8	270.8	265.4	283.8	286.5	733.4	1325.1	7265.3
Capital Expenditures	161.3	180.8	184.8	210.0	209.5	175.0	168.2	194.9	226.3	277.3	300.3	556.8	2056.5
Gross Fixed Capital Formation and Invent	30.3	31.1	36.6	37.9	51.6	53.2	53.3	52.3	74.3	72.3	100.7	556.8	1492.5
Loans to Enterprises	131.0	149.7	148.2	172.1	157.9	121.8	114.9	142.6	152.0	205.0	199.6	0.0	564.0
Central Budget Balance	**50.4**	**28.0**	**59.5**	**88.3**	**139.6**	**71.8**	**88.7**	**-97.1**	**-429.8**	**-279.1**	**137.1**	**1115.4**	**-1183.7**

a. Includes taxes on natural resources, forest revenue and duties and other collections.
b. Includes revenue from the foreign currency budget in 1991 and 1992.
c. Includes expenditure from foreign currency budget in 1992.
Source: Ministry of Finance.

Table 4.5 - Latvia: Central Government Budget - Economic Classification
(Percent Share of Total)

	1980	1981	1982	1983	1984	1985	1986	1987	1988	1989	1990	1991	Budget 1992
Total Revenues	**100.0**	**100.0**	**100.0**	**100.0**	**100.0**	**100.0**	**100.0**	**100.0**	**100.0**	**100.0**	**100.0**	**100.0**	**100.0**
Tax Revenues	94.5	93.2	86.9	83.6	85.1	84.9	84.5	91.5	94.1	89.0	92.9	92.2	89.0
Taxes on Income and Profits	41.4	40.8	37.3	37.9	39.7	40.6	41.9	46.8	44.9	40.3	38.9	31.6	34.7
Taxes on Enterprises	33.3	33.0	29.6	30.6	32.0	32.4	33.6	37.8	35.2	30.4	27.1	23.6	23.7
Taxes on Individuals	8.1	7.9	7.6	7.3	7.7	8.3	8.3	9.0	9.7	9.9	11.8	8.0	11.0
Domestic Taxes on Goods and Services	53.1	52.4	49.6	45.7	45.5	44.3	42.6	44.7	49.2	48.7	54.0	48.2	44.3
Turnover Tax and Excises	53.1	52.4	49.6	45.7	45.5	44.3	42.6	44.7	49.2	48.7	54.0	45.4	44.3
Other	0.0	0.0	0.0	0.0	0.0	0.0	0.0	0.0	0.0	0.0	0.0	2.8	0.0
Taxes on Foreign Trade	0.0	0.0	0.0	0.0	0.0	0.0	0.0	0.0	0.0	0.0	0.0	0.2	3.5
Property Taxes	0.0	0.0	0.0	0.0	0.0	0.0	0.0	0.0	0.0	0.0	0.0	1.3	0.0
Other	0.0	0.0	0.0	0.0	0.0	0.0	0.0	0.0	0.0	0.0	0.0	0.0	0.0
Other Taxes [a]	0.0	0.0	0.0	0.0	0.0	0.0	0.0	0.0	0.0	0.0	0.0	10.9	6.4
Non-Tax Revenues	5.5	6.8	13.1	16.4	14.9	15.1	15.5	8.5	5.9	11.0	7.1	7.8	11.0
Transfers from the USSR budget	2.3	3.5	8.8	9.9	4.8	4.2	5.8	1.7	4.8	2.7	1.3	0.0	0.0
Other [b]	3.2	3.3	4.3	6.6	10.1	10.8	9.7	6.8	1.1	8.3	5.7	7.8	11.0
Total Expenditures	**100.0**	**100.0**	**100.0**	**100.0**	**100.0**	**100.0**	**100.0**	**100.0**	**100.0**	**100.0**	**100.0**	**100.0**	**100.0**
Current Expenditures	95.0	94.8	95.0	94.6	94.6	95.4	95.7	95.1	94.8	93.8	92.1	88.6	91.3
Wages and Salaries	3.0	2.9	2.7	2.6	2.7	2.7	2.8	2.7	2.3	2.3	3.1	10.8	17.9
Supplies and Maintenance	2.9	2.9	2.9	2.8	3.2	3.4	3.4	3.5	2.7	3.3	4.5	18.4	16.1
Subsidies	14.3	13.8	14.2	19.3	25.9	29.3	28.4	25.4	28.3	28.2	43.5	6.0	1.9
Interest	0.0	0.0	0.0	0.0	0.0	0.0	0.0	0.0	0.0	0.0	0.0	0.0	0.6
Transfers to Local Budgets	9.1	9.1	9.2	9.1	9.1	9.1	9.1	9.1	9.1	9.1	9.1	13.4	22.8
Transfers to USSR budget	51.4	51.2	50.2	47.0	40.8	37.1	37.2	39.3	37.7	36.2	1.0	0.0	0.0
Other Transfers	7.1	7.2	7.2	6.9	7.0	7.6	8.0	8.4	8.2	8.5	11.6	12.8	1.3
Transfers to Individuals	6.9	6.7	6.7	6.5	6.9	7.4	7.9	8.3	8.2	8.4	11.2	12.5	0.9
Transfers to Enterprises	0.3	0.5	0.5	0.4	0.1	0.1	0.1	0.1	0.1	0.1	0.4	0.3	0.3
Other Current Expenditures [c]	7.2	7.8	8.5	6.9	5.9	6.2	6.9	6.7	6.5	6.4	19.3	27.2	30.7
Capital Expenditures	5.0	5.2	5.0	5.4	5.4	4.6	4.3	4.9	5.2	6.2	7.9	11.4	8.7
Gross Fixed Capital Formation & Invent	0.9	0.9	1.0	1.0	1.3	1.4	1.4	1.3	1.7	1.6	2.7	11.4	6.3
Loans to Enterprises	4.0	4.3	4.0	4.4	4.1	3.2	2.9	3.6	3.5	4.6	5.3	0.0	2.4

a. Includes taxes on natural resources, forest revenue and duties and other collections.

b. Includes revenue from the foreign currency budget in 1991.

c. Includes expenditure from foreign currency budget in 1992.

Source: Ministry of Finance.

Table 4.6 - Latvia: Central Government Budget as Share of GDP - Economic Classification
(Percent)

	1980	1981	1982	1983	1984	1985	1986	1987	1988	1989	1990	1991
Total Revenues	**41.6**	**41.1**	**42.2**	**44.8**	**43.1**	**42.9**	**43.1**	**40.8**	**39.3**	**38.6**	**32.2**	**20.9**
Tax Revenues	39.3	38.3	36.6	37.5	36.7	36.5	36.4	37.4	37.0	34.3	29.9	19.3
Taxes on Income and Profits	17.2	16.8	15.7	17.0	17.1	17.5	18.0	19.1	17.6	15.5	12.5	6.6
Taxes on Enterprises	13.9	13.6	12.5	13.7	13.8	13.9	14.5	15.4	13.8	11.7	8.7	4.9
Taxes on Individuals	3.4	3.2	3.2	3.3	3.3	3.5	3.6	3.7	3.8	3.8	3.8	1.7
Domestic Taxes on Goods and Services	22.1	21.5	20.9	20.5	19.6	19.0	18.4	18.2	19.3	18.8	17.4	10.1
Turnover Tax and Excises	22.1	21.5	20.9	20.5	19.6	19.0	18.4	18.2	19.3	18.8	17.4	9.5
Other	0.0	0.0	0.0	0.0	0.0	0.0	0.0	0.0	0.0	0.0	0.0	0.6
Taxes on Foreign Trade	0.0	0.0	0.0	0.0	0.0	0.0	0.0	0.0	0.0	0.0	0.0	0.0
Property Taxes	0.0	0.0	0.0	0.0	0.0	0.0	0.0	0.0	0.0	0.0	0.0	0.3
Other	0.0	0.0	0.0	0.0	0.0	0.0	0.0	0.0	0.0	0.0	0.0	0.0
Other Taxes [a]	0.0	0.0	0.0	0.0	0.0	0.0	0.0	0.0	0.0	0.0	0.0	2.3
Non-Tax Revenues	2.3	2.8	5.5	7.4	6.4	6.5	6.7	3.5	2.3	4.2	2.3	1.6
Transfers from the USSR budget	0.9	1.4	3.7	4.4	2.1	1.8	2.5	0.7	1.9	1.0	0.4	0.0
Other [b]	1.3	1.4	1.8	2.9	4.4	4.7	4.2	2.8	0.4	3.2	1.9	1.6
Total Expenditures	**41.0**	**40.8**	**41.5**	**43.8**	**41.6**	**42.2**	**42.1**	**41.9**	**43.6**	**41.1**	**31.1**	**17.0**
Current Expenditures	38.9	38.7	39.4	41.5	39.3	40.2	40.3	39.8	41.3	38.6	28.6	15.1
Wages and Salaries	1.2	1.2	1.1	1.1	1.1	1.2	1.2	1.1	1.0	0.9	1.0	1.8
Supplies and Maintenance	1.2	1.2	1.2	1.2	1.3	1.4	1.4	1.5	1.2	1.3	1.4	3.1
Subsidies	5.8	5.6	5.9	8.5	10.8	12.3	11.9	10.6	12.3	11.6	13.5	1.0
Interest	0.0	0.0	0.0	0.0	0.0	0.0	0.0	0.0	0.0	0.0	0.0	0.0
Transfers to Local Budgets	3.7	3.7	3.8	4.0	3.8	3.8	3.8	3.8	4.0	3.7	2.8	2.3
Transfers to USSR budget	21.1	20.9	20.8	20.6	17.0	15.6	15.7	16.4	16.4	14.9	0.3	0.0
Other Transfers	2.9	2.9	3.0	3.0	2.9	3.2	3.4	3.5	3.6	3.5	3.6	2.2
Transfers to Individuals	2.8	2.7	2.8	2.8	2.9	3.1	3.3	3.5	3.6	3.5	3.5	2.1
Transfers to Enterprises	0.1	0.2	0.2	0.2	0.1	0.1	0.0	0.0	0.0	0.0	0.1	0.1
Other Current Expenditures	3.0	3.2	3.5	3.0	2.4	2.6	2.9	2.8	2.9	2.6	6.0	4.6
Capital Expenditures	2.0	2.1	2.1	2.4	2.3	1.9	1.8	2.1	2.3	2.5	2.5	1.9
Gross Fixed Capital Formation & Invent	0.4	0.4	0.4	0.4	0.6	0.6	0.6	0.6	0.7	0.7	0.8	1.9
Loans to Enterprises	1.7	1.8	1.7	1.9	1.7	1.3	1.2	1.5	1.5	1.9	1.6	0.0
Central Budget Balance	**0.6**	**0.3**	**0.7**	**1.0**	**1.5**	**0.8**	**1.0**	**-1.0**	**-4.3**	**-2.6**	**1.1**	**3.9**

a. Includes taxes on natural resources, forest revenue and duties and other collections.
b. Includes revenue from the foreign currency budget in 1991.

Source: Ministry of Finance.

Table 4.7 - Latvia: Local Government Budget - Economic Classification
(Mln of Rubles)

	1980	1981	1982	1983	1984	1985	1986	1987	1988	1989	1990	1991	Budget 1992
Total Revenues	**389.7**	**400.7**	**403.7**	**396.6**	**417.9**	**493.0**	**518.0**	**750.3**	**1132.6**	**1063.2**	**920.8**	**2338.6**	**11345.2**
Tax Revenues	79.0	75.4	57.7	62.5	67.9	123.0	117.0	74.3	138.6	274.2	353.8	1681.8	5857.5
Taxes on Income and Profits	79.0	75.3	57.7	62.4	67.9	73.0	69.0	74.3	138.6	274.2	353.8	1226.9	4274.9
Taxes on Enterprises	79.0	75.3	57.7	62.4	67.9	73.0	69.0	74.3	138.6	274.2	353.8	669.1	1935.1
Taxes on Individuals	0.0	0.0	0.0	0.0	0.0	0.0	0.0	0.0	0.0	0.0	0.0	557.8	2339.8
Domestic Taxes on Goods and Services	0.0	0.1	0.0	0.1	0.0	50.0	48.0	0.0	0.0	0.0	0.0	0.0	527.1
Turnover Tax and Excises	0.0	0.0	0.0	0.0	0.0	0.0	0.0	0.0	0.0	0.0	0.0	0.0	527.1
Other	0.0	0.1	0.0	0.1	0.0	50.0	48.0	0.0	0.0	0.0	0.0	0.0	0.0
Taxes on Foreign Trade	0.0	0.0	0.0	0.0	0.0	0.0	0.0	0.0	0.0	0.0	0.0	0.0	0.0
Property Taxes	0.0	0.0	0.0	0.0	0.0	0.0	0.0	0.0	0.0	0.0	0.0	320.3	831.0
Taxes on Fixed Assets	0.0	0.0	0.0	0.0	0.0	0.0	0.0	0.0	0.0	0.0	0.0	0.0	0.0
Land Tax	0.0	0.0	0.0	0.0	0.0	0.0	0.0	0.0	0.0	0.0	0.0	232.3	531.0
Other	0.0	0.0	0.0	0.0	0.0	0.0	0.0	0.0	0.0	0.0	0.0	88.0	300.0
Other Taxes	0.0	0.0	0.0	0.0	0.0	0.0	0.0	0.0	0.0	0.0	0.0	134.6	224.5
Taxes on Natural Resources	0.0	0.0	0.0	0.0	0.0	0.0	0.0	0.0	0.0	0.0	0.0	40.6	54.4
Environmental Taxes	0.0	0.0	0.0	0.0	0.0	0.0	0.0	0.0	0.0	0.0	0.0	29.6	94.2
Other Taxes	0.0	0.0	0.0	0.0	0.0	0.0	0.0	0.0	0.0	0.0	0.0	64.4	75.9
Non-Tax Revenues	310.7	325.3	346.0	334.1	350.0	370.0	401.0	676.0	994.0	789.0	567.0	656.8	5487.7
Transfer from state budget	294.4	313.9	337.9	355.5	351.3	346.0	357.0	360.0	394.0	408.0	345.0	653.3	5402.4
Other Transfers	16.3	11.4	8.1	-21.4	-1.3	24.0	44.0	316.0	600.0	381.0	222.0	3.5	85.3
Total Expenditures	**427.5**	**429.7**	**451.0**	**501.1**	**495.0**	**537.1**	**568.6**	**619.6**	**648.6**	**735.5**	**927.5**	**2047.0**	**11606.7**
Current Expenditures	350.0	355.1	380.3	428.6	422.4	452.3	479.2	514.6	530.6	602.0	750.6	1745.3	10548.0
Wages and Salaries	152.1	156.5	159.9	160.4	165.7	175.0	182.9	199.6	212.0	226.6	260.3	782.5	4839.2
Supplies and Maintenance	120.3	124.7	134.8	132.0	135.1	148.0	163.1	176.9	194.8	239.9	277.5	698.1	3457.8
Subsidies	9.9	1.3	0.7	1.0	0.9	0.9	1.0	0.6	1.0	0.7	27.4	80.1	400.0
Transfers	7.8	7.8	7.7	9.5	8.1	9.6	8.3	9.9	13.1	15.6	8.5	0.2	1200.4
Transfers to Enterprises	7.8	7.8	7.6	9.4	8.0	9.5	8.2	9.8	12.9	15.4	8.4	0.0	0.0
Transfers to Individuals	0.0	0.0	0.1	0.1	0.1	0.1	0.1	0.1	0.2	0.2	0.1	0.2	1200.4
Other	59.9	64.8	77.2	125.7	112.6	118.8	123.9	127.6	109.7	119.2	176.9	184.4	650.6
Capital Expenditures	77.5	74.6	70.7	72.5	72.6	84.8	89.4	105.0	118.0	133.5	176.9	301.7	1058.7
Gross Fixed Capital Formation & Invent	64.3	63.9	61.2	62.2	60.2	66.3	69.1	78.9	85.6	90.1	116.3	301.7	1058.7
Loans to Enterprises	13.2	10.7	9.5	10.3	12.4	18.5	20.3	26.1	32.4	43.4	60.6	0.0	0.0
Local Budget Balance	**-37.8**	**-29.0**	**-47.3**	**-104.5**	**-77.1**	**-44.1**	**-50.6**	**130.7**	**484.0**	**327.7**	**-6.7**	**291.6**	**-261.5**

Source: Ministry of Finance.

Table 4.8 - Latvia: Local Government Budget - Economic Classification
(Percent Share of Total)

	1980	1981	1982	1983	1984	1985	1986	1987	1988	1989	1990	1991	Budget 1992
Total Revenues	**100.0**	**100.0**	**100.0**	**100.0**	**100.0**	**100.0**	**100.0**	**100.0**	**100.0**	**100.0**	**100.0**	**100.0**	**100.0**
Tax Revenues	20.3	18.8	14.3	15.8	16.2	24.9	22.6	9.9	12.2	25.8	38.4	71.9	51.6
Taxes on Income and Profits	20.3	18.8	14.3	15.7	16.2	14.8	13.3	9.9	12.2	25.8	38.4	52.5	37.7
Taxes on Enterprises	20.3	18.8	14.3	15.7	16.2	14.8	13.3	9.9	12.2	25.8	38.4	28.6	17.1
Taxes on Individuals	0.0	0.0	0.0	0.0	0.0	0.0	0.0	0.0	0.0	0.0	0.0	23.9	20.6
Domestic Taxes on Goods and Services	0.0	0.0	0.0	0.0	0.0	10.1	9.3	0.0	0.0	0.0	0.0	0.0	4.6
Turnover Tax and Excises	0.0	0.0	0.0	0.0	0.0	0.0	0.0	0.0	0.0	0.0	0.0	0.0	4.6
Other	0.0	0.0	0.0	0.0	0.0	10.1	9.3	0.0	0.0	0.0	0.0	0.0	0.0
Taxes on Foreign Trade	0.0	0.0	0.0	0.0	0.0	0.0	0.0	0.0	0.0	0.0	0.0	0.0	0.0
Property Taxes	0.0	0.0	0.0	0.0	0.0	0.0	0.0	0.0	0.0	0.0	0.0	13.7	7.3
Taxes on Fixed Assets	0.0	0.0	0.0	0.0	0.0	0.0	0.0	0.0	0.0	0.0	0.0	0.0	0.0
Land Tax	0.0	0.0	0.0	0.0	0.0	0.0	0.0	0.0	0.0	0.0	0.0	9.9	4.7
Other	0.0	0.0	0.0	0.0	0.0	0.0	0.0	0.0	0.0	0.0	0.0	3.8	2.6
Other Taxes	0.0	0.0	0.0	0.0	0.0	0.0	0.0	0.0	0.0	0.0	0.0	5.8	2.0
Taxes on Natural Resources	0.0	0.0	0.0	0.0	0.0	0.0	0.0	0.0	0.0	0.0	0.0	1.7	0.5
Environmental Taxes	0.0	0.0	0.0	0.0	0.0	0.0	0.0	0.0	0.0	0.0	0.0	1.3	0.8
Other Taxes	0.0	0.0	0.0	0.0	0.0	0.0	0.0	0.0	0.0	0.0	0.0	2.8	0.7
Non-Tax Revenues	79.7	81.2	85.7	84.2	83.8	75.1	77.4	90.1	87.8	74.2	61.6	28.1	48.4
Transfer from state budget	75.5	78.3	83.7	89.6	84.1	70.2	68.9	48.0	34.8	38.4	37.5	27.9	47.6
Other Transfers	4.2	2.8	2.0	-5.4	-0.3	4.9	8.5	42.1	53.0	35.8	24.1	0.1	0.8
Total Expenditures	100.0	100.0	100.0	100.0	100.0	100.0	100.0	100.0	100.0	100.0	100.0	100.0	100.0
Current Expenditures	81.9	82.6	84.3	85.5	85.3	84.2	84.3	83.1	81.8	81.8	80.9	85.3	90.9
Wages and Salaries	35.6	36.4	35.5	32.0	33.5	32.6	32.2	32.2	32.7	30.8	28.1	38.2	41.7
Supplies and Maintenance	28.1	29.0	29.9	26.3	27.3	27.6	28.7	28.6	30.0	32.6	29.9	34.1	29.8
Subsidies	2.3	0.3	0.2	0.2	0.2	0.2	0.2	0.1	0.2	0.1	3.0	3.9	3.4
Transfers	1.8	1.8	1.7	1.9	1.6	1.8	1.5	1.6	2.0	2.1	0.9	0.0	10.3
Transfers to Enterprises	1.8	1.8	1.7	1.9	1.6	1.8	1.4	1.6	2.0	2.1	0.9	0.0	0.0
Transfers to Individuals	0.0	0.0	0.0	0.0	0.0	0.0	0.0	0.0	0.0	0.0	0.0	0.0	10.3
Other	14.0	15.1	17.1	25.1	22.7	22.1	21.8	20.6	16.9	16.2	19.1	9.0	5.6
Capital Expenditures	18.1	17.4	15.7	14.5	14.7	15.8	15.7	16.9	18.2	18.2	19.1	14.7	9.1
Gross Fixed Capital Formation & Invent	15.0	14.9	13.6	12.4	12.2	12.3	12.2	12.7	13.2	12.3	12.5	14.7	9.1
Loans to Enterprises	3.1	2.5	2.1	2.1	2.5	3.4	3.6	4.2	5.0	5.9	6.5	0.0	0.0

Source: Ministry of Finance.

Table 4.9 - Latvia: Local Government Budget as Share of GDP - Economic Classification
(Percent)

	1980	1981	1982	1983	1984	1985	1986	1987	1988	1989	1990	1991
Total Revenues	**4.9**	**4.7**	**4.6**	**4.4**	**4.5**	**5.5**	**5.6**	**7.9**	**11.4**	**9.7**	**7.5**	**8.2**
Tax Revenues	1.0	0.9	0.7	0.7	0.7	1.4	1.3	0.8	1.4	2.5	2.9	5.9
Taxes on Income and Profits	1.0	0.9	0.7	0.7	0.7	0.8	0.7	0.8	1.4	2.5	2.9	4.3
Taxes on Enterprises	1.0	0.9	0.7	0.7	0.7	0.8	0.7	0.8	1.4	2.5	2.9	2.3
Taxes on Individuals	0.0	0.0	0.0	0.0	0.0	0.0	0.0	0.0	0.0	0.0	0.0	1.9
Domestic Taxes on Goods and Services	0.0	0.0	0.0	0.0	0.0	0.6	0.5	0.0	0.0	0.0	0.0	0.0
Turnover Tax and Excises	0.0	0.0	0.0	0.0	0.0	0.0	0.0	0.0	0.0	0.0	0.0	0.0
Other	0.0	0.0	0.0	0.0	0.0	0.6	0.5	0.0	0.0	0.0	0.0	0.0
Taxes on Foreign Trade	0.0	0.0	0.0	0.0	0.0	0.0	0.0	0.0	0.0	0.0	0.0	0.0
Property Taxes	0.0	0.0	0.0	0.0	0.0	0.0	0.0	0.0	0.0	0.0	0.0	1.1
Taxes on Fixed Assets	0.0	0.0	0.0	0.0	0.0	0.0	0.0	0.0	0.0	0.0	0.0	0.0
Land Tax	0.0	0.0	0.0	0.0	0.0	0.0	0.0	0.0	0.0	0.0	0.0	0.8
Other	0.0	0.0	0.0	0.0	0.0	0.0	0.0	0.0	0.0	0.0	0.0	0.3
Other Taxes	0.0	0.0	0.0	0.0	0.0	0.0	0.0	0.0	0.0	0.0	0.0	0.5
Taxes on Natural Resources	0.0	0.0	0.0	0.0	0.0	0.0	0.0	0.0	0.0	0.0	0.0	0.1
Environmental Taxes	0.0	0.0	0.0	0.0	0.0	0.0	0.0	0.0	0.0	0.0	0.0	0.1
Other Taxes	0.0	0.0	0.0	0.0	0.0	0.0	0.0	0.0	0.0	0.0	0.0	0.2
Non-Tax Revenues	3.9	3.8	3.9	3.7	3.8	4.1	4.3	7.1	10.0	7.2	4.6	2.3
Transfer from state budget	3.7	3.7	3.8	4.0	3.8	3.8	3.8	3.8	4.0	3.7	2.8	2.3
Other Transfers	0.2	0.1	0.1	-0.2	0.0	0.3	0.5	3.3	6.0	3.5	1.8	0.0
Total Expenditures	5.4	5.1	5.1	5.6	5.3	5.9	6.1	6.5	6.5	6.7	7.6	7.1
Current Expenditures	4.4	4.2	4.3	4.8	4.5	5.0	5.1	5.4	5.3	5.5	6.2	6.1
Wages and Salaries	1.9	1.8	1.8	1.8	1.8	1.9	2.0	2.1	2.1	2.1	2.1	2.7
Supplies and Maintenance	1.5	1.5	1.5	1.5	1.5	1.6	1.7	1.9	2.0	2.2	2.3	2.4
Subsidies	0.1	0.0	0.0	0.0	0.0	0.0	0.0	0.0	0.0	0.0	0.2	0.3
Transfers	0.1	0.1	0.1	0.1	0.1	0.1	0.1	0.1	0.1	0.1	0.1	0.0
Transfers to Enterprises	0.1	0.1	0.1	0.1	0.1	0.1	0.1	0.1	0.1	0.1	0.1	0.0
Transfers to Individuals	0.0	0.0	0.0	0.0	0.0	0.0	0.0	0.0	0.0	0.0	0.0	0.0
Other	0.8	0.8	0.9	1.4	1.2	1.3	1.3	1.3	1.1	1.1	1.4	0.6
Capital Expenditures	1.0	0.9	0.8	0.8	0.8	0.9	1.0	1.1	1.2	1.2	1.4	1.1
Gross Fixed Capital Formation & Invent	0.8	0.8	0.7	0.7	0.6	0.7	0.7	0.8	0.9	0.8	1.0	1.1
Loans to Enterprises	0.2	0.1	0.1	0.1	0.1	0.2	0.2	0.3	0.3	0.4	0.5	0.0
Local Budget Balance	-0.5	-0.3	-0.5	-1.2	-0.8	-0.5	-0.5	1.4	4.9	3.0	-0.1	1.0

Source: Ministry of Finance.

Table 4.10 - Latvia: Operations of the Social Security System
(Mln of Rubles)

	1980	1981	1982	1983	1984	1985	1986	1987	1988	1989	1990	1991	Plan 1992
Total Revenue	**463.0**	**502.2**	**546.4**	**576.3**	**602.6**	**632.2**	**667.2**	**696.8**	**739.5**	**783.2**	**955.6**	**3060.9**	**15869.1**
Social Insurance Contributions	138.9	158.7	243.9	250.3	265.6	210.4	279.1	288.7	309.6	329.2	442.0	2962.4	15869.1
Budgetary Transfers	324.1	343.5	302.5	326.0	337.0	421.8	388.1	408.1	429.9	454.0	513.6	98.5	0.0
of which:													
USSR & Social Insurance Budgets	307.1	326.0	284.5	308.0	318.9	402.9	367.4	386.8	408.1	430.8	487.3	0.0	0.0
Social Insurance	0.0	47.5	6.0	81.9	14.1	14.6	7.5	0.0	0.0	0.0	0.0		
Latvian Budget	15.0	15.4	15.5	15.5	15.6	16.4	18.0	18.4	18.9	20.8	23.7	0.0	0.0
Other	2.0	2.1	2.5	2.5	2.5	2.5	2.7	2.9	2.9	2.4	2.6	98.5	0.0
Total Expenditures	**463.0**	**502.2**	**526.6**	**570.1**	**602.6**	**632.2**	**667.2**	**696.8**	**739.5**	**753.2**	**865.1**	**2650.0**	**15089.4**
Wages	0.0	0.0	0.0	0.0	0.0	0.0	0.0	0.0	0.0	0.0	0.0	0.0	0.0
Administrative Costs	0.0	0.0	0.0	0.0	0.0	0.0	0.0	0.0	0.0	0.0	0.0	4.8	84.0
Pensions	353.8	396.3	420.8	444.6	468.8	498.2	531.1	554.9	595.3	609.8	682.3	2238.7	9739.0
Allowances	98.9	95.0	94.8	111.0	119.2	120.7	123.0	125.4	126.4	126.4	153.1	368.9	4983.5
of which:													
Sick Pay	82.3	77.8	75.8	79.0	84.5	86.1	87.7	88.4	89.2	90.2	106.9	156.5	706.8
Maternity Leave	14.6	15.5	17.4	30.6	33.4	33.3	34.2	35.9	36.1	34.8	44.6	32.9	138.6
Family Allowances	1.8	1.7	1.6	1.4	1.3	1.3	1.1	1.1	1.1	1.4	1.6	1.7	2065.0
Other Expenditures	10.3	10.9	11.0	14.5	14.6	13.3	13.1	16.5	17.8	17.0	29.7	37.6	282.9
Balance	**0.0**	**0.0**	**19.8**	**6.2**	**0.0**	**0.0**	**0.0**	**0.0**	**0.0**	**30.0**	**90.5**	**410.9**	**779.7**

Sources: Ministry of Welfare and Central Statistical Committee.

Table 4.11 - Latvia: Operations of Extrabudgetary Funds
(Mln of Rubles)

	1991 Budget	1991 Jan-Sept	1991 Outturn
Total Revenues	**355.3**	**175.1**	**273.8**
Enviromental Protection Fund	5.3	4.2	6.3
Privatization Fund	0.0	20.4	37.0
Agricultural Stabilization Fund [a]	350.0	150.5	230.5
Total Expenditures	**356.2**	**134.9**	**232.2**
Environmental Protection Fund of which:	6.2	1.9	4.7
Wages	0.3	0.0	N.A.
Other Administrative Costs	0.3	0.0	N.A.
Capital Investment	4.8	1.9	N.A.
Privatization Fund			
Agricultural Stabilization Fund	350.0	133.0	227.5
of which: Producer Price Subsidies	350.0	133.0	N.A.
Net Position	**-0.9**	**40.2**	**41.6**

a. Derived from special 10% levy on state enterprises for 'use of capital'.
Source: Ministry of Finance.

Table 4.12 - Latvia: Foreign Currency Budget
(Mln of Rubles and Foreign Currency)

	1991 Requests	1991 Approved	1992 Requests
Payments for Imports	9.3	4.5	4.8
Travel Expenses of Ministries	0.7	NA	NA
Pending Payments from 1990	4.4	NA	NA
1990 Payments Still to be Approved by Council of Ministries	1.4	NA	NA
Currency Reserve to be Sold for Rubles	1.5	NA	NA
Reserve to Cover Foreign Debt Guarantees	15.6	NA	NA
Additional Requests for Imports of Raw Materials (Mln of US$)	2.4	NA	NA
Total Foreign Currency Expenditures	34.3	NA	NA
Total Excluding 1990 Payments Still to be Approved	32.9	32.9	NA

Source: Ministry of Finance.

Table 4.13 - Latvia: Central Government Operations - Functional Classification
(Mln of Rubles)

	1980	1981	1982	1983	1984	1985	1986	1987	1988	1989	1990	1991	Budget 1992
Total Revenues	**3289.0**	**3480.9**	**3735.3**	**3998.8**	**4004.3**	**3878.3**	**4015.4**	**3863.4**	**3910.0**	**4213.0**	**3931.0**	**5993.9**	**22494.3**
Tax Revenues	3109.2	3243.7	3246.2	3342.0	3408.6	3294.3	3393.4	3534.4	3680.0	3749.0	3652.0	5526.5	20009.2
Taxes on Income and Profits	1362.0	1421.1	1391.7	1515.1	1588.6	1576.3	1681.4	1808.4	1757.0	1696.0	1528.0	1894.5	7812.7
Taxes on Enterprises	1095.0	1147.3	1107.0	1221.7	1281.9	1256.0	1348.0	1459.0	1376.0	1280.0	1066.0	1417.5	5333.9
Taxes on Individuals	267.0	273.8	284.7	293.4	306.7	320.3	333.4	349.4	381.0	416.0	462.0	477.0	2478.8
Domestic Taxes on Goods and Services	1747.2	1822.6	1854.5	1826.9	1820.0	1718.0	1712.0	1726.0	1923.0	2053.0	2124.0	2891.0	9960.3
Turnover Tax, Excises and VAT	1747.2	1822.6	1854.5	1826.9	1820.0	1718.0	1712.0	1726.0	1923.0	2053.0	2124.0	2723.1	9960.3
Other	0.0	0.0	0.0	0.0	0.0	0.0	0.0	0.0	0.0	0.0	0.0	167.9	0.0
Taxes on Foreign Trade	0.0	0.0	0.0	0.0	0.0	0.0	0.0	0.0	0.0	0.0	0.0	11.4	797.0
Property Taxes	0.0	0.0	0.0	0.0	0.0	0.0	0.0	0.0	0.0	0.0	0.0	77.0	0.0
Taxes on Fixed Assets	0.0	0.0	0.0	0.0	0.0	0.0	0.0	0.0	0.0	0.0	0.0	0.0	
Land Tax	0.0	0.0	0.0	0.0	0.0	0.0	0.0	0.0	0.0	0.0	0.0	0.0	
Other	0.0	0.0	0.0	0.0	0.0	0.0	0.0	0.0	0.0	0.0	0.0	0.0	0.0
Other Taxes	0.0	0.0	0.0	0.0	0.0	0.0	0.0	0.0	0.0	0.0	0.0	652.6	1439.2
Non-Tax Revenues	179.8	237.2	489.1	656.8	595.7	584.0	622.0	329.0	230.0	464.0	279.0	467.4	2485.1
Transfers from the USSR budget	74.5	120.6	329.0	394.5	191.2	164.0	232.0	65.0	187.0	113.0	53.0	0.0	0.0
Transfer from municipal budgets	0.0	0.0	0.0	0.0	0.0	0.0	0.0	0.0	0.0	0.0	0.0	0.0	0.0
Other [a]	105.3	116.6	160.1	262.3	404.5	420.0	390.0	264.0	43.0	351.0	226.0	467.4	2485.1
Total Expenditures	**3238.6**	**3452.9**	**3675.8**	**3910.5**	**3864.7**	**3806.5**	**3926.7**	**3960.5**	**4339.8**	**4492.1**	**3793.9**	**4878.5**	**23678.0**
Economy	734.5	802.6	892.0	1105.2	1290.6	1368.4	1389.5	1299.1	1496.8	1586.0	1986.6	2272.8	4157.4
Investment Expenditures	130.0	149.5	149.0	173.2	158.6	122.3	114.4	144.3	148.6	197.0	188.3	556.8	1492.5
Subsidies	8.6	15.6	19.0	16.7	4.7	2.2	2.4	2.1	2.5	3.1	12.5	295.0	456.0
Operational Expenditures	54.9	54.3	59.4	64.3	73.2	73.4	73.7	45.2	25.4	26.3	26.4	NA	NA
Price Compensation	461.6	477.1	522.6	755.8	1000.3	1114.3	1114.2	1004.9	1228.6	1264.9	1649.7	NA	NA
Other	79.4	106.1	142.0	95.2	53.8	56.2	84.8	102.6	91.7	94.7	109.7	NA	NA
Justice & Internal Security	1.4	1.4	1.5	1.6	1.6	1.6	1.8	4.7	2.5	3.3	7.2	227.1	NA
Social & Cultural Activities	461.5	478.9	510.8	524.1	559.4	587.1	627.6	654.1	712.1	756.6	848.5	1382.5	5955.0
Education & Culture	168.4	172.2	180.6	185.5	199.3	206.7	219.9	223.2	244.6	244.1	268.9	534.0	NA
Health & Sports	63.5	66.3	74.6	76.3	83.6	86.8	83.5	87.1	98.1	114.1	136.8	312.5	NA
Social Maintenance	19.7	20.9	21.6	21.7	22.9	24.3	27.4	27.5	30.0	33.1	34.0	0.0	NA
Pensions [b]	208.8	218.4	229.9	235.8	248.4	263.6	290.7	309.7	332.4	358.1	401.3	536.0	NA
Other Benefits	1.1	1.1	4.1	4.8	5.2	5.7	6.1	6.6	7.0	7.2	7.5	0.0	NA
Administration	11.9	12.7	14.7	11.3	13.6	15.3	12.6	8.1	10.6	11.4	27.8	144.3	NA
Transportation & Communications	58.0	62.1	60.3	61.2	56.5	58.5	61.0	63.2	63.0	75.4	75.1	91.4	NA
Other Activities	12.0	15.1	11.8	14.5	15.5	18.0	15.3	16.4	25.5	27.2	467.5	101.1	NA
Transfers to USSR Budget	1664.9	1766.2	1846.8	1837.1	1576.2	1411.6	1462.0	1554.9	1634.8	1623.9	36.3	0.0	0.0
Transfers to Local Budgets	294.4	313.9	337.9	355.5	351.3	346.0	356.9	360.0	394.5	408.3	344.9	653.3	5402.4
State Budget Balance	**50.4**	**28.0**	**59.5**	**88.3**	**139.6**	**71.8**	**88.7**	**-97.1**	**-429.8**	**-279.1**	**137.1**	**1115.4**	**-1183.7**

a. Includes revenue from foreign currency budget in 1991.
b. In 1991 includes social maintenance and other benefits.
Source: Ministry of Finance.

Table 4.14 - Latvia: Central Government Operations - Functional Classification
(Percent Share of Total)

	1980	1981	1982	1983	1984	1985	1986	1987	1988	1989	1990	1991	Budget 1992
Total Revenues	**100.0**	**100.0**	**100.0**	**100.0**	**100.0**	**100.0**	**100.0**	**100.0**	**100.0**	**100.0**	**100.0**	**100.0**	**100.0**
Tax Revenues	94.5	93.2	86.9	83.6	85.1	84.9	84.5	91.5	94.1	89.0	92.9	92.2	89.0
Taxes on Income and Profits	41.4	40.8	37.3	37.9	39.7	40.6	41.9	46.8	44.9	40.3	38.9	31.6	34.7
Taxes on Enterprises	33.3	33.0	29.6	30.6	32.0	32.4	33.6	37.8	35.2	30.4	27.1	23.6	23.7
Taxes on Individuals	8.1	7.9	7.6	7.3	7.7	8.3	8.3	9.0	9.7	9.9	11.8	8.0	11.0
Domestic Taxes on Goods and Services	53.1	52.4	49.6	45.7	45.5	44.3	42.6	44.7	49.2	48.7	54.0	48.2	44.3
Turnover Tax, Excises and VAT	53.1	52.4	49.6	45.7	45.5	44.3	42.6	44.7	49.2	48.7	54.0	45.4	44.3
Other	0.0	0.0	0.0	0.0	0.0	0.0	0.0	0.0	0.0	0.0	0.0	2.8	0.0
Taxes on Foreign Trade	0.0	0.0	0.0	0.0	0.0	0.0	0.0	0.0	0.0	0.0	0.0	0.2	3.5
Property Taxes	0.0	0.0	0.0	0.0	0.0	0.0	0.0	0.0	0.0	0.0	0.0	1.3	₈0.0
Taxes on Fixed Assets	0.0	0.0	0.0	0.0	0.0	0.0	0.0	0.0	0.0	0.0	0.0	0.0	!
Land Tax	0.0	0.0	0.0	0.0	0.0	0.0	0.0	0.0	0.0	0.0	0.0	0.0	
Other	0.0	0.0	0.0	0.0	0.0	0.0	0.0	0.0	0.0	0.0	0.0	0.0	0.0
Other Taxes	0.0	0.0	0.0	0.0	0.0	0.0	0.0	0.0	0.0	0.0	0.0	10.9	6.4
Non-Tax Revenues	5.5	6.8	13.1	16.4	14.9	15.1	15.5	8.5	5.9	11.0	7.1	7.8	11.0
Transfers from the USSR budget	2.3	3.5	8.8	9.9	4.8	4.2	5.8	1.7	4.8	2.7	1.3	0.0	0.0
Transfer from municipal budgets	0.0	0.0	0.0	0.0	0.0	0.0	0.0	0.0	0.0	0.0	0.0	0.0	0.0
Other [a]	3.2	3.3	4.3	6.6	10.1	10.8	9.7	6.8	1.1	8.3	5.7	7.8	11.0
Total Expenditures	**100.0**	**100.0**	**100.0**	**100.0**	**100.0**	**100.0**	**100.0**	**100.0**	**100.0**	**100.0**	**100.0**	**100.0**	**100.0**
Economy	22.7	23.2	24.3	28.3	33.4	35.9	35.4	32.8	34.5	35.3	52.4	46.6	17.6
Investment Expenditures	4.0	4.3	4.1	4.4	4.1	3.2	2.9	3.6	3.4	4.4	5.0	11.4	6.3
Subsidies	0.3	0.5	0.5	0.4	0.1	0.1	0.1	0.1	0.1	0.1	0.3	6.0	1.9
Operational Expenditures	1.7	1.6	1.6	1.6	1.9	1.9	1.9	1.1	0.6	0.6	0.7	NA	NA
Price Compensation	14.3	13.8	14.2	19.3	25.9	29.3	28.4	25.4	28.3	28.2	43.5	NA	NA
Other	2.5	3.1	3.9	2.4	1.4	1.5	2.2	2.6	2.1	2.1	2.9	NA	NA
Justice & Internal Security	0.0	0.0	0.0	0.0	0.0	0.0	0.0	0.1	0.1	0.1	0.2	4.7	NA
Social & Cultural Activities	14.2	13.9	13.9	13.4	14.5	15.4	16.0	16.5	16.4	16.8	22.4	28.3	25.1
Education & Culture	5.2	5.0	4.9	4.7	5.2	5.4	5.6	5.6	5.6	5.4	7.1	10.9	NA
Health & Sports	2.0	1.9	2.0	2.0	2.2	2.3	2.1	2.2	2.3	2.5	3.6	6.4	NA
Social Maintenance	0.6	0.6	0.6	0.6	0.6	0.6	0.7	0.7	0.7	0.7	0.9	0.0	NA
Pensions [b]	6.4	6.3	6.3	6.0	6.4	6.9	7.4	7.8	7.7	8.0	10.6	11.0	NA
Other Benefits	0.0	0.0	0.1	0.1	0.1	0.1	0.2	0.2	0.2	0.2	0.2	0.0	NA
Administration	0.4	0.4	0.4	0.3	0.4	0.4	0.3	0.2	0.2	0.3	0.7	3.0	NA
Transportation & Communications	1.8	1.8	1.6	1.6	1.5	1.5	1.6	1.6	1.5	1.7	2.0	1.9	NA
Other Activities	0.4	0.4	0.3	0.4	0.4	0.5	0.4	0.4	0.6	0.6	12.3	2.1	NA
Transfers to USSR Budget	51.4	51.2	50.2	47.0	40.8	37.1	37.2	39.3	37.7	36.2	1.0	0.0	0.0
Transfers to Local Budgets	9.1	9.1	9.2	9.1	9.1	9.1	9.1	9.1	9.1	9.1	9.1	13.4	22.8

a. Includes revenue from foreign currency budget in 1991.
b. In 1991 includes social maintenance and other benefits.
Source: Ministry of Finance of Latvia.

Table 4.15 - Latvia: Central Government Operations as Share of GDP - Functional Classification
(Percent)

	1980	1981	1982	1983	1984	1985	1986	1987	1988	1989	1990	1991
Total Revenues	**41.6**	**41.1**	**42.2**	**44.8**	**43.1**	**42.9**	**43.1**	**40.8**	**39.3**	**38.6**	**32.2**	**20.9**
Tax Revenues	39.3	38.3	36.6	37.5	36.7	36.5	36.4	37.4	37.0	34.3	29.9	19.3
Taxes on Income and Profits	17.2	16.8	15.7	17.0	17.1	17.5	18.0	19.1	17.6	15.5	12.5	6.6
Taxes on Enterprises	13.9	13.6	12.5	13.7	13.8	13.9	14.5	15.4	13.8	11.7	8.7	4.9
Taxes on Individuals	3.4	3.2	3.2	3.3	3.3	3.5	3.6	3.7	3.8	3.8	3.8	1.7
Domestic Taxes on Goods and Services	22.1	21.5	20.9	20.5	19.6	19.0	18.4	18.2	19.3	18.8	17.4	10.1
Turnover Tax, Excises and VAT	22.1	21.5	20.9	20.5	19.6	19.0	18.4	18.2	19.3	18.8	17.4	9.5
Other	0.0	0.0	0.0	0.0	0.0	0.0	0.0	0.0	0.0	0.0	0.0	0.6
Taxes on Foreign Trade	0.0	0.0	0.0	0.0	0.0	0.0	0.0	0.0	0.0	0.0	0.0	0.0
Property Taxes	0.0	0.0	0.0	0.0	0.0	0.0	0.0	0.0	0.0	0.0	0.0	0.3
Taxes on Fixed Assets	0.0	0.0	0.0	0.0	0.0	0.0	0.0	0.0	0.0	0.0	0.0	0.0
Land Tax	0.0	0.0	0.0	0.0	0.0	0.0	0.0	0.0	0.0	0.0	0.0	0.0
Other	0.0	0.0	0.0	0.0	0.0	0.0	0.0	0.0	0.0	0.0	0.0	0.0
Other Taxes	0.0	0.0	0.0	0.0	0.0	0.0	0.0	0.0	0.0	0.0	0.0	2.3
Non-Tax Revenues	2.3	2.8	5.5	7.4	6.4	6.5	6.7	3.5	2.3	4.2	2.3	1.6
Transfers from the USSR budget	0.9	1.4	3.7	4.4	2.1	1.8	2.5	0.7	1.9	1.0	0.4	0.0
Transfer from municipal budgets	0.0	0.0	0.0	0.0	0.0	0.0	0.0	0.0	0.0	0.0	0.0	0.0
Other [a]	1.3	1.4	1.8	2.9	4.4	4.7	4.2	2.8	0.4	3.2	1.9	1.6
Total Expenditures	**41.0**	**40.8**	**41.5**	**43.8**	**41.6**	**42.2**	**42.1**	**41.9**	**43.6**	**41.1**	**31.1**	**17.0**
Economy	9.3	9.5	10.1	12.4	13.9	15.2	14.9	13.7	15.0	14.5	16.3	7.9
Investment Expenditures	1.6	1.8	1.7	1.9	1.7	1.4	1.2	1.5	1.5	1.8	1.5	1.9
Subsidies	0.1	0.2	0.2	0.2	0.1	0.0	0.0	0.0	0.0	0.0	0.1	1.0
Operational Expenditures	0.7	0.6	0.7	0.7	0.8	0.8	0.8	0.5	0.3	0.2	0.2	NA
Price Compensation	5.8	5.6	5.9	8.5	10.8	12.3	11.9	10.6	12.3	11.6	13.5	NA
Other	1.0	1.3	1.6	1.1	0.6	0.6	0.9	1.1	0.9	0.9	0.9	NA
Justice & Internal Security	0.0	0.0	0.0	0.0	0.0	0.0	0.0	0.0	0.0	0.0	0.1	0.8
Social & Cultural Activities	5.8	5.7	5.8	5.9	6.0	6.5	6.7	6.9	7.2	6.9	7.0	4.8
Education & Culture	2.1	2.0	2.0	2.1	2.1	2.3	2.4	2.4	2.5	2.2	2.2	1.9
Health & Sports	0.8	0.8	0.8	0.9	0.9	1.0	0.9	0.9	1.0	1.0	1.1	1.1
Social Maintenance	0.2	0.2	0.2	0.2	0.2	0.3	0.3	0.3	0.3	0.3	0.3	0.0
Pensions [b]	2.6	2.6	2.6	2.6	2.7	2.9	3.1	3.3	3.3	3.3	3.3	1.9
Other Benefits	0.0	0.0	0.0	0.1	0.1	0.1	0.1	0.1	0.1	0.1	0.1	0.0
Administration	0.2	0.2	0.2	0.1	0.1	0.2	0.1	0.1	0.1	0.1	0.2	0.5
Transportation & Communications	0.7	0.7	0.7	0.7	0.6	0.6	0.7	0.7	0.6	0.7	0.6	0.3
Other Activities	0.2	0.2	0.1	0.2	0.2	0.2	0.2	0.2	0.3	0.2	3.8	0.4
Transfers to USSR Budget	21.1	20.9	20.8	20.6	17.0	15.6	15.7	16.4	16.4	14.9	0.3	0.0
Transfers to Local Budgets	3.7	3.7	3.8	4.0	3.8	3.8	3.8	3.8	4.0	3.7	2.8	2.3
State Budget Balance	**0.6**	**0.3**	**0.7**	**1.0**	**1.5**	**0.8**	**1.0**	**-1.0**	**-4.3**	**-2.6**	**1.1**	**3.9**

a. Includes revenue from foreign currency budget in 1991.
b. In 1991 includes social maintenance and other benefits.
Source: Ministry of Finance of Latvia.

Table 4.16 - Latvia: Local Government Budget - Functional Classification
(Mln of Rubles)

	1980	1981	1982	1983	1984	1985	1986	1987	1988	1989	1990	1991	Budget 1992
Total Revenues	**389.7**	**400.7**	**403.7**	**396.6**	**417.9**	**493.0**	**518.0**	**750.3**	**1132.6**	**1063.2**	**920.8**	**2338.6**	**11345.2**
Tax Revenues	79.0	75.4	57.7	62.5	67.9	123.0	117.0	74.3	138.6	274.2	353.8	1681.8	5857.5
Taxes on Income and Profits	79.0	75.3	57.7	62.4	67.9	73.0	69.0	74.3	138.6	274.2	353.8	1226.9	4274.9
Taxes on Enterprises	79.0	75.3	57.7	62.4	67.9	73.0	69.0	74.3	138.6	274.2	353.8	669.1	1935.1
Taxes on Individuals	0.0	0.0	0.0	0.0	0.0	0.0	0.0	0.0	0.0	0.0	0.0	557.8	2339.8
Domestic Taxes on Goods and Services	0.0	0.1	0.0	0.1	0.0	50.0	48.0	0.0	0.0	0.0	0.0	0.0	527.1
Turnover Tax and Excises	0.0	0.0	0.0	0.0	0.0	0.0	0.0	0.0	0.0	0.0	0.0	0.0	527.1
Value-Added Tax	0.0	0.0	0.0	0.0	0.0	0.0	0.0	0.0	0.0	0.0	0.0	0.0	
Other	0.0	0.1	0.0	0.1	0.0	50.0	48.0	0.0	0.0	0.0	0.0	0.0	0.0
Taxes on Foreign Trade	0.0	0.0	0.0	0.0	0.0	0.0	0.0	0.0	0.0	0.0	0.0	0.0	0.0
Property Taxes	0.0	0.0	0.0	0.0	0.0	0.0	0.0	0.0	0.0	0.0	0.0	320.3	831.0
Taxes on Fixed Assets	0.0	0.0	0.0	0.0	0.0	0.0	0.0	0.0	0.0	0.0	0.0	0.0	0.0
Land Tax	0.0	0.0	0.0	0.0	0.0	0.0	0.0	0.0	0.0	0.0	0.0	232.3	531.0
Other	0.0	0.0	0.0	0.0	0.0	0.0	0.0	0.0	0.0	0.0	0.0	88.0	300.0
Other Taxes	0.0	0.0	0.0	0.0	0.0	0.0	0.0	0.0	0.0	0.0	0.0	134.6	224.5
of which:													
Taxes on Natural Resources	0.0	0.0	0.0	0.0	0.0	0.0	0.0	0.0	0.0	0.0	0.0	40.6	54.4
Environmental Taxes	0.0	0.0	0.0	0.0	0.0	0.0	0.0	0.0	0.0	0.0	0.0	29.6	94.2
Other Taxes	0.0	0.0	0.0	0.0	0.0	0.0	0.0	0.0	0.0	0.0	0.0	64.4	75.9
Non-Tax Revenues	310.7	325.3	346.0	334.1	350.0	370.0	401.0	676.0	994.0	789.0	567.0	656.8	5487.7
Transfer from state budget	294.4	313.9	337.9	355.5	351.3	346.0	357.0	360.0	394.0	408.0	345.0	653.3	5402.4
Other													
Total Expenditures	**427.5**	**429.7**	**451.0**	**501.1**	**495.0**	**537.1**	**568.6**	**619.6**	**648.6**	**735.5**	**927.5**	**2047.0**	**11606.7**
Economy	129.3	126.5	136.2	169.6	167.0	193.5	208.4	223.8	208.2	243.8	334.3	552.5	4006.5
Investment	45.7	47.6	45.5	43.9	48.3	59.1	63.3	68.7	75.7	83.8	105.8	301.7	1058.7
Subsidies	7.8	7.9	28.2	9.5	8.0	12.9	10.0	9.7	12.9	15.3	8.3	80.1	400.0
Operational Expenditures	0.1	0.3	0.0	1.1	0.7	0.7	0.8	1.1	0.2	0.3	0.1	NA	NA
Price Compensation	9.9	1.3	0.7	1.0	0.9	0.9	1.0	0.6	1.0	0.7	27.4	NA	NA
Other	65.8	69.4	61.8	114.1	109.1	119.9	133.3	143.7	118.4	143.7	192.7	NA	NA
Social & Cultural Activities	278.2	280.7	293.6	299.7	303.1	318.4	333.9	366.6	412.8	458.9	535.8	1330.1	6885.4
Education & Culture	168.3	167.0	174.4	177.2	180.5	191.3	204.7	227.8	259.3	285.8	333.2	826.2	NA
Health & Sports	98.9	102.3	107.7	111.7	111.8	115.4	117.3	126.3	140.1	156.5	181.3	458.7	NA
Social Maintenance	11.0	11.4	11.5	10.8	10.8	11.7	11.9	12.5	13.4	16.6	21.3	45.2	NA
Administration	9.5	9.7	7.4	10.5	9.0	7.9	11.9	16.4	15.0	18.7	34.7	0.0	
Transportation & Communications	0.2	0.3	0.4	0.4	0.4	0.5	0.5	0.6	1.1	0.8	1.2	0.0	
Other Activities	10.3	12.5	13.4	20.9	15.5	16.8	13.9	12.3	11.5	13.3	21.5	164.4	714.7
Local Budget Balance	**-37.8**	**-29.0**	**-47.3**	**-104.5**	**-77.1**	**-44.1**	**-50.6**	**130.7**	**484.0**	**327.7**	**-6.7**	**291.6**	**-261.5**

Source: Ministry of Finance.

Table 4.17 - Latvia: Subsidies by Product
(Mln of Rubles)

	1980	1981	1982	1983	1984	1985	1986	1987	1988	1989	1990
Agro-Industrial Complex	487.6	517.6	642.8	1180.4	1289.4	1284.4	1162.8	1152.3	1497.3	1576.5	1261.3
Food Production	455.2	479.8	593.1	1051.4	1150.1	1138.4	1022.3	1028.5	1154.2	1201.2	977.7
Grain	11.2	13.6	12.9	-5.2	9.7	2.1	-22.7	-13.7	11.7	14.0	43.0
Cattle, Poultry, Fowl	301.3	314.5	398.1	521.5	547.3	646.1	554.4	572.4	620.0	640.9	583.0
Sugar	0.0	0.0	0.0	0.0	0.0	47.0	45.1	47.1	45.9	47.2	45.3
Starch Products	0.0	0.7	2.6	3.8	4.9	3.7	3.3	2.4	2.2	3.0	4.2
Eggs	0.4	0.4	0.5	0.8	1.6	1.5	0.5	0.2	0.0	0.0	0.0
Milk & Dairy Products	142.3	150.6	179.0	425.1	451.1	374.5	349.5	339.8	381.5	432.0	253.0
Fish	0.0	0.0	0.0	105.4	135.5	63.5	87.3	77.6	92.9	64.1	48.0
Soy-Beans & Rye	0.0	0.0	0.0	0.0	0.0	0.0	4.9	2.7	0.0	0.0	0.1
Sugar Beets	0.0	0.0	0.0	0.0	0.0	0.0	0.0	0.0	0.0	0.0	1.1
Farmers	0.0	0.0	0.0	77.6	93.3	99.2	106.5	78.9	323.1	365.3	281.3
Transfers to Low Profit Farms	0.0	0.0	0.0	77.6	93.3	99.2	106.5	78.9	10.6	0.0	0.0
Agric. Producer Price Support	0.0	0.0	0.0	0.0	0.0	0.0	0.0	0.0	312.5	365.3	281.3
Other Agro-Ind. Subsidies	32.4	37.8	49.7	51.4	46.0	46.8	34.0	44.9	20.0	10.0	2.3
Agric. Machines	9.6	9.8	22.0	22.1	23.4	24.6	20.6	23.9	8.7	1.0	0.0
Mineral Fertilizers	21.0	25.7	25.7	19.7	15.0	17.5	7.7	13.6	4.4	1.0	0.0
Flax	1.8	2.3	2.0	9.6	7.6	4.7	5.7	7.4	6.9	8.0	2.3
Industry	4.7	3.6	3.4	6.9	8.2	5.1	6.1	6.2	7.8	21.1	0.3
Leather Rat Mat.	1.7	2.0	2.5	4.2	5.1	2.7	3.1	3.7	3.8	4.4	0.0
Process. Leather	1.2	1.1	0.1	0.0	0.3	0.3	0.3	0.4	0.4	0.4	0.0
Fur	0.1	0.2	0.0	1.3	1.4	1.2	1.6	1.5	3.4	1.2	0.0
Ethyl Alcohol	1.7	0.3	0.8	1.4	1.4	0.9	1.1	0.6	0.2	0.1	0.2
Other	0.0	0.0	0.0	0.0	0.0	0.0	0.0	0.0	0.0	15.0	0.1
Other Consumer Subsidies	-20.8	-22.9	-22.6	-23.2	-15.3	-13.6	-16.7	-20.4	18.1	32.0	-16.4
Radios	-20.8	-22.9	-22.6	-23.2	-19.9	-17.4	-19.0	-19.3	-18.4	-15.0	-19.0
Consumer Goods	0.0	0.0	0.0	0.0	0.0	0.0	0.0	0.0	25.4	35.0	0.0
Canned Fruit	0.0	0.0	0.0	0.0	4.6	3.8	2.3	-1.1	11.1	12.0	2.6
Total Subsidies	471.5	498.3	623.6	1164.1	1282.3	1275.9	1152.2	1138.1	1523.2	1629.6	1245.2

Source: State Committee for Statistics.

Table 4.18 - Latvia: Tax and Other Revenues Transferred to USSR
(Mln of Rubles)

	1980	1981	1982	1983	1984	1985	1986	1987	1988	1989
Turnover tax	1747.2	1822.7	1854.5	1827.0	1820.0	1768.0	1760.0	1726.0	1923.0	2053.0
Transferred to USSR	1006.6	1058.1	1162.9	1062.4	782.6	628.0	571.6	587.1	586.5	886.9
Residual	740.6	764.6	691.6	764.6	1037.4	1140.0	1188.4	1138.9	1336.5	1166.1
Profit taxes and deductions	1142.9	1188.0	1131.2	1247.3	1304.1	1284.6	1374.6	1486.1	1452.0	1413.5
Transferred to USSR	502.4	541.4	511.0	552.5	603.8	598.3	656.5	750.2	769.2	674.1
Residual	640.5	646.6	620.2	694.8	700.3	686.3	718.1	735.9	682.8	739.4
Individual Income Tax	248.5	255.3	266.0	274.5	287.6	300.9	313.5	330.5	361.4	394.7
Transferred to USSR	124.1	127.5	132.8	137.1	143.6	150.3	156.6	164.5	179.8	0.0
Residual	124.4	127.8	133.2	137.4	144.0	150.6	156.9	166.0	181.6	394.7
Income tax from enterprises and cooperatives	18.8	21.4	20.7	20.9	21.7	21.4	22.6	24.3	26.5	52.8
Transferred to USSR	2.2	2.6	2.4	1.9	2.5	2.4	2.4	3.1	3.7	3.4
Residual	16.6	18.8	18.3	19.0	19.2	19.0	20.2	21.2	22.8	49.4
Lottery bonds	3.4	2.4	8.4	6.8	7.8	9.0	6.6	10.0	11.2	9.6
Transferred to USSR	1.7	1.2	4.2	3.4	3.9	4.5	3.3	5.0	5.6	4.8
Residual	1.7	1.2	4.2	3.4	3.9	4.5	3.3	5.0	5.6	4.8
Total revenues transferred to USSR	1642.7	1730.8	1813.3	1757.3	1536.4	1382.5	1340.4	1509.9	1544.8	1616.9
Tax	1641.0	1729.6	1809.1	1753.9	1532.5	1378.0	1337.1	1504.9	1539.2	1612.1
Non-tax	1.7	1.2	4.2	3.4	3.9	4.5	3.3	5.0	5.6	4.8
Memorandum Items:										
Tax & NonTax Revenues	3847.3	4069.9	4347.5	4616.2	4673.5	4657.5	4843.6	4950.5	5388.1	5659.0
State	3289.0	3480.9	3735.3	3998.8	4004.3	3878.3	4015.4	3863.4	3910.0	4213.0
Local	389.7	400.7	403.7	396.6	417.9	493.0	518.0	750.3	1132.6	1063.2

Sources: Ministry of Finance and Ministry of Welfare.

Table 5.1 - Latvia: Balance Sheet of Bank of Latvia [a]
(Mlns of Rubles, end of period)

	1987	1988	1989	1990	1991-Q1	1991-Q2	1991-Q3	1991-Q4
Assets								
I. Foreign Assets of which:	447.0	139.0	87.0	423.0	2702.0	1114.0	1383.0	5715.0
1. Gold [b]	4.0	0.0	0.0	0.0	0.0	0.0	0.0	4.0
2. Convertible currencies	22.0	0.0	0.0	0.0	0.0	0.0	0.0	5.0
3. Non-convertible currencies	421.0	139.0	87.0	423.0	2702.0	1114.0	1383.0	5706.0
of which: Cash	9.0	0.0	0.0	0.0	0.0	0.0	0.0	469.0
II. Domestic credits of which:	3600.0	-120.0	-69.0	73.0	-147.0	-172.0	1488.0	5040.0
1. Commercial banks	0.0	0.0	0.0	0.0	0.0	0.0	52.0	187.0
2. Savings banks	0.0	0.0	0.0	0.0	5.0	0.0	0.0	0.0
3. Specialized banks [c]	14.0	0.0	0.0	298.0	6.0	0.0	1575.0	770.0
4. Foreign trade bank [c]								
5. Enterprises & coops.	3408.0	0.0	0.0	0.0	0.0	1.0	2.0	6509.0
6. Households	103.0	0.0	0.0	0.0	0.0	0.0	0.0	63.0
7. Net lending to government [d]	75.0	-120.0	-69.0	-225.0	-158.0	-173.0	-141.0	-2489.0
III. Other domestic assets	15.0	4.0	6.0	12.0	4.0	4.0	5.0	29.0
Total Assets	4062.0	23.0	24.0	508.0	2559.0	946.0	2876.0	10784.0
Liabilities								
I. Foreign liabilities of which:	2.0	0.0	0.0	0.0	2043.0	0.0	0.0	0.0
1. Convertible currencies	2.0	0.0	0.0	0.0	0.0	0.0	0.0	0.0
2. Non-convertible currencies	0.0	0.0	0.0	0.0	2043.0	0.0	0.0	0.0
II. Total Deposits of which:	1110.0	6.0	18.0	199.0	217.0	381.0	2087.0	9928.0
1. Commercial banks	0.0	0.0	14.0	157.0	135.0	272.0	585.0	894.0
2. Savings banks	0.0	0.0	0.0	0.0	0.0	0.0	0.0	0.0
3. Specialized banks [c]	0.0	0.0	0.0	0.0	0.0	0.0	1403.0	4169.0
4. Foreign trade bank [c]	0.0	0.0	0.0	38.0	74.0	95.0	92.0	142.0
5. Enterprises & coops.	1110.0	6.0	4.0	4.0	8.0	14.0	7.0	4660.0
6. Households	0.0	0.0	0.0	0.0	0.0	0.0	0.0	3.0
III. Total Foreign exchange deposits	0.0	0.0	0.0	0.0	0.0	0.0	0.0	0.0
IV. Capital	13.0	0.0	0.0	0.0	0.0	0.0	0.0	86.0
V. Reserves	0.0	0.0	0.0	163.0	264.0	419.0	674.0	12.0
VI. Other liabilities [e]	2937.0	17.0	6.0	146.0	35.0	146.0	115.0	758.0
Total Liabilities	4062.0	23.0	24.0	508.0	2559.0	946.0	2876.0	10784.0

a. Prior to 1988, this was Gosbank and as of December 1991, it includes the three specialized banks.

b. This refers to 4.053 out of 11 tons which has been recognized and it is valued at Rb 1 per gram. During the period 1988 to 1991-Q3, this was shown in the balance sheet of the specialized banks which were merged with Bank of Latvia in December 1991.

c. Latvia branches only.

d. Includes deposits of social organizations.

e. This includes liabilities of former Gosbank to the Savings bank. As of 1988 it appears as a nonconvertible claim on Gosbank, Moscow.

Sources: Bank of Latvia and Bank staff estimates.

Table 5.2 - *Latvia: Balance Sheet of Savings Bank*
(Mlns of Rubles, end of period)

	1987	1988	1989	1990	1991-Q1	1991-Q2	1991-Q3	1991-Q4
Assets								
I. Foreign Assets of which:	3001.0	3250.0	3511.0	3539.0	3577.0	4561.0	4847.0	5103.0
1. Convertible currencies								
2. Non-convertible currencies	2995.0	3240.0	3499.0	3520.0	3559.0	4545.0	4829.0	5085.0
2.1 Savings Bank of the USSR	2928.0	3123.0	3300.0	3394.0	3559.0	4545.0	4829.0	5085.0
2.2 Other Banks	67.0	117.0	199.0	126.0	0.0	0.0	0.0	0.0
3. Currency Holdings	6.0	10.0	12.0	19.0	18.0	16.0	18.0	18.0
of which: cash	6.0	10.0	12.0	19.0	18.0	16.0	18.0	18.0
II. Domestic credits of which:	0.0	64.0	85.0	99.0	157.0	393.0	445.0	756.0
1. Savings banks	0.0	0.0	0.0	0.0	0.0	0.0	0.0	0.0
2. Specialized banks	0.0	0.0	0.0	0.0	47.0	276.0	330.0	0.0
3. Bank of Latvia	0.0	0.0	0.0	0.0	0.0	0.0	0.0	500.0
4. Enterprises & coops.	0.0	0.0	6.0	4.0	15.0	23.0	23.0	159.0
5. Households	0.0	64.0	79.0	95.0	95.0	94.0	92.0	97.0
6. Net lending to government	0.0	0.0	0.0	0.0	0.0	0.0	0.0	0.0
III. Other domestic assets	6.0	6.0	6.0	6.0	6.0	7.0	8.0	8.0
Total Assets	3007.0	3320.0	3602.0	3644.0	3740.0	4961.0	5300.0	5867.0
Liabilities								
I. Foreign liabilities of which:	0.0	0.0	0.0	0.0	0.0	86.0	0.0	0.0
1. Convertible currencies	0.0	0.0	0.0	0.0	0.0	0.0	0.0	0.0
2. Non-convertible currencies	0.0	0.0	0.0	0.0	0.0	86.0	0.0	0.0
II. Total Deposits of which:	3007.0	3320.0	3602.0	3644.0	3740.0	4875.0	5273.0	5832.0
1. Commercial banks	0.0	0.0	0.0	0.0	0.0	0.0	0.0	0.0
2. Savings banks	0.0	0.0	0.0	0.0	0.0	0.0	0.0	0.0
3. Specialized banks	0.0	0.0	0.0	0.0	0.0	0.0	0.0	0.0
4. Bank of Latvia	0.0	0.0	0.0	0.0	0.0	0.0	0.0	0.0
5. Enterprises & coops.	8.0	8.0	15.0	35.0	48.0	60.0	166.0	200.0
6. Households	2999.0	3312.0	3587.0	3609.0	3692.0	4815.0	5107.0	5632.0
III. Capital	0.0	0.0	0.0	0.0	0.0	0.0	0.0	0.0
IV. Reserves	0.0	0.0	0.0	0.0	0.0	0.0	0.0	0.0
V. Other liabilities	0.0	0.0	0.0	0.0	0.0	0.0	27.0	35.0
Total Liabilities	3007.0	3320.0	3602.0	3644.0	3740.0	4961.0	5300.0	5867.0

Sources: Bank of Latvia and Bank staff estimates.

Table 5.3 - Latvia: Consolidated Balance Sheet of Commercial Bank [a]
(Mlns of Rubles, end of period)

	1989	1990	1991-Q1	1991-Q2	1991-Q3	1991-Q4
Assets						
I. Foreign Assets	15.0	132.0	112.0	314.0	492.0	627.0
of which:						
1. Convertible currencies	0.0	0.0	0.0	0.0	0.0	0.0
2. Non-convertible currencies	0.0	0.0	0.0	0.0	0.0	619.0
3. Currency Holdings	15.0	132.0	112.0	314.0	492.0	8.0
II. Domestic credits	35.0	144.0	179.0	852.0	920.0	1446.0
of which:						
1. Savings banks	0.0	0.0	0.0	6.0	56.0	0.0
2. Specialized banks	0.0	3.0	7.0	12.0	68.0	211.0
3. Bank of Latvia	1.0	10.0	6.0	31.0	87.0	178.0
4. Enterprises & coops.	34.0	129.0	164.0	802.0	708.0	1048.0
5. Households	0.0	2.0	2.0	1.0	1.0	9.0
6. Net lending to government	0.0	0.0	0.0	0.0	0.0	0.0
III. Other domestic assets	0.0	3.0	10.0	11.0	0.0	71.0
Total Assets	50.0	279.0	301.0	1177.0	1412.0	2144.0
Liabilities						
I. Foreign liabilities	0.0	0.0	0.0	0.0	0.0	0.0
of which:						
1. Convertible currencies	0.0	0.0	0.0	0.0	0.0	0.0
2. Non-convertible currencies	0.0	0.0	0.0	0.0	0.0	0.0
II. Total Deposits	15.0	199.0	208.0	802.0	920.0	1582.0
of which:						
1. Savings banks	0.0	0.0	0.0	0.0	0.0	0.0
2. Specialized banks	0.0	25.0	50.0	44.0	47.0	198.0
3. Bank of Latvia	0.0	0.0	0.0	8.0	52.0	5.0
4. Enterprises & coops.	15.0	167.0	149.0	742.0	808.0	1286.0
5. Households	0.0	7.0	9.0	8.0	13.0	93.0
III. Capital	35.0	79.0	93.0	375.0	448.0	460.0
IV. Reserves	0.0	0.0	0.0	0.0	0.0	0.0
V. Other liabilities	0.0	1.0	0.0	0.0	44.0	102.0
Total Liabilities	50.0	279.0	301.0	1177.0	1412.0	2144.0

a. These consist of ten (10) commercial banks. They are: Latgales, Zemes, Rigas Komercbank, Baltija,
   Rigas banka, Simkas, Sakaru, Innovacijas, Ako, Daugava Bank and Latvia Commercbank.
Sources: Bank of Latvia and Bank staff estimates.

Table 5.4 - Latvia: Consolidated Balance Sheet of Specialized Banks [a]
(Mlns of Rubles, end of period)

	1988	1989	1990	1991-Q1	1991-Q2	1991-Q3
Assets						
I. Foreign Assets of which:	82.0	157.0	330.0	680.0	1591.0	1619.0
1. Gold	4.0	4.0	4.0	4.0	4.0	4.0
2. Convertible currencies	13.0	1.0	0.0	1.0	2.0	4.0
3. Non-convertible currencies	51.0	138.0	212.0	170.0	1423.0	1401.0
4. Currency Holdings	14.0	14.0	114.0	505.0	162.0	210.0
of which: cash	14.0	14.0	114.0	505.0	162.0	210.0
II. Domestic credits of which:	3443.0	3297.0	2904.0	3179.0	3072.0	4070.0
1. Savings banks	0.0	0.0	0.0	2.0	0.0	0.0
2. Specialized banks	0.0	0.0	0.0	0.0	0.0	0.0
3. Bank of Latvia	0.0	0.0	152.0	257.0	371.0	632.0
4. Enterprises & coops.	3126.0	2979.0	3080.0	3516.0	4011.0	5044.0
5. Households	103.0	104.0	93.0	91.0	91.0	70.0
6. Net lending to government [b]	214.0	214.0	-421.0	-687.0	-1401.0	-1676.0
III. Other domestic assets	11.0	11.0	12.0	196.0	84.0	28.0
TOTAL ASSETS	3536.0	3465.0	3246.0	4055.0	4747.0	5717.0
Liabilities						
I. Foreign liabilities of which:	1950.0	1778.0	1405.0	1705.0	1304.0	128.0
1. Convertible currencies	0.0	0.0	0.0	0.0	0.0	0.0
2. Non-convertible currencies	1950.0	1778.0	1405.0	1705.0	1304.0	128.0
II. Total Deposits of which:	1559.0	1595.0	1802.0	2257.0	3320.0	5399.0
1. Savings banks	0.0	0.0	0.0	49.0	220.0	329.0
2. Specialized banks	0.0	0.0	0.0	2.0	335.0	3.0
3. Bank of Latvia	0.0	0.0	32.0	38.0	46.0	1623.0
4. Enterprises & coops.	1559.0	1595.0	1756.0	2155.0	2701.0	3410.0
5. Households	0.0	0.0	14.0	13.0	18.0	34.0
III. Capital	0.0	0.0	0.0	25.0	29.0	64.0
IV. Reserves	0.0	0.0	0.0	0.0	0.0	0.0
V. Other liabilities	27.0	92.0	39.0	68.0	94.0	126.0
TOTAL LIABILITIES	3536.0	3465.0	3246.0	4055.0	4747.0	5717.0

a. These consist of Foreign Trade Bank (Vneshkonombank), Agrobank, Bank for Industry and Construction
   and Housing and Social Bank. As of December 1991, these are merged with the Bank of Latvia.
b. Includes deposits of social organizations.
Sources: Bank of Latvia and Bank staff estimates.

Table 5.5 - Latvia: Monetary Survey
(Mlns of Rubles, end of period)

	1990-Q4	1991-Q1	1991-Q2	1991-Q3	1991-Q4
Net Foreign Assets	5,005	5,502	8,424	10,880	13,442
Foreign Assets	6,410	9,250	9,814	11,008	13,442
- Convertible	13	14	106	185	576
- Nonconvertible [a]	6,397	9,236	9,708	10,823	12,866
Foreign Liabilities	1,405	3,748	1,390	128	0
Net Domestic Assets	2,715	2,872	2,398	1,665	6,569
Domestic credit [b]	2,757	3,038	3,449	4,123	5,550
Credit to households	190	188	186	163	179
Credit to enterprises	3,213	3,695	4,837	5,777	7,740
Other items, net	-42	-166	-1,051	-2,458	1,019
Revaluation, net	9	9	100	177	
Other assets, n et	-543	-613	-1,745	-2,580	
Capital and reserves	242	382	823	1,186	
Interbanking transactions [b]	249	56	-229	-1,242	
Broad Money (M2)	7,720	8,374	10,822	12,545	16,241
Currency in circulation	2,128	2,300	2,464	3,000	4,000
Deposit of enterprises	1,962	2,360	3,517	4,391	6,300
Deposit of households	3,630	3,714	4,841	5,154	5,941
Memo Items:					
Household deposits/GDP [c]	26.1	22.0	23.0	22.0	15.0
M2/GDP [c]	55.0	48.3	52.0	53.0	40.1

a. Includes the counterpart of currency in circulation, claims of the Savings Bank on Gosbank Moscow and other claims, including reserve requirements on all-union banks in Moscow.

b. Credits to households and enterprises plus net credits to the government (not shown).

c. Defined as $m_t/gdp_t = (M_t/GDP_t)(P'_t/P_t)$, where m_t and M_t are the real and nominal money stocks, gdpt and GDP_t are nominal and real GDP, respectively. P_t is the retail price index at t and P'_t is the average value of the index in 1991.

Sources: Bank of Latvia and World Bank staff estimates.

Table 5.6 - Latvia: Bank Credits to Different Sectors of Economy
(Mln Rubles at end-of-year)

	1970	1980	1981	1982	1983	1984	1985	1986	1987	1988	1989	1990	1991
Short-Term Credits	989	2,221	2,759	2,989	2,923	2,871	2,852	2,443	2,324	2,068	1,863	2,129	6,627
Industry	346	689	772	817	766	778	743	759	689	628	598	598	2,042
Agriculture	55	547	639	683	619	577	539	491	532	461	420	273	267
Excluding Collective Farms	13	248	309	346	327	300	270	251	248	215	211	159	127
Construction	31	182	425	426	406	427	429	71	68	32	15	11	56
Stock Financing	47	43	57	64	82	66	68	95	91	55	63	143	719
Trade	332	450	515	614	643	598	641	532	490	459	415	360	1,342
Other Sectors	178	310	351	385	407	425	432	445	454	433	352	744	2,201
Long-Term Credits	255	908	964	1,023	1,051	1,068	1,058	1,060	1,046	1,139	1,205	1,203	1,159
State Enterprises & Coops	252	899	950	1,001	1,020	1,024	1,001	985	945	980	1,002	1,013	934
State Farms	8	39	45	48	47	42	37	53	45	69	47	40	43
Collective Farms	191	520	573	618	623	634	621	620	608	611	603	494	263
Housing Cooperatives	25	50	48	50	55	66	78	88	94	102	104	90	65
Individuals	3	9	14	22	31	44	57	75	101	159	203	190	225
Total Credits [a]	1,244	3,129	3,723	4,012	3,974	3,939	3,910	3,503	3,370	3,207	3,068	3,332	7,786

a. Certain credits included in the other tables in this section are not reflected in this total.
Source: State Committee for Statistics.

Table 6.1 - Latvia: Retail Goods and Services Index

Year	Month	From Previous Month to Stated Month (A)	Statistical Department of the IMF (A')	From Previous 3 Months to Stated Month (B)	From Previous 6 Months to Stated Month (C)	From Previous 12 Months to Stated Month (D)
			Percentage Increase in Inter-Monthly Paasche Retail Price Index [a]			
1991	Jan	29.0		NA	NA	NA
	Feb	14.2		NA	NA	NA
	Mar	5.2		55.0	NA	NA
	Apr	15.3		39.0	NA	NA
	May	2.2		24.0	NA	NA
	Jun	2.1		20.0	86.0	NA
	Jul	1.9		6.0	47.0	NA
	Aug	1.1		5.0	31.0	NA
	Sep	8.9		13.0	35.0	NA
	Oct	5.5		16.0	24.0	NA
	Nov	9.7		26.0	33.0	NA
	Dec	49.7		73.0	95.0	262.0
1992	Jan	56.4	64.1	157.0	199.0	339.0
	Feb	38.8	48.6	225.0	310.0	434.0
	Mar	37.5	33.8	198.0	417.0	597.9
	Apr	12.1	11.0	114.0	449.5	578.6
	May	11.3	13.2	71.5	457.5	639.1
	Jun		15.2			
	Jul		19.6			
	Aug		16.3			
	Sep		12.1			
	Oct		25.1			

NA = Not available.

a. For periods greater than one month, derived by compounding relevant
   monthly increases.

Columns (B), (C) and (D) show the precentage increases in the retail price level for the various 3-monthly, 6-monthly and 12-monthly periods ending in the stated months, respectively.

Source: State Committee for Statistics.

Table 6.2 - Latvia: Consumer Price Index
(1987 = 100.0)

	1988	1989	1990	1991
Consumer Price Index	103.6	108.5	119.9	326.4
Average Prices of Goods Purchased	104.2	109.6	122.2	342.2
Price of Services	100.1	101.3	104.5	231.0
Memorandum Items:				
Percent Change from Previous Year				
Consumer Price Index	3.6	4.7	10.5	172.2
Average Prices of Goods	4.2	5.2	11.5	180.0
Purchased Price of Services	0.1	1.2	3.2	121.1

Source: State Committ ee for Statistics.

Table 6.3 - Latvia: Relationship Between Collective Farm and State Retail Prices
(State Retail Prices = 100)

	1980	1981	1982	1983	1984	1985	1986	1987	1988	1989	1990	1991
Crop Products	298	265	329	266	283	292	266	308	287	264	235	175
Potatoes	350	362	442	394	375	436	400	408	373	350	203	177
Vegetables	373	368	443	316	313	379	312	332	272	333	288	193
Cabbage	380	469	569	554	569	287	407	372	268	314	186	149
Onions	295	294	302	234	277	326	390	256	194	211	257	160
Beets	935	890	870	1350	787	820	720	750	810	794	318	183
Carrots	542	555	675	600	975	491	462	500	619	743	511	215
Fruits	231	193	247	219	251	222	216	266	284	210	209	155
Vegetable Oil	306	306	306	306	356	366	356	356	380	385	413	198
Livestock Products	251	274	325	282	251	244	260	249	256	280	365	244
Meat	247	269	321	278	248	249	260	248	255	305	404	252
Milk & Milk Products	337	387	401	369	273	372	407	379	437	503	574	347
All Products	276	269	327	272	271	280	265	291	279	275	263	206

State retail prices refer to prices paid by consumers at the retail level. Collective farm prices refer to prices paid
by the State to the collective farms.
Source: Latvian authorities.

Table 6.4 - Latvia: *Average Monthly Salary of Workers*
(Rubles per Month)

	1980	1981	1982	1983	1984	1985	1986	1987	1988	1989	1990	1991
Agriculture	157.0	166.8	174.1	185.7	203.6	214.2	224.4	226.6	235.1	259.2	281.2	473.4
Industry	186.3	189.8	195.7	198.2	205.6	212.1	217.5	225.4	248.2	270.8	309.1	602.3
Construction	203.8	207.9	218.4	228.2	235.8	241.7	249.6	265.6	295.0	332.9	385.4	674.4
Education	142.1	144.3	145.4	145.5	148.5	154.6	159.6	168.1	171.6	177.7	195.5	459.2
Health	133.2	135.8	139.5	138.5	139.5	141.7	144.2	154.0	162.9	176.4	203.8	451.5
Average Salary in State Enterprises	171.4	175.0	180.4	183.6	190.3	195.9	201.4	208.9	227.0	249.9	290.9	561.4
Average Salary in:												
Agricultural Cooperatives	151.9	159.7	168.4	183.4	205.2	212.7	222.7	230.9	243.1	264.1	300.5	457.7
Other Cooperatives	NA	NA	NA	NA	NA	NA	NA	NA	495.0	668.0	507.0	694.0

Source: State Committee for Statistics.

Table 6.5 - Latvia: Annual Family Money Income and Expenditures
(Thousand Rubles per 100 Families)

	1980	1985	1989	1990	1991
Money Income	158.0	181.3	223.0	257.7	497.3
Wages	108.0	122.4	150.0	168.4	284.0
Earnings from Collective Farms	9.6	11.8	15.0	18.1	25.3
Pensions & Other Social Payments	21.3	23.5	27.1	28.9	104.1
Pensions	14.0	14.7	16.5	18.1	37.8
Other Income	19.1	23.7	30.9	42.3	83.9
Earnings from Own Farm Production	7.3	10.0	13.2	15.7	28.6
Money Expenditure	151.8	164.6	203.0	235.9	470.6
of which:					
Food	49.4	52.7	61.5	69.4	177.8
Other Consumer Goods	52.2	56.7	71.7	88.8	166.5
Fabrics	2.5	1.7	2.2	3.0	5.9
Clothing	12.4	12.9	14.6	18.8	32.4
Knitted Garments	4.9	5.8	7.5	9.7	17.4
Footwear	5.4	6.6	6.5	9.3	19.1
Household Appliances & Furniture	6.0	6.7	8.5	9.8	21.8
Sports & Recreation Goods	5.5	6.9	8.9	12.0	23.1
Sanitation & Hygiene	2.7	3.3	4.9	5.9	9.5
Construction Materials	0.7	0.9	1.6	1.9	4.7
Fuel	0.3	0.3	0.3	0.2	0.4
Alcoholic Beverages	6.4	5.6	6.9	10.3	15.7
Cultural and Social Services	15.5	17.5	21.8	22.9	34.3
Rent & Communal Services	4.6	5.0	5.8	6.0	8.1
Taxes and Contributions	13.1	15.5	19.5	21.2	37.2
Other Expenditure	15.1	16.5	21.7	23.3	39.1
Money Savings	6.3	16.7	20.0	21.9	26.7

Source: State Committee for Statistics.

Table 6.6 - Latvia: Family Budget of Workers
(Rubles Per Person in a Year)

	1970	1980	1981	1982	1983	1984	1985	1986	1987	1988	1989	1990	1991
Sources of Income	1202.8	1705.4	1730.7	1792.1	1842.6	1878.1	1912.6	1972.0	2030.5	2164.7	2358.2	2710.2	5480.7
Wages & Salaries	973.7	1350.4	1354.8	1397.7	1442.2	1482.4	1505.5	1514.2	1581.0	1690.5	1813.5	2052.9	3462.0
Pensions & Oth Soc Pmts	104.8	167.2	174.6	171.1	176.4	183.4	179.7	180.6	192.5	198.4	214.9	229.7	908.3
Income from Priv Plots	56.2	51.2	58.4	62.0	66.6	66.7	62.4	78.8	66.3	75.9	101.9	102.4	291.5
Income from Oth Srvcs	68.1	136.6	142.9	161.3	157.4	145.6	165.0	198.4	190.7	199.9	227.9	325.2	818.9
Expenditure	1147.9	1620.9	1617.6	1712.1	1716.4	1701.0	1727.7	1763.2	1901.2	1944.5	2116.4	2472.4	5130.4
Food	459.7	564.0	567.1	572.7	587.9	583.9	594.1	610.9	648.2	659.9	688.2	771.5	2165.4
Other Consumer Goods	351.0	568.6	560.2	623.8	601.1	586.5	604.0	623.2	684.2	674.2	762.9	953.2	1786.5
Alcoholic Bvgs.	46.1	62.8	63.2	69.2	67.6	64.1	56.1	49.3	56.3	59.6	69.9	102.6	154.9
Cultural & Social Srvcs	131.5	167.2	174.7	183.7	190.1	186.6	185.9	190.2	201.5	212.0	228.8	243.3	365.5
Rent & Community Srvc	35.5	47.3	47.3	48.0	49.3	49.4	49.7	55.7	55.0	55.2	57.3	60.2	79.4
Taxes & Contributions	106.8	162.3	162.2	168.1	176.4	185.8	188.4	189.9	198.3	215.7	233.3	255.3	428.2
Other	52.8	96.0	90.2	94.6	93.3	94.1	99.2	99.7	112.7	123.1	133.3	146.5	229.9
Savings [a]	54.9	84.5	113.1	80.0	126.2	177.1	184.9	208.8	129.3	220.2	241.8	237.8	350.3
Savings Ratio	4.6	5.0	6.5	4.5	6.8	9.4	9.7	10.6	6.4	10.2	10.3	8.8	6.4

a. Increase in cash lendings and deposits.
Source: State Committee for Statistics.

Table 6.7 - Latvia: Household Monetary Incomes and Outlays
(Millions of Rubles)

	1987	1988	1989	1990
Total Labor Income	4144	4573	5307	6371
Regular Wages	3285	3522	3780	4184
Wages Paid by Cooperatives	0	82	392	858
Other Wages and Compensations	105	116	128	158
Income Paid by Collective Farms	421	440	505	588
Income from Sale of Farm Products	333	413	503	582
Total Transfer Receipts	1208	1323	1513	1684
Pensions and Allowances	728	775	810	925
Scholarships	23	26	26	29
Income from the Financial System (insurance, interest, etc.)	192	236	261	369
Other Income	265	286	416	361
Adjustment	0	0	0	0
Total Income	5352	5896	6821	8056
Total Purchases	4902	5281	5793	6866
Retail Trade purchases	4419	4741	5196	6204
Purchased Services of which:	483	540	596	662
Rent and Utilities	134	144	153	153
Communications	44	48	50	56
Health and other Services	9	9	9	10
Cooperatives	1	21	39	70
Transfers and Savings of which:	830	976	1048	963
Taxes, Fees, Dues and Other	565	628	744	857
Savings	257	333	305	105
Other	8	15	0	0
Adjustment	0	0	0	0
Total Outlays	5732	6257	6841	7828

Source: State Committee on Statistics (GOSKOMSTAT).

Table 6.8 - Latvia: Wages, Prices, and Minimum Social Benefits in 1991
(Rubles and Index: 1990, Quarter IV = 100.0)

	1990	1991												1992									
		Jan	Feb	Mar	Apr	May	Jun	Jul	Aug	Sep	Oct	Nov	Dec	Jan	Feb	Mar	Apr	May	Jun	Jul	Aug	Sep	Oct
WAGES																							
Average wage (in Ruble)																							
Yearly	321.0						600.0																
Quarterly	N.A.	393.0	393.0	393.0	480.0	480.0	480.0	562.0	562.0	562.0	935.0	935.0	935.0	1985.0	1985.0	1985.0	3810.0	3810.0	3810.0	N.A.	N.A.	N.A.	N.A.
Average wage (Dec = 100.0) Dec																							
Minimum wage (in Ruble)	100.0	100.0	100.0	100.0	190.0	190.0	190.0	190.0	190.0	260.0	260.0	280.0	280.0	460.0	670.0	670.0	1000.0	1000.0	1500.0	1500.0	1500.0	1500.0	1500.0
Minimum level of living	100.0	202.0	236.0	248.0	304.0	N.A.	333.0	N.A.	N.A.	336.0	339.0	409.0	796.0	1244.0	1758.0	2199.0	2462.0	2882.0	3325.0	3826.0	3992.0	4542.0	N.A.
Minimum pension payment	100.0	146.0	146.0	146.0	166.0	166.0	166.0	166.0	N.A.	230.0	230.0	250.0	305.0	305.0	540.0	540.0	540.0	800.0	1200.0	1200.0	1200.0	1200.0	1200.0
Minimum pension	100.0	100.0	100.0	100.0	100.0	100.0	100.0	100.0	100.0	100.0	100.0	100.0	100.0	..	..	..	..	..	..	..	..	..	..
Price compensation [a]	N.A.	46.0	46.0	46.0	66.0	66.0	66.0	66.0	66.0	130.0	130.0	150.0	205.0	..	..	..	..	..	..	..	300.0	800.0	800.0
Social pension	N.A.	116.8	116.8	116.8	132.8	132.8	132.8	132.8	132.8	184.0	184.0	200.0	244.0	244.0	290.0	681.0	818.0	1035.0	1571.0	1571.0	N.A.	N.A.	N.A.
PRICES																							
CPI																							
(December 1990 = 100.0)	100.0	129.0	147.3	155.0	178.7	182.6	186.5	190.0	192.1	209.2	220.7	242.1	362.4	566.8	786.8								
Monthly inflation rate	N.A.	29.0	14.2	5.2	15.3	2.2	2.1	1.9	1.1	8.9	5.5	9.7	49.7	56.4	38.8								
CPI of minimum level of living																							
(December 1990 = 100.0)	100.0	169.2	197.4	206.0	228.8	232.8	228.3	223.1	255.5	276.5	291.2	336.7	706.3	1170.3	1801.1	2534.1	3101.7	3514.2	4044.8	5027.7	5550.6	6422.0	N.A.
Monthly inflation rate	N.A.	69.2	16.7	4.4	11.1	1.7	-1.9	-2.3	14.5	8.2	5.3	15.6	109.8	65.7	53.9	40.7	22.4	13.3	15.1	24.3	10.4	15.7	N.A.
o/w Food																							
(December 1990 = 100.0)	100.0	206.2	221.0	221.8 [r]	219.5	225.5	228.6	207.5	263.2	291.3	306.2	336.1	942.4	1328.8	1863.0	2254.2	2432.3	2592.8	3051.7	3680.4	3945.4	4505.6	N.A.
Monthly inflation rate	N.A.	106.2	7.2 [r]	0.4	-1.0	2.7	1.4	-9.2	26.7	10.7	5.1	9.8	180.4	41.0	40.2	21.0	7.9	6.6	17.7	20.6	7.2	14.2	N.A.

a. Paid only during 1991 and resumed payment in Aug 1992.

Source: Data provided by the Latvia authorities (January and October 1992).

Table 7.1 - Latvia: Number of Pensions as of December 31, by Type
(Thousands)

	1985	1986	1987	1988	1989	1990	1991	1991 1 June	1992 1 July	1992 1 October
Old-age pensions	356	367	380	391	400	412	498	497	493	493
Disability pensions	56	57	58	59	60	61	87	90	99	104
Survivor's pensions	38	38	36	34	32	30	32	31	30	28
Others	104	103	101	99	100	99	5	7	8	8
Personal pensions [a]	8	8	8	8	9	8	...	...	...	
Collective farm workers [a]	91	89	87	85	84	83	...	...	...	
Service pensions	1	1	1	1	1	1	4.5	...	...	...
Special invalid pensions	4	5	5	5	6	7	...	...	...	
Tschernobil pensions	...	...	...	...	...	...	0.5	...	...	...
Social pension	...	...	...	...	...	...	20	19	20	20
Total	554	565	575	583	592	602	641	644	650	655

Memorandum item:

b

	1985	1986	1987	1988	1989	1990	1991	1 June
Population (in thousand)	2587.7	2612.1	2641.1	2665.8	2673.5	2667.9	2657.0	2653.3
Employed (in thousand)	1394.8	1403.7	1412.6	1413.1	1406.9	1408.7	1396.8	1369.9

Total number of pensions
in percent of

	1985	1986	1987	1988	1989	1990	1991	1 June
Employed	39.7	40.3	40.7	41.3	42.1	42.7	45.9	47.0
Population	21.4	21.6	21.8	21.9	22.1	22.6	24.1	24.3

a. Transformed into old-age and disability pensions in 1991.
b. World Bank staff estimates.
Sources: Ministry of Welfare, Labor and Health and World Bank Staff estimates.

Table 7.2 - Latvia: Monthly Amount of Pensions by Type
(Rubles)

	1985	1986	1987	1988	1989	1990	1991 1/	1992 Plan
Old-age pensions								
Average benefit	89	91	94	96	94	100	422	4500
Minimum benefit	50	50	50	50	70	70	305	980
Disability pensions								
Average benefit	68	70	72	74	76	82	650	4500
Minimum benefit							475	1825
Group I	75	75	75	75	85	85	...	...
Group II	50	50	50	50	70	80	...	...
Group III	30	30	30	30	30	40	...	...
Survivor's pensions								
Average benefit	42	43	44	44	46	47	435	4000
Minimum benefit							305	4000
for 1 beneficiary	28	28	28	28	28	...	...	...
for 2 beneficiaries	50	50	50	50	50	...	...	...
for 3+ beneficiaries	75	75	75	75	75	...	...	...
Others	55.5	57.9	63.3	64.9	80.8	83.6	202.8	...
Personal pensions [a]	97	100	103	108	114	125	...	...
Collective farm workers [a]	53	55	61	62	80	81	...	...
Service pensions	76	79	85	105	109	114	153	290
Special invalid pensions	24	38	36	38	37	63	...	...
Tschernobil pensions	...	...	...	...	...	...	632	4000
Social pension	...	...	...	...	...	...	383	4015
Average pension	77.4	79.6	83.3	85.5	87.3	92.8	452.0	4018.0
Memorandum item:								
Minimum wage	70	70	70	70	70	100	460	4500
Average wage	196	201	209	227	250	321	...	...
Consumer price index (1987=100)	...	...	100	103.6	108.5	119.9	326.4	...

a. End-of-year values.
Sources: Ministry of Welfare, Labor and Health and World Bank Staff estimates.

Table 7.3 - Latvia: Pension Expenditure
(Millions of Rubles)

	1985	1986	1987	1988	1989	1990	1991	1992 Draft b
Old-age pensions [a]	368.3	394.3	414.0	448.5	443.4	503.0	...	7086.8
Disability pensions [a]	44.3	47.1	48.4	52.2	53.8	61.1	...	1819.6
Survivor's pensions [a]	18.6	19.3	18.4	17.9	17.4	17.2	...	443.1
Others [a]	67.1	70.4	74.1	76.8	95.3	101.1	...	389.6
Total expenditure	498.2	531.1	554.9	595.3	609.8	682.3	2238.7	9739.1
Memorandum Items: GDP (Mln Rubles)	9030.2	9325.0	9462.3	9956.1	10928.2	12201.0	28665.0	...
Pension expenditure in percent of GDP	5.5	5.7	5.9	6.0	5.6	5.6	7.8	...

a. Expenditure distribution estimated from Tables 7.1 and 7.2.
b. For the first three quarters.
Sources: Ministry of Welfare, Labor and Health and World Bank Staff estimates.

Table 7.4 - Latvia: Family Benefits

	1985	1986	1987	1988	1989	1990	1991 Plan	1991 Prelim. 2/	1991 Prelim.	1992 Jan-Jun
Number of Beneficiaries (in thousands)										
Birth Grant	...	...	...	...	29.6	27.8	...	...	30.7	15.6
Maternity leave	9.9	9.5	9.7	10.2	9.1	8.3	...	...	12.9	...
Child Care Allowance	27.4	27.9	28.8	28.8	26.9	32.5	95.0	...	83.0	87.2
Up to age of 1	27.4	27.9	28.8	28.8	26.9	32.5	...	...	...	...
Child aged 0 to 1 1/2	...	...	...	...	...	...	...	...	46.1	44.6
Child aged 1 1/2 to 3	...	...	...	...	...	...	...	...	36.9	42.6
Family allowances	25.0	27.0	29.0	31.0	32.0	34.0	560.0	...	559.6	578.6
Low-income multi-child allowance	25.0	27.0	29.0	31.0	32.0	34.0	...	...	...	...
Child aged 0 to 8	...	...	...	...	...	...	...	...	288.9	296.6
Child aged 8 to 15	...	...	...	...	...	...	...	...	240.8	262.0
Child in higher education	...	...	...	...	...	...	...	...	29.9	29.0
Kindergarten subst. allowance	...	...	...	...	...	61.0	85.0	...	86.1	98.0
Others	...	...	...	...	...	3.0	...	...	...	...
Average Benefits (in ruble, per month)										
Birth Grant	...	...	...	...	74.0	75.0	249.0	...	303.0	570.0
Maternity leave	164.0	167.0	168.0	171.0	171.0	194.0	...	...	286.0	1386.0
Child Care Allowance										
Up to age of 1	35.0	35.0	35.0	35.0	33.0	54.0	...	...	...	...
Child aged 0 to 1 1/2	...	...	...	...	...	...	...	...	132.0	549.0
Child aged 1 1/2 to 3	...	...	...	...	...	...	...	...	101.0	451.0
Family allowances										
Low-income multi-child allowance	19.0	19.0	19.0	19.0	20.0	19.0	...	...	...	...
Child aged 0 to 8	...	...	...	...	...	...	...	...	65.0	259.0
Child aged 8 to 15	...	...	...	...	...	...	...	...	79.0	299.0
Child in higher education	...	...	...	...	...	...	...	...	79.0	301.0
Kindergarten subst. allowance	...	...	...	...	...	50.0	58.0	...	58.0	101.0
Expenditure (in millions of rubles)										
Birth Grant	2.6	2.7	2.7	2.6	2.2	2.1	9.0	3.6	6.0	9.2
Maternity leave	19.4	19.1	19.5	21.0	18.6	19.3	49.8	23.1	32.9	73.7
Child Care Allowance	11.5	11.7	12.1	12.1	16.8	21.2	135.5	73.6	113.0	273.1
Up to age of 1	11.5	11.7	12.1	12.1	16.8	21.2	...	...	...	...
Child aged 0 to 1 1/2	...	...	...	...	...	...	...	...	67.5	148.2
Child aged 1 1/2 to 3	...	...	...	...	...	...	...	...	45.5	124.9
Family allowances	1.3	1.1	1.1	1.1	1.4	1.6	524.2	330.4	514.8	980.8
Low-income multi-child allowance	1.3	1.1	1.1	1.1	1.4	1.6	...	...	...	...
Child aged 0 to 8	...	...	...	...	...	...	...	...	233.4	461.0
Child aged 8 to 15	...	...	...	...	...	...	...	...	238.0	472.3
Child in higher education	...	...	...	...	...	...	...	...	29.4	47.0
Kindergarten subst. allowance	...	...	...	...	...	...	57.4	31.0	52.1	68.2
Others	0.2	0.2	0.2	0.2	0.1	1.0	2.5	1.1	1.9	0.0
Total expenditure	35.0	34.8	35.6	37.0	39.1	45.2	778.4	462.8	720.7	2069.0

Source: Ministry of Welfare, Labor and Health (February 1992 and updated October 1992).

Table 8.1 - Latvia: Agricultural Land Area by Farm Categories
(Thousand Hectares)

	1940	1960	1965	1970	1975	1980	1985	1990	1991
All Area Categories:									
Agricultural Land	3713.6	3076.5	2982.3	2907.8	2554.4	2580.6	2589.4	2567.0	2567.8
Arable Land	2171.4	1736.4	1786.2	1603.8	1658.2	1712.3	1716.7	1687.4	1689.1
Forest and Woodland Area	1899.0	2398.6	2527.9	2561.7	2726.8	2728.6	2739.5	2803.2	2802.4
State Farms and Rural Enterprises	NA	2668.7	2612.6	2555.8	2320.0	2359.9	2374.1	2235.6	2203.0
Arable Land	NA	1580.5	1643.3	1466.3	1552.8	1614.7	1619.4	1500.5	1478.6
Private & Subsidiary Farms	NA	123.3	127.3	133.7	126.7	118.7	117.6	237.2	270.9
Arable Land	NA	99.0	97.9	95.0	89.3	84.2	83.8	172.8	196.5
Private Farms	NA	NA	NA	NA	NA	NA	NA	108.7	132.2
Arable Land	NA	NA	NA	NA	NA	NA	NA	79.1	96.7
Total Land in Agricultural Use:									
Agricultural Land	NA	2792.0	2739.9	2689.5	2446.7	2478.6	2491.7	2472.8	2473.9
Arable Land	NA	1679.5	1741.2	1561.3	1642.1	1698.9	1703.2	1673.3	1675.1

There were no private farms before 1985.
Source: State Committee for Statistics.

Table 8.2 - Latvia: Agricultural Production

	1970	1975	1980	1981	1982	1983	1984	1985	1986	1987	1988	1989	1990	1991
(Mln of Current Rubles)														
Total Gross Agricultural Production	1575.3	1766.3	2052.7	2308.4	2568.0	2973.8	3285.3	3355.7	3338.1	3210.2	3751.8	3843.6	4132.0	8881.3
Crop Production of which:	634.5	627.0	730.7	908.1	1009.0	1080.6	1165.4	1046.6	1144.5	1035.8	1210.8	1290.0	1421.4	3387.2
Grains	113.6	112.2	136.3	146.1	190.9	215.1	153.9	235.9	247.7	262.5	279.7	298.0	328.3	782.4
Fibers	3.2	3.1	1.8	4.6	6.1	16.8	4.7	6.4	11.8	9.2	9.7	10.3	11.4	27.1
Sugarbeet	7.0	6.9	5.5	11.0	13.9	23.5	28.2	17.4	17.4	17.1	19.4	20.6	22.7	54.2
Potatoes	177.0	174.9	180.2	255.0	303.0	290.4	323.4	223.6	243.1	191.0	247.0	263.2	290.0	691.0
Vegetables	83.1	82.1	99.9	116.4	129.3	134.2	98.2	90.3	84.0	90.7	99.3	105.8	116.6	277.8
Animal Production of which:	940.8	1139.3	1322.0	1400.3	1559.0	1893.2	2119.9	2309.1	2193.6	2174.4	2541.0	2553.6	2710.6	5494.1
Livestock for Slaughter of which:	467.4	593.3	710.3	773.0	877.3	1026.0	1107.0	1212.1	1197.5	1187.2	1368.6	1375.4	1459.9	2961.3
Cattle	211.4	294.7	305.6	312.5	354.4	433.8	510.9	550.0	563.9	536.8	628.1	631.2	670.0	1357.0
Pigs	202.3	231.2	315.6	361.9	421.5	469.3	460.3	521.0	500.6	503.8	580.3	583.2	619.1	1252.7
Sheep	20.0	16.8	11.1	12.7	12.2	17.5	24.4	22.1	20.5	20.6	24.1	24.2	25.7	54.9
Poultry	29.2	44.4	74.3	82.9	85.7	100.7	107.1	114.6	109.1	121.3	131.3	132.0	140.1	285.7
Milk	349.9	413.8	452.9	455.2	486.7	646.8	761.1	843.8	775.9	786.8	915.8	920.3	976.9	1977.9
Eggs	44.9	56.8	68.1	71.1	69.0	79.9	80.8	82.3	84.6	84.4	95.5	46.0	101.9	208.8
Material Inputs of which:	701.5	953.5	1355.6	1405.7	1437.8	1604.5	1664.9	1726.9	1778.8	1838.8	1949.8	2038.7	2201.5	3685.3
Crop Production	NA	NA	425.4	465.2	487.1	521.6	550.6	546.0	566.3	595.9	627.1	674.8	678.1	1103.8
Animal Production	NA	NA	930.2	940.5	950.7	1082.9	1114.3	1180.9	1212.5	1242.9	1322.7	1363.9	1523.4	2581.5
Net Material Product [a] of which:	873.8	812.8	697.1	902.7	1130.2	1369.3	1620.4	1628.8	1559.3	1371.7	1802.0	1804.9	1930.5	5196.0
Crop Production	NA	NA	305.3	442.9	521.9	559.0	614.8	500.6	578.2	439.9	583.7	615.2	743.3	2283.4
Animal Production	NA	NA	391.8	459.8	608.3	810.3	1005.6	1128.2	981.1	931.8	1218.3	1189.7	1187.2	2912.6
(Mln of 1983 Rubles)														
Total Gross Agricultural Production	2298.5	2293.4	2398.5	2514.3	2547.6	2776.5	2971.9	2878.0	3035.3	2984.1	2940.4	3054.4	2743.1	2636.2
Crop Production of which:	861.6	689.9	680.8	809.7	830.4	905.2	1020.0	860.2	977.0	898.3	863.4	990.3	793.2	835.3
Grains	131.3	126.3	105.7	117.0	144.7	157.5	209.8	166.1	200.0	213.2	148.7	201.0	205.8	161.2
Fibers	9.3	9.2	5.7	6.5	10.2	15.3	12.4	10.0	11.3	14.2	11.4	14.5	7.5	9.0
Sugarbeet	12.1	10.5	9.3	15.9	14.8	20.1	24.9	18.3	18.6	18.1	23.2	20.3	22.6	19.4
Potatoes	445.1	285.0	229.3	245.9	283.9	278.3	352.5	243.2	299.3	216.9	212.2	251.5	194.3	180.5
Vegetables	146.6	116.1	108.1	113.8	114.2	75.6	127.3	110.7	69.2	65.0	68.1	62.1	54.1	64.2
Animal Production of which:	1436.9	1603.5	1717.7	1704.6	1717.1	1871.3	1951.9	2017.8	2058.3	2085.8	2077.0	2064.1	1949.9	1800.9
Livestock for Slaughter of which:	695.0	828.0	924.6	926.6	926.1	1024.4	1074.6	1093.1	1112.6	1127.7	1112.3	1101.1	1029.1	949.8
Cattle	351.2	450.4	434.8	423.9	430.4	474.5	507.4	529.2	525.4	536.6	525.5	526.5	501.6	478.8
Pigs	275.9	294.0	379.9	387.9	379.1	422.1	433.9	428.8	448.6	444.2	439.8	423.7	396.9	346.8
Sheep	25.2	21.1	12.4	12.5	12.6	12.7	14.8	13.0	12.1	12.0	12.9	15.0	14.1	14.6
Poultry	37.1	55.4	93.4	98.1	100.2	109.8	112.9	116.9	121.7	130.1	129.0	131.1	112.7	105.6
Milk	678.4	708.0	671.7	646.2	651.9	694.8	730.0	775.3	776.1	787.5	782.2	783.2	750.1	689.9
Eggs	47.9	63.3	69.9	70.7	71.6	78.8	82.4	84.3	88.4	88.2	88.1	85.2	78.4	72.8
Material Inputs of which:	NA	1001.6	1326.1	1363.2	1377.2	1504.4	1566.5	1579.5	1646.2	1690.4	1649.7	1622.1	1612.9	1821.5
Crop Production	NA	360.6	477.4	513.9	514.0	549.3	567.9	529.9	568.0	594.7	519.7	572.0	537.7	679.8
Animal Production	NA	641.0	848.7	849.3	863.2	955.1	998.6	1049.6	1078.2	1095.7	1130.0	1050.1	1075.2	1141.7
Net Material Product [a] of which:	NA	1291.8	1072.4	1151.1	1170.4	1272.1	1405.4	1298.5	1389.1	1293.7	1290.7	1432.3	1130.2	814.7
Crop Production	NA	329.3	203.4	295.8	316.4	355.9	452.1	330.3	409.0	303.6	343.7	418.3	255.5	155.5
Animal Production	NA	962.5	869.0	855.3	854.0	916.2	953.3	968.2	980.1	990.1	947.0	1014.0	874.7	659.2

a. May not add up due to rounding.

Note: Data for 1983 in constant prices do not match 1983 data in current prices because prices used are prices as of January, 1983 rather than the average prices for 1983.

Source: State Committee for Statistics.

Table 8.3 - Latvia: Total Harvest and Productivity of Certain Grain Crops

	1980	1985	1986	1987	1988	1989	1990	1991
			Production (Thousand Tons)					
Winter Grain	259.1	386.9	474.7	485.7	509.4	697.2	698.0	342.1
of which:								
Winter Wheat	129.9	217.1	228.3	295.6	270.2	360.0	370.2	185.9
Winter Rye	129.2	169.8	245.8	189.4	239.0	336.8	323.6	145.8
Spring Crops	555.7	906.6	1034.0	1144.0	632.6	900.1	923.9	993.4
of which:								
Barley	439.1	710.8	802.2	906.7	500.2	700.3	692.8	761.9
Oat	96.4	129.7	151.9	151.1	89.7	149.3	176.1	177.2
Legumes	4.1	55.8	62.5	54.9	28.5	27.7	22.7	20.7
			Average Yield (Centner per Hectare)					
Winter Grain	13.4	19.8	23.2	26.3	24.8	28.3	25.6	24.0
of which:								
Winter Wheat	15.7	23.0	23.6	28.9	25.8	30.6	26.3	26.6
Winter Rye	11.6	16.9	22.9	23.1	23.6	26.2	24.8	21.1
Spring Crops	11.1	17.0	19.4	22.3	14.1	20.7	22.4	19.3
of which:								
Barley	11.1	17.9	19.7	22.5	14.2	22.1	22.6	19.2
Oat	11.8	14.2	19.7	22.4	13.7	19.7	21.4	19.1
Legumes	10.1	15.3	17.1	20.2	14.0	19.6	21.6	23.0

Source: Latvian Statistical Yearbook, 1990.

Table 8.4 - Latvia: Livestock and Poultry

	1980	1985	1989	1990	1991
(Thousand Heads)					
Cattle	1427	1485	1472	1439	1383
(milking cows)	580	563	544	535	531
Swine	1759	1721	1555	1401	1247
Sheep	203	177	159	165	190
Goats	6	5	5	5	6
Horses	35	33	32	31	30
Poultry	11158	12667	11246	10321	10395
(Production)					
Average Yield of Milk per Cow (kilograms)	2920	3417	3636	3476	3289
Collective & State Farms	2770	3363	3604	3379	3044
Average Yield of Wool per Sheep (kilograms)	1.8	2.3	2.3	2.2	2.2
Collective & State Farms	3.3	3.5	3.1	3.1	2.9
Average Egg Production per Hen (pieces)	215	198	219	210	205

Source: Latvian Statistical Yearbook, 1990.

Table 9.1 - Latvia: Industrial Output at Current Prices

	1970	1975	1980	1981	1982	1983	1984	1985	1986	1987	1988	1989	1990	1991
					Mln of Current Rubles									
Electrical Power Engineering	72.1	80.0	120.8	122.1	158.4	155.2	128.0	166.3	169.2	182.4	173.6	200.3	228.5	648.9
Fuel Industry	30.0	32.5	35.8	35.5	43.9	46.8	49.0	47.4	51.0	47.1	45.4	48.6	43.6	70.8
Ferrous Metallurgy	53.9	91.4	113.1	115.5	142.9	143.3	148.2	150.9	154.4	156.6	159.5	161.1	152.9	217.0
NonFerrous Metallurgy	6.1	9.8	12.1	12.6	13.7	14.2	14.6	14.8	14.2	13.9	14.0	12.4	11.7	15.2
Chemical & Petrochemical	296.2	406.8	511.4	557.8	570.1	583.8	629.2	672.8	708.3	730.5	762.5	811.8	794.7	1810.7
Mechanical Engg & Metalworking	1062.4	1423.0	1980.5	2093.5	2098.0	2186.7	2324.5	2429.0	2561.8	2680.3	2766.2	2843.6	2884.8	5305.1
of which:														
Mechanical Engg	812.4	1068.7	1487.7	1585.6	1546.7	1603.3	1682.4	1742.3	1858.4	1932.4	2052.5	2130.4	2199.1	4195.3
Building Materials	176.4	245.6	236.4	233.2	278.5	288.4	304.3	301.6	319.0	334.0	346.5	335.4	348.2	798.5
of which:														
Cement Production	24.4	29.3	22.9	22.4	27.3	27.8	27.7	26.6	29.0	28.2	27.3	18.3	27.2	92.5
Prefabricated Reinforced	73.3	109.7	97.5	93.1	117.1	121.2	127.4	126.0	130.4	133.9	137.9	137.2	137.9	314.3
Wall Materials	18.0	13.0	20.0	20.7	24.9	24.7	26.4	25.6	26.8	38.8	41.7	45.0	49.7	123.8
Inert Materials	10.1	30.9	29.1	32.8	37.7	41.2	43.9	42.8	45.9	51.0	53.8	46.7	43.6	50.7
Glass & Porcelain	30.4	44.4	55.6	56.2	55.3	56.9	58.2	60.1	62.3	65.4	67.3	67.9	67.7	230.0
Forest, Timber, Cellulose and Paper	382.5	378.4	399.0	424.8	504.8	534.4	555.9	566.4	588.3	618.1	639.4	622.0	612.8	1819.1
Timber Preparation	98.4	64.0	63.0	64.1	83.2	88.4	89.8	93.0	96.7	101.0	102.6	101.1	96.9	310.1
Woodworking	210.4	234.6	269.6	289.9	328.1	342.6	358.5	363.2	382.7	403.6	419.4	402.4	400.6	1021.2
Cellulose & Paper	73.7	79.8	66.4	70.8	93.5	103.4	107.6	110.2	108.9	113.5	117.4	118.5	115.3	487.8
Light Industry	1257.0	1638.6	1749.4	1767.9	1896.2	1892.0	1877.6	1885.3	1900.8	1932.2	1974.8	2007.0	1977.0	5854.5
of which:														
Textile	820.5	1154.1	1263.1	1262.4	1361.9	1358.4	1346.6	1338.5	1358.2	1359.9	1387.1	1407.6	1390.7	3769.0
Clothing	285.6	301.1	290.7	307.3	312.5	307.8	305.9	314.7	309.1	323.4	328.6	336.5	344.0	1013.9
Leather, Fur & Shoe Ind.	146.8	175.7	188.7	190.9	213.9	217.8	217.1	223.0	223.9	238.8	246.4	248.3	227.6	1003.8
Food Industry	1374.9	1808.3	1997.5	2003.0	2126.2	2199.6	2302.3	2421.6	2475.4	2602.4	2725.1	2827.4	2739.2	6648.8
Food & Spices	419.3	563.0	711.6	694.0	765.4	742.9	738.1	787.9	775.7	847.2	909.6	1021.5	1030.4	2044.3
Meat & Milk	606.0	779.5	823.3	835.6	819.8	898.0	974.3	1020.2	1062.6	1117.4	1131.9	1130.4	1083.2	3441.5
Fish Industry	349.6	465.8	462.6	473.4	541.0	558.7	589.9	613.5	637.1	637.8	683.6	675.5	625.6	1162.9
Printing Industry	24.9	33.4	39.9	39.6	40.0	41.6	43.1	44.8	43.2	37.9	39.9	25.0	28.8	120.6
Other Fields	220.7	339.3	500.4	511.9	504.4	521.4	580.4	618.2	638.5	651.9	737.8	865.3	1096.9	2427.7
Total Gross Output	4987.5	6531.5	7751.9	7973.6	8432.4	8664.3	9015.3	9379.2	9686.4	10052.7	10452.0	10827.8	10986.8	25966.9
Intermediate & Capital Goods	2631.7	3737.1	4488.4	4624.7	4840.2	4891.1	5183.8	5315.0	5560.0	5730.0	5863.6	5987.8	5943.9	
Consumer Goods	2355.8	2794.4	3263.5	3348.9	3592.2	3773.2	3831.5	4064.2	4126.4	4322.7	4588.4	4840.0	5042.9	

Source: State Committee for Statistics.

Table 9.2 - Latvia: Industrial Output at Constant Prices

	1970	1975	1980	1981	1982	1983	1984	1985	1986	1987	1988	1989	1990	1991
					Mln of Rubles at January 1, 1982 Prices									
Electrical Power Engineering	66.0	74.4	115.1	118.0	115.8	114.7	106.3	130.2	133.3	150.5	136.5	150.1	170.1	234.8
Fuel Industry	32.7	37.6	40.4	40.0	43.9	46.8	51.1	48.4	50.8	48.4	46.3	49.0	43.7	68.3
Ferrous Metallurgy	74.0	114.6	139.9	143.0	144.6	143.3	148.2	150.9	154.5	156.8	160.0	161.8	156.1	217.0
NonFerrous Metallurgy	6.7	10.6	13.2	13.7	13.7	14.2	14.6	14.9	14.2	13.9	14.0	12.4	11.7	15.2
Chemical & Petrochemical	228.7	368.1	490.0	530.2	573.0	586.5	629.3	674.5	711.4	742.5	764.3	809.7	797.0	1509.4
Mechanical Engg & Metalworking	844.2	1304.4	1852.0	1992.8	2100.2	2193.7	2348.3	2481.8	2628.6	2779.0	2877.6	2950.9	2990.6	4678.8
of which:														
Mechanical Engg	594.8	918.2	1354.2	1466.6	1546.9	1609.0	1704.3	1796.0	1916.4	2028.9	2158.6	2234.4	2302.2	3690.9
Building Materials	199.0	288.2	278.2	281.6	279.5	289.0	305.0	301.4	318.4	333.7	345.8	333.3	333.7	679.3
of which:														
Cement Production	28.9	31.7	28.3	27.7	27.3	27.8	27.7	26.7	29.0	28.3	27.4	18.3	25.7	83.3
Prefabricated Reinforced	83.3	122.4	116.0	114.7	117.3	121.6	127.6	126.1	130.3	133.8	137.8	136.7	131.3	252.5
Wall Materials	14.7	21.5	23.9	24.5	24.9	24.7	26.4	25.6	26.7	38.6	41.7	44.9	46.4	107.7
Inert Materials	11.5	37.0	36.9	36.7	38.0	41.1	44.4	43.3	46.2	51.5	53.8	46.7	43.3	45.9
Glass & Porcelain	23.9	41.6	53.5	54.5	55.2	56.7	58.1	59.9	62.2	64.8	66.9	67.3	67.1	161.3
Forest, Timber, Cellulose and Paper	394.7	411.3	430.2	460.7	493.1	521.2	540.2	548.1	572.4	599.1	622.2	599.7	583.1	1686.5
Timber Preparation	99.5	69.4	67.3	61.1	72.7	76.4	76.3	76.3	80.9	84.6	87.5	84.1	79.7	297.9
Woodworking	207.2	244.5	278.2	309.3	326.9	341.4	356.3	361.6	382.4	400.7	416.8	397.0	388.1	946.0
Cellulose & Paper	88.0	97.4	84.7	90.3	93.5	103.4	107.6	110.2	109.1	113.8	117.9	118.6	115.3	442.5
Light Industry	1336.0	1671.9	1851.2	1882.6	1896.0	1895.9	1889.7	1903.2	1927.9	1964.2	2008.0	2033.0	1997.5	4536.9
of which:														
Textile	946.3	1203.7	1335.2	1351.2	1361.7	1358.3	1349.3	1345.5	1365.9	1369.7	1398.9	1408.6	1389.7	2942.0
Clothing	222.0	262.8	297.0	310.1	312.3	310.3	310.6	320.7	320.2	337.4	340.5	354.4	359.2	760.9
Leather, Fur & Shoe Industry	156.3	194.6	208.1	210.4	213.8	219.1	221.7	227.8	232.3	247.1	255.9	248.3	234.0	783.6
Food Industry	1477.9	1955.8	2112.5	2118.8	2149.7	2217.2	2311.6	2365.8	2414.4	2537.9	2634.6	2740.6	2646.2	5815.2
Food & Spices	474.4	619.9	736.5	751.9	761.3	739.3	735.4	725.6	716.3	793.0	853.7	968.7	982.5	1653.8
Meat & Milk	630.7	810.7	821.4	834.5	813.0	886.9	952.0	996.0	1029.3	1077.7	1090.1	1092.0	1042.4	3092.9
Fish Industry	372.8	525.2	554.6	532.4	575.4	591.0	624.2	644.2	668.8	667.2	690.8	679.9	621.2	1068.5
Printing Industry	20.9	29.3	36.5	39.4	40.0	41.7	43.2	44.6	43.2	37.9	39.9	25.2	28.2	91.8
Other Fields	127.3	273.2	493.0	507.0	505.4	521.4	580.2	611.1	633.6	624.9	673.1	742.4	903.8	2192.8
Total Gross Output	4832.0	6581.0	7905.7	8182.3	8410.1	8642.3	9025.8	9334.8	9664.9	10053.6	10389.2	10675.4	10728.8	21887.3
Intermediate & Capital Goods	2556.1	3673.3	4488.0	4635.3	4734.0	4860.2	5120.1	5281.4	5514.5	5687.6	5777.5	5859.1	5745.7	
Consumer Goods	2275.9	2907.7	3417.7	3547.0	3676.1	3782.1	3905.7	4053.4	4150.6	4366.0	4611.7	4816.3	4983.1	

Note: Data for 1982 in constant prices do not match 1982 data in current prices because prices used are prices as of January, 1982 rather than the average prices for 1982.

Source: State Committee for Statistics.

Table 9.3 - Latvia: State Industrial Enterprises by Number of Employees
(Yearly Average)

Number of Employees in the Productive Sphere	1987	1990
Less than 50	3	12
51 - 100	16	31
101 - 200	41	69
201 - 300	35	52
301 - 500	66	82
501 - 1,000	80	72
1,001 - 2,000	40	33
2,001 - 5,000	37	21
5,001 - 10,000	6	5
Over 10,000	2	1
TOTAL	326	378

Source: State Committee for Statistics.

Table 9.4 - Latvia: Gross and Net Capital Formation by Industrial Branches
(Mln Rubles)

	1975	1980	1981	1982	1983	1984	1985	1986	1987	1988	1989	1990	1991
Industry Gross Total:	3515.9	4204.7	4438.0	4686.4	4768.3	5029.8	5239.9	5470.9	5639.5	5749.4	5943.4	6170.3	6423.5
Net	2484.8	2673.8	2751.4	2837.8	2778.8	2877.0	2895.3	2954.0	2729.8	2959.6	2990.3	3049.9	3397.4
Power Gross	671.3	856.3	878.7	907.6	932.2	968.3	996.8	1021.4	1034.8	1061.3	1087.5	1115.4	1141.5
Net	495.0	594.5	598.9	605.3	610.3	625.4	630.2	633.4	625.4	623.4	620.4	619.6	617.6
Fuel Industry Gross	58.5	67.7	69.7	71.5	72.1	73.0	74.1	74.6	72.9	69.2	69.3	63.2	65.2
Net	38.7	39.6	39.5	38.5	37.5	36.4	35.1	33.7	32.1	29.3	28.2	24.0	28.8
Ferrous Metal. Gross	72.4	80.1	83.1	88.3	88.2	88.9	90.8	96.5	99.2	100.9	103.8	100.9	105.8
Net	53.0	45.1	45.3	47.0	44.8	48.0	41.2	43.6	45.0	42.7	42.3	39.1	49.7
Non-Ferrous Met. Gross	1.6	1.9	2.0	3.5	3.8	3.9	4.0	4.0	5.1	5.4	5.9	5.8	5.2
Net	1.2	1.2	1.2	2.8	2.9	2.9	2.9	2.8	3.7	3.9	4.2	3.9	3.3
Chemical & Oil Gross	240.1	500.3	526.4	557.4	453.0	481.1	492.1	514.1	512.2	506.1	518.1	532.9	541.7
Net	174.7	356.2	359.8	367.6	264.6	272.2	259.9	259.3	243.7	233.7	225.8	208.8	263.8
Machine Con. & Wrk Gross	637.7	926.2	975.3	1047.6	1123.7	1204.9	1278.9	1359.6	1441.6	1518.3	1615.5	1671.1	1727.2
Net	448.7	580.8	595.3	621.0	646.6	683.3	699.4	729.0	741.6	755.8	783.9	787.4	912.5
Wood, Pulp & Paper Gross	195.1	272.1	287.5	309.4	320.9	332.2	340.3	362.9	417.5	425.0	421.6	417.8	445.7
Net	116.0	155.5	152.4	168.3	167.1	162.7	157.7	170.8	174.3	202.3	190.8	178.5	235.4
Constr. Mat. Gross	208.7	249.1	258.2	269.3	282.7	299.7	325.5	331.8	378.1	349.8	342.9	354.6	378.1
Net	142.4	141.7	142.4	144.0	148.7	155.9	170.6	166.9	169.5	183.6	172.8	178.2	201.2
Glass & Ceramics Gross	34.8	41.8	42.7	43.7	44.8	45.2	45.9	46.3	48.1	50.0	51.6	53.0	55.1
Net	24.2	24.2	23.8	23.0	22.3	21.4	19.9	18.6	18.3	18.1	17.4	16.9	23.0
Light Industry Gross	299.7	365.0	380.2	401.4	420.1	438.1	465.2	486.3	502.3	531.1	580.0	617.0	670.0
Net	211.2	224.5	226.4	234.1	239.0	242.0	254.5	259.1	255.7	271.5	305.6	331.6	372.0
Food Industry Gross	613.5	717.4	800.3	839.6	872.1	934.1	957.1	989.4	931.4	926.6	928.6	1011.9	1044.6
Net	418.4	423.7	472.6	484.2	490.5	521.9	515.8	521.5	298.6	471.8	468.2	530.6	545.0
Flour-Grain Ind. Gross	38.6	55.1	60.1	66.5	69.8	71.4	75.9	86.0	90.1	95.8	103.1	108.9	120.4
Net	31.7	39.3	46.2	50.8	52.3	52.1	54.4	61.2	63.6	65.2	71.3	75.4	81.8
Other	443.9	71.7	73.8	80.6	84.9	89.0	93.3	98.0	106.2	109.9	115.5	117.8	123.0
Net	329.6	47.5	47.6	51.2	52.2	52.8	53.7	54.1	58.3	58.3	59.4	55.9	63.3

Source: State Committee for Statistics.

Table 9.5 - Latvia: Construction Activity
(Mln Rubles)

	1970	1975	1980	1981	1982	1983	1984	1985	1986	1987	1988	1989	1990	1991
Current Prices														
Investment	898.0	1228.0	1234.0	1324.0	1367.0	1374.0	1621.0	1790.0	1964.0	1829.0	1888.0	2000.0	1887.0	2342.0
State	750.0	1036.0	1012.0	1111.0	1139.0	1105.0	1319.0	1489.0	1614.0	1484.0	1506.0	1665.0	1500.0	1614.0
Cooperatives	138.0	168.0	202.0	193.0	206.0	244.0	271.0	271.0	304.0	302.0	337.0	284.0	343.0	668.0
Social Organizations	4.0	12.0	8.0	10.0	10.0	11.0	10.0	7.0	11.0	8.0	8.0	7.0	8.0	15.0
Private	6.0	12.0	12.0	10.0	12.0	14.0	21.0	23.0	35.0	35.0	37.0	44.0	36.0	45.0
Constant 1984 Prices														
Investment	1004.0	1414.0	1428.0	1535.0	1589.0	1598.0	1716.0	1894.0	2074.0	1955.0	1952.0	2034.0	1867.0	1183.0
State	845.0	1187.0	1187.0	1304.0	1345.0	1313.0	1417.0	1585.0	1727.0	1612.0	1570.0	1655.0	1455.0	815.0
Cooperatives	146.0	202.0	220.0	210.0	221.0	259.0	268.0	279.0	301.0	299.0	337.0	328.0	368.0	337.0
Social Organizations	7.0	13.0	9.0	11.0	11.0	12.0	10.0	7.0	11.0	8.0	8.0	7.0	8.0	8.0
Private	6.0	12.0	12.0	10.0	12.0	14.0	21.0	23.0	35.0	36.0	37.0	44.0	36.0	23.0

Note: Data for 1984 in constant prices do not match 1984 data in current prices because prices used are prices as of January, 1984 rather than the average prices for 1984.
Source: State Committee for Statistics.

Table 10.1 - Latvia: Energy Balance Sheet
(Thousands of Tons Coal Equivalent)

	1970	1975	1980	1985	1990
Domestic Sources	1299	1095	815	685	557
Coal	NA	NA	NA	NA	NA
Other Solid Fuels	1299	1095	815	685	557
Liquid Fuel	NA	NA	NA	NA	NA
Other [a]	NA	NA	NA	NA	NA
Imports	7505	8233	9952	11455	11076
Liquid Fuel	4388	4047	5814	7708	6478
of which:					
USSR	4361	3977	5658	7572	6300
Others	27	70	156	136	178
Gas	1282	1561	2041	2890	3634
of which:					
USSR	1282	1561	2041	2890	3634
Others	NA	NA	NA	NA	NA
Coal	1780	2540	1993	787	840
of which:					
USSR	1335	1796	1380	340	362
Others	445	744	613	447	478
Other Primary Energy Imports from the USSR	55	85	104	70	124
Change in Stocks	140	254	135	-112	306
Domestic Use of Primary Energy of which for:	8944	9582	10902	12028	11939
Electricity Generation [a]	NA	420	405	368	428
Other Purposes of which by:	NA	9162	10497	11660	11511
Industry	NA	2284	2312	2518	2044
Agriculture	NA	486	754	495	300
Households	NA	469	534	764	817

a. Excluding hydro- and nuclear-generated electricity.
Source: Latvian authorities.

Table 10.2 - Latvia: Electric Energy Balance Sheet
(Millions of kwh)

	1970	1975	1980	1981	1982	1983	1984	1985	1986	1987	1988	1989	1990	1991
Electroenergy Produced	2695	2893	4681	4793	4695	4491	3843	4961	5184	5937	5110	5801	6647	5645
Electroenergy Received from Other Republics	2914	4720	5908	7104	8167	9419	9340	8373	7850	8175	8500	7740	7138	7054
Total Electroenergy Used of which:	4611	6361	8230	8530	8742	8980	9239	9451	9680	10211	10361	10257	10230	9870
Industry	2239	2943	3398	3425	3467	3538	3615	3682	3786	3914	3970	3933	3766	3606
Agriculture	505	884	1439	1519	1566	1612	1728	1833	1860	2074	2116	2102	2166	2033
Transport	228	274	351	364	383	398	419	400	421	445	434	423	390	350
Others	1001	1386	1845	1916	2000	2087	2150	2302	2406	2484	2606	2591	2722	2719
Transmission Loss	638	874	1197	1306	1326	1345	1327	1234	1207	1294	1235	1208	1186	1161
Electroenergy Supplied to Other Republics	998	1252	2359	3367	4120	4930	3944	3883	3354	3901	3249	3284	3555	2829

Source: Summary of Annual Report of Industrial Enterprises and Establishments.

Table 11.1 - Latvia: Death Rates by Cause, Selected Diseases, 1970-90
(per 100,000 population)

Causes of Death	1970	1980	1985	1990
Tuberculosis	16.0	8.5	5.2	5.6
Infectious and parasitic diseases	4.6	6.4	5.7	5.7
Cancer	170.1	178.0	194.6	204.9
Circulatory disease	662.0	789.6	843.6	756.5
Cerebrovascular disease	165.9	211.8	254.1	227.4
High blood pressure	56.9	47.5	56.1	63.3
Myocardial infarction	-	28.4	41.5	52.2
Other ischemic cardiopathologies	441.8	501.9	491.9	413.6
Diseases of the respiratory system	65.2	58.3	54.8	44.0
Chronic obstructive pulmonary disease	-	-	35.2	30.2
Perinatal causes	6.6	4.7	7.6	7.9
Accidents, poisoning, trauma	126.1	149.0	123.3	138.9

Source: Ministry of Welfare, Department of Health, Medical Statistics Bureau, Riga, Latvia 1992.

Table 11.2 - Latvia: Exports and Imports of Raw Material for Pharmaceutical Production, 1980-90
In Convertible Currency

	1980	1985	1990
Exports in million dollars	3.5	4.5	4.5
Imports in million dollars	60.5	65.5	70.5

Source: Department of Drugs, Ministry of Welfare, Riga, Latvia, 1992

Table 11.3 - Latvia: Exports, Imports, and Domestic Production of Drugs, 1980-90

	1980	1985	1990
Total trade, in million rubles			
Exports	362.2	429.9	439.9
Imports	3539.5	3838.3	4152.1
Trade in ruble market, in million rubles			
Exports	160	170	180
Imports	45	55	80
Trade in convertible currency market, in million dollars			
Exports (raw material)	3.5	4.5	4.5
Imports	60.5	65.5	70.5
Domestic production of drugs, in million dollars	19	20	23

Source: Department of Drugs, Ministry of Welfare, Riga, Latvia, 1992

Table 12.1 - Latvia: Enrolment and Resources in Formal Education, 1991

	Schools		Vocational Schools	Higher Education
	Primary and low secondary	Upper secondary		
Number of students (a)	309 990	28 220	67 409	45 953
Percentage of age group enrolled (b)				
Age 15 - 16	10	41	45	-
17 - 18	-	20	51	9
20 - 24	-	-	8	19
Number of institutions	979	377	153	10
Average no. students per institution	317	75	440	4 177
Students - teacher ratio (c)	10.2	8.1	7.1	8.0
Expenditure per student (d) (RBL)	957	1 220	2 660	4 116

Notes: - rounded to zero

      (a)   The schoold data includes students enrolled in special schools. The vocational schools data 10 per cent of enrolment is part-time.

      (b)   All data refer to 1989.

      (c)   The school data exclude special schools.

Source: Andris Piebalgs, "Latvia: System of Education", Riga, November 1991

Table 12.2 - Latvia: Schools, Students and Academic Personal
For Academic Year 1991/92

1. Number of Schools

	Latvian	Russian	Polish	Ukrainian	Mixed (Latvian and Russian)	Total
Primary schools	47	10	2		10	69
Basic schools	337	53			53	443
Secondary schools	170	145	1	1	60	377
Total	554	208	3	1	123	889
Special schools	27	10			17	54
Special classes	24	9			3	36

2. Number of Students

	Latvian	Russian	Polish	Ukrainian	Total
Primary schools (1-4 classes)	2727	1568	91		4386
Basic schools (1-9 classes)	52942	13926			66868
Secondary schools (1-12 classes)	122565	136532	81	36	259214
Total	178234	152026	172	36	330468
Special schools	4454	2351			6805
Special classes	578	359			937
Total	183266	154736	172	36	338210

3. Division of Number of Students According to the Teaches Stages

	Latvian	Russian	Polish	Ukrainian	Total
Primary schools (1-4 classes)	80149	62108	172	36	142465
Basic schools (5-9 classes)	80938	78984			159922
Secondary schools (10-12 classes)	17147	10934			28081

4. Personnel

	Teachers	Part time teachers	Administrators	Class teachers	Other personnel
Primary schools	468	86	73	116	354
Basic schools	8615	648	1117	1528	4099
Secondary schools	20593	1579	1668	1664	7453
Total	29676	2313	2858	3308	11906
Special schools	1628	95	164	748	1037

Table 12.3 - Latvia: Workers Training and Increasing of Qualification
(thousands, persons)

	1985	1986	1987	1988	1989	1990
Qualified workers trained in vocational schools	22,6	20,8	20,7	20,2	19.4	18,1
Trained workers having acquired additional profession	76,1	71,3	70,0	67,5	53,6	45,0
Workers trained in qualification courses	580,7	592,7	612,0	442,9	307,3	195,8

Source: State Committee for Statistics of the Republic of Latvia.

Table 12.4 - Latvia: Higher and Secondary Special Educational Institutions

	1985/86	1986/87	1987/88	1988/89	1989/90	1990/91	1991/92
Number of higher educational institutions	10	10	10	10	10	10	14
Number of students therein	43914	43316	43705	44247	45615	45953	46279
Number of secondary educational institution	55	55	57	57	57	57	56
Number of pupils therein	40799	40753	40742	40007	38091	36109	31823

Source: State Committee for Statistics of the Republic of Latvia.

BIBLIOGRAPHY

Baltic Council on Cooperation Commission. *On Work in the Baltic Council on Cooperation.* Tallinn, Riga and Vilnius, December 1990.

"Baltic Republics." *Central European: Finance and Business in Central and Eastern Europe (UK)* 6:34-39, October 1991.

Bond, S., Devereux, M. and H. Freeman. *Inflation Non-Neutralities in the UK Corporation Tax.* Fiscal Studies. November 1990.

Brown, Stuart, and Misha Belkindas. "Who's Feeding Whom? An Analysis of Soviet Interrepublican Trade." Washington, D.C. January 1992 (Mimeograph).

Calvo, G. A., and J.A. Frenkel. "From Centrally Planned to Market Economy." *IMF Staff Papers* 38(2), Washington, D.C. June 1991.

Clemens, Walter, Jr. *Baltic Independence and Russian Empire.* New York: St. Martin's Press. 1991.

Commission of the European Communities. *Stabilization, Liberalization and Devolution. Assessment of the Economic Situation and Reform Process in the Soviet Union.* Brussels: European Economy 75. 1990.

Corden, W. "The Normative Theory of International Trade". In R. Jones, ed., *International Trade: Surveys of Theory and Policy.* New York: North-Holland, 1986.

Dreifeld, Juris. "Immigration and Ethnicity in Latvia." *Journal of Soviet Nationalities (US),* 1:43-81. Winter 1990-1991.

Feldstein, M., and Lawrence Summers. "Inflation and the Taxation of Capital Income", *National Tax Journal.* December 1979.

Fischer, S., and Alan H. Gelb. "Issues in the Reform of Socialist Economies". In V. Corbo, F. Coricelli, and J. Bossak, eds., *Reforming Central and Eastern European Economies.* World Bank, Washington D.C. September 1991.

Gelb, Alan H., and Cheryl W. Gray. *The Transformation of Economies in Central and Eastern Europe.* Policy and Research Series Working Paper 17. World Bank, Washington D.C. June 1991.

Geron, Leonard. "Baltic Challenge." *World Today (UK)* 46:40-41. March 1990.

Goldschmidt, Y., and J. Yaron, *Inflation Adjustments of Financial Statements.* World Bank, PRE Working Paper 670, May 1991.

Greene, J., and P. Isard. "Currency Convertibility and the Transformation of Centrally Planned Economies." *IMF Occasional Paper #81*, Washington D.C. June 1991.

Hanson, Philip. "External Economic Relations of the Baltic States." (Manuscript to an article to be published in the *Economic Bulletin for Europe* 43, November 1991.) United Nations Economic Commission for Europe, New York.

_____. "The Baltic States". *The Economist Intelligence Unit Briefing, Special Report 2033*. London: EIU. 1990.

_____. "Property Rights in the New Phase of Reforms." *Soviet Economy*. VI(2). 1990.

Hinds, Manuel. "Issues in the Introduction of Market Forces in Eastern European Socialist Economies". In Simon Commander, ed., *Managing Inflation in Socialist Economies in Transition,* World Bank, Washington D.C. June 1991.

Hiden, John and Patrick Salmon. *The Baltic Nations and Europe: Estonia, Latvia, and Lithuania in the Twentieth Century.* New York: Longman, 1991.

Hofheinz, Paul. "Opportunity in the Baltics." *Fortune Magazine (US)*, 124:68-74, October 21, 1991.

International Monetary Fund (IMF), World Bank, OECD, and EBRD. *A Study of the Soviet Economy.* Paris. 1991.

_____. Various issues. *International Financial Statistics.* Washington, D.C.

Koropeckyi, I. S. and Gertrude Schroeder. *Economics of the Soviet Regions.* New York: Praeger, 1981.

Latvian Ministry of Economics. "Economic and Demographic Information." Riga, 1990.

Latvian State Committee for Statistics. Various issues. *Latvijas Tautas Saimnieciba: Statistikas Gadagramata (National Economy of Latvia: Statistical Yearbook).* Riga, 1992.

Matolcsy, Z., "The Micro Effects of Inflation on Corporate Taxation and Profitability." *The Economic Record,* December 1984.

Ministry of Industry and Energetics, Estonia; Ministry of Energy and Industry, Latvia; and Ministry of Industry, Lithuania. *Energy in Estonia, Latvia and Lithuania. Energy Efficiency and Technology Transfer.* Tallinn, Riga and Vilnius, 1991.

Oxenstierna, Susanne. "Labour Market Policies in the Baltic Republics." *International Labour Review.* ILO 130, 2:255-74, 1991.

Page, Stanley. *The Formation of the Baltic States: A Study of the Effects of Great Power Politics Upon the Emergence of Lithuania, Latvia and Estonia.* New York: H. Fertig Press, 1970.

PlanEcon. *Review and Outlook for the Former Soviet Republics.* Washington, D.C. April 1992.

Sachs, J., and D. Lipton. *Remaining Steps to Achieve a Market-Based Monetary System.* Paper presented at the Conference on the Change of Economic System in Russia, Stockholm School of Economics. Stockholm, June 15-16, 1992.

Salvatore, D. *International Economics.* New York: MacMillan, 1983.

Sweden Ministry of Foreign Affairs. *Economic Survey of the Baltic Countries*, Stockholm, June 1991.

Tarr, D.G. "The Terms-of-Trade Effects on Countries of the Former Soviet Union of Moving to World Prices". World Bank, Washington, D.C. August 1992.

Thirsk, W., "Lessons from Tax Reform: An Overview". In J. Khalilzadeh-Shirazi, and Shah A., eds., *Tax Policy in Developing Countries.* World Bank, Washington D.C., 1991.

US Department of Health and Human Services. *Social Security Programs Throughout the World - 1989.* US Government Printing Office, Washington, D.C., 1991.

Van Arkadie, Brian and Mats Karlsson. *Economic Survey of the Baltic States.* New York: New York University Press, 1992.

Von Rauch, Georg. *The Baltic States. The Years of Independence. Estonia, Latvia. Lithuania, 1917-1940.* London: C. Hurst & Co. Ltd., 1974.

Wadekin, Karl Eugen. *Agriculture in Inter-System Comparison: Communist and Non-Communist Cases.* Berlin: In Kommission Bei Duncker and Humblot, 1985.

World Bank, *Diagnostic Study of the Foreign Direct Investment Environment in Latvia.* Foreign Investment Advisory Services (FIAS), World Bank, Washington, D.C., October 1992.

World Bank. *Issues in Central and East European Land Transport.* June 1991.

_____. *World Development Report, 1991.* New York: Oxford University Press.

Distributors of World Bank Publications

ARGENTINA
Carlos Hirsch, SRL
Galeria Guemes
Florida 165, 4th Floor-Ofc. 453/465
1333 Buenos Aires

**AUSTRALIA, PAPUA NEW GUINEA,
FIJI, SOLOMON ISLANDS,
VANUATU, AND WESTERN SAMOA**
D.A. Books & Journals
648 Whitehorse Road
Mitcham 3132
Victoria

AUSTRIA
Gerold and Co.
Graben 31
A-1011 Wien

BANGLADESH
Micro Industries Development
   Assistance Society (MIDAS)
House 5, Road 16
Dhanmondi R/Area
Dhaka 1209

   Branch offices:
   156, Nur Ahmed Sarak
   Chittagong 4000

   76, K.D.A. Avenue
   Kulna 9100

BELGIUM
Jean De Lannoy
Av. du Roi 202
1060 Brussels

CANADA
Le Diffuseur
C.P. 85, 1501B rue Ampère
Boucherville, Québec
J4B 5E6

CHILE
Invertec IGT S.A.
Americo Vespucio Norte 1165
Santiago

CHINA
China Financial & Economic
   Publishing House
8, Da Fo Si Dong Jie
Beijing

COLOMBIA
Infoenlace Ltda.
Apartado Aereo 34270
Bogota D.E.

COTE D'IVOIRE
Centre d'Edition et de Diffusion
   Africaines (CEDA)
04 B.P. 541
Abidjan 04 Plateau

CYPRUS
Center of Applied Research
Cyprus College
6, Diogenes Street, Engomi
P.O. Box 2006
Nicosia

DENMARK
SamfundsLitteratur
Rosenoerns Allé 11
DK-1970 Frederiksberg C

DOMINICAN REPUBLIC
Editora Taller, C. por A.
Restauración e Isabel la Católica 309
Apartado de Correos 2190 Z-1
Santo Domingo

EGYPT, ARAB REPUBLIC OF
Al Ahram
Al Galaa Street
Cairo

The Middle East Observer
41, Sherif Street
Cairo

FINLAND
Akateeminen Kirjakauppa
P.O. Box 128
SF-00101 Helsinki 10

FRANCE
World Bank Publications
66, avenue d'Iéna
75116 Paris

GERMANY
UNO-Verlag
Poppelsdorfer Allee 55
D-5300 Bonn 1

HONG KONG, MACAO
Asia 2000 Ltd.
46-48 Wyndham Street
Winning Centre
2nd Floor
Central Hong Kong

INDIA
Allied Publishers Private Ltd.
751 Mount Road
Madras - 600 002

   Branch offices:
   15 J.N. Heredia Marg
   Ballard Estate
   Bombay - 400 038

   13/14 Asaf Ali Road
   New Delhi - 110 002

   17 Chittaranjan Avenue
   Calcutta - 700 072

   Jayadeva Hostel Building
   5th Main Road, Gandhinagar
   Bangalore - 560 009

   3-5-1129 Kachiguda
      Cross Road
   Hyderabad - 500 027

   Prarthana Flats, 2nd Floor
   Near Thakore Baug, Navrangpura
   Ahmedabad - 380 009

   Patiala House
   16-A Ashok Marg
   Lucknow - 226 001

   Central Bazaar Road
   60 Bajaj Nagar
   Nagpur 440 010

INDONESIA
Pt. Indira Limited
Jalan Borobudur 20
P.O. Box 181
Jakarta 10320

IRELAND
Government Supplies Agency
4-5 Harcourt Road
Dublin 2

ISRAEL
Yozmot Literature Ltd.
P.O. Box 56055
Tel Aviv 61560

ITALY
Licosa Commissionaria Sansoni SPA
Via Duca Di Calabria, 1/1
Casella Postale 552
50125 Firenze

JAPAN
Eastern Book Service
Hongo 3-Chome, Bunkyo-ku 113
Tokyo

KENYA
Africa Book Service (E.A.) Ltd.
Quaran House, Mfangano Street
P.O. Box 45245
Nairobi

KOREA, REPUBLIC OF
Pan Korea Book Corporation
P.O. Box 101, Kwangwhamun
Seoul

MALAYSIA
University of Malaya Cooperative
   Bookshop, Limited
P.O. Box 1127, Jalan Pantai Baru
59700 Kuala Lumpur

MEXICO
INFOTEC
Apartado Postal 22-860
14060 Tlalpan, Mexico D.F.

NETHERLANDS
De Lindeboom/InOr-Publikaties
P.O. Box 202
7480 AE Haaksbergen

NEW ZEALAND
EBSCO NZ Ltd.
Private Mail Bag 99914
New Market
Auckland

NIGERIA
University Press Limited
Three Crowns Building Jericho
Private Mail Bag 5095
Ibadan

NORWAY
Narvesen Information Center
Book Department
P.O. Box 6125 Etterstad
N-0602 Oslo 6

PAKISTAN
Mirza Book Agency
65, Shahrah-e-Quaid-e-Azam
P.O. Box No. 729
Lahore 54000

PERU
Editorial Desarrollo SA
Apartado 3824
Lima 1

PHILIPPINES
International Book Center
Suite 1703, Cityland 10
Condominium Tower 1
Ayala Avenue, Corner H.V. dela
   Costa Extension
Makati, Metro Manila

POLAND
International Publishing Service
Ul. Piekna 31/37
00-677 Warzawa

For subscription orders:
IPS Journals
Ul. Okrezna 3
02-916 Warszawa

PORTUGAL
Livraria Portugal
Rua Do Carmo 70-74
1200 Lisbon

SAUDI ARABIA, QATAR
Jarir Book Store
P.O. Box 3196
Riyadh 11471

**SINGAPORE, TAIWAN,
MYANMAR, BRUNEI**
Information Publications
   Private, Ltd.
Golden Wheel Building
41, Kallang Pudding, #04-03
Singapore 1334

SOUTH AFRICA, BOTSWANA
For single titles:
Oxford University Press
   Southern Africa
P.O. Box 1141
Cape Town 8000

For subscription orders:
International Subscription Service
P.O. Box 41095
Craighall
Johannesburg 2024

SPAIN
Mundi-Prensa Libros, S.A.
Castello 37
28001 Madrid

Librería Internacional AEDOS
Consell de Cent, 391
08009 Barcelona

SRI LANKA AND THE MALDIVES
Lake House Bookshop
P.O. Box 244
100, Sir Chittampalam A.
   Gardiner Mawatha
Colombo 2

SWEDEN
For single titles:
Fritzes Fackboksforetaget
Regeringsgatan 12, Box 16356
S-103 27 Stockholm

For subscription orders:
Wennergren-Williams AB
P. O. Box 1305
S-171 25 Solna

SWITZERLAND
For single titles:
Librairie Payot
1, rue de Bourg
CH 1002 Lausanne

For subscription orders:
Librairie Payot
Service des Abonnements
Case postale 3312
CH 1002 Lausanne

TANZANIA
Oxford University Press
P.O. Box 5299
Maktaba Road
Dar es Salaam

THAILAND
Central Department Store
306 Silom Road
Bangkok

**TRINIDAD & TOBAGO, ANTIGUA
BARBUDA, BARBADOS,
DOMINICA, GRENADA, GUYANA,
JAMAICA, MONTSERRAT, ST.
KITTS & NEVIS, ST. LUCIA,
ST. VINCENT & GRENADINES**
Systematics Studies Unit
#9 Watts Street
Curepe
Trinidad, West Indies

TURKEY
Infotel
Narlabahçe Sok. No. 15
Cagaloglu
Istanbul

UNITED KINGDOM
Microinfo Ltd.
P.O. Box 3
Alton, Hampshire GU34 2PG
England

VENEZUELA
Libreria del Este
Aptdo. 60.337
Caracas 1060-A